Amazon

How the world's most relentless retailer will continue to revolutionize commerce

SECOND EDITION

Natalie Berg
Miya Knights

KoganPage

First published in Great Britain and the United States in 2019 by Kogan Page Limited
Second edition published 2022

2nd Floor, 45 Gee Street	8 W 38th Street, Suite 902	4737/23 Ansari Road
London EC1V 3RS	New York, NY 10018	Daryaganj
United Kingdom	USA	New Delhi 110002
		India

www.koganpage.com

ISBNs

Hardback   978 1 3986 0144 4
Paperback   978 1 3986 0142 0
Ebook   978 1 3986 0143 7

British Library Cataloguing-in-Publication Data

A CIP record for this book is available from the British Library.

Library of Congress Control Number

2021944898

Typeset by Integra Software Services, Pondicherry
Print production managed by Jellyfish
Printed and bound by Henry Ling Limited, at the Dorset Press, Dorchester, DT1 1HD

PRAISE FOR *AMAZON 2ND EDITION*

'If you believe in the philosophy of knowing your enemy then *Amazon* is a must-read for any omnichannel retailer.'
Tim Mason, CEO, Eagle Eye Solutions

'As well as being a comprehensive and authoritative insight on how the Amazon model relentlessly evolved to create more Amazon, it's also a must-read insight into the future of shopping and how retail must adapt to stay relevant to the "on-my-terms" customer.'
Robin Phillips, CEO, The Watch Shop

'Berg and Knights keep us up to date with what is hot in the Amazon ecosystem today. While many retailers claim to be customer-centric, the disjointed nature of their businesses allows Amazon to continue to forge ahead. This book is essential reading for anyone who believes Amazon is a competitor. Read it and learn from it.'
Clive Humby OBE, Co-founder of dunnhumby and chief architect of Tesco's Clubcard

'Berg and Knights thoughtfully and thoroughly dissect all of Amazon's consumer and competitive competencies. Their analysis dives deep into Amazon's business strategies and provides ample advice on what competitors need to do to thrive alongside Amazon.'
Sucharita Kodali, Vice President and Principal Analyst, Forrester Research

'In this book, Berg and Knights comprehensively and accessibly unpack Amazon's multi-layered strategy with a perspective that understands Amazon as a technology company, but is rooted in the authors' deep knowledge of the retail space. A clear-eyed and engaging assessment that, in this latest edition, incorporates the dramatic acceleration in e-commerce brought about by a global pandemic and the ways in which Amazon has capitalized on that for future growth. Essential reading for anyone trying to understand retail's Amazon-centric future.'
Bryan Gildenberg, SVP, Commerce at Omnicom Commerce Group

'Berg and Knights have identified the strength and might in the rise of Amazon as being a technology company first and retailer second. Amazon's relentless focus on the customer has informed the details of their infrastructure and they own the last mile. Removing aspects of store shopping that consumers cannot abide, such as queuing, waiting, missing sizes or inventory items, have all been addressed. The Amazon physical experience will undoubtedly result in high satisfaction rates. With the last mile firmly sorted, here they have the competitive advantage, Amazon must now focus on making the physical experience exciting and engaging – this isn't yet a core competency. How will retailers respond to this new and emerging threat posed by Amazon? There remain only three options: compete, concede or collaborate.'
Ruth Harrison, Global Head of Industry Domains, Thoughtworks and former GM, Selfridges

'Berg and Knights deliver surgical insights on Amazon's progress and impact during the global pandemic while curating an updated end-to-end landscape view of the industries affected by the Amazon. While many businesses struggled due to COVID, the pandemic served as kindling to fuel Amazon further, strengthening its flywheel, enabling it to spin its impact even wider. This second edition of *Amazon* is the go-to primer for those wanting to learn about Amazon, and returning experts will realize that it has always been "Infrastructure Week" at Amazon and said infrastructure will be key to keeping today and tomorrow always "Day 1" for Amazon.'
Anh Nguyen Lue, North America Open Innovation and eCom Category Management Leader, P&G

CONTENTS

01   It's an Amazon world 1
     Notes 4

02   Why Amazon is not your average retailer: introduction to
     retail strategy 5
     Losing money to make money 7
     Amazon's core principles 8
     Uneven playing field: tax 18
     Three pillars: Marketplace, Prime, AWS 21
     Tech company first, retailer second 23
     Notes 27

03   Pandemic pivots: how COVID upended the retail industry 33
     COVID: the great retail accelerant 34
     Demise of 'status-quo retail' 35
     Digital transformation: COVID will finish what Amazon started 36
     The future of e-commerce is stores 39
     Customer experience is the new currency 41
     Conscious consumption 43
     Notes 46

04   Amazon's pandemic power grab 50
     Amazon's golden age 51
     Cementing its status: a shopping and entertainment behemoth 51
     Alexa, join my Zoom meeting 57
     Showcasing Amazon's technological prowess 59
     Notes 61

05   The Prime ecosystem: redefining loyalty for today's modern shopper 65

Shipping, shopping, streaming and more 67
But is Prime actually a loyalty programme? 71
What does Amazon get out of Prime? 72
Can Prime work in a physical setting? 74
Prime 2.0 76
Notes 79

06   Retail apocalypse or rebirth? 82

The on-my-terms shopper is born 83
Amazon Effect: killing the category killer 86
Overspaced, with questionable relevance 87
Notes 92

07   End of pure-play e-commerce: Amazon's transition to bricks and mortar retailing 96

Next-generation retail: the quest for omnichannel 97
Key drivers of convergence of physical and digital retail 99
Clicks chasing bricks – incentives for getting physical 106
Amazon makes its move 111
Notes 117

08   Amazon's grocery ambitions: create a platform to sell you everything else 122

US online grocery: a slow burner 123
Food: the final frontier and importance of frequency 126
Amazon's food fight: life before Whole Foods Market 127
Notes 138

09   Supermarkets: a brave new era 142

Applying its thirst for invention to the supermarket sector 143
Why Whole Foods Market? 146
The wake-up call 148
Goodbye Whole Foods, hello Amazon Fresh? 150
Notes 152

10   A private label juggernaut: here comes the squeeze 154

The post-great recession mindset 155
Amazon's private label ambitions 156
Notes 172

11   Technology and frictionless retail 176

Customer obsession 177
One click to no click 184
Notes 188

12   AI and voice: the new retail frontier 190

The value of recommendation 191
The importance of interaction 193
Supply chain complexity 194
The untapped potential of voice 197
Notes 210

13   Store of the future: how digital automation will enrich the customer experience 213

Research online, buy offline 215
Location as a proxy for relevance 218
The store as a showroom 222
The digital customer experience 224
Notes 234

14   Redefining the store: shifting from transactional to experiential 236

From shop to lifestyle centre: ensuring brand values align 239
A place to eat 240
A place to work 242
A place to play   244
A place to discover, a place to learn 249
A place to rent 252
In summary 255
Notes 256

15   Retail fulfilment: winning the customer over the final mile 260

The promise to deliver 260
Developing the last mile 265
Building out the last mile 269
Notes 273

16   The last-mile infrastructure 275

Last-mile labour 276
Growing physical infrastructure 280
Real estate demand 283
Amazon as a carrier 287
Fulfilment by Amazon 288
Race for the last mile 289
Remote innovation 293
Notes 296

17   Conclusion: peak Amazon? 299

Notes 303

Index 305

01

It's an Amazon world

Relevant 'rɛləv(ə)(cl)nt *appropriate to the current time, period, or circumstances; of contemporary interest.*

Retail is going through a transition. The naysayers will call it an apocalypse; to others, it's digital transformation. But one thing we can all agree on is that this is a period of profound structural change.

The pandemic-induced shift to online shopping, combined with broader changes in consumer values and spending habits, has exposed an overbuilt retail landscape. Traditional business models are being displaced and retailers are left scrambling for survival, with stores closing at record rates and bankruptcies now rife in the industry. This is retail Darwinism – evolve or die.

But there's one word that often gets overlooked in all this talk of an impending apocalypse – relevance. The most important rule in retail is being relevant to customers. If you can't deliver on the basic principles of giving customers what they want or standing out from the competition, then you don't stand a chance. For these retailers, yes, the Doomsday clock is ticking.

For those willing to embrace change, however, we believe this is a fantastically exciting time to reinvent retail. The future is fewer, more impactful stores. The future is offering shoppers a more blended online and offline experience. And the future is excelling at WACD: What Amazon Can't Do.

The titan of 21st-century commerce, Amazon has grown from online bookseller to become one of the most valuable public companies in the world. At the time of writing, Amazon accounted for around half of US e-commerce sales.[1] In 2010, the retailer employed approximately 30,000 people. A decade later, that figure rose to 1.3 million. In fact, Amazon added a whopping 500,000 people to its workforce in 2020 alone.[2] A pandemic year like no other. Not even Walmart, the largest private employer in the US, has ever added so many workers in a single year.[3] Amazon has become the undisputed market leader in everything from cloud computing to voice technology. It is the number one destination for product search ahead of Google[4] and it has also overtaken Walmart to become the largest US clothing retailer.[5] In 2021, at the time of writing, Amazon was worth more than Walmart, Netflix, Target, Nike and Costco combined. In fact, founder Jeff Bezos' *personal worth* is more than the market valuation of some of those businesses.[6] Those cardboard boxes are certainly changing retail.

As if that's not enough, Amazon has been busy ramping up its global operations. In 2010, Amazon's international presence was limited to seven markets: Canada, UK, Germany, France, Japan, China and Italy. A decade later, operations outside of the US accounted for around one-third of sales, spanning more than 20 foreign markets, from the bright lights of Mexico City to the remote hills of the Himalayas.[7]

By 2020, Amazon owned or leased more than 400 million square feet of space around the world.[8] Amazon has added more than 30 new product categories since its site was launched,[9] and now boasts over 200 million Prime members around the world willing to pay roughly $100 a year to shop with them.[10]

Amazon has become one of the most influential businesses of the 21st century due to its unwavering commitment to an initial vision: to relentlessly innovate in a bid to create long-term value for customers. Amazon's success stems from its constant dissatisfaction with the status quo, its appetite for disruption, its desire to build lifelong loyalty among its shoppers. Amazon is full of surprises, but every action is ultimately guided by a vision that hasn't changed since its inception.

As with most disruptors, Amazon is an outsider. It is a technology company with deep pockets and the luxury of long-term thinking. Amazon would not be where it is today if it weren't for its ability to play by its own rules, shunning short termism and other traditional constraints faced by public retailers. It has relentlessly built out its retail offer, not just through category expansion – upending entire sectors in the process – but also by enhancing entertainment, fulfilment and technology capabilities to create a unique, frictionless and fully embedded experience for the customer.

To competitors, Amazon is ruthless and fearsome. To customers, Amazon is effortless and, increasingly, indispensable. It has hit the ultimate shopper sweet spot by combining access to millions of products with ever faster delivery. And that's just the beginning. Capitalizing on the strength and trust of its brand, Amazon continues to spread its tentacles across entirely new industries. The mere whisper that Amazon might enter a sector is enough to send stocks tumbling. And it's getting clearer by the day that Amazon is not satisfied with just being the retailer; it also wants to be the infrastructure.

Today, Amazon is firing on all cylinders. The pandemic-driven shift towards a more digital world has strengthened every aspect of its business – retail, Amazon Web Services (AWS), Prime, Alexa, advertising – and, in the absence of regulatory intervention, Amazon's growth shows no signs of abating.

But Amazon is at an inflection point. The king of e-commerce has recognized that, for all its conveniences, online-only is no longer enough. The convergence of physical and digital retail is accelerating. If Amazon wants to crack the grocery and pharmacy sectors, it needs stores. If Amazon wants to offset rising fulfilment and customer acquisition costs, it needs stores. And if Amazon wants to further drive Prime membership, adoption of voice technology and one-hour delivery, guess what? It needs stores.

The future of retail is clicks and mortar. Amazon will redefine the supermarket for the 21st-century shopper – stripping out checkouts, digitizing the experience, utilizing stores for fast delivery and, crucially, engaging with shoppers in a way that it could never do online. The store of the future will become more experiential and service-led.

Grocery will unlock a very big piece of the puzzle for Amazon: frequency. As a former Whole Foods Market boss puts it, 'food is the platform for selling you everything else'.[11] This is why Amazon's move into groceries should worry all retailers, not just supermarkets. It's another step closer to achieving total retail dominance.

As we'll portray throughout this book, Amazon is, in many ways, uncatchable. It has woven itself into the fabric of our everyday lives, and many are now questioning whether Amazon's ubiquity is good for the economy – and for democracy as a whole. Efforts to curtail Amazon's dominance will continue to grow, and a company of Amazon's size, power and influence should be scrutinized, particularly in the wake of the pandemic. Landmark reforms to the global tax system and what could be the most significant changes to US antitrust law in decades will help to level the playing field. We must also acknowledge, however, that Amazon has been a force for good in that the retail sector has seriously raised its game. Amazon's unrelenting focus on enhancing the customer experience has been a catalyst for wider industry change. As we look ahead, we will see a deepening of the bifurcation of retail's winners and losers. The undifferentiated and underperforming retailers will be weeded out, and the retailers left standing will be much stronger for having reinvented themselves – ensuring relevance and, ultimately, survival.

Notes

1 Vena, Danny (2018) Amazon dominated e-commerce sales in 2017, *The Motley Fool*, 12 January. Available from: https://www.fool.com/investing/2018/01/12/amazon-dominated-e-commerce-sales-in-2017.aspx (archived at https://perma.cc/RA3R-8XZ7) [Last accessed 12/6/2018].

2 Securities and Exchange Commission (2020) Amazon 10-K for the fiscal year ended December 31, 2020. Available from: https://www.sec.gov/ix?doc=/Archives/edgar/data/1018724/000101872421000004/amzn-20201231.htm (archived at https://perma.cc/RYU3-H2S5) [Last accessed 18/6/2021].

3 Wakabayashi, Daisuke, Weise, Karen, Nicas, Jack and Isaac, Mike (2020) The economy is in record decline, but not for the tech giants, *The New York Times*, 30 July. Available from: https://www.nytimes.com/2020/07/30/technology/tech-company-earnings-amazon-apple-facebook-google.html (archived at https://perma.cc/Z45B-4KMP) [Last accessed 18/6/2021].

4 Nickelsburg, Monica (2017) Chart: Amazon is the most popular destination for shoppers searching for products online, *Geekwire*, 6 July. Available from: https://www.geekwire.com/2017/chart-amazon-popular-destination-shoppers-searching-products-online/ (archived at https://perma.cc/R25Z-Y3H3) [Last accessed 12/6/2018].

5 Repko, Melissa (2021) Walmart acquires virtual fitting room company Zeekit as it makes push into fashion, *CNBC*, 13 May. Available from: https://www.cnbc.com/2021/05/13/walmart-acquires-virtual-fitting-room-company-zeekit-.html (archived at https://perma.cc/9TP2-QRJX) [Last accessed 18/6/2021].

6 Author research; Google Finance.

7 Author research; Amazon 10-Ks for 2010 and 2020.

8 Securities and Exchange Commission (2020) Amazon 10-K for the fiscal year ended December 31, 2020. Available from: https://www.sec.gov/ix?doc=/Archives/edgar/data/1018724/000101872421000004/amzn-20201231.htm (archived at https://perma.cc/RYU3-H2S5) [Last accessed 18/6/2021].

9 Sender, Hanna, Stevens, Laura and Serkez, Yaryna (2018) Amazon: the making of a giant, *Wall Street Journal*, 14 March. Available from: https://www.wsj.com/graphics/amazon-the-making-of-a-giant/ (archived at https://perma.cc/NT42-M56B) [Last accessed 12/6/2018].

10 Amazon 2020 Letter to Shareholders. Available from: https://www.aboutamazon.com/news/company-news/2020-letter-to-shareholders (archived at https://perma.cc/5AHF-5UFB) [Last accessed 18/6/2021].

11 Kowitt, Beth (2018) How Amazon is using Whole Foods in a bid for total retail domination, *Fortune*, 21 May. Available from: http://fortune.com/longform/amazon-groceries-fortune-500/ (archived at https://perma.cc/V4LT-5XYS) [Last accessed 12/6/2018].

02

Why Amazon is not your average retailer: introduction to retail strategy

Flywheel *A heavy revolving wheel in a machine, which is used to increase the machine's momentum and thereby provide greater stability or a reserve of available power.*

Amazon is full of contradictions. The retailer whose strategy was to be 'unprofitable for a long time' is now one of the most valuable companies in the world. Amazon is a retailer that doesn't own most of the stuff it sells. Amazon is both a feared competitor and, increasingly, retail partner. Depending on who you ask, the phrase 'The Amazon Effect' can either mean putting a company out of business or drastically enhancing the customer experience.

What is Amazon's USP? Near-infinite assortment and competitive prices are critical components of its marketplace model – but they alone don't differentiate Amazon enough from its rivals to explain its profound success in the world of retailing. The tech giant has spun an intricate web around its customers through its Prime membership programme, yet ultimately its USP is convenience. Cold, hard convenience. Customers are loyal to the service, the frictionless experience, the sheer effortlessness of buying through Amazon's platform. Time is a precious commodity and Amazon knows it. Over one quarter of purchases on Amazon take place in three minutes or less, and half of all purchases are finished in less than 15 minutes.[1]

FIGURE 2.1   Market capitalization: select US companies, billions (as of 21 June 2021)

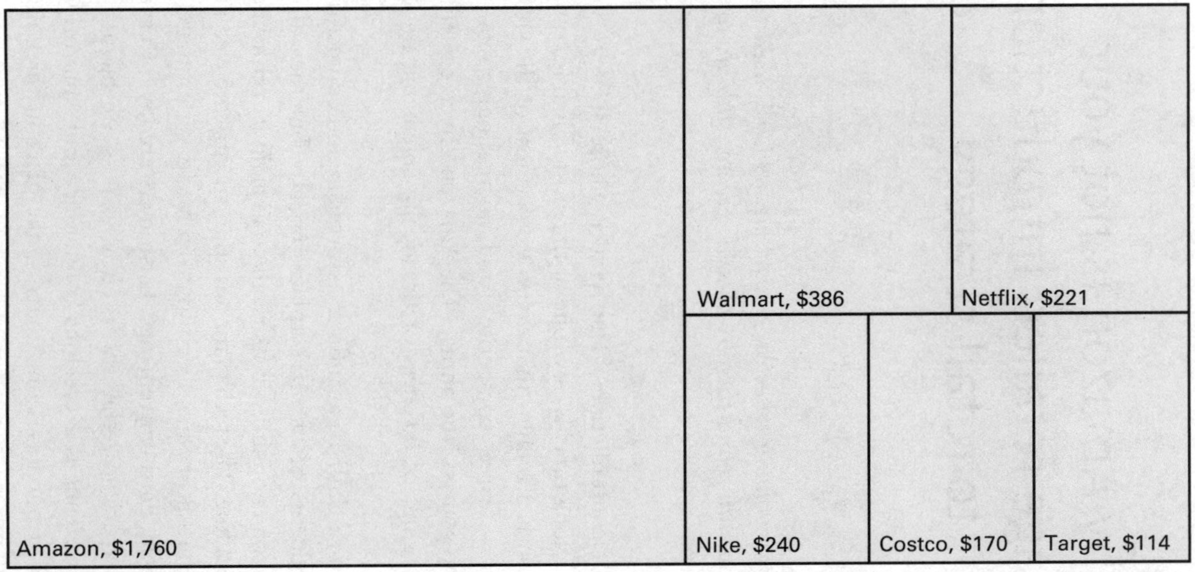

Amazon, $1,760

Walmart, $386

Netflix, $221

Nike, $240

Costco, $170

Target, $114

SOURCE Author research; Google Finance

A question we often get asked is: What is Amazon? Amazon sells everything from nappies to treadmills, but it also produces hit television shows and provides cloud computing services to clients as diverse as McDonald's, Zalando and NASA. Amazon is a hardware manufacturer, payment processor, advertising platform, virtual tour operator, ocean freight business, publisher, wi-fi system, delivery network, fashion designer, private label business and airline. It doesn't stop there. Amazon operates the largest civilian surveillance network in the US. It is also a supermarket, pharmacy and healthcare provider. Amazon has dabbled in restaurant delivery, luxury goods, financial services and hair salons. The tech giant has even tried to cure the common cold (yes, really). By the time you're reading this, it's likely Amazon will be on the cusp of solving yet another problem or disrupting yet another sector.

Amazon is aware that, to the outside world, such diversification seems scattered and illogical. Is Amazon simply a jack of all trades but master of none? 'As we do new things, we accept that we may be misunderstood for long periods of time,'[2] the retailer stated on its website in 2021. To understand Amazon, you first need to understand its strategic framework: the flywheel (see Figure 2.2).

Losing money to make money

Created by management theorist Jim Collins, the flywheel effect describes a virtuous cycle that makes companies ever more successful. On his website, Collins states: '[T]here is no single defining action, no grand program, no one killer innovation, no solitary lucky break, no miracle moment. Rather, the process resembles relentlessly pushing a giant, heavy flywheel, turn upon turn, building momentum until a point of breakthrough, and beyond.'[3]

FIGURE 2.2   The flywheel: the key to Amazon's success

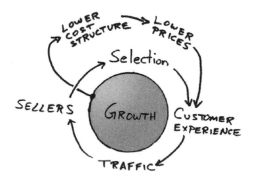

So how does this apply to Amazon? In his book, *The Everything Store*, Brad Stone explains the initial thinking:

> Bezos and his lieutenants sketched their own virtuous cycle, which they believed powered their business. It went something like this: lower prices led to more customer visits. More customers increased the volume of sales and attracted more commission-paying third-party sellers to the site. That allowed Amazon to get more out of fixed costs like the fulfilment centres and the servers needed to run the website. This greater efficiency then enabled it to lower prices further. Feed any part of this flywheel, they reasoned, and it should accelerate the loop.[4]

After more than two decades of investment, the flywheel is now spinning. Amazon continues to diversify its business, looking well beyond the borders of retail, to feed the flywheel. Amazon isn't satisfied with being the Everything Store, it also wants to be the Everywhere Store. Intentions to disrupt entirely new industries like financial services and healthcare may seem incongruous with the core retail division, but we have to remember two things:

1 Every new service is another spoke on the wheel. Amazon's success cannot be measured by looking at one business unit in isolation.

2 The one thing linking all of Amazon's seemingly irrational moves is the opportunity to improve the customer experience, further embedding itself with shoppers in the process.

It's important to bear in mind here here that Amazon is not actually a retailer but a tech company always looking at ways to improve through innovation. Trust and loyalty to the Amazon brand are now well established and can be translated across other sectors, although this will not come without greater scrutiny.

Now let's take a closer look at how Amazon's values have shaped its strategy to become one of the most disruptive and influential retail businesses of the 21st century.

Amazon's core principles

'We're a company of pioneers. It's our job to make bold bets, and we get our energy from inventing on behalf of customers. Success is measured against the possible, not the probable.'
Amazon, 2021[5]

Winning combo: customer obsession and passion for invention

Most retailers would consider themselves innovative, customer-centric and results-oriented. The difference with Amazon is that it really means it.

It may have started out in books, but for well over a decade now Amazon's bold mission has been to become 'Earth's most customer-centric company' – full stop. It has remained unwaveringly committed to this goal, ensuring that every decision made will ultimately add value to the customer. The whole point of retail, after all, is to serve the shopper.

'If you want to get to the truth about what makes us different, it's this. We are genuinely customer-centric, we are genuinely long-term-oriented and we genuinely like to invent. Most companies are not those things.'
Jeff Bezos, Amazon Founder and Executive Chairman [6]

Amazon is clearly not the first retailer in the world to obsess over its customers. In fact, one might argue that inspiration was taken from the late Sam Walton, founder of Walmart, who genuinely embraced the 'customer is king' mantra and once famously said, 'There is only one boss. The customer. And he can fire everybody in the company from the chairman on down, simply by spending his money somewhere else.'[7]

What sets Amazon apart, however, is its relentless dissatisfaction with the status quo. It is genuinely infatuated with the customer experience. It continuously looks for better ways of serving its shoppers and stamping out friction from the overall experience. When retailers talk of innovation, they tend to mean things like pop-up stores and digital displays. With Amazon, it's underwater warehouses and robotic postmen.

In a past letter to shareholders, Jeff Bezos wrote:

There are many advantages to a customer-centric approach, but here's the big one: customers are always beautifully, wonderfully dissatisfied, even when they report being happy and business is great. Even when they don't yet know it, customers want something better, and your desire to delight customers will drive you to invent on their behalf.[8]

Bezos makes the point that no one ever asked Amazon to create the Prime membership programme 'but it sure turns out they wanted it'.[9] Amazon has the solution before the customer need even exists.

Speaking to the authors in an exclusive interview, Amazon's UK boss John Boumphrey stressed the importance of selection, price and convenience. 'You'll never have customers say to you, "I wish there was less choice. I wish the prices were a bit higher. I wish deliveries came a bit slower." One of the reasons that retail is so exciting is because it is so dynamic. What is innovative one year becomes the new normal in years to come.'

Amazon spends billions of dollars on research and development, possibly more than any other company in the world.[10] Yet despite Amazon's deep pockets for R&D, the company considers frugality to be a key leadership principle as it helps to breed resourcefulness, self-sufficiency and invention.

Frugality is a common trait among the world's most successful retailers. In the early days, Amazon famously used doors as desks. Walmart got its very name because it only had seven letters, which was shorter than the alternative suggestions and therefore cheaper to install and light the exterior neon sign. Meanwhile, senior executives at Spain's largest retailer, Mercadona, are thought to keep a one-euro-cent coin in their pockets to remind them that they are working to cut costs for the shopper.[11]

Similarly, Amazon will only spend money when there's a clear benefit to the customer. 'Jeff would never dream of changing a pixel, a button, a place on the checkout or anything on that website unless you articulated to Jeff what it was going to do to the customer,' said Brian McBride, former Amazon UK boss. 'Unless there was something in it for the customer, why do it?'[12]

AMAZON'S LEADERSHIP PRINCIPLES

1 Customer obsession.

2 Ownership.

3 Invent and simplify.

4 Leaders are right, a lot.

5 Learn and be curious.

6 Hire and develop the best.

7 Insist on the highest standards.

8 Think big.

9 Bias for action.

10 Frugality.

11 Earn trust.

12 Dive deep.

13 Have backbone; disagree and commit.

14 Deliver results.

An 'Always Day One' philosophy enables Amazon to maintain its entrepreneurial agility in spite of its size. In addition to obsessing over and anticipating customer needs, this start-up mentality means that Amazon focuses on results over process, makes high-quality decisions quickly and embraces external trends. Is there ever a Day Two? Not according to Bezos. 'Day Two is stasis. Followed by irrelevance. Followed by excruciating, painful decline. Followed by death. And *that* is why it is *always* Day One.'[13]

Innovating at scale

So how does Amazon create a culture of continuous improvement? One that thrives on agility? How does it innovate at scale?

One example is the 'working backwards' approach. Amazon has always been quite a vocal critic of PowerPoint slides (easy for the presenter, difficult for the audience). Instead, meetings are structured around six-page narratives which are silently read at the start of each meeting. The memos, according to Bezos, force a deeper clarity, particularly when it comes to new product development. They're designed to read as a mock press release announcing the finished product while conveying the benefits to the customer in layman's terms – or as former Amazon director Ian McAllister calls it, 'Oprah-speak', not 'Geek-speak'.

'Working backwards makes you accountable for how it will work for the customer.'
Paul Misener, Amazon Vice President for Global Innovation Policy and Communications[14]

These are 'centred around the customer problem, how current solutions (internal or external) fail, and how the new product will blow away existing solutions.' If the benefits don't sound appealing, then the product manager continues to tweak the internal document. 'Iterating on a press release is a lot less expensive than iterating on the product itself (and quicker!)', McAllister observed in his blog.[15]

FIGURE 2.3 Playing the long game: Amazon sales vs profits

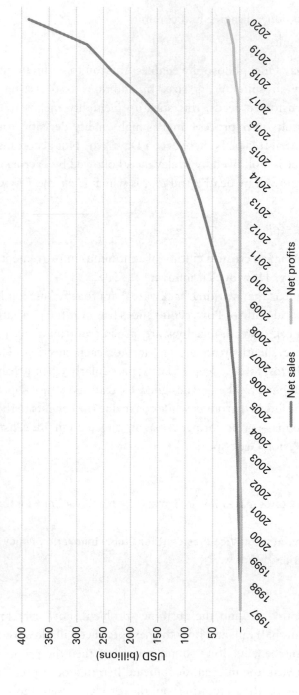

USD (billions)

1997 1998 1999 2000 2001 2002 2003 2004 2005 2006 2007 2008 2009 2010 2011 2012 2013 2014 2015 2016 2017 2018 2019 2020

Net sales   Net profits

SOURCE Author research; Amazon 10-Ks

FIGURE 2.4   Are Amazon's profit struggles finally over?

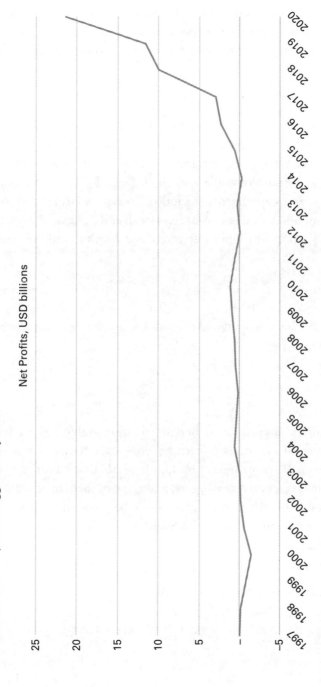

Net Profits, USD billions

SOURCE Author research; Amazon 10-Ks

The result? Rapid innovation. A great example of this is Prime Now, as Amazon's one- to two-hour delivery service was initially branded, which went from product idea to launch in just 111 days.[16] This is how Amazon differentiates: its unique approach to product development enables it to marry a start-up mentality with the scale and resources of a large company.

The best place in the world to fail

Amazon values curiosity and risk taking, but not everything it touches turns to gold. Bezos himself has admitted that Amazon has made 'billions of dollars of failures'.[17] Its biggest flop was arguably the Fire phone, which was no match for iPhones and Androids and eventually led to a $170 million write-off. Other short-lived experiments included: travel website Amazon Destinations, Groupon-like deals site Amazon Local, and Amazon Wallet, an app that allowed shoppers to store gift cards and loyalty cards on their phone.

> 'Many of life's failures are people who did not realize how close they were to success when they gave up.'
> **Thomas Edison**

Innovation and failure, according to Bezos, are 'inseparable twins'. It is Amazon's acceptance of failure as a learning experience that sets it apart from other businesses. '[E]very single important thing that we have done has taken a lot of risk taking, perseverance, guts, and some of them have worked out, most of them have not,' says Bezos. Let's be clear, the ones that have worked out – for example, Prime, AWS and Alexa – have been colossal successes for the company.

The 20-year bet and importance of consistency

> 'We're going to be unprofitable for a long time. And that's our strategy.'
> **Jeff Bezos, 1997**[18]

Wall Street is inherently short-termist, leaving most public companies focused on maximizing profitability and stock performance from quarter to quarter. Amazon does the exact opposite.

Since Day One, Amazon has prioritized growth over profitability, measuring its own success by customer and revenue growth, the degree to which customers purchase from it on a repeat basis, and brand equity. The plan has always been to establish market leadership, which in turn would strengthen Amazon's economic model.

It looks like that time has finally come. Amazon has had a rocky history when it comes to making money, but in 2020 the retailer reported $21.3 billion in net income, making it one of the most profitable companies in the world (see Figures 2.3 and 2.4).[19] And that was no pandemic blip – Amazon had been steadily improving profitability in the years leading up to the COVID crisis. The flywheel concept isn't designed for overnight success, it's about building long-lasting relationships with customers. Decades of enhancing the customer experience coupled with investment in high-growth, high-margin businesses have finally come to fruition.

Not to be overlooked here is the importance of consistency in Amazon's strategy: its first-ever shareholder letter from 1997 reads as if it was written yesterday. Bezos didn't predict the future, he created it. More than two decades ago, he laid out his vision to focus relentlessly on customers in a bid to create long-term value for both shoppers and shareholders. Don't forget that in 1997 Amazon was an online bookseller, nothing like the retail goliath it has become today, but nonetheless its strategy was crystallized.

For Bezos' plan to work, he had to be in it for the long haul. He spent the next 24 years at the helm, which was critical to keep Amazon from wavering from its original vision.

It was only in 2021 that Bezos finally handed over the reins to former AWS boss Andy Jassy. Bezos, however, is not far from the action today – he followed a similar path to Bill Gates at Microsoft and Eric Schmidt at Google by transitioning to an executive chairman role.

Taking a step back after a quarter of a century has allowed Bezos to pursue his other interests – from newspapers to space exploration. Amazon's founder may no longer be involved in the day-to-day running of the business but he still wields a great deal of influence. Let's not forget that we are talking about one of the richest people on the planet – with much of his net worth tied up in Amazon stock. As CFO Brian Olsavsky puts it: 'Jeff is really not going anywhere. It's more of a restructuring of who's doing what.'[20]

'It took more than 50 meetings for me to raise $1 million from investors, and over the course of all those meetings, the most common question was, "What's the internet?".'
Jeff Bezos, 2020[21]

Bezos' persuasiveness, his resilience and faith in the Amazon model would ultimately pay off. But back in those early days, a thick skin and extraordinary focus were needed to shrug off the critics and quell shareholder fears. A whole lot of people were betting against Amazon in its infancy. 'Back then there wasn't a blind faith that every Jeff idea was going to be a home run,' said former Amazon director Vijay Ravindran.[22] By 2000, the year the dot-com bubble burst and Amazon's sixth in operation, the retailer had yet to report a profit and was haemorrhaging millions of dollars in losses. Wall Street analysts were convinced Bezos was building a house of cards,[23] with Lehman Bros analyst Ravi Suria predicting Amazon would run out of cash in a matter of months unless it could 'pull another financing rabbit out of its rather magical hat.'[24] Suria wasn't alone here. The same year, finance magazine *Barron's* put out a list of 51 internet companies that were expected to go bust by the end of 2000. The Burn Rate 51 included now-forgotten names like CDNow and Infonautics – and Amazon.

Headlines such as 'Can Amazon survive?'[25] and 'Amazon: Ponzi scheme or Wal-Mart of the web?'[26] illustrated doubts over Amazon's future. Amazon was expected to be yet another victim of the dot-com bubble.

Despite the broader scepticism and genuine befuddlement over its unconventional business model, Amazon managed to persuade enough shareholders by telling a compelling story. Bezos requested their patience and surprisingly they agreed. 'I think it comes down to a consistent message and consistent strategy, one that doesn't deviate when the stock goes down or goes up,' said Bill Miller, the Chief Investment Officer at Miller Value Partners.[27]

Former Amazon executive Brittain Ladd believes that companies either play a finite or infinite game. With a finite game, the company believes it can beat its competitors. It is characterized by an agreed set of rules and clearly defined mechanisms for scoring the game.

Speaking to the authors, Ladd commented:

Amazon, however, plays an infinite game where the goal is to outlast competitors. Amazon understands that competitors will come and go. Amazon understands that it can't be the best at all things. Amazon has made a strategic decision to place its focus on outlasting its competitors by creating an ecosystem that flawlessly meets and serves the needs of consumers across an ever-expanding array of products, services and technology.

Cheap capital and sustainable moats

Amazon clearly plays by its own set of rules. Without Bezos' vision, it wouldn't have earned the confidence of the investment community. Without the confidence of its shareholders, it wouldn't have been able to invest in the necessary infrastructure for the core e-commerce business or to innovate well beyond the borders of retail, adding those critical spokes to the flywheel. There would be no AWS, no Prime, no Alexa. Amazon wouldn't be Amazon.

But is this fair? NYU Professor of Marketing Scott Galloway doesn't think so. He explains: 'They have access to cheaper capital than any company in modern history. Amazon can now borrow money for less than the cost of what China can borrow money [for]. As a result, they're able to throw up more stuff against the wall than any other firm.'[28]

As a competitor, how can you possibly keep up with a company that has zero obligation to report a profit? A company whose primary expectation from its investors is to keep ploughing money into new areas of growth? A company that has no qualms about crushing those that stand in its way?

'You really develop very sustainable moats around a business when you run it at low margins,' says Mark Mahaney, RBC Capital Managing Director, who has covered internet stocks since 1998. 'Very few companies want to come into Amazon's core businesses and try to compete with them at 1 per cent margins or 2 per cent margins.'[29]

And that's just the retail business. Many of Amazon's 'non-core' businesses are in fact loss leaders. Prime subscription fees may now be a healthy top-line contributor, but does it genuinely cover the cost of shipping for an entire year's worth of purchases? Unlikely, especially when you consider all the other perks that come with it.[30] Meanwhile, its devices such as Kindles and Echos[31] are typically sold at cost price or at a loss. Bezos has stated that when sold at their full retail price, Echo speakers are not loss-making[32]– but just how often is that? According to Amazon price tracker site Camelcamelcamel. com, devices like the Echo Dot and Echo Show are on sale as often as not.

Like Google, Amazon aims to lock in as many shoppers as possible and then make money on the content purchased through the device[33] (as well as gain valuable data about buying habits). Given that Echo owners spend 66 per cent more than the average Amazon shopper, the retailer is very clearly incentivized to subsidize sales[34] of its devices.

Uneven playing field: tax

We can't talk about Amazon's competitive advantages without mentioning tax. Amazon was one of the first companies to hit $1 trillion in market value and is now one of the world's largest retailers, in revenue terms.[35]

But companies don't pay tax on revenues – they pay tax on profits. Amazon's unconventional profit-sacrificing strategy has allowed it to minimize, sometimes even eliminate, its tax burden. After paying nothing in federal taxes for a couple of years, the result of various tax credits and tax breaks for executive stock options, Amazon started paying federal income tax again in the US in 2019.[36]

As an online retailer, Amazon has historically – and controversially – benefited from a 1992 Supreme Court ruling – Quill Corp. vs North Dakota – that prevented states from collecting sales tax from e-commerce companies unless those retailers had a physical presence in that state (in the form of an office or warehouse, for example). This was one of the reasons why Bezos was initially attracted to Washington as Amazon's headquarters: the state had a small population and its capital Seattle was becoming a technology hub. It's worth pointing out here that Bezos' first choice is said to have been a Native American reservation near San Francisco, which would have presented generous tax breaks had the state not intervened.

Amazon spent its early days building warehouses in small states like Nevada and Kansas, allowing it to deliver to nearby populous states like California and Texas, but without collecting sales taxes.[37] For years, the ability to sell stuff tax-free gave Amazon and other online retailers a gargantuan edge over bricks and mortar rivals. However, as Amazon continued to expand and its focus shifted to ever faster delivery, it had little choice but to open more fulfilment centres in closer proximity to its customers. 'When that strategy no longer became tenable, and as Amazon wanted to add more warehouses in more states to support its growing Prime two-day delivery program, the company often negotiated to get the taxes delayed, deferred, or reduced as a condition of collecting them',[38] wrote Jeremy Bowman of *The Motley Fool*.

Many states subsequently signed on to an agreement that allowed retailers to voluntarily collect sales tax. By 2017, Amazon was collecting sales tax from all 45 states that had a state-wide sales tax,[39] which meant that by the following year, when the Supreme Court finally overturned the 1992 ruling, the impact on Amazon was fairly minimal. It did, however, mean that Amazon's third-party merchants had to begin charging sales tax on their products (Amazon had previously only collected tax on the items it owned).[40]

> 'Amazon use various loopholes so they pay not a single solitary penny in federal income tax. I don't want to punish them, but that's just wrong.'
> **US President Joe Biden, 2021[41]**

When Amazon was on the hunt for a second headquarters, it solicited bids from cities and regions across North America, promising $5 billion in investment and 50,000 new jobs over the next decade. The *Hunger Games*-style competition resulted in over 200 bids, with extraordinary offers ranging from New Jersey's $7 billion in tax incentives to Chicago's promise that employees would have to pay part of their salary back to Amazon as 'income tax'.

In Europe, Amazon's tax structure has been equally controversial. After over a decade of channelling sales through entities in Luxembourg, in 2015 Amazon began accounting for sales and paying taxes in Britain, Germany, Spain and Italy. The EU has since ordered Amazon to pay back €250 million in taxes, the result of an unfair tax break the company was previously given by Luxembourg, and has proposed a 3 per cent digital services tax on revenues – rather than profits – of large tech companies. In the meantime, individual markets are taking it upon themselves to enact change at a country level: as of 2021, about half of all European OECD countries had either announced, proposed or implemented a digital services tax.[42]

Meanwhile, in the UK, a revaluation of business rates in 2017 disproportionately benefited Amazon and other online retailers. The rates, deemed by many as archaic, were calculated to take into account the rise in property prices since the Great Recession; as most of Amazon's warehouses are located out of town, they actually saw their value (and therefore

FIGURE 2.5   When do we stop calling Amazon a retailer? Net sales by business segment

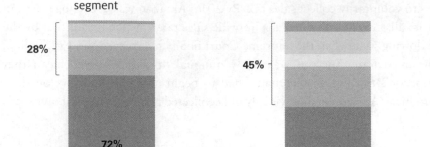

business levy) decline while many high street retailers saw their bill go up – some by up to 400 per cent. Another massive competitive advantage for Amazon.

But Amazon's tax fight is only just heating up. In 2021, the Biden administration proposed raising the US corporate tax rate to 28 per cent (this was then changed to a 15 per cent tax floor in a bid to win congressional support) and changing the tax code to close loopholes that allow companies to move profits overseas. At least 55 of America's biggest companies paid zero in federal taxes for 2020, despite a collective $40.5 billion in pre-tax earnings.[43] Although it's entirely legal for companies to move between countries, many governments, and increasingly consumers, believe that the likes of Amazon have a moral obligation to pay more tax, particularly in the wake of the pandemic.

In 2021, the G7 nations – Canada, France, Germany, Italy, Japan, the UK and the US – signed a landmark deal to reform the global tax system to more accurately reflect today's digital era. The historic G7 tax deal set a minimum global corporation tax rate of 15 per cent and requires multinational companies to pay tax on profits they generate in a given country, rather than where the company is headquartered for tax purposes. This means that companies like Amazon could be taxed in any market where they generate more than 10 per cent profit on sales. Although Amazon's retail margins are consistently below this threshold, its cloud computing business, Amazon Web

FIGURE 2.6   Spot the cash cow: Amazon operating margin by segment

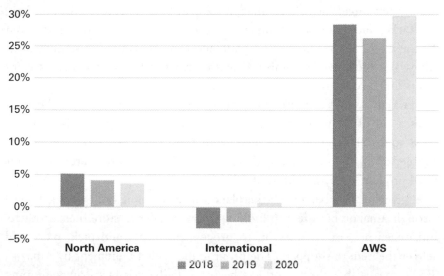

Services, consistently delivers an operating margin in the 25–30 per cent range. There's no hiding from this one: the days of big tech tax avoidance are coming to an end.

Three pillars: Marketplace, Prime, AWS

Tax loopholes and unique access to cheap capital have historically given Amazon a sustained competitive advantage over its bricks and mortar rivals. As we've touched on previously, this allowed Amazon to more rapidly invest in new areas for growth, resulting in what it describes as the three pillars of the business: Marketplace, Prime and AWS.

These diverse revenue streams have played an instrumental role in accelerating Amazon's flywheel. With the exception of AWS (which can perhaps be excused given this is Amazon's main profit engine), these businesses have directly added value to customers. What is more, they are largely unique to Amazon.

Marketplace

As one of the first retailers to open its site to third-party sellers, Amazon has been able to achieve its dream of offering 'Earth's biggest selection'.

Customers benefit by having millions of products across dozens of categories at their fingertips, while Amazon reduces both inventory cost and risk.
Its Marketplace has enabled Amazon to become the first port of call for even
the most obscure products – from silicone wine glasses to cat scratch turn-
tables – which, when combined with Prime delivery, becomes a very
compelling proposition.

Marketplace has also proved to be a fruitful revenue stream, as Amazon
takes a cut of about 15 per cent of the price of the merchandise.[44] From
2018 to 2020, revenues generated from third-party seller services nearly
doubled to $81 billion, making this Amazon's largest source of revenue after
retail product sales and ahead of AWS.[45]

A growing number of Marketplace sellers are not only opting to sell
through Amazon but are also looking to the retailer to store their products
and, when an order comes in, to process payments and pick, pack and
deliver the item to shoppers. The programme, called Fulfilment by Amazon
(FBA), means that these products become eligible for fast Prime shipping
and also have a greater chance of winning the Buy Box (so that the product
appears in the first 'Add to Basket' button on the product detail page). For
Amazon, FBA allows it to make better use of excess capacity while simultaneously increasing shipping volumes, and therefore leverage, with the likes
of UPS and FedEx. But perhaps the best part of FBA is that it would take
decades for another retailer to replicate.

Prime

Amazon's membership scheme has proven to be the glue of its ecosystem.
The tech giant has cleverly taken Prime from a scheme that initially centred
on delivery perks to an all-encompassing digital content-streaming, book-
lending, photo-storing beast of a membership programme. The result?
Higher spend, shopper frequency and retention. As we'll explore in the
coming chapters, today Prime is so much more than a loyalty programme –
it's become a way of life.

Amazon Web Services

Amazon's cloud storage service may not directly benefit shoppers, but it has
certainly proven to be Amazon's white knight (and therefore it's no surprise
that the person who built this business would go on to succeed Bezos).

Operating margins are consistently in double digits compared with the paltry 3–5 per cent range often coming from the retail unit (see Figure 2.6). In 2020, AWS was responsible for approximately two-thirds of Amazon's total operating profit. In some years, it's been as high as 100 per cent.[46] Remember Brad Stone's point about feeding *any* part of the flywheel to accelerate it? A uniquely profitable division within Amazon means greater opportunity to reinvest in the core retail division.

> 'Many characterized AWS as a bold – and unusual – bet when we started. "What does this have to do with selling books?" We could have stuck to the knitting. I'm glad we didn't.'
> **Jeff Bezos**[47]

AWS is the clear market leader in the public cloud business, powering hundreds of thousands of businesses in nearly 200 countries around the world,[48] allowing Amazon, in analyst Ben Thompson's words, to 'take a cut of all economic activity'.[49] Unsurprisingly, major competitors like Walmart and Kroger are steering clear of AWS (much to the advantage of other cloud providers like Google and Microsoft), but Amazon still provides cloud computing services to a number of retail brands which, as of 2021, included Interflora, Under Armour and Ocado.

AWS might be the outlier of an already eclectic and wide-ranging mix of business units at Amazon, but it still bears all the traditional Amazonian hallmarks: customer-obsessed, inventive and experimental, and long-term-oriented.

Tech company first, retailer second

As we established earlier in the chapter, Amazon's technology roots and passion for invention are what sets it distantly apart from rivals. In fact, many of Amazon's past innovations can be easily forgotten because they have simply become today's normal. Cast your mind back to the late '90s: online shopping used to be quite a laborious process. Amazon cut out the friction by launching 1-click shopping, personalized product recommendations and user-generated ratings and reviews.

> 'Invention is the root of our success. We've done crazy things together, and then made them normal.'
> **Jeff Bezos, 2021**[50]

Delivery, meanwhile, wasn't always fast and free. Prime significantly raised customer expectations, leaving competitors with little choice but to invest in their own fulfilment capabilities. Amazon tackled one of the biggest barriers to online shopping – missed deliveries – with the 2011 launch of Amazon Lockers. Today, virtually every major Western retailer offers click & collect. 'The only real constant in retail is customers' desire for lower prices, better selection, and convenience,' said Jeff Bezos in 2020.[51]

Meanwhile, e-readers sounded like science fiction before Amazon introduced the Kindle. Although the broader category has seen a slowdown in sales (we can blame screen fatigue), the convenience of storing hundreds of books on a single device was a gamechanger at launch.

> 'We may be a retailer, but we are a tech company at heart. When Jeff started Amazon, he didn't start it to open [a] book shop.'
> **Amazon CTO Werner Vogels**[52]

Amazon is the ultimate disruptor. These are just a handful of initiatives that have revolutionized shopping and consumption habits. Most of Amazon's innovations catch competitors on the back foot, leaving them in the undesirable position of reacting to rather than leading change. 'We weren't the first place you go when it's time to buy products online,' Walmart CEO Doug McMillon said in 2021. 'We're trying to change that, obviously. You've got to earn that. You've got to have the assortment. You got to have the price. You got to provide service. You got to deliver when you're supposed to deliver.'[53]

Amazon has capitalized on its first-mover advantage in the digital space and one party in particular has benefited – the customer. Ceaseless innovation from Amazon raises customer expectations, which in turn leads competitors to raise their game and ultimately creates a better experience for the shopper. What would the world be like if Amazon didn't exist? In a nutshell, customers would be way more tolerant of mediocre service.

'If you get it right, a few years after a surprising invention, the new thing has become normal. People yawn. And that yawn is the greatest compliment an inventor can receive.'
Jeff Bezos, 2021[54]

The big question is, of the experiments currently brewing, which will be the ones to stick and transform the industry once again? Amazon has already been a phenomenal catalyst for change in areas like delivery, checkout and voice technology, and is almost singlehandedly shaping the future of retailing in the Western world. Here are our predictions:

- **The store is dead. Long live the store!** Amazon's growing appetite for stores is validation that physical retail is evolving, not dying. Pure-play e-commerce is no longer enough. As technology breaks down the barriers between physical and digital, those retailers without a bricks and mortar presence – already under pressure to offset shipping and customer acquisition costs – will be severely disadvantaged.

- **There will be a greater divergence between functional and fun shopping.** In the future, consumers will spend significantly less time buying the essentials. Our homes, powered by Amazon, will do all the mundane reordering so shoppers will never have to go into a supermarket to buy bleach or toilet paper again. Instead, these products will be automatically replenished – the ultimate test of brand loyalty. Amazon's quest to take the chore out of food shopping and facilitate a frictionless experience creates an opportunity for competitors to focus on WACD: What Amazon Can't Do.

- **Winning in retail today means excelling where Amazon cannot, and therefore focusing less on product and more on experience, curation, community and discovery.** The store of the future will go from transactional to experiential as competitors look to distance themselves from the utilitarian aspect of buying online. Amazon is great for purchasing, not so compelling for shopping. We believe the design, layout and broader purpose of the physical store will evolve to better reflect shifting consumer priorities. It won't just be a place to buy, but also a place to eat, work, play, discover, learn and even rent products.

- **Amazon will democratize online grocery, as technology dismantles the barriers traditionally associated with grocery e-commerce in the US.** More anti-Amazon alliances will form, with the likes of Instacart, Deliveroo, Ocado and Google particularly benefiting from Amazon's grocery ambitions. Once Amazon convinces shoppers that it is a credible alternative to the supermarkets, then it has cleared that final hurdle to becoming the Everything Store. Capturing that high-frequency purchase makes it easier to cross-sell and bait shoppers into its broader ecosystem, making Amazon the default shopping option. And that's when things get ugly, not just for the supermarkets but for all of retail: Amazon shoppers tend to be loyal, lifelong customers.

- **As Prime transitions to a bricks and mortar setting, retailers will have to drastically rethink their own loyalty schemes.** The notion of swiping a plastic card at the till in exchange for points is dated. The next evolution of loyalty will see retailers ditch the 'more you shop, more you earn' concept. Points-based schemes will become a thing of the past as the loyalty battleground shifts from saving customers money to saving them time, energy and effort. Hyper-personalization through real-time mobile rewards will become the norm. There is an urgency to go beyond the transaction, developing a deep, emotional bond with shoppers.

- **One-hour delivery or less will become the norm in urban areas, as legacy retailers reconfigure their best assets – their stores – to act as mini warehouses.** Retailers must also utilize their physical locations to appease today's 'on my terms' shopper with instore collection and to address the Achilles heel of online retail – returns. Expect to see more collaboration, even with Amazon itself, in this area as retailers join forces to better serve the customer. The store of the future won't just become a hub for experience but also for fulfilment.

- **Amazon will continue to relentlessly innovate on behalf of the customer, wowing shoppers and disrupting more sectors in the process.** In the future, the notion of skipping the checkout will feel natural (and not like we're shoplifting); in-home or in-car delivery will be an acceptable alternative to traditional unattended delivery; and the main barrier to buying clothes online – sizing – will be largely diminished. Meanwhile, the combination of more sophisticated AI and the penetration of Alexa into the home and on our phones could lead to the era of the truly personalized shopping assistant.

- **Amazon will transition into a predominantly service-based company.** Retail, as a percentage of overall sales, continues to decline (from 72 per cent in 2015 to 55 per cent in 2020) (see Figure 2.5).[55] We believe the tipping point, when the majority of Amazon's sales come from services rather than first-party goods, will take place before 2025. Although there is still plenty of opportunity to grow its core retail offering internationally, Amazon is building out a portfolio of wide-ranging services for consumers (through continuous Prime enhancements) and also for other businesses such as Marketplace, AWS, Just Walk Out and advertising. What is more, as third-party sales continue to grow as a percentage of total paid units, Amazon's stated sales become less reflective of the gross merchandise volume moving through Amazon (because this only accounts for its take of the third-party vendor's sale, not the full order value). Amazon is moving from retail merchant to indispensable infrastructure.

- **In the future, more retailers will run on Amazon's rails.** Retailers themselves are increasingly content to overlook the huge competitive threat posed by Amazon to take advantage of its physical and digital infrastructure. Some may consider it playing with fire – certainly retailers like Toys R Us, Borders and Circuit City would. They were among Amazon's very first 'frenemies' in the early noughties when they outsourced their e-commerce businesses to the giant – all three have since gone bankrupt. But we believe more retailers will cozy up to Amazon if it helps them to achieve greater reach (Marketplace), drive traffic to stores (Amazon pop-ups, click & collect, instore returns) or improve the customer experience (same-day delivery, checkout-free shopping, voice shopping). The unique dual role of competitor and service provider is becoming more apparent by the day. 'Co-opetition' is a key theme for the future.

In summary, Amazon is not your average retailer because it's not actually a retailer. It's a tech company whose sole purpose is perpetual innovation on behalf of its customers. And it happens to sell a lot of stuff in the process.

Notes

1 Amazon 2020 Letter to Shareholders. Available from: https://www.aboutamazon.com/news/company-news/2020-letter-to-shareholders (archived at https://perma.cc/WYZ9-8FSF) [Last accessed 18/6/2021].

2 Amazon's website (2018). Available from: https://www.amazon.jobs/en/ principles (archived at https://perma.cc/2ZEK-FV4Y) [Last accessed 19/6/2018].

3 https://www.jimcollins.com/concepts/the-flywheel.html (archived at https://perma.cc/24DK-G7V7).

4 Stone, B (2013) *The Everything Store: Jeff Bezos and the age of Amazon*, Bantam Press, London.

5 Amazon's website (2021). Available from: https://www.amazon.jobs/en/ jobs/1139963/systems-development-engineer (archived at https://perma.cc/ M6DE-9FMV) [Last accessed 18/6/2021].

6 Stone, B (2013) *The Everything Store: Jeff Bezos and the age of Amazon*, Bantam Press, London.

7 Tonner, Andrew (2016) 7 Sam Walton quotes you should read right now, *The Motley Fool*, 8 September. Available from: https://www.fool.com/ investing/2016/09/08/7-sam-walton-quotes-you-should-read-right-now.aspx (archived at https://perma.cc/3N6J-PTKK) [Last accessed 19/6/2018].

8 Amazon staff (2017) 2016 Letter to Shareholders, 17 April. Available from: https://www.aboutamazon.com/news/company-news/2016-letter-to-shareholders (archived at https://perma.cc/BXF9-55GV) [Last accessed 12/7/21].

9 Amazon 2016 letter to shareholders (2017), *Amazon.com*. Available from: http://phx.corporate-ir.net/phoenix.zhtml?c=97664&p=irol-reportsannual (archived at https://perma.cc/485J-9M5M) [Last accessed 19/6/2018].

10 Fox, Justin (2021) Amazon spends billions on R&D. Just don't call it that, *Bloomberg*, 11 February. Available from: https://www.bloomberg.com/opinion/ articles/2021-02-11/amazon-spends-billions-on-r-d-just-don-t-call-it-that (archived at https://perma.cc/C82K-GNPZ) [Last accessed 18/6/2021].

11 Delgado, Cristina (2013) Butcher's boy who has discreetly risen to become Spain's second-richest man, *El Pais*, 11 November. Available from: https:// elpais.com/elpais/2013/11/11/inenglish/1384183939_312177.html (archived at https://perma.cc/GQU5-ABF6) [Last accessed 19/6/2018].

12 Sillitoe, Ben (2018) 10 tips from a UK retail stalwart: ASOS chairman Brian McBride, *Retail Connections*, 9 May. Available from: http://www. retailconnections.co.uk/articles/10-tips-uk-retail-boss-brian-mcbride/ (archived at https://perma.cc/HU48-Z7FY) [Last accessed 19/6/2018].

13 Amazon staff (2017) 2016 Letter to Shareholders, 17 April. Available from: https://www.aboutamazon.com/news/company-news/2016-letter-to-shareholders (archived at https://perma.cc/BXF9-55GV) [Last accessed 12/7/21].

14 Misener, Paul (13 September 2017) Retail innovation at Amazon presentation, *Retail Week*. Tech event, 2017 Agenda. Available from: http://rw.retail-week.

com/Video/TECH/AGENDA/PDF/MAINSTAGE_AGENDA.pdf (archived at https://perma.cc/K3TW-HH9V) [Last accessed 2/4/2018].

15 McAllister, Ian (2012) What is Amazon's approach to product development and product management? *Quora*, 18 May. Available from: https://www. quora.com/What-is-Amazons-approach-to-product-development-and-product-management (archived at https://perma.cc/2FY2-YKA7) [Last accessed 19/6/2018].

16 Gonzalez, Angel (2016) For Amazon exec Stephenie Landry, the future is Now, *Seattle Times*, 21 May. Available from: https://www.seattletimes.com/business/ amazon/for-amazon-exec-stephenie-landry-the-future-is-now/ (archived at https://perma.cc/47KE-YW5Q) [Last accessed 19/6/2018].

17 Statement by Jeffrey P. Bezos Founder & Chief Executive Officer, Amazon before the U.S. House of Representatives Committee on the Judiciary Subcommittee on Antitrust, Commercial, and Administrative Law (2020). Available from: https://www.congress.gov/116/meeting/house/110883/ witnesses/HHRG-116-JU05-Wstate-BezosJ-20200729.pdf (archived at https:// perma.cc/F9H3-5W5K) [Last accessed 18/6/2021].

18 MacLean, Rob (2000) What business is Amazon.com really in? *Inc.*, 21 February. Available from: https://www.inc.com/magazine/20000201/16854. html (archived at https://perma.cc/8CMY-VUBT) [Last accessed 19/6/2018].

19 Amazon 10-K for the fiscal year ended December 31, 2020. Available from: https://www.sec.gov/ix?doc=/Archives/edgar/data/1018724/ 000101872421000004/amzn-20201231.htm (archived at https://perma.cc/ QG5L-YE6G) [Last accessed 18/6/2021].

20 Neate, Rupert (2021) What will Amazon founder Jeff Bezos do next?, *The Guardian*, 3 February. Available from: https://www.theguardian.com/ technology/2021/feb/03/what-will-amazon-founder-jeff-bezos-do-next (archived at https://perma.cc/2NCU-K3EQ) [Last accessed 18/6/2021].

21 Statement by Jeffrey P. Bezos Founder & Chief Executive Officer, Amazon before the U.S. House of Representatives Committee on the Judiciary Subcommittee on Antitrust, Commercial, and Administrative Law (2020). Available from: https://www.congress.gov/116/meeting/house/110883/ witnesses/HHRG-116-JU05-Wstate-BezosJ-20200729.pdf (archived at https:// perma.cc/35DH-GR3N) [Last accessed 18/6/2021].

22 Del Ray, Jason (2019) The making of Amazon Prime, the internet's most successful and devastating membership program, *Vox*, 3 May. Available from: https://www.vox.com/recode/2019/5/3/18511544/amazon-prime-oral-history-jeff-bezos-one-day-shipping (archived at https://perma.cc/B6H7-YBT8) [Last accessed 18/6/2021].

23 Khan, Lina (2017) Amazon's antitrust paradox, *Yale Law Journal*. Available from: https://www.yalelawjournal.org/note/amazons-antitrust-paradox (archived at https://perma.cc/84P6-KHL6) [Last accessed 19/6/2018].

24 Pender, Kathleen (2000) Scathing report of Amazon is a must-read for stock owners, *SF Gate*, 30 June. Available from: https://www.sfgate.com/business/ networth/article/Scathing-Report-of-Amazon-Is-a-Must-Read-for-2750932.php (archived at https://perma.cc/9DNV-P5A5) [Last accessed 19/6/2018].

25 Anonymous (2000) Can Amazon survive? *Knowledge at Wharton*, 30 August. Available from: http://knowledge.wharton.upenn.edu/article/can-amazon-survive/ (archived at https://perma.cc/D3P4-S9AR) [Last accessed 19/6/2018].

26 Anonymous (2000) Amazon: Ponzi scheme or Wal-Mart of the web? *Slate*, 8 February. Available from: http://www.slate.com/articles/business/moneybox/ 2000/02/amazon_ponzi_scheme_or_walmart_of_the_web.html (archived at https://perma.cc/7ADG-4SQN) [Last accessed 19/6/2018].

27 Corkery, Michael and Wingfield, Nick (2018) Amazon asked for patience. Remarkably, Wall Street complied, *New York Times*, 4 February. Available from: https://www.nytimes.com/2018/02/04/technology/amazon-asked-for-patience-remarkably-wall-street-complied.html (archived at https://perma.cc/ UH9T-9BZ8) [Last accessed 19/6/2018].

28 Lee, Nathaniel, Lebowitz, Shana and Kovach, Steve (2017) Scott Galloway: Amazon is using an unfair advantage to dominate its competitors, *Business Insider*, 11 October. Available from: http://uk.businessinsider.com/scott-galloway-why-amazon-successful-2017-10 (archived at https://perma.cc/ 2S7E-9P88) [Last accessed 28/6/2018].

29 Fox, Justin (2013) How Amazon trained its investors to behave, *Harvard Business Review*, 30 January. Available from: https://hbr.org/2013/01/ howamazon-trained-its-investo (archived at https://perma.cc/5HX2-RXMF) [Last accessed 28/6/2018].

30 Hern, Alex (2013) How can Amazon pay tax on profits it doesn't make? *The Guardian*, 16 May. Available from: https://www.theguardian.com/ commentisfree/2013/may/16/amazon-tax-avoidance-profits (archived at https:// perma.cc/C9XY-NUDV) [Last accessed 28/6/2018].

31 Nellis, Stephen and Paresh, Dave (2018) Amazon, Google cut speaker prices in market share contest: analysts. Reuters, 3 January. Available from: https:// www.reuters.com/article/us-amazon-alphabet-speakers/amazon-google-cut-speaker-prices-in-market-share-contest-analysts-idUSKBN1ES0VV (archived at https://perma.cc/6YXX-Z3K5) [Last accessed 28/6/2018].

32 Hollister, Sean (2020) Amazon doesn't sell Echo speakers at a loss, says Bezos-unless they're on sale, *The Verge*, 29 July. Available from: https://www. theverge.com/2020/7/29/21347121/amazon-echo-speaker-price-undercut-rivals-loss-sale-antitrust-hearing (archived at https://perma.cc/E6XS-WXEG) [Last accessed 18/6/2021].

33 Santos, Alexis (2012) Bezos: Amazon breaks even on Kindle devices, not trying to make money on hardware, *Engadget*, 12 October. Available from: https:// www.engadget.com/2012/10/12/amazon-kindle-fire-hd-paperwhite-hardware-no-profit/ (archived at https://perma.cc/KD2F-MMM6) [Last accessed 28/6/2018].

34 Williams, Robert (2018) Study: Amazon Echo owners are big spenders, *Mobile Marketer*, 4 January. Available from: https://www.mobilemarketer.com/news/study-amazon-echo-owners-are-big-spenders/514050/ (archived at https://perma.cc/5CKQ-FRZN) [Last accessed 28/6/2018].

35 La Monica, Paul R (2018) Apple is leading the race to $1 trillion, *CNN*, 27 February. Available from: http://money.cnn.com/2018/02/27/investing/apple-google-amazon-microsoft-trillion-dollar-market-value/index.html (archived at https://perma.cc/9PKS-K4BP) [Last accessed 28/6/2018].

36 Bose, Nandita (2021) Biden singles out Amazon for not paying federal taxes, Reuters, 1 April. Available from: https://www.reuters.com/article/us-usa-biden-amazon-taxes-idUSKBN2BN3LL (archived at https://perma.cc/H5ZX-R22C) [Last accessed 18/6/2021].

37 Soper, Spencer, Townsend, Matthew and Browning, Lynnley (2017) Trump's bruising tweet highlights Amazon's lingering tax fight, *Bloomberg*, 17 August. Available from: https://www.bloomberg.com/news/articles/2017-08-17/trump-s-bruising-tweet-highlights-amazon-s-lingering-tax-fight (archived at https://perma.cc/65LD-2HGJ) [Last accessed 28/6/2018].

38 Bowman, Jeremy (2018) Analysis: Trump is right. Amazon is a master of tax avoidance, *USA Today*, 9 April. Available from: https://www.usatoday.com/story/money/business/2018/04/09/trump-is-right-amazon-is-a-master-of-tax-avoidance/33653439/ (archived at https://perma.cc/4NJZ-BG9B) [Last accessed 28/6/2018].

39 Isidore, Chris (2017) Amazon to start collecting state sales taxes everywhere, *CNN*, 29 March. Available from: http://money.cnn.com/2017/03/29/technology/amazon-sales-tax/index.html (archived at https://perma.cc/9G9Q-NEVH) [Last accessed 28/6/2018].

40 Finley, Klint (2018) Why the Supreme Court sales tax ruling may benefit Amazon, *Wired*, 21 June. Available from: https://www.wired.com/story/why-the-supreme-court-sales-tax-ruling-may-benefit-amazon/ (archived at https://perma.cc/6K69-WGDK) [Last accessed 27/82018].

41 Bose, Nandita (2021) Biden singles out Amazon for not paying federal taxes, Reuters, 1 April. Available from: https://www.reuters.com/article/us-usa-biden-amazon-taxes-idUSKBN2BN3LL (archived at https://perma.cc/3N7R-E22M) [Last accessed 18/6/2021].

42 Asen, Elke (2021) What European OECD Countries Are Doing about Digital Services Taxes, *The Tax Foundation*, 25 March. Available from: https://taxfoundation.org/digital-tax-europe-2020/ (archived at https://perma.cc/6VPF-ADCL) [Last accessed 18/6/2021].

43 White, Martha C (2021) Biden's plan to overhaul tax code would close offshore tax loopholes, NBC News, 7 April. Available from: https://www.nbcnews.com/business/economy/biden-s-plan-overhaul-tax-code-would-close-offshore-tax-n1263372 (archived at https://perma.cc/6VPF-ADCL) [Last accessed 18/6/2021].

44 Ovide, Shira (2018) How Amazon's bottomless appetite became corporate America's nightmare, *Bloomberg*, 14 March. Available from: https://www. bloomberg.com/graphics/2018-amazon-industry-displacement/ (archived at https://perma.cc/9FAL-MFLG) [Last accessed 28/6/2018].

45 Amazon 10-K for the fiscal year ended December 31, 2020. Available from: https://www.sec.gov/ix?doc=/Archives/edgar/data/1018724/ 000101872421000004/amzn-20201231.htm (archived at https://perma.cc/ LG7M-T3P2) [Last accessed 18/6/2021].

46 Amazon 10-K for the fiscal year ended December 31, 2020. Available from: https://www.sec.gov/ix?doc=/Archives/edgar/data/1018724/ 000101872421000004/amzn-20201231.htm (archived at https://perma.cc/ EP6J-QTGP) [Last accessed 18/6/2021].

47 Amazon 2015 letter to shareholders (2016) Amazon.com, Available from: http://phx.corporate-ir.net/phoenix.zhtml?c=97664&p=irol-reportsannual (archived at https://perma.cc/99QT-STRX) [Last accessed 28/6/18]

48 Amazon's website (nd) https://aws.amazon.com/about-aws/ (archived at https://perma.cc/X27N-EQV4) [Last accessed 28/6/18].

49 Thompson, Ben (2017) Amazon's new customer, *Stratechery*, 19 June. Available from: https://stratechery.com/2017/amazons-new-customer/ (archived at https://perma.cc/6S9W-LPD3) [Last accessed 28/6/2018].

50 Email from Jeff Bezos to employees (2021). Available from: https://www. aboutamazon.com/news/company-news/email-from-jeff-bezos-to-employees (archived at https://perma.cc/4WGB-PET5) [Last accessed 18/6/2021].

51 Statement by Jeffrey P. Bezos, Founder & Chief Executive Officer, Amazon before the U.S. House of Representatives Committee on the Judiciary Subcommittee on Antitrust, Commercial, and Administrative Law (2020). Available from: https://www.congress.gov/116/meeting/house/110883/ witnesses/HHRG-116-JU05-Wstate-BezosJ-20200729.pdf (archived at https:// perma.cc/JV78-ZHA5) [Last accessed 18/6/2021].

52 Miller, Ron (2016) At Amazon the Flywheel Effect drives innovation, *TechCrunch*, 10 September. Available from: https://techcrunch.com/2016/09/10/ at-amazon-the-flywheel-effect-drives-innovation/ (archived at https://perma.cc/ 5F8J-9BCJ) [Last accessed 28/6/2018].

53 Wal-Mart Stores Inc. (WMT) Q4 2021 earnings call transcript (2021). Available from: https://www.fool.com/earnings/call-transcripts/2021/02/19/wal-mart-stores-inc-wmt-q4-2020-earnings-call-tran/ (archived at https://perma.cc/ 9ZZQ-MDRA) [Last accessed 18/6/2021].

54 Email from Jeff Bezos to employees (2021). Available from: https://www. aboutamazon.com/news/company-news/email-from-jeff-bezos-to-employees (archived at https://perma.cc/5P8G-THM7) [Last accessed 18/6/2021].

55 Amazon 10-K for the fiscal year ended December 31, 2020. Available from: https://www.sec.gov/ix?doc=/Archives/edgar/data/1018724/ 000101872421000004/amzn-20201231.htm (archived at https://perma.cc/ E7GV-75JK) [Last accessed 18/6/2021].

03

Pandemic pivots: how COVID upended the retail industry

'Pan' + 'Demos' = 'All' + 'People'

The retail sector is no stranger to disruption, yet nothing in our lifetime has jolted the industry like COVID-19. As the COVID crisis unfolded in early 2020, consumer behaviour changed dramatically and instantaneously. Everyday certainties dissolved and consumers' needs dropped right down to the bottom of Maslow's pyramid – physiological and safety. As 21st-century shoppers, we had become used to having the world at our fingertips, yet seemingly overnight COVID redefined our needs, values and expectations.

As retailers learned to safely operate in the midst of the pandemic, they had no choice but to temporarily sacrifice most of the joy and pleasure of shopping instore: closing fitting rooms and cafés, encouraging customers to shop alone, requiring shoppers to wear face coverings, follow one-way systems and even queue to get in at busy times.

> 'There are decades where nothing happens, and there are weeks where decades happen.'
> **Lenin**

But here's the good news – we believe there will be a post-pandemic revival of the physical store. This century will experience its own Roaring Twenties. We are social creatures, after all, and the notion of 'going shopping' is inherently a leisure activity. After the last major pandemic in 1918, we saw the emergence of department stores, cinemas and stadiums. The future of retail in a post-COVID world is fewer but far better stores that will tap into emotion, human connection, discovery and community. Bricks and mortar retail will become a high-touch, sensory-driven experience once again.

Shopping habits, however, have been upended by the pandemic. Our lives are no longer just digitally influenced, they have become overwhelmingly digital. We have learned to work, educate, shop, socialize and even exercise online, and many of these habits will outlast the pandemic. In the future, it will be difficult to know where the physical world ends and the digital one begins.

COVID: the great retail accelerant

As retail analysts, we are continuously evaluating industry trends in an attempt to predict the next ones. Making retail predictions can be tricky at the best of times, but no one could have planned for the mysterious illness that was beginning to spread more than 5,000 miles away in Wuhan, China. And certainly no one could have predicted the rapid speed at which the COVID crisis would unfold, changing our world for ever.

On the very last day of the decade, Chinese authorities alerted the World Health Organization (WHO) to a growing number of pneumonia-like cases and by early March, the coronavirus outbreak was declared a pandemic. What followed was a devastating year of incalculable loss, a perpetual cycle of lockdowns, physical and mental health struggles and, consequently, a radical shift in consumer behaviour. Even as we write this book in mid-2021, over a year into the pandemic, changes are happening on what feels like a daily basis, highlighting the unprecedented nature of the COVID crisis and the resulting shockwaves that continue to ripple through the retail industry.

> 'The Covid-19 crisis will cause five years' change to our high streets in less than 12 months.'
> **Sir John Timpson, Chairman of Timpson, 2021**[1]

The unparalleled disruption caused by the pandemic resulted in an acceleration of many retail trends that had long been brewing. What would have taken years was now, incredibly, happening in weeks. As analysts, we had been warning of Retail Darwinism for years; now, for the first time, retailers were genuinely forced to evolve to ensure their survival. Agility was no longer a nice-to-have.

EARLY PANDEMIC PIVOTS: RESPONDING TO AN UNFOLDING CRISIS

The actions taken by retailers in those early, uncertain days will define them in the future, whether that's converting perfume factories to make hand sanitizer (LVMH) or turning car parks into coronavirus testing sites (Walmart). In the UK, beauty retailer Lush was the first high street retailer to take action against the virus, encouraging shoppers to come in and wash their hands without any pressure to make a purchase. Retailers began putting people before profit. UK frozen food retailer Cook offered customers a free frozen meal to take back to an ill or elderly neighbour. Carrefour in France and Iceland in Northern Ireland were two of the first supermarkets to open earlier, exclusively for customers aged 70 and over. To protect its staff and the community, clothing company Patagonia was one of the first retailers to shut not only its shops but its e-commerce operations too. Meanwhile, British grocery retailer Morrisons switched to paying its small suppliers immediately to help them with cash flow during the early days of the pandemic.

Now let's explore the trends that were fast-tracked by the pandemic.

Demise of 'status-quo retail'

Retailers are finding that if they weren't relevant before the pandemic, they're definitely not now. COVID exacerbated the many challenges plaguing the sector – an oversupply of retail space, the rise of more nimble competition, the need to adapt to seismic technology-driven changes in shopping habits.

Retail's tectonic plates were shifting well before 2020, so there had already been a natural filtering of those retailers that failed to stay relevant. The pandemic simply exposed the remaining dinosaurs, the mediocre retailers, the digital laggards. For years, we had been urging retailers to 'adapt or die'. When COVID hit, it was more like 'adapt or die an imminent death'.

'It's only when the tide goes out that you learn who's been swimming naked.'
Warren Buffett[2]

A key theme of this crisis has been a deepening of the disparity between retail's winners and losers. It has accelerated the bifurcation of retail and the importance of agility has been reinforced. COVID has been the final nail in the coffin for those retailers with underlying structural issues, many now paying the price for years of inaction.

In the UK, we have bid farewell to struggling retailers such as Topshop and TM Lewin – iconic brands but ones that ultimately failed to stay relevant. The very same week that Amazon announced a combined 85,000 new jobs across North America and the UK,[3,4] we witnessed Debenhams, a retailer that had traded on British high streets for over *200 years*, close its last stores. But perhaps it doesn't get any more Darwinian than dead mall space in the US being converted into Google offices and Amazon fulfilment centres. COVID has simply accelerated the demise of irrelevant retail.

Digital transformation: COVID will finish what Amazon started

Imagine if the pandemic had hit in 2000 instead of 2020. Quarantine days would have looked quite different without the likes of Zoom, Netflix, Spotify, Facebook and Uber Eats to keep us connected, fed and entertained. Back in 2000, Amazon was primarily a book and music/video retailer – and you had to spend $100 to qualify for free shipping!

In contrast, today we live in a ubiquitously connected world. A world that is digitally accessible, where amenities are on tap and meals turn up within minutes of ordering. A world where we can while away the hours consuming digital content, a world of home comforts and infinite choice. A world with instant access to millions of products to buy, songs to listen to and movies to watch. There has never been a more empowering time to be a consumer.

In many ways 21st-century retail has been well equipped to handle a global lockdown thanks to considerable investment in both e-commerce fulfilment capabilities and technologies that connect online and physical retail. This meant that when stores were required to shut, retailers could continue to serve customers from the only channel available – e-commerce (see Figures 3.1 and 3.2).

Looking ahead, COVID will supercharge digital transformation. This is a pivotal moment for e-commerce, a once-in-a-lifetime opportunity for online retailers to hit the gas. COVID has accelerated the broader shift to digital

FIGURE 3.1   The great acceleration: e-commerce as a share of total US retail sales

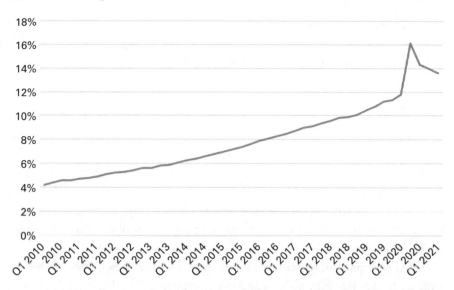

SOURCE US Census Bureau
NOTE Seasonally adjusted data

FIGURE 3.2   Retail e-commerce sales growth by region, 2020

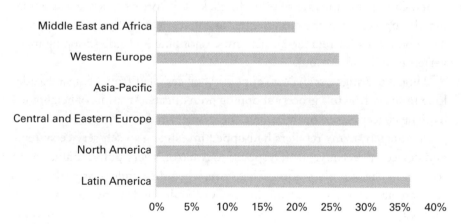

SOURCE   eMarketer

and, as we will explore throughout the book, the big question now is whether habits learned so swiftly during lockdown will outlast the pandemic. In China, the SARS epidemic in 2003 led to a permanent shift in consumer behaviour and contributed to the launch of digital payments and online shopping. The after-effects of this global pandemic will be far greater and wider reaching: there will be no return to the status quo.

'The [pandemic-induced] shift to online doesn't look like a 12-month/18-month phenomenon: this is something that will permanently change people's shopping habits.'
Dame Sharon White, John Lewis Chairman, 2020[5]

Pre-COVID, if you asked us to name a disruptive force other than Amazon that would rapidly accelerate the shift to online shopping, we would have been genuinely stumped. For years, Amazon was the primary catalyst for change in the retail sector, from fast delivery to one-click checkout. Amazon has a track record of stamping out complacency, enhancing the customer experience and steering competitors towards a more digital world. But it ultimately took a pandemic for many retailers to address their own complacency and recognize the importance of digital strength. Necessity is, after all, the mother of invention.

In a post-pandemic world, digital transformation will no longer be optional: COVID will finish what Amazon started.

The digital store: frictionless shopping and no-touch checkout

When COVID hit, the race to offer the slickest instore experience was immediately superseded by the need to offer one that was safe, hygienic and quick. The good news for retailers? Frictionless shopping and safe shopping inadvertently go hand in hand.

Almost overnight, scan & go apps and devices went from being a decade-long industry trial to a grocery shopping prerequisite. At a time of heightened hygiene concerns, no-touch became the new normal.

Fortunately, many retailers had upped investment in self-service systems and devices in recent years in response to Amazon's very public ambitions to roll out its checkout-less stores. Therefore, when the pandemic struck, retailers were able to rapidly extend this as COVID drove demand for low-touch physical shopping environments. For example, Marks & Spencer became the first British retailer to commit to offering checkout-free technology options across its entire store estate. A trial no more.

'The "new normal"… isn't new anymore. It's just normal. Call it a pivot, a new dawn or a fresh start, but one thing is clear: things will never be the same again.'
James Bailey, Executive Director, Waitrose, 2021[6]

In fact, the pandemic presented an opportunity to really scale technologies that retailers previously had written off. These included QR codes, as well as adoption of other mobile-enabled self-service options such as contactless payments. The US went from being a mobile payments laggard to the second-largest market, with $465 billion worth of mobile payment transactions processed in 2020. Usage is on track to surpass half of all smartphone users by 2025.[7]

Store technology rollouts had hitherto been stifled, where not enough retailers were willing to adopt and offer it on a large enough scale to give consumers a chance to discover their true appetite for it. But COVID took care of that. Who would have thought the arrival of Amazon's Just Walk Out technology on British shores would be welcomed for its no-touch advantages over its perceived threat to cashier jobs?

Checkout-free shopping is here to stay. It will be a gamechanger for travel retail and other time-sensitive shopping missions, such as office workers on their lunch break or those attending live events. However, there is a fine balance between 'seamless' and 'soulless'. There is a danger that too much automation can make stores feel cold and uninspiring, so as retailers look to technology to bring the physical store into the 21st century, they must ensure that it is *friction* that they're killing – and not the *experience*.

The future of e-commerce is stores

A decade ago, retailers were preparing for a future world centred around online shopping. This meant prioritizing investment in e-commerce fulfilment capabilities while rightsizing store portfolios to reflect shifting consumer demand. However, what most retailers failed to recognize at the time was the critical role that their very own stores would play in the sector's digital transformation.

Fast forward to the 2020s and the most successful retailers are those that view their stores as assets, not liabilities. The most successful retailers today use their stores as fulfilment hubs. They recognize that the key to growing e-commerce sales, as contradictory as it may sound, is by leveraging their physical infrastructure. The future of e-commerce? Stores.

The ability to continue serving customers throughout a pandemic via click & collect and curbside pickup will have cemented the critical role that stores play in facilitating e-commerce transactions, both in terms of customer experience and more favourable economics.

Over the past decade, click & collect has gone from being a quirky business model typically associated with British retailer Argos (unknowingly ahead of its time) to a retailing prerequisite. During the pandemic, nearly 100,000 brands around the world began offering curbside pickup, according to Shopify.[8]

Even in the UK, where this service has become ingrained in the shopper psyche, we witnessed click & collect reach new heights in 2020. For example, when demand for online grocery surged, click & collect became an attractive option for budget supermarkets whose business models were not compatible with home delivery. Aldi launched its first click & collect offering in the UK, rolling it out to over 200 stores, while many others – independent retailers, fish & chip shops and even libraries – also went digital in 2020.

Meanwhile, French retailers, the pioneers of the 'drive' concept, saw huge growth in this space during the pandemic. Carrefour's drive-through business reported nearly a 50 per cent increase in 2020, while Auchan extended this service internationally to stores in Poland, Ukraine and Senegal.[9]

The real acceleration, however, took place across the Atlantic where adoption of click & collect and curbside pickup had historically been slow. In 2020, US click & collect sales more than doubled and double-digit growth is expected to be sustained through 2024, according to eMarketer.[10] Many legacy retailers were forced to pivot quickly: Walmart launched curbside pickup in just six days.[11]

'In March, we didn't have curbside in any form; in April, we had curbside up-and-running; and in May it was rolled out in every store.'
Jeff Gennette, Macy's CEO, 2020[12]

Target chairman Brian Cornell also observed an increase in demand for both same-day collection and delivery. And here's the important part – this behaviour will outlast the pandemic. 'We expect those services to be very sticky over time … I think we've matured the awareness and the use of those same-day services by two, three, if not four years,' Cornell said.[13]

Local is very much the new digital, according to Google. During the pandemic, searches for 'who has' + 'in stock' increased by more than 8,000 per cent. Searches for 'local' + 'business(es)' meanwhile jumped by over 80 per cent.[14] It's becoming clearer that traditional metrics for success are no longer valid. Most transactions today are digitally influenced, yet the mounting cost of online deliveries and returns is unsustainable – physical stores play a vital role in addressing these shifts in consumer behaviour. The future of retail isn't online or instore but a seamless convergence of physical and digital channels.

> 'We all know that the pandemic has driven shopping behaviours online; what's often overlooked are the millions of people now going online to search for things locally on the high street.'
> **Nick Brackenbury, co-Founder of NearSt, Google-backed retail technology start-up, 2021[15]**

British fashion retailer Next understood this early on. As one of the more agile high street fashion chains and with its roots in catalogue retailing, Next was unusual in that it went into the pandemic with over half of its sales already coming from e-commerce. It is also one of the few British retailers to allow customers to view real-time local product availability for a one-hour click & collect service. This is how you leverage stores in a digital era. Next, however, believes that stores now face a 'fundamental and irreversible disadvantage' to online, and like-for-like sales declines will remain the new normal.[16]

So are stores facing an existential crisis or a rebirth? In a post pandemic world, the role of the store will be three-fold – transact, inspire and facilitate online shopping. If the role of the store is no longer purely to sell, then how should we be measuring its success? In a post-COVID world, metrics like dwell time, conversion rates, staff satisfaction and percentage of online orders collected/returned instore are going to be a whole lot more meaningful than measuring the inevitable decline in transactions made within a retailer's four walls.

Customer experience is the new currency

As we portray throughout this book, retail must continue to adapt to the emergence of the digitally-enabled, hyper-informed 21st-century shopper. The customer who shops on their terms and is intolerant of mediocre service.

The customer who is spoilt for choice and looks to bricks and mortar for all the things that a screen cannot deliver.

Therefore, prior to the pandemic, the concept of 'experiential retail' had been gaining momentum, positioned as the catch-all solution to the physical store's problems. While some retailers interpreted this as chucking a few gyms and prosecco bars into their stores, others understood that it required a titanic cultural shift.

Due to safety and hygiene concerns, the pandemic may have relegated 'experiential retail' to the buzzword archives, but the notion of offering an immersive, memorable and sensory-filled bricks and mortar experience will come back with a vengeance. We will see the democratization of a white-glove service previously limited to high-value customers.

In order to achieve this, retailers must radically rethink the rules of engagement. They must redefine the role of the sales associate (should we even use this term at all?), enabling store employees to become trusted shopping companions, equipped with new skills and digital tools, and incentivized to provide stellar service. After all, brand evangelism starts with the employee.

Clienteling will no longer be a luxury experience, and it certainly won't be confined to the physical store. During the pandemic, more retailers looked to connect online shoppers with instore staff via text, chat or even video. Some of the nimbler retailers transferred entire instore services such as interior design, personal styling and nursery advice to virtual sessions – and this will stick.

Similarly, for major brands like IKEA and Nike, augmented reality (AR) went from a nice-to-have to an indispensable tool when stores were forced to shut. COVID fast-tracked the shift towards more immersive e-commerce experiences, with livestreaming, virtual showrooms and social commerce gaining momentum in 2020/21. In the future, expect more retailers to invest in experiences that combine discovery with the effortlessness of transacting online.

'We are democratising the right to laziness.'
Turancan Salur, UK general manager, 10-minute delivery app Getir, 2021[17]

One silver lining of the pandemic was that it unleashed a wave of innovation and spawned a number of start-ups, particularly in the rapid delivery space.

Utilizing hyper-local dark stores, these ultra-fast delivery providers targeted the convenience-led, top-up shopping mission. Forget one hour-delivery – 15-minute delivery of fresh groceries is becoming the norm in urban areas.

Meanwhile, the battle for in-home – where we have spent an unprecedented amount of time during the pandemic – will continue to heat up. Even before COVID hit, retailers were cosying up to shoppers in their homes in a bid to follow their customers in the most literal sense. The advent of 5G will make not only our devices but also our homes smarter and more connected than ever before.

'You can imagine a future where we'll be able to reach customers on their devices in their homes to help them think about their healthcare in terms of what they eat, how much they move, and then what types of healthcare services they need and where they get them.'
Doug McMillon, Walmart CEO, 2021[18]

Be prepared for the rise of in-home services, as consumers continue to sacrifice privacy for convenience. In the future, retailers won't just deliver groceries to your fridge but perhaps cook you a meal once there. The possibilities for concierge-level service are endless – personal styling, health assessments, collecting online returns. Retailers will find new ways to transcend the transaction and capitalize on the trust they've already established with their shoppers. The concept of shopping will no longer be limited to stores or screens.

Conscious consumption

In a *Journal of Retailing* essay in 1955, economist and retail analyst Victor Lebow wrote:

'Our enormously productive economy demands that we make consumption our way of life, that we convert the buying and use of goods into rituals, that we seek our spiritual satisfactions, our ego satisfactions, in consumption. The measure of social status, of social acceptance, of prestige, is now to be found in our consumptive patterns. The very meaning and significance of our lives today is expressed in consumptive terms... We need things consumed, burned up, worn out, replaced and discarded at an ever-increasing pace.'[19]

For the past century, Western culture has been defined by consumerism. Yet COVID changed that overnight. The pandemic exposed both the fragility and the interconnectedness of our world. It served as a reminder of the human impact on our environment and will have a lasting impact on consumption.

Consumers are reassessing their values as they awaken to the reality of an even bigger threat – climate change. COVID has humbled us. It has accelerated the transition from mindless to mindful consumption. More consumers are prioritizing values over value, longevity over fashionability.

The resale, repair and rental economies have been thrust into the spotlight as circularity goes mainstream. Etsy's $1.6 billion acquisition of second-hand clothing app Depop, Selfridges' 'Let's change the way we shop' campaign, resale apps Poshmark and ThredUp going public, Levi's circular-focused concept store and Rent the Runway's expansion into resale – these are all signs of genuine change in an industry notorious for waste. Over the past two decades, the volume of clothes American consumers throw away has doubled.[20] The fashion industry is responsible for 20 per cent of global wastewater, according to the United Nations, and emits roughly the same quantity of greenhouse-gas emissions per year as the entire economies of France, Germany and the UK combined.[21]

> 'Historic attitudes towards consumption are not a realistic way for humanity to live and aren't a practical solution for anyone.'
> **Jesper Brodin, CEO of Ingka Group (IKEA's parent company), 2021[22]**

So how can retail, an industry that relies on consumption, take action to reduce its environmental impact and embrace a green recovery? We're in for major changes ahead. The 'Greta Thunberg effect' will hit retail hard as consumerism becomes a dirty word. The days of throwaway fashion are numbered. In the future, more consumers will think twice before buying new – the perfect antidote to fast fashion. Retailers must do more to extend the product lifecycle and address our culture of waste.

H&M, for example, now offers shoppers loyalty points for 'conscious behaviour' such as recycling old clothes, and in 2021 it rolled out its second-hand clothing site Sellpy across Europe. The retailer has also expanded its

'Take Care' service after initial success in Germany, which aims to help shoppers extend the life of their clothes with free repairs and advice on removing stains. This is a delicate message for an industry that is founded on consumption, but a vital one as we address the climate emergency. Consumers will look to brands whose values align with their own – and of course not just on climate change but also issues such as social justice and gender equality. Now more than ever, shoppers are voting with their wallets – brand tribalism is here to stay.

Retailers must also acknowledge the elephant in the room – e-commerce fulfilment. Many retail businesses have created a rod for their own backs with fast and free delivery. Can consumers be retrained to opt for slower, greener alternatives? We believe that no-rush delivery will make a comeback in the 2020s as retailers look to protect both profits and planet.

In accelerating the shift towards a more digital world, the pandemic has also magnified the returns challenge. Online returns may be part and parcel of modern-day shopping, but retailers must do more to address the root cause (sizing in many cases) while steering customers towards more sustainable ways to return unwanted goods, as we'll explore later in the book.

Retailers can also help consumers to make more informed decisions by providing greater transparency around provenance and sourcing. Online marketplaces, for example, could embed a 'buy local' or 'ethically sourced' filter as consumers become more mindful in their spending.

The hyper-local retail movement will also gain momentum throughout the 2020s as consumers continue to spend more time in their communities. This is a once-in-a-lifetime opportunity for local high streets – they must become greener, more digitally connected, people-friendly spaces. They must go beyond retail to stay relevant, embracing opportunities to convert surplus retail space to alternative uses such as residential and co-working.

> 'I think people will go back to a much more hybrid way of living and working, with more of a focus on localism.'
> **Steve Murrells, CEO of The Co-operative Group**[23]

There will be no return to the old normal of working. The world's largest work-from-home experiment has been broadly successful and although much uncertainty lies ahead, it is fair to assume that the days of 9–5 are over. The world of work will become more hybrid and flexible.

This will naturally have huge implications for our urban landscape, particularly when we consider the simultaneous changes to street space across a number of cities around the world. During the pandemic, urban spaces underwent radical change as local governments reallocated road space to pedestrians and cyclists in order to allow for social distancing and avoid a car-based recovery.

The 15-minute city concept, where most essentials are in close proximity to your home, has gained momentum across Europe and will have major implications for retail. Cities like Barcelona, London and Milan have transformed, and in Paris half of all parking spaces are expected to be removed by 2025. COVID's one silver lining is the opportunity to reshape our world for the better.

So how do we make sense of all of these changes? In a nutshell, retailers must be prepared for a world where the only constant is change. A world where:

- laggards die;
- customers are tribes;
- stores are showrooms and fulfilment hubs;
- brands sell values, not stuff;
- purpose meets profit.

Notes

1 Drennan, Mia (2021) Covid was the final lever for the creative destruction of the high street: it's not gone, just changing, City A.M., 8 March. Available from: https://www.cityam.com/covid-was-the-final-lever-for-the-creative-destruction-of-the-high-street-its-not-gone-just-changing/ (archived at https://perma.cc/2UVG-TDGS) [Last accessed 20/6/2021].

2 Maxfield, John (2014) Warren Buffett: How to avoid going broke, *The Motley Fool*, 2 August. Available from: https://www.fool.com/investing/general/2014/08/02/warren-buffett-broke.aspx (archived at https://perma.cc/W4NU-HN2M) [Last accessed: 21/6/2021].

3 Palmer, Annie (2021) Amazon to hire 75,000 workers and pay $100 bonus if they get Covid vaccine, CNBC, 13 May. Available from: https://www.cnbc.com/2021/05/13/amazon-hiring-75000-more-workers-in-latest-job-spree.html (archived at https://perma.cc/J5QM-TXLX) [Last accessed 12/7/2021].

4 Sweney, Mark (2021) Amazon creates 10,000 UK jobs on back of online shopping boom, *Guardian*, 14 May. Available from: https://www.theguardian. com/technology/2021/may/14/amazon-creates-10000-uk-jobs-on-back-of-online-shopping-boom-coronavirus (archived at https://perma.cc/ XN72-HK4R) [Last accessed 12/7/2021].

5 Carrick, Angharad (2020) Dame Sharon White: It is too early to predict the end of the high street, City A.M., 15 October. Available from: https://www. cityam.com/dame-sharon-white-it-is-not-the-end-of-the-high-street-yet/ (archived at https://perma.cc/XX9Q-XXH8) [Last accessed 20/6/2021].

6 Waitrose & Partners Food & Drink Report 2021 (2021) Available from: https://www.waitrose.com/ecom/content/inspiration/at-home-with-us/more-stories/waitrose-food-and-drink-report (archived at https://perma.cc/ S7LY-VWTP) [Last accessed 20/6/2021].

7 Perez, Sarah (2021) Fueled by pandemic, contactless mobile payments to surpass half of all smartphone users in US by 2025, *TechCrunch*, 5 April. Available from: https://techcrunch.com/2021/04/05/fueled-by-pandemic-contactless-mobile-payments-to-surpass-half-of-all-smartphone-users-in-u-s-by-2025/ (archived at https://perma.cc/3Z4W-LGQN) [Last accessed 20/6/2021].

8 Shopify: The Future of Ecommerce Report 2021 (2021) Available from: https:// enterprise.plus.shopify.com/rs/932-KRM-548/images/Shopify_Future_of_ Commerce.pdf (archived at https://perma.cc/E5CY-QMLT) [Last accessed 20/6/2021].

9 Annual reports: Carrefour 2020 Annual Report (2020) Available from: file:///C:/Users/Natalie%20Berg/Downloads/EN_Carrefour_RA2020_Complet_ BAT_Web_1.pdf (archived at https://perma.cc/5FPV-XGT6) [Last accessed 20/6/2021]. Auchan Holding Annual Results Presentation (2021) Available from: https://groupe-elo.com/uploads/files/modules/publications/1614938444_ 6042014c55d38.pdf (archived at https://perma.cc/5FPV-XGT6) [Last accessed 20/6/2021].

10 Anonymous (2021) Click-and-Collect 2021: Buy Online, Pick-up In Store (BOPIS) industry trends, *Business Insider*, 5 May. Available from: https://www. businessinsider.com/click-and-collect-industry-trends?r=US&IR=T (archived at https://perma.cc/F4ME-N9PM) [Last accessed 20/6/2021].

11 Wal-Mart Stores Inc. (WMT) Q4 2021 Earnings Call Transcript (2021) Available from: https://www.fool.com/earnings/call-transcripts/2021/02/19/ wal-mart-stores-inc-wmt-q4-2020-earnings-call-tran/ (archived at https:// perma.cc/26MY-FCDY) [Last accessed 20/6/2021].

12 Morgan Stanley Global Consumer and Retail Conference (2020) Transcript available from: https://seekingalpha.com/article/4392308-macys-m-ceo-jeff-gennette-presents-morgan-stanleys-global-consumer-and-retail-conference [Last accessed 12/7/2021].

13 Target (TGT) Q1 2021 Earnings Call Transcript (2021) Available from: https://www.fool.com/earnings/call-transcripts/2021/05/19/target-tgt-q1-2021-earnings-call-transcript/ (archived at https://perma.cc/9TN8-E4FF) [Last accessed 20/6/2021].

14 Target (TGT) Q1 2021 Earnings Call Transcript (2021) Available from: https://www.fool.com/earnings/call-transcripts/2021/05/19/target-tgt-q1-2021-earnings-call-transcript/ (archived at https://perma.cc/385F-DR9E) [Last accessed 20/6/2021].

15 Grosvenor Group press release (2021) Grosvenor Group backs retail tech start-up NearSt, 5 January. Available from: https://grosvenor.com/news-and-insight/all-articles/grosvenor-group-backs-retail-tech-start-up-nearst (archived at https://perma.cc/2KTY-F62Z) [Last accessed 20/6/2021].

16 Next plc (2021) Results for the year ending January 2021. Available from: https://www.nextplc.co.uk/~/media/Files/N/Next-PLC-V2/documents/2021/Website-pdf-Jan21.pdf (archived at https://perma.cc/E2ND-3R57) [Last accessed 15/7/2021].

17 Wallop, Harry (2021) 'We are democratising the right to laziness': the rise of on-demand grocery deliveries, *The Guardian*, 12 June. Available from: https://www.theguardian.com/lifeandstyle/2021/jun/12/the-rise-of-on-demand-grocery-deliveries (archived at https://perma.cc/V35A-AAMK) [Last accessed 20/6/2021].

18 Walmart WMT Q1 2022 Earnings Call Transcript (2021) Available from: https://www.rev.com/blog/transcripts/walmart-wmt-q1-2022-earnings-call-transcript (archived at https://perma.cc/9TPZ-QAZS) [Last accessed 20/6/2021].

19 Lebow, Victor (1955) Price competition in 1955, *Journal of Retailing*, Spring.

20 Monroe, Rachel (2021) Ultra-fast fashion is eating the world, *The Atlantic*, 6 February. Available from: https://www.theatlantic.com/magazine/archive/2021/03/ultra-fast-fashion-is-eating-the-world/617794/ (archived at https://perma.cc/SG9B-Z43B) [Last accessed 20/6/2021].

21 Monroe, Rachel (2021) Ultra-fast fashion is eating the world, *The Atlantic*, 6 February. Available from: https://www.theatlantic.com/magazine/archive/2021/03/ultra-fast-fashion-is-eating-the-world/617794/ (archived at https://perma.cc/9X4Z-SS7J) [Last accessed 20/6/2021].

22 Fleming, Sean (2021) IKEA fits in a world that wants to buy less, says Ingka Group's CEO, World Economic Forum, 26 January. Available from: https:// www.weforum.org/agenda/2021/01/jesper-brodin-ikea-circular-economy/ (archived at https://perma.cc/W7ZH-ARMH) [Last accessed 20/6/2021].

23 Cavazza, Manfreda (2021) Analysis: Shops and the 15-minute city – how to win in a hyper-local world, *Retail Week*, 15 April. Available from: https://www. retail-week.com/15-minute-city (archived at https://perma.cc/XJ7M-ME7M) [Last accessed 20/6/2021].

04

Amazon's pandemic power grab

COVID may have sounded the death knell for many businesses, but one retailer in particular has come out stronger. Amazon is hands-down the undisputed winner of this pandemic.

Its business model may not have been intentionally built for a pandemic, but it has turned out to be highly relevant in such a climate – and for reasons that go well beyond retail. As we have seen, Amazon is not a retailer but a disparate collection of businesses that, on the surface, appear to have little to do with one another. The tech giant continues to spawn new business segments at a bewildering rate. Despite the seemingly disjointed nature of the Amazon model, from cloud computing to video streaming, its various divisions have one thing in common: they have all benefited from the pandemic-induced shift towards a more digital world.

> 'No industry or business will be spared from the impact of these changes. Millions of companies risk disappearing and many industries face an uncertain future; a few will thrive.'
> **Klaus Schwab, Founder, World Economic Forum, 2020**[1]

2020 was therefore a big year for big tech. Amazon's net income nearly doubled to reach $21.3 billion,[2] its market cap rose by over $700 billion and Jeff Bezos' net worth grew by $75 billion – more than the annual GDP of Costa Rica or Lithuania.[3]

With crisis comes opportunity – for Amazon at least. While many retailers muddled their way through the pandemic, Amazon propelled itself into new industries, made blockbuster acquisitions, launched new products and brands, and doubled down on technology. The retailer hired hundreds of thousands of employees, unveiled new store formats, turned disused malls into warehouses, and even added a couple of new markets to its roster. A key theme of this crisis is that the strong will emerge stronger. These days, Amazon is seemingly invincible.

Amazon's golden age

COVID has enabled Amazon to tighten its grip on consumers and bolster its broader ecosystem by:

- reinforcing its status as the indispensable route to market;
- further embedding itself in consumers' homes;
- accelerating its vision as a technology vendor.

Cementing its status: a shopping and entertainment behemoth

Amazon scooped up trade during the pandemic for all the obvious reasons – its ubiquity, ease, near-infinite assortment, fast delivery, the list goes on. You don't need analysts like us to explain the very direct correlation between a global lockdown and subsequent surge in sales coming from the titan of e-commerce. Talk about first-mover advantage. Amazon has devoted decades to perfecting the online shopping experience, so when stores were forced to shut and consumers forced to hunker down, Amazon became the main show in town.

And we mean that in a more literal sense as well. Amazon had spent the previous decade building out its digital content, putting it in an enviable position when COVID struck. At the start of the pandemic, Amazon made a selection of books, video and music available for free on Kindle, Audible, Prime Video and Amazon Music. Goodwill or prime customer acquisition opportunity? Perhaps a bit of both. In March 2020, the month that COVID was declared a pandemic by the World Health Organization, the number of first-time Prime viewers nearly doubled[4] and by the end of 2020, a year of confinement with little else for consumers to do, total Prime Video streaming hours had increased 70 per cent. A whopping 175 million Prime members streamed video that year.[5]

Meanwhile, Amazon's Fire TV reached more than 50 million monthly active global users during the pandemic.[6] The tech giant secured new content deals with premium streaming providers, including HBO Max, discovery+ and Xfinity in the US; Disney+ in Mexico and Brazil; NOW TV in the UK; and CANAL+ in France. The final quarter of 2020 also marked Prime Video's strongest viewership for live sports globally. In fact, Prime Video's exclusive coverage of the San Francisco 49ers vs. Arizona Cardinals game on 26 December attracted an estimated 11.2 million viewers and delivered the highest digital average-minute audience ever for an NFL regular season game.[7]

Meanwhile, Amazon's live-streaming platform Twitch had its best ever year: hours watched on Twitch nearly doubled in the first quarter of 2021 and at the time of writing the site averages more than 35 million daily visitors.[8]

In mid-2021, Amazon made its most ambitious move yet in the entertainment industry – acquiring MGM Studios. The tech giant shelled out $8.5 billion for the iconic Hollywood studio in a bid to keep up with burgeoning demand for streaming content. The acquisition, Amazon's second largest to date, boosted Prime Video's offering with about 4,000 films, including the James Bond franchise, and 17,000 television shows such as 'Shark Tank' and the 'Handmaid's Tale' series.

> 'For Prime customers, I think the value proposition was very relevant in 2020.'
> **John Boumphrey, Amazon UK Country Manager**

This might sound like an obscenely expensive deal given that it's essentially a free bolt-on for Prime members, but don't forget that increased digital engagement ultimately strengthens Amazon's retail proposition. As Bezos has said, 'When we win a Golden Globe, it helps us sell more shoes.'[9] Amazon's broader Prime membership scheme is pretty generous to begin with, but now we know there is no catalyst like a pandemic to get customers signed up. As of 2021, Amazon had over 200 million customers around the globe signed up to Prime. That's *over 200 million people* willing to pay to shop on Amazon and have access to its services. And for context, at the start of 2020, Amazon reported having over 150 million members.[10] Prime became a whole lot more appealing in a pandemic year.

As we'll explore in the next chapter, Prime customers spend more on Amazon, they buy more frequently and they stick around. This was particularly pronounced at the start of the pandemic – Amazon found that not only were Prime members buying more regularly but basket sizes were also going up.[11] Prime shoppers naturally made Amazon their first port of call, while stay-at-home lockdown orders provided the perfect conditions for acquiring new customers as well. In the early stages of the pandemic, Amazon shoppers were spending $11,000 a second on its products and services.[12]

'Renewal rates are going up and the engagement is going up,' Amazon CFO Brian Olsavsky said in 2020. 'And so people are buying more frequently and across more categories, they're using more of our digital benefits ... and we think that will have lasting value.'[13] COVID has been a customer acquisition tool like none before.

In 2020, Amazon solidified its status as the indispensable route to market – for brands but also increasingly for other retailers. During the first lockdown, online marketplaces like Amazon became a lifeline for many smaller businesses which had no choice but to pivot online. And some large businesses too: in the US, footwear brand Birkenstock reversed a decision not to sell on Amazon once wholesale orders started drying up during the pandemic.[14] In the UK, coffee shop Pret began selling on Amazon's platform in a bid to offset a steep fall in sales in its city-centre stores. 'Simply put, Covid-19, in our view, has injected Amazon with a growth hormone,' said Tom Forte, an analyst at the investment bank D.A. Davidson & Company.[15]

Amazon's relevance in a pandemic was by no means limited to its home market. In Australia, a relatively new market for the online behemoth, COVID enabled Amazon to accelerate growth, with sales nearly doubling to AU$1 billion in 2020.

> 'Our expansion plans, in terms of putting down a footprint ... have probably just been brought forward a little bit.'
> **Craig Fuller, Director of Operations, Amazon Australia, 2021[16]**

Perhaps capitalizing on newfound demand, the retailer doubled its fulfilment network by opening 11 new Australian sites during the pandemic.[17] Amazon also launched in Poland and Sweden (dubbed 'Project Dancing Queen') while simultaneously strengthening its position in more mature markets. Frédéric Duval, the head of Amazon France, said in late 2020 that online activity increased in the 40–50 per cent range: 'Business has grown with the lock-down.'[18] Meanwhile, in the UK, Amazon is expected to overtake Tesco to become the country's largest retailer by 2025.[19]

The pandemic also presented a once-in-a-lifetime chance to accelerate Amazon's strategic goals, and perhaps shift customer perception, in nascent sectors. Take healthcare, for example. During the pandemic, a couple of years after acquiring online pharmacy PillPack, Amazon made its most concerted push into this industry. The retailer launched a dedicated pharmacy storefront with exclusive discounts for Prime members on top of the usual speedy delivery. Building on this momentum, in 2021, Amazon embarked on a national rollout of its healthcare service, Amazon Care. This may not have been in direct response to the pandemic, but there couldn't have been a more apt time to make its mark in this industry. Could we see the launch of physical Amazon-branded pharmacies in the future?

Amazon isn't just coming for health. During the COVID crisis, the retailer made its much-anticipated, though somewhat underwhelming, foray into the luxury sector. At the start of the pandemic, Amazon launched a digital storefront with Vogue to help connect designers directly with shoppers. Later that year, the retailer unveiled Luxury Stores, an invite-only shopping experience available via the Amazon app that features both established and emerging luxury fashion and beauty brands.

As quarantined consumers traded suits for sweats, many retailers saw clothing sales fall off a cliff. Luxury, however, was relatively insulated from the pandemic and therefore ripe for online growth for two reasons: 1) the uncomfortable truth that the rich got richer during the COVID crisis; and 2) it is a category that has arguably been as much about the in-person experience as the product – and therefore underpenetrated online.

While Chinese retailers like Alibaba have successfully navigated the luxury market, brands had been reluctant to sell on Amazon due to counterfeit concerns. But with stores forced to shut and Amazon's dominance in e-commerce, this was the opportune time to prove to luxury brands that alongside selling teeth-whitening kits and tennis rackets, Amazon could also dish out a $1,500 Oscar de La Renta bag.

The pandemic also presented Amazon with a unique opportunity to finally make its mark in grocery. Several years after acquiring Whole Foods Market, Amazon was still very much in experimentation mode and struggling to convince shoppers, particularly outside the US, that it was a bona fide grocery destination. With such established competition, what would

FIGURE 4.1 A shopper 'just walks out' of an Amazon Fresh supermarket, one of several grocery formats launched during the pandemic

make a shopper switch to Amazon? Price? No. Ease? No, all that experimentation meant that its grocery site was uncharacteristically clunky and hard to navigate. How about a global pandemic? Tick.

Seemingly overnight, securing an online delivery slot with any of the major supermarkets became harder than getting tickets to Glastonbury, giving Amazon the long-awaited opportunity to raise awareness and establish credibility in its grocery offering. And Amazon seized the moment, expanding delivery capacity by 60 per cent[20] in the first few months of the pandemic and going on to launch new private-label ranges and accelerate its bricks and mortar ambitions with the rollout of Amazon Go convenience stores and the launch of a new supermarket chain at home – Amazon Fresh (see Figure 4.1) – while also debuting its first checkout-free store outside of the US with the launch of Amazon Fresh in London (same name, different concept). During the pandemic, Amazon hit the nuclear button in the UK, one of the most competitive grocery e-commerce markets in the world, by offering Prime members free same-day delivery on groceries (having already made groceries a free Prime benefit in the US just before the pandemic hit).

'What we did over the past year [in grocery] was responsive to customer demand. But it was also a continuation of experimentation in the category,'

Amazon's UK boss John Boumphrey told us. 'Demand for online grocery went up significantly and a lot of businesses weren't able to keep up.' This was a once-in-a-lifetime opportunity for Amazon to hit the accelerator.

> 'Grocery has been a great revelation during the post-pandemic period here. I think people really value the ability to get home delivery. And we've seen that as numbers go up considerably pre and post-pandemic.'
> **Brian Olsavsky, Amazon CFO, 2021**[21]

A by-product of Amazon's strengthened retail platform? More brands looking to advertise on it. Advertising might be a relatively new business stream for the tech giant, but for context, it is important to understand that Amazon went into the pandemic as the third-largest US ad publisher behind Google and Facebook. In other words, not exactly the underdog.

Think back to Amazon's flywheel: more shoppers turning to its e-commerce platform during a pandemic would have attracted more merchants, which would have attracted higher advertising spend – in a bid to get seen. 'We just had a lot more traffic, and we do a good job of turning that traffic into valuable real estate for our advertisers,' said Olsavsky.[22]

Despite many businesses reining in advertising spend in those early uncertain months of 2020, Amazon saw a clear recovery as the year progressed. So why is advertising on Amazon so important during a pandemic? Beyond the obvious reasons of visibility and data, it's important to remember that the majority of shoppers begin their product search on Amazon – not Google or another search engine. Marketers can therefore reach shoppers as they research products as well as when they are looking to make a purchase. Amazon is now even attracting advertising from businesses like carmakers and insurance companies that have zero intention of selling on its platform but see the value in acquiring Amazon's purchasing data. Ads on Amazon have the power to drive sales through other non-Amazon channels, increasing the importance of its platform.

Amazon's advertising business was already on the path to becoming yet another high-growth, high-margin business stream. COVID just cemented that. A Feedvisor survey of 1,000 major brands suggested the number advertising on Amazon rose to 73 per cent in 2020, compared with just 57 per cent in 2019.[23] In the fourth quarter of 2020, growth in Amazon's 'Other' category, which is mainly comprised of advertising, surpassed Prime subscription services for the first time and grew at a higher rate than any other business segment.[24] As of mid-2021, Amazon's advertising unit was 2.4 times as large as Snap, Twitter, Roku and Pinterest combined – and growing nearly twice as quickly.[25]

Alexa, join my Zoom meeting

Over the past decade, while most retailers were busy catching up in e-commerce, Amazon was quietly embedding itself in people's homes. From the now-defunct Dash reordering buttons to modern-day Alexa, the smart home has been the focus of much of Amazon's recent innovations. By making our home environments more intelligent and connected, Amazon has been able to provide a new level of convenience and deepen engagement with its most important customers. Naturally in exchange for customer data – something that not all customers are on board with.

But when COVID struck, Amazon's grip on the physical home went from creepy to coveted. Its various gadgets were suddenly wildly relevant for the quarantined consumer – and Amazon recognized the opportunity. A number of new devices and services were launched mid-pandemic to cater to the newfound demand for videoconferencing, home security and, as discussed, video streaming.

> 'Nobody anticipated the pandemic, and we certainly didn't plan for it. But I think our homes are now our offices, they're our schools, they're our movie theaters. A lot of our products became even more applicable in this environment.'
> **Dave Limp, Amazon SVP, Devices and Services, 2020[26]**

Need a reliable Wi-Fi connection at home? Amazon's Eero has got you covered. Need to connect with quarantined family members? Amazon's Care Hub lets you monitor their activity feeds with Echo devices. Need help homeschooling? The Reading Sidekick lets your children practise reading with Alexa.

AMAZON'S CURE FOR CABIN FEVER

Never one to shy away from an idea, the tech giant launched Amazon Explore during the pandemic. With travel ground to a halt and consumers stuck at home, Amazon decided to bring the holiday directly into the home. Its virtual travel platform lets users book from over 250 interactive tours and experiences around the globe, including pasta-making workshops in Italy, a virtual tour of NYC's Central Park and a stroll through the Gardens by the Bay in Singapore.

Unlike other virtual tours, these are one-to-one experiences and, naturally, there is a shopping element. Amazon Explore users have the option to shop in local stores via a tour guide. Amazon is clearly building on the momentum for livestreaming which became the next best thing to shopping in-store during the pandemic, and a trend that we believe will stick post-COVID as physical and digital retail continue to merge. There is also an opportunity to use virtual experiences to bolster Amazon's core retail offering. Need a shaker for that virtual cocktail tour in Argentina? We know just the place.

Alexa kept people informed, connected, productive and entertained while stuck indoors. At the start of the pandemic, Alexa even helped to diagnose COVID cases and its handwashing timer sang to users for the recommended 20 seconds of scrubbing.

Unsurprisingly, as people spent an unprecedented amount of time in their homes, Alexa features like video calling and Drop In (a two-way intercom-like conversation between Echo devices) became more popular than ever before. Amazon's Echo Show – the one with a screen – became the fastest growing of Echo devices and made nearly three times the number of video calls globally than in the prior year.[27] 'I think people are finding more benefit from Alexa when they're at home, they're listening to more music, asking questions, particularly questions related to COVID and issues around it. They're using it in education with their children and I think we're seeing a lot more on the communication side, people using Alexa calling and Drop In,' said Olsavsky.[28]

New routines like Work from Home and Stay at Home reminded Alexa users when to begin their day, when to eat, join meetings and take breaks. Alexa's role as a trusted assistant was cemented during the pandemic. This is significant because it allows Amazon to harness valuable insights into customers in the most intimate of settings (that data can then be used to promote other business areas such as e-commerce and Prime Video) while also directly strengthening Amazon's retail proposition. Alexa seamlessly funnels purchases through to Amazon's platform and, thanks to COVID, she is now truly part of the family.

Showcasing Amazon's technological prowess

Retailer or tech vendor? We know which is more lucrative.

We've already touched on how the pandemic has propelled checkout-free shopping into the mainstream, much to Amazon's benefit. Not only did the retailer accelerate expansion plans for Amazon's own checkout-free stores during the pandemic, but it was also an opportune time to begin licensing the technology to rivals.

In March 2020, Amazon launched justwalkout.com, inviting retailers to enquire about licensing Amazon's automated checkout technology. The main difference is that shoppers enter the store by tapping a credit card rather than the Amazon app.

'This has pretty broad applicability across store sizes, across industries, because it fundamentally tackles a problem of how you get convenience in physical locations, especially when people are hard-pressed for time,' said Dilip Kumar, Amazon's Vice President of Physical Retail and Technology.[29]

The ultimate frenemy, Amazon has a history of disrupting the customer experience and then courting rivals with a solution. During the pandemic, Amazon signed agreements to license its Just Walk Out technology to a variety of third parties in the travel and entertainment industries:

- OTG: Newark Liberty and LaGuardia airports;
- Hudson: Chicago Midway and Dallas Love Field airports;
- TD Garden: New England's largest sports and entertainment arena and home of the NBA's Boston Celtics and the NHL's Boston Bruins;
- Levy Restaurants: a concessionaire in Chicago's United Center which is the home of the Chicago Blackhawks hockey team and Chicago Bulls basketball team.

Another innovation launched in the COVID era was Amazon One, a scanner that registers an image of the user's palm to not only pay for items but also enter a building or identify yourself. You can see where this is going: 'We believe Amazon One has broad applicability beyond our retail stores, so we also plan to offer the service to third parties like retailers, stadiums, and office buildings so that more people can benefit from this ease and convenience in more places,' said Kumar.[30]

With Amazon, things are not always what they seem. Amazon is quietly becoming the rails – not just in retail but across a variety of industries. And many of Amazon's moves are designed to strengthen other aspects of the business. For example, its checkout-free systems are underpinned by its cloud computing business, AWS, so an increase in demand for Just Walk Out technology also bolsters Amazon's most profitable business segment.

> 'I have a feeling that the pandemic will have accelerated cloud adoption in the enterprise by a few years.'
> **Andy Jassy, Amazon CEO, 2020**[31]

AWS immediately benefited during the pandemic as businesses were forced to swiftly adapt to remote working. Zoom, a leading video conferencing service and AWS customer, became a household name during the pandemic. But it had to move at lightning speed in order to meet rising demand, scaling from 10 million daily meeting participants to 300 million in a mere matter of weeks.[32] In the UK alone, Zoom went from having a few hundred thousand users in the first two months of 2020 to more than 13 million in April and May.[33] AWS enabled Zoom to set up hundreds of thousands of servers in less than a month instead of the several months it would have taken to set them up physically.

As is often the case during a crisis, businesses tend to step back and think more strategically about future operations. Amazon noted that many businesses accelerated their plans to move to AWS, having observed how cloud-based businesses were able to continue operating with minimal disruption during a crisis, compared with the challenge of having to manage the infrastructure themselves.

No business is going to boast about profiting from a pandemic, but Amazon has genuinely thrived in these conditions. There is no denying that the dramatic shift in customer behaviour – less time in stores, offices, cinemas and restaurants – has been a boon to Amazon's business. COVID has reinforced its strategic advantages and made Amazon even more powerful and even more influential.

Amazon went from being described as an 'evil face of capitalism' to a kind of 'corporate Red Cross' during the pandemic.[34] In this chapter, we've highlighted the forceful tailwinds that COVID has accelerated for Amazon's business – but in doing so it has also strengthened headwinds. The key question now is how Amazon's pandemic success is viewed in the eyes of policymakers, who could yet hold its fate as a retail technology behemoth in the balance with the threat of 'big tech' and antitrust legislation.

Notes

1 Schwab, Klaus and Malleret, Thierry (2020) COVID-19's legacy: This is how to get the Great Reset right, World Economic Forum, 14 July. Available from: https://www.weforum.org/agenda/2020/07/covid19-this-is-how-to-get-the-great-reset-right/ (archived at https://perma.cc/3JD6-QA5Z) [Last accessed 20/6/2021].

2 Amazon 10-K for the fiscal year ended December 31, 2020. Available from: https://www.sec.gov/ix?doc=/Archives/edgar/data/1018724/000101872421000004/amzn-20201231.htm (archived at https://perma.cc/F9FG-2XMX) [Last accessed 18/6/2021].

3 Taylor, Kate (2021) A chart shows how Jeff Bezos's net worth exploded by $75 billion in 2020, reaching $188 billion before he stepped down as Amazon's CEO, Business Insider, 2 February. Available from: https://www.businessinsider.com/amazon-ceo-jeff-bezos-net-worth-explodes-in-2020-chart-2020-12?r=US&IR=T (archived at https://perma.cc/K74X-XCCZ) [Last accessed 20/6/2021].

4 Amazon press release (2021) Amazon.com announces financial results and CEO transition, 2 February. Available from: https://press.aboutamazon.com/news-releases/news-release-details/amazoncom-announces-financial-results-and-ceo-transition (archived at https://perma.cc/NL7L-W465) [Last accessed 20/6/2021].

5 Spangler, Todd (2021) Amazon tops Q1 expectations, Bezos touts more than 175 million Prime Video viewers, Variety, 29 April. Available from: https://variety.com/2021/digital/news/amazon-q1-2021-prime-video-viewers-1234963065/ (archived at https://perma.cc/9JHB-QEFV) [Last accessed 20/6/2021].

6 Amazon press release (2021) Amazon.com announces financial results and CEO transition, 2 February. Available from: https://press.aboutamazon.com/news-releases/news-release-details/amazoncom-announces-financial-results-and-ceo-transition (archived at https://perma.cc/2DKD-6GQQ) [Last accessed 20/6/2021].

7 Ibid.

8 Bijan, Stephen (2021) Twitch ended 2020 with its biggest numbers ever, The Verge, 11 January. Available from: https://www.theverge.com/2021/1/11/22220528/twitch-2020-aoc-among-us-facebook-youtube (archived at https://perma.cc/4XLQ-JREH) [Last accessed 20/6/2021]; Amazon (AMZN) Q1 2021 earnings call transcript (2021) Available from: https://www.fool.com/earnings/call-transcripts/2021/04/29/amazon-amzn-q1-2021-earnings-call-transcript/ (archived at https://perma.cc/C83J-H8R9) [Last accessed 20/6/2021].

9 https://www.businessinsider.com/amazon-ceo-jeff-bezos-said-something-about-prime-video-that-should-scare-netflix-2016-6?r=US&IR=T (archived at https://perma.cc/23K5-FC8M).

10 Amazon press release (2021) Amazon.com announces fourth quarter sales up 21% to $87.4 billion, 30 January. Available from: https://ir.aboutamazon.com/news-release/news-release-details/2020/Amazoncom-Announces-Fourth-Quarter-Sales-up-21-to-874-Billion/default.aspx (archived at https://perma.cc/KN4Q-SBL6) [Last accessed: 20/6/2021].

11 Amazon.com Inc (AMZN) Q1 2020 earnings call transcript (2020). Available from: https://www.fool.com/earnings/call-transcripts/2020/04/30/amazoncom-inc-amzn-q1-2020-earnings-call-transcrip.aspx (archived at https://perma.cc/J54J-A6CC) [Last accessed 20/6/2021].

12 Neate, Rupert (2020) Amazon reaps $11,000-a-second coronavirus lockdown bonanza, *The Guardian*, 15 April. Available from: https://www.theguardian.com/technology/2020/apr/15/amazon-lockdown-bonanza-jeff-bezos-fortune-109bn-coronavirus (archived at https://perma.cc/Y6LE-KMR8) [Last accessed 20/6/2021].

13 Edited transcript of AMZN.OQ earnings conference call or presentation 29-Oct-20 9:30pm GMT (2020). Available from: https://finance.yahoo.com/news/edited-transcript-amzn-oq-earnings-213000784.html (archived at https://perma.cc/2HJ3-HTZ3) [Last accessed 20/6/2021].

14 Del Ray, Jason (2020) Amazon was already powerful. The coronavirus pandemic cleared the way to dominance, *Vox*, 10 April. Available from: https://www.vox.com/recode/2020/4/10/21215953/amazon-fresh-walmart-grocery-delivery-coronavirus-retail-store-closures (archived at https://perma.cc/ZZQ8-8QJE) [Last accessed 20/6/2021].

15 Wakabayashi, Daisuke, Weise, Karen, Nicas, Jack and Isaac, Mike (2020) The economy is in record decline, but not for the tech giants, *The New York Times*, 30 July. Available from: https://www.nytimes.com/2020/07/30/technology/tech-company-earnings-amazon-apple-facebook-google.html (archived at https://perma.cc/2AD7-C8HL) [Last accessed 18/6/2021].

16 Powell, Dominic (2021) Amazon's Australian growth beating expectations thanks to COVID, *Sydney Morning Herald*, 2 June. Available from: https://www.smh.com.au/business/companies/amazon-s-australian-growth-beating-expectations-thanks-to-covid-20210602-p57xb0.html (archived at https://perma.cc/3Y8Q-BPKS) [Last accessed 20/6/2021].

17 Ibid.

18 Anonymous (2020) Amazon France CEO says French lockdown boosted sales, Reuters, 18 November. Available from: https://www.fr24news.com/a/2020/11/amazon-france-ceo-says-french-lockdown-boosted-sales-3.html (archived at https://perma.cc/8S3Z-CD3D) [Last accessed 20/6/2021].

19 Onita, Laura (2021) Amazon to overtake Tesco as Britain's biggest retailer by 2025, 2 June. Available from: https://www.telegraph.co.uk/business/2021/06/02/amazon-overtake-tesco-britains-biggest-retailer-2025/ (archived at https://perma.cc/4HQF-VASV) [Last accessed 20/6/2021].

20 Amazon.com Inc (AMZN) Q1 2020 earnings call transcript (2020) Available from: https://www.fool.com/earnings/call-transcripts/2020/04/30/amazoncom-inc-amzn-q1-2020-earnings-call-transcrip.aspx (archived at https://perma.cc/P8EP-DH8L) [Last accessed 20/6/2021].

21 Amazon (AMZN) Q1 2021 earnings call transcript (2021) Available from: https://www.fool.com/earnings/call-transcripts/2021/04/29/amazon-amzn-q1-2021-earnings-call-transcript/ (archived at https://perma.cc/VGD8-SGEE) [Last accessed 20/6/2021].

22 Edited transcript of AMZN.OQ earnings conference call or presentation 29-Oct-20 9:30pm GMT (2020) Available from: https://finance.yahoo.com/news/edited-transcript-amzn-oq-earnings-213000784.html (archived at https://perma.cc/7C88-WKKR) [Last accessed 20/6/2021].

23 Lee, Dave (2020) Amazon's advertising business booms in pandemic, *Financial Times*, 29 December. Available from: https://www.ft.com/content/095d73d5-a7a6-4acc-9dcc-9ee3e3d1fff4 (archived at https://perma.cc/89Q8-PH9V) [Last accessed 20/6/2021].

24 Ibid.

25 Graham, Megan (2021) Amazon's ad revenue is now twice as big as Snap, Twitter, Roku and Pinterest combined, CNBC, 25 May. Available from: https://www.cnbc.com/2021/05/25/amazon-ad-revenue-now-twice-as-big-as-snap-twitter-roku-and-pinterest-combined.html#:~:text=The%20major%20growth%20in%20Amazon's,quickly%2C%20according%20to%20Loop%20Capital (archived at https://perma.cc/9DAG-5Q2G) [Last accessed 20/6/2021].

26 Rubin, Ben Fox (2020) Alexa is more vital than ever during coronavirus, and Amazon knows it, CNET, 25 September. Available from: https://www.cnet.com/home/smart-home/alexa-is-more-vital-than-ever-during-coronavirus-and-amazon-knows-it/ (archived at https://perma.cc/HW6E-9F6V) [Last accessed 20/6/2021].

27 Amazon: Email from Dagmar Wickham (2021).

28 Amazon.com Inc (AMZN) Q1 2020 earnings call transcript (2020) Available from: https://www.fool.com/earnings/call-transcripts/2020/04/30/amazoncom-inc-amzn-q1-2020-earnings-call-transcrip.aspx (archived at https://perma.cc/YAB6-3GCF) [Last accessed 20/6/2021].

29 Dastin, Jeffrey (2020) Amazon launches business selling automated checkout to retailers, Reuters, 9 March. Available from: https://www.reuters.com/article/us-amazon-com-store-technology-idUSKBN20W0OD (archived at https://perma.cc/Q3BE-Q53Y) [Last accessed 6/20/2021].

30 Kumar, Dilip (2020) Introducing Amazon One – a new innovation to make everyday activities effortless, Amazon blog, 29 September. Available from: https://www.aboutamazon.com/news/innovation-at-amazon/introducing-amazon-one-a-new-innovation-to-make-everyday-activities-effortless (archived at https://perma.cc/2PJZ-HER4) [Last accessed 20/6/2021].

31 Palmer, Annie (2020) AWS CEO Andy Jassy: Offices will become more like shared workspaces after the pandemic, CNBC, 1 December. Available from: https://www.cnbc.com/2020/12/01/aws-ceo-jassy-people-wont-be-in-offices-100percent-of-the-time-after-covid.html (archived at https://perma.cc/579P-QFZJ) [Last accessed 20/6/2021].

32 Amazon: Email from Dagmar Wickham (2021).

33 Ofcom Online Nation 2021 Report (2021). Available from: https://www.ofcom.org.uk/__data/assets/pdf_file/0013/220414/online-nation-2021-report.pdf (archived at https://perma.cc/4TKJ-4866) [Last accessed 19/6/2021].

34 Dumaine, Brian (2020) Amazon was built for the pandemic – and will likely emerge from it stronger than ever, *Fortune*, 18 May. Available from: https://fortune.com/2020/05/18/amazon-business-jeff-bezos-amzn-sales-revenue-coronavirus-pandemic/ (archived at https://perma.cc/59JH-J6BC) [Last accessed 20/6/2021].

05

The Prime ecosystem: redefining loyalty for today's modern shopper

'"All-you-can-eat" express shipping.'[1] This is how Jeff Bezos described Amazon Prime when it launched back in 2005. The idea was simple – shoppers pay an annual fee in exchange for unlimited two-day shipping. No longer would customers have to worry about consolidating orders or minimum purchase requirements. Bezos wanted fast shipping to become an everyday experience rather than an 'occasional indulgence'.[2]

The company had already been offering Super Saver Shipping, which catered to those time-rich customers who didn't mind waiting a bit longer for their orders to arrive (this still exists today, but is just called free shipping). This set the stage for new delivery services such as Prime, an idea first proposed by Amazon engineer Charlie Ward. In his book, *The Everything Store*, Brad Stone writes:

> Why not create a service for the opposite type of customer, Ward suggested, a speedy shipping club for consumers whose needs were time sensitive and who weren't price conscious? He suggested that it could work like a music club, with a monthly charge.[3]

Amazon is no stranger to risk taking, and this was quite a gamble. 'Prime was very bold and it very much reflected the strategy that we've come to expect from Amazon – that this was a multi-decade time horizon. They're not playing a quarter-to-quarter game,' said former eBay executive Michael Dearing.[4] Not only would the promise of unlimited two-day shipping disproportionately raise customer expectations and add significant cost pressure, particularly in the short term, but were customers willing to pay for the privilege of shopping with Amazon? Sure, warehouse clubs like

Costco were charging a membership fee – but this was recouped in the form of lower prices instore. Could Amazon convince shoppers that fast shipping alone was worth the initial $79 fee?

> 'It was never about the seventy-nine dollars. It was really about changing people's mentality so they wouldn't shop anywhere else.'
> **Vijay Ravindran, ex-Amazon Director, 2013**[5]

It appears so. By 2021, Amazon was shipping more than 45 million items worldwide and had over 200 million paid Prime members globally, making it one of the world's largest online subscription schemes.

Amazon has exported its Prime model to almost all international countries of operation. Shoppers in Amazon's three largest global markets – Germany, Japan and the UK – were naturally the first to get a taste for Prime when it went global in 2007 (see Table 5.1). However, in recent years, Amazon has been backfilling existing markets with Prime, which is arguably a far more compelling proposition today than when it was first exported over a decade ago. From 2016 to 2021, Amazon more than doubled the number of markets offering Prime. As of mid-2021, Prime was available in every Amazon market except for Poland and Sweden. As these are relatively new markets, it's likely that Amazon will launch Prime in both European countries before 2025.

TABLE 5.1   Amazon Prime international presence

Year Launched	Market
2005	US
2007	Germany
2007	UK
2007	Japan
2008	France
2011	Italy
2011	Spain
2013	Canada
2014	Austria*
2016	Belgium*
2016	China

(continued)

TABLE 5.1 (Continued)

Year Launched	Market
2016	India
2017	Luxembourg*
2017	Mexico
2017	Netherlands
2017	Singapore
2018	Australia
2019	UAE
2019	Brazil
2020	Turkey
2021	Saudi Arabia

*Markets without a dedicated country site
Source: Author research; Amazon

Shipping, shopping, streaming and more

The Prime model is classic Amazon – customer-obsessed with a long-term view of success. Today, Prime is about so much more than just shipping perks (see Table 5.2). Amazon has spent the past decade relentlessly building out the Prime flywheel to the extent that it is now described as 'the gateway to the best of Amazon', according to Prime Director Lisa Leung.[6] The retailer has significantly expanded an already impressive range of Prime-eligible products while also continuing to tack on entertainment perks in a bid to drive both customer acquisition and retention.

'They come for shipping. They stay for digital.'
Aaron Perrine, Amazon General Manager[7]

In an effort to increase Prime's stickiness and as part of Amazon's broader strategy to spread its tentacles across new sectors, in 2011 the retailer launched what is now known as Prime Video – unlimited, commercial-free, instant streaming of thousands of TV shows and films.

Why include this as a free perk for Prime members? Just as Netflix didn't charge more when it transitioned from DVDs to digital streaming, Amazon felt that bundling Prime Video would offer members additional value while taking pressure off the company to provide best-in-class content.

'I remember Jeff used those exact words. It's an, "Oh, by the way",' said Bill Carr, former Amazon Vice President of Digital Music and Video, in a 2019 *Vox* interview. "'Yeah, Prime is $79 a year. Oh, by the way, there's free movies and TV shows with it." And how much could consumers complain about the quality of movies and TV shows if it's free?'[8]

Amazon spent the next decade sweetening the deal, building out its content for rent or purchase and signing exclusive deals to stream live sports (i.e. Premier League and NFL). Members can now subscribe to content from channels like HBO and Showtime for additional fees, and Amazon has taken greater control of production through its Amazon Studios subsidiary to offer subscribers exclusive content such as the TV shows *The Marvellous Mrs Maisel*, *Transparent* and *The Grand Tour*. And now with its block-buster acquisition of MGM, as discussed in the previous chapter, Amazon has become a bona fide alternative to Netflix. It's a truly global streaming service that is available in more than 200 countries and territories around the world.[9]

The main benefit for Amazon? Prime Video customers not only shop more with Amazon, they have higher renewal rates and are more likely to convert a free trial into a monthly or annual Prime membership.

'So what we find is that customers who watch a movie that they love, they buy more Tide ... video viewers are telling us with their actions that video is an important part of the Prime experience,' said Jeff Wilke, former CEO of Amazon's Worldwide Consumer Business.[10]

Prime Video has been a powerful customer acquisition tool in interna-tional markets as well, particularly those where Amazon isn't as dominant in e-commerce. Brazil, for example, is one of Amazon's more challenging markets due to strong local competition and logistical complexities. Amazon entered Brazil in 2012 but primarily sold e-readers and books until it opened up its site to third-party vendors five years later. Prime, too, followed an unconventional path – Amazon launched a video-only subscription as a way to build awareness before offering its broader Prime subscription to Brazilian shoppers. In Japan, meanwhile, membership increased 16 per cent just three months after the launch of Prime Video. In India, where Amazon is heavily investing in Prime Video, Amazon added more new Prime members in its first year than any other market in the company's history. Although China

TABLE 5.2   Prime is about much more than free shipping

Category	Amazon (US) Prime Membership Benefits
Shipping	Free two-day delivery on millions of items
	Free one-day delivery on more than 10 million items with no minimum purchase
	Free same-day delivery, in select areas, on over 3 million items for qualifying orders over $35
	Release day delivery by 7pm on new videos, games, books, music, movies and more
	1- and 2-hr grocery delivery available from Amazon Fresh and Whole Foods Market
	Scheduled, in-home, in-car and in-garage delivery
	No-rush delivery: earn rewards for slow delivery
Digital	Prime Video: stream or download thousands of TV shows and movies including Amazon Originals
	Prime Gaming: free games, in game items, free Twitch channel subscription every month
	Prime Music: stream over 2 million songs without any ads
	Prime Reading: Read from over 1,000 top Kindle books, magazines, comics, kids' books and more
	Amazon Photos: unlimited, full-resolution photo storage
Shopping	Prime Wardrobe: 'try before you buy' clothes
	Alexa: voice shopping and deals
	Just for Prime: early access to deals and exclusive access to deals including Prime Day
	Exclusive savings on groceries and prescriptions
	5% cashback with the Amazon Prime Rewards Visa Card
	Access to online prices when shopping in-store (Amazon 4-Star and Amazon Books)

SOURCE Author research; Amazon, as of June 2021

remains one of the only markets in the world where Prime Video is not available due to strict media regulations, in 2018 Amazon added the first entertainment benefit – Prime Reading – to its offering. Despite local market nuances, the strength of Amazon's Prime bundle proposition makes it easier today to drive member adoption and retention internationally.

Convenience has always been the premise, but these days Amazon is taking Prime to the next level by granting shoppers access to an entire *life-style of convenience*. Want one-hour delivery? Want Alexa to add something to your basket? Want in-garage or in-car deliveries? Guess what – you need to be a Prime member.

'Our goal with Amazon Prime, make no mistake, is to make sure that if you are not a Prime member, you are being irresponsible.'
Jeff Bezos[11]

Prime is also increasingly about access to *products* as much as it is *services*. As part of Amazon's efforts to tap into the food and fashion sectors, the retailer has been quietly building out a wide-ranging portfolio of private label products, many of which are reserved for members. This creates a heightened sense of exclusivity, and one that is impossible to replicate in a physical setting. Can you imagine Walmart banning certain customers from taking Great Value products off its shelves? Amazon cleverly gets away with this in a digital environment and is clearly motivated to grow its private label portfolio as a means of providing greater value to customers while differentiating from its peers in a margin-accretive manner.

It's important to point out that Prime membership used to act as a gate-way to those services with additional fees. For example, up until 2019, Prime members had to pay a $15 monthly add-on fee for food delivery, a reflection of the higher costs associated with delivery of perishable foods. But that was a big pill to swallow on top of the annual Prime fee – and certainly would have slowed adoption in this all-important category. As we touched on earlier, by making online grocery a 'free' Prime benefit for US shoppers in 2019, Amazon was in an ideal position to capture share a few months later when the pandemic hit.

Prime offers exceptional value to its members but without promising rock-bottom prices. In fact, in the early days, Amazon employees wanted to call the programme Super Saver Platinum, which Bezos rejected on the basis that it was not designed to be a money-saving scheme.[12] (It is thought that the name Prime was eventually chosen due to the prime position of fast-track pallets in fulfilment centres.[13]) Today, however, there are a growing number of financial incentives to become a Prime member. In addition to the main shipping benefit, members have access to exclusive deals, can get cash-back on purchases by using a Prime-branded Visa card and, as Amazon moves further into bricks and mortar, members will have access to 'online prices' in stores.

What is more, Amazon has created an entire shopping event – Prime Day – exclusively for its members. The Black Friday-esque event, guised as a celebration of Amazon's 20th birthday for its 2015 launch, is designed to artificially stimulate demand in an otherwise sluggish period while simulta-neously rewarding members of the Prime club with more than 24 hours' worth of deals. But make no mistake, Prime Day is as much about brazen customer acquisition as it is about reminding existing members of the value of Prime.

In summary, the aim is to make Prime so attractive that, in Bezos' own words, shoppers would be 'irresponsible' not to join. By clustering its services under one umbrella, with each intended to make the customer's life either easier or more enjoyable, Amazon can tap into consumer needs that far supersede price. It doesn't just want share of wallet, it wants share of life.

But is Prime actually a loyalty programme?

It's a hotly debated question in the retail industry – can we really call Prime a loyalty programme? In their essence, these schemes are designed to drive repeat business by rewarding a retailer's most important customers. In this sense, Amazon Prime is the very epitome of a loyalty scheme. After all, not many other retailers have millions of customers paying for the privilege of shopping with them.

However, the term 'loyalty scheme' is often associated with the plastic cards we carry around in our wallets, habitually swiping them at the till in exchange for (often unquantifiable) points. Let's be very clear here – these types of loyalty schemes are on the way out.

The term 'loyalty card' is a misnomer. They don't drive loyalty. By focus-ing on discounts and vouchers, these schemes often end up encouraging the very opposite behaviour as shoppers cherry-pick the best deals. This is also a reflection of changing shopping habits and proliferation of choice, particu-larly in markets like the UK where consumers have ditched the weekly shop. Instead, shoppers are buying more frequently, in smaller quantities and across a range of different retailers. The idea of being loyal to one and only one supermarket is a thing of the past.

So when it comes to driving loyalty today, retailers must ditch the 'more you shop, more you earn' concept in favour of convenience, service and experience. With Prime, Amazon is spearheading this next evolution of loyalty – the battleground is quickly shifting from saving customers money to saving them time, energy and effort. Retailers will drive loyalty through greater personalization and by delighting shoppers with instore perks. Waitrose, for example, has been wildly successful in offering its loyalty card-holders free coffee and tea, welcoming shoppers into its stores as you would welcome a guest into your home.

In recent years, loyalty cards have naturally evolved to become more digi-tally led – after all, there is nowhere to swipe your plastic card in a checkout-free store! As we touched on in the last chapter, the pandemic was a catalyst to accelerate the adoption of the digital wallet, merging digital rewards and payment instrument. Loyalty schemes are morphing to become part of a wider bundle that not only rewards shoppers for their custom but also sends them personalized, real-time offers instore and reduces friction by allowing them to find and pay for products – all in one app.

Price-oriented retailers, of course, are the exception here and will continue to drive loyalty by offering their shoppers exceptional value for money. We would argue that there is merit to ditching costly loyalty schemes altogether, in this case to invest in everyday low prices. After all, Aldi and Primark don't operate loyalty schemes and they have some of the most devoted customers out there. At the end of the day, the key to driving loyalty is understanding what your customers value.

For Amazon, this is ease and convenience. It's instant gratification. And increasingly it's about entertaining them in the process. If Amazon achieves this, then the benefits to its wider business are bountiful.

What does Amazon get out of Prime?

Extreme loyalty. Lifelong, monogamous shoppers. Customers who wear Prime blinders and don't bother checking other retail sites. They shop on autopilot, making Amazon their first port of call, their default shopping option, even if it's not always the cheapest. Addicted to the convenience offered by Prime, shoppers become less price-sensitive – all to the advantage of Amazon's algorithms. This is behavioural modification at its best.

So what does that look like in numbers?

- **Spend**: according to Consumer Intelligence Research Partners, the average Prime member spends $1,400 annually – more than twice the amount spent by non-members.[14] As with most subscriptions, members typically feel the need to get their money's worth, which can lead to irrational decision making: in this case, shoppers justify the annual Prime fee by spending more with Amazon. The sunk cost fallacy works to Amazon's advantage.

- **Frequency**: Prime customers tend to be 'super users', shopping with Amazon far more regularly than non-Prime members. According to a Feedvisor survey, 85 per cent of Prime members browse for products at least once a week, and nearly half (45 per cent) place an order at least once a week, making Bezos' initial vision – using Prime as a tool to remove barriers to more frequent shopping – a reality.[15]

- **Retention**: it is estimated that retention rates are higher than 90 per cent.[16]

Through Prime, Amazon also gets access to a treasure trove of customer data, giving it an unrivalled understanding of the online purchasing behaviour of its most important shoppers. This allows for greater personalization, from helpful product recommendations to perhaps less-than-welcome dynamic pricing (according to Profitero, Amazon changes its prices more than 2.5 million times a day).

Prime also enables upsell opportunities, and perhaps more importantly, baits shoppers into Amazon's wider ecosystem. While other retailers' loyalty schemes focus on top-tier customers, Amazon cleverly draws as many shoppers as it can into its ecosystem, thereby maximizing customer value over their lifetime. There's a good reason the retailer practically gives Prime memberships away to college students and offers Prime members discounts on nappies and baby food – it can capture tomorrow's consumers at critical life stages, locking them in as loyal members of the club.

'The two times in your life when you were most likely to change your shopping behavior are when you're a student ... and when you have children. So as [these customers] got older, they were already sort of addicted to Amazon being the best place for them to get their stuff.'
Julie Todaro, former Amazon executive[17]

Another bonus for Amazon? Prime is nearly impossible to replicate. It is wide-reaching, probably too generous and certainly unique in scope, giving Amazon a compelling point of differentiation. Not many other retailers have the scale, infrastructure or cross-sector dominance to produce a copy-cat version.

The one retailer that just may give Amazon a run for its money, however, is Walmart. In 2020, the retailer launched its own Prime-like membership scheme called Walmart+ and within two weeks 11 per cent of Americans signed up to the service.[18] For $98 a year, members get access to unlimited 'free' delivery, fuel discounts and access to scan & go (somewhat bizarre to include this last one as a 'perk' given it is fast becoming the norm, plus it's in the retailer's interest to encourage this kind of behaviour in terms of both customer experience and labour cost savings).

In any case, it's fascinating to see Walmart take a leaf from Amazon's book and shift its focus away from purely saving customers money – and instead saving customers time. It's much easier to charge a premium on this, with time becoming the ultimate commodity. A few years prior to the launch of Walmart+, the retailer took its first punch at Prime with 'ShippingPass', a similar scheme that offered unlimited two-day shipping but for a lower fee of $49. Walmart scrapped the short-lived programme in 2017, instead offering free two-day shipping on more than 2 million items – no membership required.

We believe Walmart+ will sharpen the retailer's competitive edge, but given its current lack of streaming services and smaller assortment for same-day delivery (160,000 versus Amazon's 3 million), we see it as complementary rather than cannibalistic.

Can Prime work in a physical setting?

It's been fascinating for industry analysts like us to watch how Prime would unfold in a physical setting. Sure, it's easy to tier shoppers online where you can enable or disable access to certain products and services. In a physical setting, it's slightly more delicate. However, Prime forms the very DNA of Amazon's retail business. As Amazon moved further into the physical world of retail, omitting Prime was never going to be an option. We caught the first glimpse of how Amazon would translate Prime in a bricks and mortar setting through Amazon Books – its first full-size, traditional store concept.

We'll discuss the details of this unique concept later in the book but for now it's important to understand that at its 2015 launch, there were no tangible benefits for Prime members. However, less than a year later, Amazon very boldly moved towards a tiered pricing model – prices for Prime customers are now equivalent to those offered on Amazon's website, and everyone else must pay the list price.

Amazon went on to launch another unconventional bricks and mortar concept, Amazon 4-Star, in 2018. As its name implies, stores only stock items that have online ratings of 4 stars and above. Like Amazon Books, Prime members have access to online prices while non-members pay the list price – unless, of course, they want to start a free trial of Prime.

Now you can argue that Amazon's tiered pricing model isn't entirely different to what American supermarkets have done for decades by scanning a loyalty card at the checkout. However, the supermarkets give shoppers a discount on *select* items, while Amazon's scheme is designed for every *single* item to have two prices. If you're not a Prime member, there is no reason to shop there – aside from perhaps testing out Amazon devices like the Echo or Kindle. It's one step short of charging admission to enter the store.

It should come as no surprise to learn that these stores don't contribute much to the top line. In fact, we would argue that they should be considered a marketing expense as their sole intention is to raise awareness of the benefits, and ultimately drive adoption, of Prime.

But how would this work in a supermarket setting? Amazon can't get away with such a visibly tiered pricing policy, as shoppers would simply vote with their feet. It must strike the right balance of rewarding Prime shoppers in a discreet enough way so as not to lose customers, while still conveying the benefits of Prime to those non-members.

Amazon's acquisition of Whole Foods Market was a watershed moment for the industry – and for Amazon itself. We'll explore this in great detail in the coming chapters but it's important to call out here that, aside from some discounted Thanksgiving turkeys in that first year, Prime members had to wait a while for any meaningful perks. Today, however, Amazon is much bolder about rewarding its best grocery shoppers while instore: Prime members now find exclusive savings and deals when shopping in Whole Foods Market as well as Amazon's eponymous supermarkets. Prime members get an additional 10 per cent off sale items and have access to perks like free two-hour grocery delivery and one-hour pickup from store. Bricks and mortar is a whole new ball game, but with Prime underpinning

Amazon's grocery strategy, we are confident that Amazon's tech-infused supermarkets can make a meaningful impact.

Prime 2.0

The future is certainly a greater physical presence, but Prime's core digital proposition will also evolve to become even more attractive, increasingly flexible and ultimately more expensive for shoppers.

More bells and whistles

Amazon will continue to enrich the Prime offer, adding new benefits that either add to the stickiness of Prime or tie in with Amazon's broader strategic focus. For example, Amazon launched its first fashion benefit – Prime Wardrobe – in 2017 as part of its efforts to build trust and credibility in the category while simultaneously tackling the main barrier to buying clothes online: size-related returns. The service brings the fitting room to the shopper by allowing Prime members to receive up to eight items of clothing, shoes or accessories to try in the comfort of their own homes. Shoppers are provided with prepaid labels and resealable boxes for free returns, and they are charged only when they decide what they'd like to keep.

Inspired by the niche services offered by brands like Stitch Fix and Trunk Club, Prime Wardrobe was the first of its kind among mainstream clothing retailers. Within months of its launch, however, UK-based online fashion retailer ASOS introduced its own try-before-you-buy service along with same-day. This is the Amazon Effect in action, kicking competitors into gear and improving the experience for the customer.

Today, it's become common for shoppers to buy with the intention of returning, but that's not always such a bad thing considering that those who return the most also typically spend the most. Retailers are right to stamp out wardrobing – when customers purchase, wear once and return for a refund. But should they be discouraging bracketing as well? This is what Prime Wardrobe does – allowing a customer to order multiple sizes to find the best fit – and it is entirely rational behaviour in the context of free returns and flexible payment options. Amazon may not be known for its fashion credentials, but once again its ability to stamp out friction shows how it is capable of disrupting an entire industry.

Looking to new demographics for growth

According to a Piper Jaffray survey, a whopping 82 per cent of US households that earn more than $112,000 per year hold a Prime membership.[19] Amazon has cornered the affluent market and now must look outside its core customer demographic for future growth. The same survey shows that Amazon's reach is lowest among those who earn less than $41,000.

The main barriers for this lower-income customer group have historically been the annual Prime fee, limited internet access and lack of a credit card. More than a quarter of American households have no or limited access to checking and savings accounts.[20]

In recent years, Amazon has ramped up efforts to target lower-income shoppers. For example, it launched a pay-monthly Prime membership scheme in 2016. For shoppers, this option actually works out more expensive on an annual basis ($156 versus $119) but provides an alternative way to access Amazon if customers are unwilling or unable to pay the annual fee in one lump sum.

Meanwhile, Amazon has homed in on the unbanked/underbanked consumer by launching a discounted Prime membership for those receiving government assistance, as well as Amazon Cash, a scheme that allows shoppers to deposit cash into their Amazon account by scanning a barcode at participating stores. This has since been rolled out in the UK as well, where it is branded Top Up.

The retailer has also extended its partnership with Coinstar to allow customers to deposit spare change directly into their Amazon accounts. In 2019, meanwhile, Amazon offered US shoppers an alternative way to shop with cash. Amazon PayCode, which had already been running in 19 countries around the world at the time of its US launch, allows customers to choose Amazon PayCode at checkout and then pay for their purchase in cash at one of 15,000 Western Union locations.

This is a blatant attempt to win share from a demographic that was traditionally served by bricks and mortar retailers, most notably Walmart. It's estimated that around 20 per cent of Walmart's shoppers pay for groceries with food stamps and, for years, Walmart has allowed customers to 'pay with cash' online (payments are made at Walmart's stores).[21]

So what's Amazon's next move? Could we see the launch of an Amazon-branded checking account? This would be a natural extension of the services

Amazon already provides and is also being offered by global e-commerce retailers like Alibaba and Rakuten.

But more fee hikes are inevitable

Amazon is clearly very motivated to grow its Prime membership base for the dual purpose of feeding the flywheel (or, in simple terms, growing sales) and offsetting rising shipping costs. As discussed, alternative revenue streams such as AWS, advertising and increasingly subscriptions (around 90 per cent of which is Prime revenues) are vital for Amazon to continue to invest in the core retail division.

Prime revenue growth will be achieved through international customer acquisition, but also good old-fashioned fee hikes. In 2005, the original Prime fee was $79 – but let's not forget that at the time of launch Prime was purely about shipping. After nearly a decade of maintaining that original price, Amazon raised the fee for the first time to $99 in 2014. This was a reflection of rising shipping costs and investments in the Prime offer with new services such as video streaming. Prime got more expensive again in 2018, jumping 20 per cent to $119, and it's fair to say this won't be the last increase.

Amazon spends billions of dollars on shipping, something we'll explore in greater detail later in the book. In theory, as shoppers spend more, volumes increase and shipping costs go down, resulting in better deals with suppliers and consequently lower prices for customers. However, as Amazon moves further into fast-moving consumer goods categories, this becomes harder to achieve given the low-value/high-frequency nature of the category. It's estimated that Prime makes up about 60 per cent of shipping costs[22] and that in order to break even on Prime, Amazon would have to increase the fee to $200. That won't happen. Yes, we can expect to see additional fee hikes every few years but let's not forget the all-important flywheel effect that is at the very heart of the Prime scheme. As intangible as it may be, Prime encourages shoppers to spend more and Amazon must strike the right balance so as not to jeopardize that.

For many, Amazon is now so deeply embedded in their everyday lives that they will accept future price increases. It's imperative that Amazon continues to invest in digital content and the core shipping offer, while also exploring new loyalty avenues, in order to maintain its incredibly high consumer value proposition. But it's fair to say that Prime will remain the engine of Amazon's retail machine.

Notes

1 Amazon press release, 2005. Amazon.com announces record free cash flow fueled by lower prices and free shipping; introduces new express shipping program – Amazon Prime, *Amazon.com*, 2 February. Available from: http://phx.corporate-ir.net/phoenix.zhtml?c=176060&p=irol-newsArticle&ID=669786 (archived at https://perma.cc/2BRK-BUZT) [Last accessed 28/6/2018].

2 Ibid.

3 Stone, Brad (2013) *The Everything Store: Jeff Bezos and the age of Amazon*, Bantam Press, London.

4 Del Ray, J (2019) The making of Amazon Prime, the internet's most successful and devastating membership program, *Vox*, 3 May. Available from: https://www.vox.com/recode/2019/5/3/18511544/amazon-prime-oral-history-jeff-bezos-one-day-shipping (archived at https://perma.cc/K2R7-CGYS) [Last accessed 18/6/2021].

5 Stone, Brad (2013) *The Everything Store: Jeff Bezos and the age of Amazon*, Bantam Press, London.

6 Amazon UK Analyst Briefing, London, July 2018.

7 Stevens, Laura (2018) Amazon targets Medicaid recipients as it widens war for low-income shoppers, *Wall Street Journal*, 7 March. Available from: https://www.wsj.com/articles/amazon-widens-war-with-walmart-for-low-income-shoppers-1520431203 (archived at https://perma.cc/A8S5-P2J4) [Last accessed 28/6/2018].

8 Del Ray, Jason (2019) The making of Amazon Prime, the internet's most successful and devastating membership program, *Vox*, 3 May. Available from: https://www.vox.com/recode/2019/5/3/18511544/amazon-prime-oral-history-jeff-bezos-one-day-shipping (archived at https://perma.cc/C5ZN-YDB6) [Last accessed 19/6/21].

9 Barraclough, Leo (2016) Amazon Prime Video goes global: Available in more than 200 territories, *Variety*, 14 December. Available from: https://variety.com/2016/digital/global/amazon-prime-video-now-available-in-more-than-200-countries-1201941818/ (archived at https://perma.cc/7MPT-D7QT) [Last accessed 19/6/21].

10 Del Ray, Jason (2019) The making of Amazon Prime, the internet's most successful and devastating membership program, *Vox*, 3 May. Available from: https://www.vox.com/recode/2019/5/3/18511544/amazon-prime-oral-history-jeff-bezos-one-day-shipping (archived at https://perma.cc/C5ZN-YDB6) [Last accessed 19/6/21].

11   Kim, Eugene (2016) Bezos to shareholders: It's 'irresponsible' not to be part of
     Amazon Prime, *Business Insider*, 17 May. Available from: http://uk.
     businessinsider.com/amazon-ceo-jeff-bezos-says-its-irresponsible-not-to-be-
     part-of-prime-2016-5 (archived at https://perma.cc/JWY9-ZZLX) [Last
     accessed 28/6/2018].

12   Stone, Brad (2013) *The Everything Store: Jeff Bezos and the age of Amazon*,
     Bantam Press, London.

13   Stone, Brad (2013) *The Everything Store: Jeff Bezos and the age of Amazon*,
     Bantam Press, London.

14   Green, Dennis (2018) Prime members spend way more on Amazon than other
     customers - and the difference is growing, *Business Insider*, 21 October.
     Available from: https://www.businessinsider.com/amazon-prime-customers-
     spend-more-than-others-2018-10?r=US&IR=T (archived at https://perma.
     cc/255M-3FLS) [Last accessed 19/6/2021].

15   Kline, Daniel B. (2018) How often do Prime members buy from Amazon?, *The
     Motley Fool*, 19 January. Available from: https://www.fool.com/
     investing/2018/01/19/how-often-do-prime-members-buy-from-amazon.aspx
     (archived at https://perma.cc/K8SY-Z784) [Last accessed 19/6/21].

16   Soper, Spencer (2018) Bezos says Amazon has topped 100 million Prime
     members, *Bloomberg*, 18 April. Available from: https://origin-www.bloomberg.
     com/news/articles/2018-04-18/amazon-s-bezos-says-company-has-topped-
     100million-prime-members (archived at https://perma.cc/JWY9-ZZLX) [Last
     accessed 28/6/2018].

17   Del Ray, J (2019) The making of Amazon Prime, the internet's most successful
     and devastating membership program, *Vox*, 3 May. Available from: https://
     www.vox.com/recode/2019/5/3/18511544/amazon-prime-oral-history-jeff-
     bezos-one-day-shipping (archived at https://perma.cc/K2R7-CGYS) [Last
     accessed 18/6/2021].

18   Monteros, Maria (2021). Walmart+ gains traction 5 months after launch,
     Retail Dive, 12 February. Available from: https://www.retaildive.com/news/
     walmart-gains-traction-5-months-after-launch/595029/ (archived at https://
     perma.cc/ZYT2-JKKD) [Last accessed: 19/6/21].

19   Molla, Rani (2017) For the wealthiest Americans, Amazon Prime has become
     the norm, *Recode*, 8 June. Available from: https://www.recode.net/2017/
     6/8/15759354/amazon-prime-low-income-discount-piper-jaffray-demographics
     (archived at https://perma.cc/Q4F3-F7M4) [Last accessed 28/6/2018].

20   Hirsch, Lauren (2018) Amazon plans more Prime perks at Whole Foods, and
     it will change the industry, *CNBC*, 1 May. Available from: https://www.cnbc.
     com/2018/05/01/prime-perks-are-coming-to-whole-foods-and-it-will-change-
     the-industry.html (archived at https://perma.cc/4GF4-STX6) [Last accessed
     28/6/2018].

21 Anonymous (2017) Amazon to discount Prime for US families on welfare, *BBC*, 6 June. Available from: https://www.bbc.com/news/technology-40170655 (archived at https://perma.cc/G26M-MLPU) [Last accessed 28/6/2018].

22 Saba, Jennifer (2018) Priming the pump, *Reuters*, 19 April. Available from: https://www.breakingviews.com/considered-view/amazons-10-bln-subsidy-is-prime-for-growth/ (archived at https://perma.cc/RJR9-J8UL) [Last accessed 28/6/2018].

06

Retail apocalypse or rebirth?

'For so long, people have predicted the demise of movie theatres, but people still like to go to the movies.'
Jeff Bezos[1]

You don't have to look very hard today to find an article or piece of research that positions e-commerce as the Grim Reaper of retail. The phrase 'retail apocalypse' has officially entered the industry lexicon and is arguably too well documented in the media these days – it even has its own Wikipedia page.

Doom and gloom make good headlines, but it's premature to start writing physical retail's obituary. We'll spend most of this chapter defying the apocalypse narrative. However, first let's make one thing very clear: we have too many stores. Today, we have an oversupply of retail space; we have retail space that is no longer fit for purpose.

Earlier in the book, we discussed how the pandemic has accelerated the demise of mediocre retail – but let's not forget that retail has been shrinking its physical footprint for years. According to Coresight Research, there were nearly 9,000 store closures in the US in 2020.[2] This was actually a slight deceleration compared with the previous year, but likely to be a pandemic blip driven by government stimulus and the shift in consumer spending (towards goods and away from services).

The reality is that many major brands, such as Zara, H&M, Gap, Victoria's Secret, Disney and Nike, continue to rightsize their store portfolios to reflect the broader shift to digital. And there's no sign of a slowdown – UBS predicts that 80,000 retail stores across the US will close by 2026.[3]

While this is especially pronounced in the overbuilt suburbs of the US, it's by no means an American phenomenon. In the UK, more than 17,500 retail outlets closed in 2020, marking the biggest decline in store numbers in over a decade.[4] As of mid-2021, one in seven British shops were lying empty.[5]

Meanwhile, global shopper demand and expectations for online retail are booming. In the UK, it took seven years for online share of retail sales to go from 9 per cent to 19 per cent (2012 to 2019), but when the pandemic struck it took a mere four months to get from 19 per cent to 33 per cent (January–May 2020).[6]

According to McKinsey, China now has more online shoppers than any other nation and accounts for approximately half of all of global e-commerce sales.[7] In the US, meanwhile, UBS predicts that e-commerce sales are expected to account for 27 per cent of total US retail sales by 2026. We'll say it again – there will be no return to the status quo.[8]

There is no denying that the pandemic-driven surge in e-commerce is partially happening at the expense of legacy brick and mortar chains – but is it all Amazon's fault? Not entirely. In a nutshell, mature modern retail markets are overstored, there has been a titanic shift in shopping habits, digital has turned retail on its head, disruptive bricks and mortar retailers – think fast fashion and discount grocers – continue to steal share from more established players, and (despite a temporary reversal of this trend during the pandemic) people are generally spending less on stuff and more on experiences. We are at the intersection of major technological, economic and societal changes that are profoundly reshaping the retail sector.

Now let's take a closer look at these shifts, and more specifically, how they're leading retailers to rightsize their store portfolios.

The on-my-terms shopper is born

'The idea that there is somehow an inherent opposition between online and physical retail is simply wrong. There is a total blend. When you see the way customers shop, it's very interchangeable between the physical store and online.'

John Boumphrey, Amazon UK Country Manager, 2021[9]

Technology isn't just raising customer expectations and creating new ways to shop – it's fundamentally revolutionizing retail. This will naturally be a key theme throughout the book, but here we'd like to specifically explore how technology is resetting customer expectations by enabling a more convenient, frictionless shopping experience.

First, we must acknowledge that the world is much more joined up than it was a decade ago: more than two-thirds of the global population is now connected via mobile[10] and by 2023 there are expected to be more than three times more networked devices on Earth than humans.[11] It's hard to imagine that the iPhone, a device that has become such an integral part of our everyday lives, has only been around since 2007. Google believes that we no longer 'go online'; today we 'live online'. In fact, with the average American spending almost nine years of their lifetime staring at their tiny screens,[12] it's fair to say that our mobile phones have simply become an extension of us as consumers.

Amazon is naturally well positioned here. In the UK, where 94 per cent of the adult online population use apps on their smartphones and tablets, Amazon's app has the greatest reach (19.2 million) of all retailers. In fact, as of 2020, Amazon was the eighth most-used app in the country. Users in the UK spend 2 hours and 5 minutes on Amazon per day, roughly the same amount of time spent checking Google Maps.[13]

In this age of ubiquitous connectivity, the consumer is king. Retailers have been challenged to cater to these 'always on' and constantly connected consumers since the introduction of e-commerce, accessible through increasingly portable computing devices. The ability to shop on a mobile phone while sitting on a train or waiting for the dentist has empowered consumers with a whole new level of convenience and accessibility, while also bridging the divide between physical and digital retail which we will discuss further in the next chapter.

Another technological development that has transformed the way we shop is, as discussed earlier, the way we pay. PayPal, which saves time and adds extra security on entering payment information, introduced consumers to online payments in the same way that contactless cards paved the way for instore mobile payment schemes, including mobile wallets such as Apple Pay and Google Pay.

Mobile has only served to accelerate the growth of e-commerce retailers including Amazon. Additional technology developments, fuelled by the demand for more immersive and portable experiences, have included mobile-optimized websites, apps, and larger devices such as tablets, with bigger touchscreens to interact with them on, as well as wearable devices, including watches, other smart jewellery and fitness trackers. And security is also evolving from the use of myriad forgettable passwords, single sign-on access via Google, Facebook, etc, two-factor authentication, biometric fingerprint and facial recognition.

Likewise, retail has evolved in its use of these technology advances to make the online shopping experience as simple as possible. Amazon's 'one-click' patent revolutionized online checkout, while brands are working out how to make social shopping pay, with shoppable media, gamified augmented reality store experiences and WeChat's app-within-app payments dominance in China as notable successes. But in future the quest for ease and convenience, driven by customer expectations set by online, will advance beyond mobile and touchscreen technology. We can already see this happening with accelerated smart home developments, so appliances can reorder their own supplies, as well as the integration of voice assistants into more and more devices, including in-car systems.

These technological improvements, which have put billions of products right at shoppers' fingertips, have been matched by similar advances in fulfilment. Lead times are getting shorter as online retailers look to replicate the sense of immediacy that was once reserved for bricks and mortar retailers. Today, customers expect shipping to be fast, reliable and free.

The result of all of this? Online shopping has become utterly effortless. Mobile commerce in particular is booming and is poised for impressive future growth. By 2024, global m-commerce sales are expected to more than double to reach US $4.5 trillion, accounting for an astounding 70 per cent of the global e-commerce market.[14]

Bricks and mortar retailers must ensure they can appease today's supercharged shopper who enters their store with heightened, and at times conflicting, expectations. On one hand, customers are demanding ultra-convenience, a frictionless shopping experience, transparency and instant gratification. But on the other hand, they also expect the environment in which they shop to be hyper-personalized and, increasingly, experiential.

The future is certainly fewer but more impactful stores: we expect retailers to continue rightsizing – while simultaneously investing in the store experience – as they adjust to this new reality of shifting spending patterns. Those retailers lacking the agility to re-engineer themselves for today's modern consumer will find themselves with no choice but to shutter stores.

Amazon Effect: killing the category killer

Like the phrase 'retail apocalypse', the 'Amazon Effect' is also effective click-bait for many retail articles today. Stores closing? It's the Amazon Effect. Retailers investing online? The Amazon Effect. Acquisitions, bankruptcies, redundancies… These days, we can find a way to link, however tenuously, most retail developments to the Seattle-based behemoth.

Nonetheless, the notion of being 'Amazoned' is very real for some. When the actual product can be delivered digitally – think music, video, games, books – and e-commerce penetration nears the 50 per cent mark, there is little hope for the physical space selling those goods. 'Category killers', highly focused retailers that are typically dominant in one product category, were naturally the first casualties of e-commerce. The likes of Blockbuster, Circuit City, CompUSA and, more recently, Toys R Us have been consigned to the pages of the history books. Many of these companies went from being the disruptor to the disrupted, a stark reminder of the danger of complacency.

Borders, for example, used to be America's second-largest bookstore chain. In a fateful interview back in 2008, transcribed on hedge fund manager Todd Sullivan's site, Borders CEO George Jones said, 'I do not think that technology and self-service in our stores will even vaguely replace the fact that you can come into our stores and there is someone who greets you and is knowledgeable about books. That is and will always be a huge part of our business.'[15] Borders went bust three years later.

What was once a competitive advantage for the category killer – a deep product assortment and large store network – ultimately led to its own demise. It's no coincidence that Amazon started out selling books as this was a commodity category that early internet shoppers would feel comfortable buying online. It's also important to understand that when Amazon was getting into books, there were three million books in print worldwide, far more than any bookstore could ever stock.[16] Cue the beginning of the end for category killers.

Amazon's very existence impacts every single retail business. It is hands down the most disruptive retailer in the Western world. No other retailer has been so effective at eliminating complacency and irrelevance in the sector, ultimately driving change for the benefit of the customer. But naturally, this means a future with less bricks and mortar retail space: 28 per cent of shoppers globally cite Amazon as the key reason for visiting physical stores less often.[17]

Overspaced, with questionable relevance

According to the International Council of Shopping Centers, the number of American shopping centres grew by 300 per cent – or more than twice as fast as the population – from 1970 to 2015.[18] Today, the US is by far the most over-retailed country in the world. It is estimated that US retail space ranges from 23.5 to 46.6 square feet per person. For context, there is just 2.4 square feet of retail space per capita in Germany and 1.5 square feet per capita in Mexico. A retail apocalypse has long been looming.[19]

The demise of the shopping centre has been exacerbated by the Great Recession, growth of online shopping and, most recently, the COVID crisis. After all, the online marketplace is simply a modernized, digital version of the shopping mall – but open 24/7 and with infinite assortment.

However, the US retail sector was considered overstored well before the e-commerce boom. According to Bloomberg, this was the 'result of investors pouring money into commercial real estate decades earlier as the suburbs boomed. All those buildings needed to be filled with stores, and that demand got the attention of venture capital. The result was the birth of the big-box era of massive stores in nearly every category – from office suppliers like Staples Inc. to pet retailers such as PetSmart Inc. and Petco Animal Supplies Inc.'[20]

Shopping malls, meanwhile, are becoming an endangered species – one quarter of US malls are expected to shut by 2025.[21] A public health crisis has exacerbated the mall's biggest challenge: staying relevant. Mall visits have been in decline for well over a decade now. During the pandemic, the temporary closure of cinemas, gyms and restaurants meant shoppers had even less of an incentive to ditch their screens. It should come as no surprise that a number of US mall-based retailers, including J.C. Penney, Neiman Marcus, Lord & Taylor, Brooks Brothers and J. Crew, filed for bankruptcy protection in 2020. Retailers that struggled to remain relevant pre-COVID found themselves clinging on for survival during a crisis. This is retail Darwinism on steroids.

While it's clear there will need to be considerable rationalization of mall space in the future, there will also be an opportunity for reinvention. In fact, malls might even be granted a new lease of life as remote working takes hold and shopping behaviour shifts once again.

Of course, it's not just malls that are overspaced and lacking relevance today. Following the demise of the category killer, we believe that out-of-town superstores and department stores are the most at-risk retail formats today. Despite the many differences between these two formats, the original premise of both department stores and superstores is the same: one-stop shopping. In the past, it made sense to dedicate 100,000-plus square feet of retail space to these 'palaces of consumption', aggregating a significant number of brands under one roof. Macy's boasts about its 2.5 million-square-foot flagship New York store being the 'World's Largest Store' – it does cover an entire city block – while in Europe some Carrefour and Tesco hypermarkets were so massive that employees used to wear roller skates to get around. Piling it high may have worked in the past; today, however, with Amazon alone stocking millions of Prime-eligible products, the idea that a bricks and mortar retailer can still offer 'everything under one roof' becomes laughable.

But retail moves fast. It was only a couple of decades ago that Walmart was banking on its Supercenter concept as the future of retail. And let's not forget, for its time, it was incredibly innovative. No longer did shoppers have to visit multiple speciality retailers; the convenience of one-stop shopping and low prices was a winning combination. Back in 1997, then CEO of Walmart David Glass predicted: 'I believe Supercenters will be to the next decade what discount stores were to the last.' It's worth pointing out that at the time Walmart, like most retailers, were only just beginning to explore 'futuristic ideas [such] as Internet shopping.'[22]

Glass was certainly right with his predictions (although we're pretty sure Bezos could update that claim with e-commerce being to the following decade what superstores were to the previous one). From 1996–2016, Walmart opened an average of 156 Supercenters each year. The majority of these openings were conversions of existing discount stores as opposed to new builds; however, this was the most significant food retailing conversion process in US history. Walmart was able to bring its winning formula of low prices and wide grocery assortment to previously underserved areas.

Back in 2012, Natalie and esteemed retail analyst and co-author Bryan Roberts predicted that Walmart would reach saturation with its Supercenter format by 2020.[23] This was based on three factors: discount conversion opportunities drying up, slow population growth and the cannibalization of bricks and mortar sales by online retail.

The 'death of the hypermarket' however, is far more pronounced in markets such as the UK where the retail sector is more heavily influenced by online and discount channels which pose the largest threat to superstores. According to the Office for National Statistics, at the time of writing in mid-2021, e-commerce made up 30 per cent of total retail sales[24] in the UK. Meanwhile, Aldi and Lidl alone account for 14 per cent of the grocery sector, according to Kantar.[25] The explosive growth in these two channels even prior to the pandemic has led to titanic shifts in shopping behaviour and expectations, the most significant of which has been the death of the weekly shop.

We may have witnessed a revival of the weekly shop in 2020 as shoppers looked to consolidate trips; however, as pandemic concerns dissipate, we believe shoppers will revert to shopping more frequently. Even prior to COVID, an astounding 65 per cent of British shoppers were visiting a super-market more than once a day. No longer do customers need to trek to an out-of-town superstore for low prices or wide assortment. Online retail is well and truly eroding the superstore proposition; meanwhile, proximity retailing no longer comes with a premium price tag. Shoppers today buy little and often; they are shopping 'for tonight' and as a result they are visit-ing a multitude of brands. In fact, we believe this trend will be accelerated by the emergence of rapid delivery providers such as Gorillas, Weezy, Getir and Dija, which all share the ambition of taking the top-up shop digital by delivering groceries in 15 minutes or less. The days of planning a week's worth of meals are gone.

The most tangible evidence of this fundamental shift in shopping habits can be found at the very entrance of a supermarket. Traditionally, the aver-age Waitrose store provided 200 large shopping carts and 150 shallow ones for the 'daily shopper'. These days, shoppers will find 250 shallow trolleys and just 70 large ones.[26] 'The notion that you are going to go and push a trolley around for the week is a thing of the past,' said former Waitrose boss, Lord Mark Price.

Department stores, meanwhile, won't be as fortunate. This channel has been in freefall for over two decades, a trend that has most recently been exacerbated by the pandemic.

A fundamental rule in retail is being relevant to your customers. This is essential in the best of times but becomes all the more critical when the backdrop is an overstored retail landscape and a digitally-enabled consumer with shifting priorities. Being all things to all people is no longer an option. In fact, we'd argue that Amazon is probably the only retailer in the world today that can get away with being all things to all people thanks to its unrivalled assortment and accessibility – in both the financial and logistical senses. For everyone else, it's essential to have both a crystal-clear vision of your target customer and a truly differentiated proposition in order to stand out from the crowd.

By their very nature, traditional department stores are simply less relevant today:

- *Online encroachment.* Although Amazon does not break out category figures, it is considered to be the largest apparel retailer in the US. We don't believe that online retailers can ever fully replace the physical store experience in categories like fashion and food, but that doesn't mean they won't try. Faster delivery, more generous returns policies and sizing improvements are helping to instil greater confidence in shoppers looking to buy clothes online.

- As we touched on earlier in the chapter, online retail is encroaching on the core premise of the department store: one-stop shopping. According to Cowen and Company, US department stores generate approximately 15–25 per cent of their sales online; however, many analysts believe that 35–40 per cent is the maximum penetration level for apparel sales online.[27] So while there is an opportunity to grow department store sales online, this will indeed lead to a glut of empty space in stores. Even the leanest, most digitally-savvy department store chains are feeling the pinch. In 2020, the UK's John Lewis saw e-commerce account for three quarters of the retailer's sales, up from an already impressive 40 per cent before the pandemic.[28] In the expectation that this trend will not 'materially reverse', John Lewis, like many others, did not re-open all of its stores following lockdown. 'The reality is that we have too much store space for the way people want to shop now,' the retailer stated in 2020.[29]

- It's also important to remind ourselves that, at one time, shoppers turned to department stores for the knowledge and assistance that could be provided by store employees. It was also an opportunity to discover and get inspired by new products. Of course, that is less relevant today as mobile phones have become the shopper's trusted advisor of choice and people often browse online before going into the stores. That said, we believe that department stores could do more to capitalize on personal shopping and the fitting room experience more broadly.

- *Product sameness and mid-market positioning.* The department store's pitfalls go far beyond *breadth* of assortment; the range itself is undifferentiated and less compelling these days. In fact, consultants at AlixPartners estimate that there is a 40 per cent overlap in product mix among traditional department stores. But these stores weren't always so homogeneous.[30] At one time, the Sears Wish Book represented the largest selection of toys you could find in one place and, up until the 1980s, JCPenney was still selling home appliances and auto products. The subsequent rise of the big-box discounters like Walmart and Target forced the major department store chains to rationalize their general merchandise offerings and shift their focus to fashion. These days, apparel, footwear and accessories make up around 80 per cent of most department stores' sales compared to just 50 per cent a few decades ago.[31]

- An increased focus on fashion may have once helped to differentiate from a growing superstore threat but today, despite their best efforts to invest in exclusive ranges and collaborate with other brands, department stores are left looking quite stale. The fast fashion chain Zara releases 500 new designs a week and can take a coat from design stage to the sales floor in 25 days.[32] Off-price retailers meanwhile offer prices up to 70 per cent lower than traditional department stores.[33] The rise of these bricks and mortar disruptors means that department stores are no longer the cheapest, nor are they the most fashionable or the most convenient. And we all know that in retail the middle ground is a very dangerous place to position yourself.

- The initial knee-jerk reaction to these new competitive threats was a period of seemingly perpetual discounting; however, this race to the bottom simply eroded margins, devalued brand perception and trained shoppers to only buy on promotion. Now department stores are opting for a more sustainable 'if you can't beat 'em, join 'em' approach by ramping up their own off-price presence. Despite the risk of cannibalizing existing stores, this format is far more relevant for today's modern shopper.

Department stores are no stranger to reinvention, and we will discuss in more detail how they can co-exist with Amazon and other online retailers later in the book; however, for now there is no denying that there will be fewer of them in the future. In summary? An apocalypse for some, but transformation for most.

Notes

1 Kumar, Kavita (2018) Amazon's Bezos calls Best Buy turnaround 'remarkable' as unveils new TV partnership, *Star Tribune*, 19 April. Available from: http://www.startribune.com/best-buy-and-amazon-partner-up-in-exclusive-deal-to-sell-new-tvs/480059943/ (archived at https://perma.cc/4V3H-9VED) [Last accessed 2/11/2018].

2 Thomas, Lauren (2021) 10,000 stores are expected to close in 2021, as pandemic continues to pummel retailers, *CNBC*, 28 January. Available from: https://www.cnbc.com/2021/01/28/10000-stores-set-to-close-in-2021-covid-keeps-pummeling-retailers.html (archived at https://perma.cc/L386-N4CC) [Last accessed 19/6/2021].

3 Thomas, Lauren (2021) More retail pain ahead: UBS predicts 80,000 stores will close in the U.S. by 2026, *CNBC*, 5 April. Available from: https://www.cnbc.com/2021/04/05/store-closures-ubs-predicts-80000-stores-will-go-dark-by-2026.html (archived at https://perma.cc/RHT3-X4P8) [Last accessed 19/6/2021].

4 Bowden, Grace (2021) Store closures hit record high of 48 per day in 2020, *Retail Week*, 15 March. Available from: https://www.retail-week.com/stores/store-closures-hit-record-high-of-48-per-day-in-2020/7036946.article?authent=1 (archived at https://perma.cc/B2BG-WTLZ) [Last accessed: 6/18/2021].

5 The British Retail Consortium (2021) Empty shop fronts continue to soar. Available from: https://brc.org.uk/news/corporate-affairs/empty-shop-fronts-continue-to-soar/ (archived at https://perma.cc/R2RN-LUTF) [Last accessed 6/18/2021].

6 Martin, Josh (2020) Shopping may never be the same again, Office for National Statistics, 29 June. Available from: https://blog.ons.gov.uk/2020/06/29/shopping-may-never-be-the-same-again/ (archived at https://perma.cc/47KT-LPRV) [Last accessed 19/6/2021].

7 McKinsey & Company (2021) China consumer report 2021. Understanding Chinese consumers: Growth engine of the world. Available from: https://www.mckinsey.com/~/media/mckinsey/featured%20insights/china/china%20still%20the%20worlds%20growth%20engine%20after%20covid%2019/mckinsey%20china%20consumer%20report%202021.pdf (archived at https://perma.cc/KE7D-EWNS) [Last accessed 19/6/2021].

8 Thomas, Lauren (2021) More retail pain ahead: UBS predicts 80,000 stores will close in the U.S. by 2026, *CNBC*, 5 April. Available from: https://www.cnbc.com/2021/04/05/store-closures-ubs-predicts-80000-stores-will-go-dark-by-2026.html (archived at https://perma.cc/RHT3-X4P8) [Last accessed 19/6/2021].

9 Interview with John Boumphrey, 24 May 2021, Amazon HQ, London.

10 Kemp, Brian (2021) 60 per cent of the world's population is now online, *We are Social*, 21 April. Available from: https://wearesocial.com/blog/2021/04/60-percent-of-the-worlds-population-is-now-online (archived at https://perma.cc/8MNX-AB79) [Last accessed 19/6/2021].

11 Hill, Kelly (2020) Connected devices will be 3x the global population by 2023, Cisco says, *RCR Wireless News*, 14 February. Available from: https://www.rcrwireless.com/20200218/internet-of-things/connected-devices-will-be-3x-the-global-population-by-2023-cisco-says (archived at https://perma.cc/FHM7-4EV9) [Last accessed 19/6/2021].

12 Al-Heeti, Abrar (2020) We'll spend nearly a decade of our lives staring at our phones, study says, *CNET*, 12 November. Available from: https://www.cnet.com/news/well-spend-nearly-a-decade-of-our-lives-staring-at-our-phones-study-says/ (archived at https://perma.cc/L8ER-SN8U) [Last accessed 19/6/2021].

13 Ofcom Online Nation 2021 Report (2021). Available from: https://www.ofcom.org.uk/__data/assets/pdf_file/0013/220414/online-nation-2021-report.pdf (archived at https://perma.cc/FHM7-4EV9) [Last accessed 19/6/2021].

14 https://www.emarketer.com/topics/industry/mcommerce (archived at https://perma.cc/9ALD-BDAA)

15 Sullivan, Ted (2008) Borders: Interview with CEO George Jones, *Seeking Alpha*, 7 October. Available from: https://seekingalpha.com/article/98837-borders-interview-with-ceo-george-jones (archived at https://perma.cc/QX8F-RBAM) [Last accessed 28/6/2018].

16 Stone, Brad (2013) *The Everything Store: Jeff Bezos and the age of Amazon*, Bantam Press, London.

17 PwC (2017) 10 retailer investments for an uncertain future. Available from: https://www.pwc.com/gx/en/industries/assets/total-retail-2017.pdf (archived at https://perma.cc/FC7M-S26K) [Last accessed 29/3/2018].

18 Fung Global Retail & Technology (2016) Deep dive: the mall is not dead: part 1. Available from: https://www.fungglobalretailtech.com/wp-content/uploads/2016/11/ Mall-Is-Not-Dead-Part-1-November-15-2016.pdf (archived at https://perma.cc/H6QW-Y893) [Last accessed 29/3/2018].

19 Hadden Loh, Tracy and Vey, Jennifer S. (2019) Retail isn't dead. It's just changing, CNN, 24 December. Available from: https://edition.cnn.com/2019/12/24/perspectives/retail-2020/index.html (archived at https://perma.cc/4G6U-MKR4) [Last accessed 19/6/2021].

20 Townsend, Matt et al (2017) America's 'retail apocalypse' is really just beginning, *Bloomberg*, 8 November. Available from: https://www.bloomberg.com/graphics/2017-retail-debt/ (archived at https://perma.cc/29K4-ZELC) [Last accessed 29/3/2018].

21 Thomas, Lauren (2020) 25% of U.S. malls are expected to shut within 5 years. Giving them a new life won't be easy, *CNBC*, 27 August. Available from: https://www.cnbc.com/2020/08/27/25percent-of-us-malls-are-set-to-shut-within-5-years-what-comes-next.html (archived at https://perma.cc/ S9ZZ-3HCB) [Last accessed 19/6/21].

22 Walmart 1997 Annual Report. Available from: http://stock.walmart.com/ investors/financial-information/annual-reports-and-proxies/default.aspx (archived at https://perma.cc/V467-MXQJ) [Last accessed 28/6/2018].

23 Berg, Natalie and Roberts, Bryan (2012) *Walmart: Key insights and practical lessons from the world's largest retailer*, Kogan Page, London.

24 Office for National Statistics (2018) Retail sales, Great Britain: February 2018. Available from: https://www.ons.gov.uk/businessindustryandtrade/ retailindustry/bulletins/retailsales/february2018#whats-the-story-in-online-sales (archived at https://perma.cc/JQ99-JMD2) [Last accessed 29/3/2018].

25 Kantar Worldpanel data (2021). Available from: https://www.kantarworldpanel. com/global/grocery-market-share/great-britain (archived at https://perma.cc/ NB76-RQ7G) [Last accessed 19/6/2021].

26 John Lewis Partnership (2017) The Waitrose Food & Drink Report 2017 – 2018. Available at: http://www.johnlewispartnership.co.uk/content/dam/cws/ pdfs/Resources/the-waitrose-food-and-drink-report-2017.pdf (archived at https://perma.cc/ZUS5-5UJ8) [Last accessed 29/3/2018].

27 Cowen and Company (2017) Retail's disruption yields opportunities – store wars! Available from: https://distressions.com/wp-content/uploads/2017/04/ Retail_s_Disruption_Yields_Opportunities_-_Ahead_of_the_Curve_Series__ Video_-_Cowen_and_Company.pdf (archived at https://perma.cc/FML9-NJMG) [Last accessed 19/6/2021].

28 John Lewis Partnership plc Annual Report and Accounts 2021 (2021). Available from: https://www.johnlewispartnership.co.uk/content/dam/cws/pdfs/ Juniper/ARA-2021/2021-Annual-Report-and-Accounts-Report.pdf (archived at https://perma.cc/J398-V2SQ) [Last accessed 19/6/2021].

29 Reuters staff (2020) UK retailer John Lewis says unlikely all its stores will re-open, Reuters, 1 July. Available from: https://www.reuters.com/article/ john-lewis-stores-idUSL8N2E84K0 (archived at https://perma.cc/Z7RV-NV6T) [Last accessed 19/6/2021].

30 Wahba, Phil (2017) Can America's department stores survive? *Fortune*, 21 February. Available from: http://fortune.com/2017/02/21/department-stores-future-macys-sears/ (archived at https://perma.cc/P9J6-WPEF) [Last accessed 29/3/2018].

31 Ibid.

32 Bain, Marc (2017) A new generation of even faster fashion is leaving H&M and Zara in the dust, *Quartz*, 6 April. Available from: https://qz.com/951055/ a-new-generation-of-even-faster-fashion-is-leaving-hm-and-zara-in-the-dust/ (archived at https://perma.cc/V79E-QK2R) [Last accessed 29/3/2018].

33 Klepacki, Laura (2017) Why off-price retail is rising as department stores are sinking, *Retail Dive*, 1 February. Available from: https://www.retaildive.com/ news/why-off-price-retail-is-rising-as-department-stores-are-sinking/434454/ (archived at https://perma.cc/S7NM-3P86) [Last accessed 29/3/2018].

07

End of pure-play e-commerce: Amazon's transition to bricks and mortar retailing

'Being a pure e-commerce player is less unique than it was. There is more competition. Increasingly, consumers won't think about online and offline – they will just think about retail.'
Sir Terry Leahy, former CEO of Tesco[1]

Now that we have established that many more stores will need to close in order to adapt to the change in shopping habits, you might rightly ask why we are now talking about the death of e-commerce and not death of the store.

The simple answer is because, despite the explosive growth of online retail, more than 80 per cent of all global retail sales take place in bricks and mortar stores.[2] Physical retail must evolve, but it certainly isn't dying. The underperformers will be weeded out. The undifferentiated will be exposed. The overcapacity issue will be addressed. But make no mistake – the bricks and mortar store will continue to play a crucial role in retail for decades to come.

'Physical stores aren't going anywhere. E-commerce is going to be a part of everything, but not the whole thing.'
Jeff Bezos[3]

In fact, we would argue that as technology continues to break down the barriers between online and offline, those retailers *without* a physical presence are the ones looking vulnerable today. Gone are the days when pure-play online retailers could boast lower overhead costs – and consequently lower prices – due to forgoing physical space requirements. The structural economic advantages once held by online-only retailers have disappeared.

Back in 2015, Natalie authored a report predicting that pure-play e-commerce would largely cease to exist by 2020.[4] This was met with a degree of scepticism at the time, the most notable of which was perhaps when the very well-regarded Alex Baldock, then CEO of Shop Direct, publicly rebutted our claim in his speech at a *Retail Week* conference.[5] But would you expect the boss of a pure-play e-commerce retailer to do anything other than to make a case for pure-play e-commerce?

Today the notion of moving 'online to offline' has become a justified trend and even has its own acronym: O2O. Since our report was published, we've seen dozens of prominent, digitally native brands make the leap into the physical realm. The most notable of these are e-commerce giants such as Amazon and Alibaba which, through the launch of new retail concepts ranging from tech-infused bookstores to checkout-free supermarkets, are sending a clear signal to the retail community that their vision of the future very much includes physical stores.

Jack Ma, founder of Alibaba, has since taken our initial prediction one step further with his belief that 'pure e-commerce will be reduced to a traditional business and replaced by the concept of New Retail – the integration of online, offline, logistics and data across a single value chain.'[6]

In this chapter, we will explore the factors driving the online to offline trend, how Amazon specifically is shifting gears to take on bricks and mortar retailing, and how the accelerated convergence of physical and digital worlds will require retailers to adapt their own business models.

Next-generation retail: the quest for omnichannel

Before we dive into the O2O trend, it's important to understand the broader convergence of physical and digital retail. Consumers today are genuinely channel- and device-agnostic. 'The consumer does not care about online and offline,' says Terry von Bibra, Alibaba's General Manager of Europe. 'No consumer in the world gets up in the morning and says, "I'm going to buy some shoes online", or goes into an electronics store and says, "I'm going to buy a refrigerator offline". The only people that care about that are the people that sell shoes or refrigerators.'[7]

What the consumer does want is a frictionless experience. Seamless shopping is now a firmly embedded expectation, regardless of the number of channels or devices used to research, browse, purchase or collect an item. Meeting this demand is no easy feat. In fact, we have calculated that there are more than 2,500 ways to shop today. The path to purchase is no longer linear – new customer touchpoints are popping up outside of traditional retail channels which, when combined with the proliferation of delivery services, means shoppers have more choice than ever before.

It's no surprise then that terms like *omnichannel, connected, seamless* and *frictionless retail* and – dare we use the horrific portmanteau – *phygital* have dominated industry discussions over the past decade. Despite having an element of buzzword bingo to it, their intent is valid – bricks and mortar retailers must not only invest in digital capabilities, but also ensure a genuinely cohesive online and offline experience. In other words, retailers need to start thinking like their shoppers.

> 'All retailers are acutely aware that, regardless of how the best features of "online" and "physical" stores are combined, we are all competing for and serving the same customers.'
> **Amazon, 2021[8]**

So what does omnichannel retailing look like in practice? A mom needs to buy her son a new pair of shoes. She researches online – desktop, mobile or tablet – then goes to the store to have her son's feet measured. The shoe she'd like is out of stock, so the store associate offers to check availability at another branch or to have it delivered to the customer's home. In this instance, the customer has left satisfied despite not walking out with the product she intended to buy. The retailer was able to offer excellent customer service – enabled by technology.

This might sound fairly simplistic by today's standards, but many retailers lack a single view of inventory and are simply not structured in a way that allows for this level of service. Despite an industry-wide focus on creating a unified customer experience, many retail businesses are still operating in silos, with online and bricks and mortar divisions working towards different sets of objectives.

But we have come a long way since the very early days of the smartphone when it wasn't unheard of for anxious retailers to deploy wireless signal jammers to prevent shoppers using their devices to search for a better price. Little did they then know how the advent of 'showrooming', as it became known, would have as profound an impact on shopping as we know it as the growth of e-commerce itself.

Equally, in the early days of e-commerce, retail store managers complained that customers who had bought an unwanted product from the retailer online increasingly wanted to return it to the store. This is easiest from the perspective of the customer, who does not want to repack and potentially pay for postage. Why should they make an extra trip to the post office when the retailer has a branch a few metres away on their main, local shopping street?

But many retailers weren't prepared for the impact on their reverse logistics, which led in some early cases to store managers refusing to accept online returns. And, yet, retailers soon realized the value of the convenience in offering this service, turning it to their advantage by enabling online fulfilment instore, with click & collect. Nowadays, if a shopper doesn't like the shoes she chose and had delivered, she can often return them via post free of charge or return them to the store, while the store is often credited with sale (and return) by virtue of where the order is placed or paid for.

For those retailers who have seen their business model come under threat from the dual whammy of the Amazon Effect and 'showrooming', digital store integration or transformation has become an important strategic imperative. Not only does this mean, perhaps counterintuitively, embracing showrooming by offering free, secure customer Wi-Fi (especially where mobile data signals fail to reach), but using that connection to capture more detailed information about customer footfall, traffic flows, dwell times and purchase behaviour, and using it to improve the customer experience and offer in a store.

As technology rapidly breaks down the barriers between online and offline, retailers are being pushed to offer a more connected retail experience that results in greater customer satisfaction. Let's now look at the specific technologies and innovations that are making this happen.

Key drivers of convergence of physical and digital retail

The pivotal role of mobile

As discussed in the previous chapter, mobile has genuinely transformed the way we shop, not only by creating endless new shopping opportunities but also by acting as a much-needed bridge between online and offline retail.

KNOWLEDGE IS POWER

Armed with their personal shopping companion, consumers can make far more informed decisions both in and out of the store. So how has this impacted the bricks and mortar shopping experience? Put simply, it's given the customer a heightened sense of empowerment. The assistance of our mobile phones has greatly improved the instore experience – and raised expectations in the process – when it comes to access, speed and convenience. Today, the majority of sales are digitally influenced.[9] Gone are the days when price comparisons meant visiting multiple physical locations. And today, when shoppers want to learn more about a product, it's often quicker to consult our phones than to seek out a store associate.

As we touched on earlier, the number one destination for online product search isn't Google – it's Amazon.[10] The combination of Amazon's unrivalled assortment and treasure trove of customer reviews makes it both a trustworthy and convenient source for consumers looking to gain product information. In fact, 80 per cent of US consumers have a favourable impression of Amazon overall. 'Who do Americans trust more than Amazon "to do the right thing"? Only their primary physicians and the military,' said Jeff Bezos.[11]

For bricks and mortar retailers, this highlights the dual challenge of price transparency and availability. If the product is out of stock or the price isn't right, then Amazon is in a prime position to gobble up that sale in the form of a mobile transaction.

> 'Many people think our main competition is Bing or Yahoo. But, really, our biggest search competitor is Amazon.'
> **Ex-Google Chairman Eric Schmidt**[12]

FRICTIONLESS, PERSONALIZED EXPERIENCE – MOBILE AND BEYOND

Mobile devices have also opened countless opportunities for retailers to create a more convenient and tailored experience for their customers. But prior to even entering the store, retailers should have a compelling online offer to win at the online 'search, browse and discovery' phase that is clearly linked to physical presence. Once this 'basic hygiene' is covered, retailers need to then give the customer a compelling reason to visit the physical store. Many already try to drive online customers into stores by offering wish lists, and recipe or shopping lists, as well as discounts, special events and local promotions that can be accessed instore.

But once there, retailers must address two of the biggest shopping bugbears (particularly in a grocery setting), which are finding products and then waiting in a queue to pay for them. Mobile has and continues to play a huge role in both areas. First, in terms of improving navigation, retailers are embracing instore mapping systems using a range of technologies including Wi-Fi, Bluetooth, audio, video and magnetic positioning, AR and 3D virtualization, allowing customers to use their mobile devices to find the products they are looking for more quickly. Some retailers have innovated to expose wait times in-app, and many were able to capitalize on consumers' willingness to forgo human interaction at the height of the pandemic, fuelling a huge uptick in contactless payments.

In a future where we're all already more used to using our mobile devices to self-serve instore, expect more retailers to bundle the likes of navigation services with personalized, real-time offers in a bid to replicate the deeply tailored experience that traditionally could only be experienced online. Wireless communications and augmented reality, accessible via mobile, are also creating new opportunities for retailers to target instore shoppers with more relevant and timely offers. In this way, retailers are always treading that fine line between convenient and creepy when using technology to infer and respond to a customer's intent. But research suggests that the majority of shoppers are receptive to receiving real-time offers that are relevant to them. As retailers look to digitize loyalty schemes and those plastic, points-based loyalty cards become a thing of the past, mobile technologies will continue to play a pivotal role here.

Secondly, reducing friction at the checkout has been a hot topic for some time, with Amazon most famously allowing shoppers to skip the checkout entirely with its Just Walk Out technology. We'll discuss this in greater detail later in the book but here it's important to point out that digital integration and the more pragmatic move towards more cashless transactions is being applied instore to speed up the authorization and therefore queuing process. Grocers, for example, are no strangers to self-checkout, relying on the customer to scan, bag and check out their own goods to deliver a faster throughput rate than a manned checkout. Or even queue-busting systems can enable a sales associate to check out customers waiting in a queue. Accepting 'tap and go' contactless or mobile wallet payments is another step to helping customers bypass the friction of queuing at the checkout altogether. But only time will tell if other retailers have the will to tackle the challenges of implementing a checkout-free experience.

In addition, digital displays, replacing traditional paper tags and posters, are increasingly becoming convenient connection points for customers to access information – on the digital shelf tag itself, by connecting to the customer's mobile device, or via an app. While mobile plays a growing, essential role in digitizing the instore experience, it's important to highlight additional technologies that are helping to break down the barriers between online and offline retail. Digital displays, including electronic shelf labels (ESLs), for example, also have the benefit of enabling the retailer to change prices and promotions dynamically, and so exploit another way to keep pace with online. Fashion retailers can use so-called smart or 'magic' mirrors to help shoppers see complementary and alternative product recommendations, share their outfit plans with friends on social networks, or even simply call an assistant to request more sizes, for example. Meanwhile, instore, endless aisle ordering and mobile kiosks allow retailers to offer an infinite assortment beyond traditional, physical constraints.

Those retailers furthest ahead in terms of integrating digital technologies into their stores understand how these efforts can combine the best that online has to offer, in terms of means of access and availability, with those attributes that cannot be replicated online and only the physical store can offer: the ability to feel and touch the product. In this instance, a few have equipped their store staff with the same access to product, pricing and availability information as their customers, so they can 'save the sale' by having products shipped from another store for collection or ordered from the store online, for home delivery and collection. For example, shoe retailer Dune's single view of stock allows it to move thousands of pairs of shoes each week and, during end of season clearance sales, it can ensure the correct merchandise is sent to the appropriate store. Crucially, it also gives the retailer the agility to fulfil from any channel, even if they are down to their last pair of shoes.

Meanwhile, retailers are blurring the boundaries even further by employing AR and virtual reality (VR) experiences. For example, fashion chain Zara, under increased competition from pure-play online rivals like ASOS and Boohoo, began testing an AR experience in 2018. Instore shoppers hold their mobile phones to a store window or sensor where they can then see models superimposed over the image on their screens. Not only does this enable passing and instore shoppers to click through to buy the item, but online shoppers can also use the app to view their purchase by hovering their phone over their freshly delivered package before opening it. In this way, mobile devices are truly enabling a far more blended shopping in the future.

Click, collect and return

When it comes to fulfilment, the boundaries between online and offline have blurred in recent years. For many shoppers today, visiting a physical location is the preferred method of receiving and returning online orders. Retailers are equally incentivized to drive this behaviour, as leveraging their stores as pick-up points is far more cost-effective than delivering to individual homes and typically results in additional spend once instore. At Target, it's been reported that one-third of shoppers that collect online orders instore go on to buy something else, while at Macy's shoppers typically spend an additional 25 per cent instore once their order has been picked up.[13]

> 'Customers are increasingly flocking to services invented by other stores that Amazon still can't match at the scale of other large companies, like curbside pickup and in-store returns.'
> **Jeff Bezos, 2020[14]**

Today, particularly in the wake of the pandemic, it's difficult to think of any retailer in a mature retail market that doesn't allow its customers to pick up their online orders instore. The phenomenal growth of click & collect (and, in less urban areas, its sister offering curbside pick-up) is proof that shoppers want to marry the benefits of online shopping – assortment and convenience – with the ease of collecting instore. After all, 90 per cent of Americans live within 10 miles of a Walmart store[15] and, in France shoppers can find a Carrefour store within an eight-minute drive.[16] Let's not underestimate the physical infrastructure advantage held by the large multinationals.

We believe, however, that there is room for improvement. The collection process can be arduous at times and shoppers are often still subject to queuing. Retailers can take steps to cut friction here, bringing dedicated collection points to the front of store, utilizing automated self-service pickup solutions (as done by Zara), and looking to technology to reduce wait times and simplify the identification process. Retailers are also reconfiguring their stores to cope with a higher volume of returns. Historically, the return rate for retail has been just under 10 per cent of sales. Today, thanks to the growth of e-commerce and heightened customer expectations, it's more like 30 per cent and in categories like apparel it can be as high as 40 per cent.[17] Shoppers today naturally expect to be able to return unwanted online orders to wherever is most convenient for them – regardless of channel used for purchase.

Once again, this highlights the critical, though evolving, role of the physical store. Retailers like Next in the UK and Home Depot in the US get it – over 80 per cent of their online returns take place in stores. BORIS (the affectionate acronym for Buy Online Return In Store) is yet another opportunity for retailers to leverage their physical stores to piggyback off the growth of online retail – and not only from the point of view of pleasing today's very demanding customer. If returning to store, the chances of an exchange over return are higher, as well as the propensity to make an incremental purchase.

It's no coincidence that Amazon's foray into physical retail – and one of the first changes to Whole Foods stores following the acquisition – was the implementation of Amazon Hub Lockers, providing shoppers with an alternative to the post office for collecting and returning online orders. Amazon has since rolled out collection kiosks, branded Amazon Hub Counters, in its own supermarkets as well as in other retailers' shops, as we'll shortly explore.

More and more pure-play e-commerce retailers continue to find value in collaborating with bricks and mortar retailers to provide shoppers with greater choice and convenience. For example, in the UK, supermarket chain Asda's wildly successful 'toyou' programme allows shoppers to collect and return orders from a slew of online retailers including ASOS, Wiggle, Gymshark, Boohoo, PrettyLittleThing, Feel Unique and AO.com. A fantastic footfall driver for Asda, the retailer now dedicates more space to its click/collect/return service and was the first UK retailer to launch an automated parcel collection tower (essentially a 5-metre-tall parcel vending machine) to make the experience even more seamless.

Collaboration is the name of the game in the UK. We've seen similar partnerships with Next/Morrisons and Waitrose/Sweaty Betty, among others, and you can expect this trend to take off globally as more retailers recognize the benefits of collect/returns collaboration – better serving the customer by creating a more unified physical and digital retail experience.

Pervasive computing: shopping without stores or screens

Finally, we can't talk about a blended online and offline shopping experience without mentioning the Internet of Things. When we think about the shopping experience blending into the background of consumers' homes, we can already see the impact that AR and VR, as well as voice and simplified replenishment solutions, are having. They are supercharging consumers' already high expectations, set by online, for speed, convenience, value and personalization. And they take advantage of the blended reality that informs most customer decisions today.

VR, for example, can enable a retailer to bring the store into the home using immersive digital displays viewed using a special headset – customers can even buy simply by nodding their head in Alibaba's Buy+ VR mall. This still might sound like science fiction to some, but the pandemic has ushered in an era of more immersive online retail experiences. In 2020, brands such as Made, Balmain and Diesel launched virtual showrooms in order to continue engaging with customers at a time when stores were forced to shut. In normal times, shoppers can also bring their home into the store – prior to the pandemic, retailers like IKEA, Macy's and Lowe's were also using VR instore to enable endless aisle capabilities. Blended retail experiences are the future.

Amazon meanwhile continues to open the industry's eyes up to the possibility of transplanting retail real estate directly into consumers' homes – from Echo devices that allow shoppers to ask Alexa to add it to their list, all the way through to what the authors consider the holy grail of frictionless commerce – auto-replenishment of goods, where the shopper can completely opt out of the purchasing decision. All share the same aim: for the means of engagement between the shopper and retailer to fade into the background, using more pervasive computing interfaces than keyboard, mouse and even touchscreen.

Amazon may be the trailblazer in this space, but its biggest bricks and mortar competitor is aggressively moving in the same direction. 'In the future, people will still want to shop in compelling stores. But more and more, there will be occasions where they prefer to pick up an order or have it delivered,' said Walmart CEO Doug McMillon in 2021. 'Some customers will eventually allow us and pay us to keep them replenished in their homes on the items they routinely purchase. For an increasing number of customers, Walmart will be seen more like a service. Customers will think of us as the merchant that serves their wants and needs, but in ways that take less time and effort. We won't just be utilitarian for them.'[18]

So, online and offline retail are no longer mutually exclusive. The most successful retailers will be those that, while recognizing the urgency for digital investment, are able to simultaneously reconfigure their stores with the ultimate view that these are assets and not liabilities. Bricks and mortar stores will play a major role in shaping the future of retail as a more convenient, connected and customer-dictated industry.

So what happens if you don't have any stores?

Clicks chasing bricks – incentives for getting physical

Now that we've established the factors driving the convergence of digital and physical worlds, let's look at what this means for pure-play e-commerce retailers.

In a nutshell, it means that online-only is no longer enough.

Yes, online retail will always win on assortment. But as we have previously established, physical space constraints aside, bricks and mortar retailers are increasingly leveraging technology to offer a more fused customer experience and in doing so they are encroaching on attributes that were traditionally solely associated with online retail – convenience, personalization, transparency of information.

Meanwhile, in the face of rising shipping and customer acquisition costs, online-only retailers are recognizing that there are a growing number of benefits – financial, logistical and marketing – to having bricks and mortar space. As e-commerce becomes a more prominent part of retailers' businesses, it's exposing the often-underreported costs of trading online. According to global consulting firm AlixPartners, these include:

- shipping and handling charges: free and/or fast shipping and packaging costs;
- costs associated with increased returns and restocking, reverse logistics, and lost margin on SKUs returned to a channel that was not intended to sell it;
- corporate headcount growth to support e-commerce divisions (including merchandising, planning, marketing, content creation, web development and IT, to name a few);
- balancing additional online marketing expenses with traditional expenses;
- incremental distribution and warehousing costs associated with piece picking;

- deleveraged store base and diluted store labour;
- incremental labour and technology expenses associated with omnichannel capabilities (ship from store, buy online, pick up in store, order from store, etc);
- complications associated with inventory management – deciding to share or not to share online and stores' inventory and the costs associated with either decision.[19]

How do these costs stack up against those incurred by a bricks and mortar retailer? Take clothing, for example. According to AlixPartners, a typical $100 clothing purchase made by a shopper in a bricks and mortar outlet comes with a cost of goods sold of about $40. The associated operating costs such as rent, overhead and labour would be $28, leaving the retailer with a profit margin of 32 per cent.[20]

The same $100 clothing transaction made online and intended for home delivery also comes with a cost of goods sold of about $40. However, the costs associated with processing that order are slightly higher than if it had been sold in a physical store. In this instance, the individual order must be picked, packed and shipped from a distribution centre (DC) to the shopper's home, which is naturally more expensive than shipping a truckload of inventory from DC to store. In this instance, operating costs would be $30, which leaves the retailer with a profit margin of 30 per cent, or slightly less profitable than if the item had been sold instore.[21]

SHIPPING COSTS

Now retailing, of course, is not as black and white as this case study may imply – there are a number of variables that would impact cost such as product category, store format and efficiencies in the supply chain. However, it's worth highlighting how physical space is becoming an attractive option for digitally native brands looking to mitigate costs. And looking ahead, there's no sign of online volumes – and therefore costs – slowing down. Global parcel volume surpassed 100 billion in 2019 and is expected to more than double by 2026.[22]

With Amazon taking roughly 40 cents of every dollar Americans spend online,[23] it's no surprise the retailer is especially motivated to optimize its supply chain and reduce shipping costs. In 2020, the cost of sorting and delivering products to customers increased by over 60 per cent to $61.1 billion.[24]

Amazon was no less affected and redoubled its characteristically relentless efforts to retain end-to-end control of its fulfilment capabilities. In December 2019, consulting firm MWPVL International found Amazon delivered just 50 per cent of its packages itself. By August 2020, at the height of the pandemic, this had increased to 67 per cent and was projected to grow to 85 per cent by the end of 2022.

Amazon continuously stirs the pot, raising customer expectations for free and ever faster delivery as it looks to bolster the value of its broader Prime ecosystem. As a historically online-only retailer, Amazon's ability to compete with bricks and mortar peers on immediacy has been vital. But now the genie has been let out of the bottle. Today, near-instant gratification is a firmly embedded customer expectation, as other retailers have had no choice but to invest in next-day and increasingly same-day delivery capabilities.

The problem? It's not sustainable. And we're beginning to see the first cracks. In recent years, Amazon has raised transportation fees for suppliers of beverages, nappies and other heavy products that are expensive to ship, while also limiting the number of single, low-priced items (soap and toothbrushes, for example) that shoppers can purchase. It also introduced Amazon Delivery Day exclusively for Prime members, touting the reassurance of being able to nominate a specific day of the week for all orders to be delivered, but also saving Amazon the cost of making multiple deliveries. As previously discussed, we have even seen Amazon increase Prime fees across its array of subscription options – annual, monthly and student – and there will most certainly be more price hikes to come. Shoppers should expect to pay more for 'free' shipping in the future.

Amazon is very transparent with investors here, stating that the cost of shipping will continue to increase as more shoppers around the globe become active Prime users and Amazon reduces shipping rates, uses more expensive shipping methods and offers additional services. In the meantime, it continues to explore ways to take greater control of the distribution and fulfilment supply chain down to the last mile to make shipping more cost-effective – drones, robotics, rewarding shoppers for choosing slow delivery, Amazon Flex, Delivery Service Partners, the list goes on. Having a physical presence – whether through lockers, instore concessions, mall pop-up sites or stores themselves – is another piece of this very big fulfilment puzzle.

RETURNS: THE ACHILLES HEEL OF E-COMMERCE

Another incentive for getting physical? Returns.

Many retailers are so focused on the pre-purchase experience that what happens after the transaction tends to be an afterthought rather than a strategic priority. Consumer expectations continue to soar, exacerbating the disconnect between the effortlessness of placing an online order and the inconsistent and often friction-filled experience of making a return. Returns are fantastically out of sync with an otherwise frictionless e-commerce experience.

Returns have plagued the industry for over a decade, but the issue was particularly magnified during the pandemic. As discussed earlier in the book, COVID accelerated the shift to online shopping and in the process exacerbated retail's perennial problem.

And, let's face it, returns are a problem. They have always been the Achilles heel of e-commerce. In fact, they've become so troublesome in recent years that retailers have taken to extreme measures, from banning serial returners to refunding customers for low-value or bulky items without asking for the product back. Clearly, some returns are not worth it for retailers, particularly when you factor in shipping and handling costs plus the dent to the item's resale value.

That said, a return or exchange is better than no transaction in the first place. How well retailers prepare for and manage the post-purchase experience will determine how likely it is that a shopper will buy from them again.

But should retailers make it easier for customers to return unwanted items or should customers be nudged towards fewer returns? On the face of it, keeping a lid on returns might seem like a sound strategy. However, those shoppers who return the most are often those who spend the most. Therefore, retailers must recognize that not all shoppers are created equal and consider the lifetime value of a customer when adapting their returns strategies: those with more generous policies tend to have a very loyal following.

Retailers must simultaneously take measures to mitigate the cost of returns – and this is where stores come in. There are also untapped opportunities to incentivize customers to change their behaviour, for example by rewarding shoppers for faster returns or returning to a particular location, or by offering longer exchange (versus returns) windows. It's worth highlighting here that Amazon has quietly clamped down on 'free returns' in recent years, a move that may empower other retailers to follow suit.

Clearly, the best return is no return at all, but that is nigh on impossible in this digital era. This is a pivotal moment for the retail sector, but as long as e-commerce is growing, the returns problem will continue to swell. Technology will play a growing role in helping retailers to address the root of the issue and ultimately stemming the tide of returns. However, returns must no longer be viewed purely as a cost of doing business but, for those that manage it well, an opportunity to increase conversion and build loyalty.

COST OF CUSTOMER ACQUISITION

The mounting cost of fulfilment isn't the only challenge – the cost of attracting new shoppers is also higher without stores. In fact, the customer acquisition costs for buy-online, ship-from-warehouse models include overhead IT and marketing costs that can make distribution costs four times higher than instore methods.[25]

A shopper may stumble upon a bricks and mortar store and decide to pop in for a browse, but the concept of 'walk-in traffic' doesn't translate online,[26] particularly for small and medium-sized retailers. Real estate in the digital realm is becoming increasingly crowded and expensive. There are millions of online retailers all vying for the customer's attention via one main portal – Google.[27] Despite millions being spent on digital marketing, paid search listings make up only around 20 per cent of clicks from Google results, according to a report by Wedbush Securities.[28] The remaining 80 per cent goes to organic listings, which suggests that natural search optimization is essential for retailers when it comes to maintaining online traffic.

Meanwhile, the first organic result in Google Search has an average click-through rate (CTR) of 28.5 per cent, according to a 2020 study by Sistrix. This drops significantly as you scroll down – the second and third positions have a CTR of 15 per cent and 11 per cent respectively. By the time a user reaches the tenth result, this falls to a mere 2.5 per cent. And it's widely known that users rarely go on to the second page of Google search results – each listing there has a CTR of less than 1 per cent.[29]

A bricks and mortar store, however, can act as a billboard for the brand, allowing shoppers to engage with the retailer in a way that can't be achieved via a screen. Ironically, this helps to drive online sales. A 2019 study from CACI showed that UK retailers without a physical store presence experience 50 per cent lower online sales compared with those that do within a certain catchment area.[30] Similarly, a study by the International Council of Shopping Centers (ICSC) found that when a clothing retailer's store closed in a market, web traffic dropped 10 per cent. Department store chains and home-goods retailers suffered a similar fate, experiencing a decline of 8 per cent and 16 per cent respectively.[31]

Amazon makes its move

Jeff Bezos was asked in a 2012 interview whether he would ever consider opening stores. 'We would love to but only if we can have a truly differentiated idea. One of the things that we don't do very well at Amazon is do a me-too product offering.'

He continued, '…when I look at physical retail stores, it's very well served. The people who operate physical retail stores are very good at it. The question we would always ask before we would embark on such a thing is, what's the idea? What would we do that would be different? How would it be better?'[32]

Since that interview, Bezos has experimented with:

- Amazon-branded kiosks in shopping centres across America;
- collection lockers in retail stores, malls, libraries, universities and even apartment buildings;
- from LA to London, pop-up stores that swap price tags for scannable barcodes;
- bookstores that aren't really designed to sell books;
- America's first cashier-less supermarket;
- Alexa concessions and Amazon product returns areas in some of its most feared competitors' stores;
- Treasure Truck (essentially Black Friday on wheels);
- a 4-star store that only stocks products with high online ratings;
- a hair salon layered with augmented reality and other tech features;
- and a couple of drive-through supermarkets.

No, Amazon is not a me-too retailer.

Historically, Amazon's physical space was designed to serve one of two purposes: showcase their devices or act as a collection site for online orders. As you can see from Table 7.1, Amazon's initial move into bricks and mortar retailing was through collection lockers, college campus drop-off/pick-up sites and mall pop-ups.

However, it was Amazon's rather ironic launch of physical bookstores in 2015 (see Figure 7.1) that marked a genuine shift in strategy, as this was the first time Amazon mimicked digital merchandising and pricing in a physical setting. 'We've applied 20 years of online bookselling experience to build a

TABLE 7.1 Evolution of Amazon's bricks and mortar presence

Year launched	Concept	Primary function	Description
2011	Amazon Lockers	Fulfilment	Parcel delivery lockers found in retail stores, shopping centres, offices, libraries, gyms and even music festivals. Allows Amazon to overcome two of the biggest barriers to online shopping: missed deliveries and inconvenient returns.
2015	Campus Pickup-Point	Fulfilment	Amazon's first fully-staffed pickup and drop-off collection point. Caters to college students across US campuses. In 2017, this was enhanced with the launch of Instant Pickup, allowing shoppers to collect from a nearby locker within two minutes of placing the order.
2014 (closed 2019)	Amazon pop-up	Technology	300–500 sq ft sites that allowed shoppers to interact with Amazon's devices such as Kindles, Fire tablets and Echo devices in real life. Started out in malls and expanded to Whole Foods and Kohls stores before all locations were closed in 2019.
2015	Amazon Books	Retail/Technology	Bookstores with uniquely digital features: book covers face out and Prime members receive preferential pricing. Designed to drive Prime membership and get shoppers interacting with Amazon technology in a physical setting.
2016	Treasure Truck	Retail	Amazon handpicks daily deals which are communicated to shoppers by text. Shoppers are then alerted to the location of the truck to collect their goods. Creates an urgency to buy and adds an element of fun to what is typically a functional shopping experience.
2017	AmazonFresh Pickup	Fulfilment	Online grocery collection service very similar to popular French 'Drive' concept. Amazon uses licence plate recognition technology to reduce waiting times, and orders are delivered directly into the trunk of the shopper's car.
2017	The Hub	Fulfilment	Parcel delivery lockers for apartment buildings. Like the famous yellow Amazon lockers, The Hub is fully self-service, open 24/7, and accepts deliveries from all carriers.
2017	Whole Foods Market	Retail	Acquisition of 450+ supermarkets across North America and the UK. Amazon was attracted to Whole Foods for its strong perishable offer, strong own label, urban presence, and overlap with Prime customer base. Amazon is officially no longer a pure-play online retailer.
2017	Amazon Returns	Fulfilment	Unique agreement with Kohl's department stores where Amazon shoppers can return unwanted online orders to their local Kohl's. Addresses the perennial headache that is online returns, while driving footfall to Kohls. We expect this to be rolled out internationally.

Year	Name	Category	Description
2017	Amazon Pop Up (formerly 'presented by Amazon')	Retail	Frequently updated themed stores that bring a selection of the hottest and most exciting items from Amazon.com to shopping malls around the country, giving customers an immersive try-before-you-buy experience.
2018	Amazon Go	Retail	One of Amazon's first physical grocery formats and the first store to open with Just Walk Out Technology. Shoppers scan their Amazon app to enter. The checkout-free shopping experience is made possible by a combination of computer vision, sensor fusion and deep learning. A larger format 'Amazon Go Grocery' was launched in 2020 but rebranded as 'Amazon Fresh' the following year.
2018	Amazon 4-star	Retail	Stores that carry a highly curated selection of products from top categories across amazon.com including devices, consumer electronics, toys, games, books, kitchen, home, and more. Every product in the store is rated 4 stars and above by customers, a top seller, or s new and trending on Amazon.com.
2019	Amazon Counter	Fulfilment	A network of staffed pick-up points that allows customers to collect their Amazon parcels in-store at a partner location. At launch, Amazon partnered with UK fashion retailer Next and Italian bookstore chain Giunti and the network of Fermopoint and SisalPay stores across Italy.
2020	Amazon Fresh	Retail	Another physical supermarket concept bearing the same name as Amazon's legacy online grocery offering. Designed from the ground up, Amazon Fresh stores offer conveniences such as the Amazon Dash Cart, which enables customers to skip the checkout line, and Alexa features to help customers manage their shopping lists and navigate aisles. Stores offer same-day delivery and in-store/curbside pickup.
2021	Amazon Salon	Retail/Technology	One of the retailer's more unconventional moves. The Amazon-branded hair salon in London's Spitalfields trials the latest industry technology, from augmented reality (AR) hair consultations to point-and-learn technology.
2022 and beyond			Amazon needs stores but does it need its own stores? We expect further store innovation to be centred around efforts to bolster its core e-commerce offering. Pharmacies, fashion and homeware stores cannot be ruled out.

NOTE Amazon Go officially opened its doors to the public in 2018
SOURCE Amazon; author research as of June 2021

FIGURE 7.1   Amazon's first-ever bricks and mortar retail concept – Amazon Books

store that integrates the benefits of offline and online book shopping', said Jennifer Cast, former Vice President of Amazon Books.[33]

The most helpful online review is displayed as well as the overall rating and number of customer reviews. Product recommendations in the form of 'if you like this, then you'll love…' signage has been brought to the physical shelf. Book covers face out as they would do online, and books must have at least 4-star recommendations to make it on to the shelf. This means a much more curated assortment; the stores only stock about five titles per three linear feet of shelving, while most bookstores offer more than triple that figure.[34] Initially, only 25 per cent of the space was dedicated to sales of non-book items such as Bose speakers and French presses, but also a lot of Amazon's own devices – Kindles, Echo speakers, Fire tablets as well as its own-label Basics range of electronic accessories.

Perhaps what's most intriguing about the Amazon Books concept, however, is its bold approach to pricing. The books do not feature price tags; instead, shoppers must scan the item and if they are a Prime member they will be offered the Amazon.com price while non-members pay the list price. As we touched on briefly in a previous chapter, the stores are clearly designed to drive Prime membership and, like Amazon Pop-Ups, to encourage shoppers to interact with Amazon devices, both of which feed the broader ecosystem. Selling books is secondary.

HAIR SALON OR LABORATORY?

Never one to rest on its laurels, in 2021 the retailer surprised the industry once again by opening its first hair salon. The 1,500 square foot salon in London's Spitalfields offers a full range of hairdressing services. It just happens to be layered with a lot of technology.

Customers can experiment with different virtual hair colours using augmented reality technology and magazines have been swapped for Fire tablets. The salon serves as a test bed for Amazon's point-and-learn technology, where customers simply point at the product they are interested in on a display shelf and the relevant information, including brand videos, appears on a display screen. Shoppers can order products by scanning the relevant QR code on the shelf.

In an exclusive interview with the authors, Amazon's UK boss John Boumphrey noted: 'The salon really gives us three things. Number one, it gives us an opportunity to work with brands on latest technologies. Number two, beauty is a very personal, experiential industry and this is a new area for us. And the third thing is that it allows us to offer more selection for customers in professional beauty.'

This should serve as yet another reminder that Amazon is not a retailer – and certainly not a hair salon – but a tech company that loves to find ways to do things better.

Over the next few years, Amazon continued to experiment with bricks and mortar both as a retailer and technology provider. It would go on to launch new grocery formats such as Amazon Go and Amazon Fresh, which we'll discuss in the coming chapters, while also partnering with existing bricks and mortar retailers such as Kohl's, Best Buy and less well-known examples like mattress DTC brand Tuft & Needle.

Tuft & Needle, another retailer that started life online though has since merged with Serta Simmons, has worked with Amazon to enhance the customer experience as it moves further into physical retailing. Its Seattle store features tablets for shoppers to read product reviews on Amazon, Echo devices to answer customer questions and QR codes that allow for one-click purchasing through the Amazon app. Daehee Park, Tuft & Needle's co-founder, said that after much debate about how to go head-to-head with Amazon, they decided to go in the exact opposite direction.

'We've decided, why not just embrace them? It is the future of retail and e-commerce… We focus on what we're good at and plug in Amazon technology for the rest.'[35]

This could be a model for other brands that are already reliant on Amazon for online sales (Tuft & Needle generates around 25 per cent of its sales through Amazon).[36]

For other brands considering selling on Amazon, Tuft & Needle co-founder J T Marino advises:

- Measuring conversion rate to determine if Amazon is increasing direct sales;
- Considering whether brands run the risk of becoming dependent on Amazon;
- Evaluating the customer experience of each channel.

'You need to have credibility markers. We need something to point to that gives customers confidence to take a chance on it,' said Marino.[37]

Similarly, we believe that Amazon will look to forge more retail partnerships as a means of addressing the ticking time bomb that is online returns. In 2017, Amazon teamed up with department store chain Kohl's for designated Amazon returns areas in its Chicago and LA department stores. Initially, naysayers argued that this was 'too Trojan Horse-like, especially as Amazon builds up its arsenal of fashion brands, but it has been a roaring success for both parties and has since been rolled out to Kohl's stores across the US.

So how does it work? Shoppers simply hand over any unwanted Amazon goods to a Kohl's store associate, without needing to box or label the item. Kohl's will package and transport the returns to Amazon for free, and for added convenience, some stores feature designated Amazon returns parking spaces near the store entrance. We believe this is a unique proposition that drives some much-needed traffic to stores without giving away tons of customer data. It's certainly one of the least risky co-opetition routes.

'Amazon is working. This returns program is working. We're seeing the traffic. We're getting new customers,' Kohl's CEO Michelle Gass said in 2021.[38]

Since partnering with Amazon, Kohl's has acquired two million new customers, around one-third of which fall into the coveted younger shopper group that department stores struggle to reach these days.[39] And they're not all just walking in, returning and walking out, as many had predicted. Gass says that 'some of them' are buying and in 2020, a larger percentage of Amazon 'returners' also purchased something instore.

The Kohl's model works because of its exclusivity. But what would happen if Amazon returns hubs were to start appearing on every corner?

This is clearly where Amazon is heading. It has since launched Counter, a similar initiative comprising a network of staffed pick-up points that allows customers to collect their Amazon parcels in-store at a partner location. Initially, Amazon launched the service in 2019 at hundreds of Next clothing stores in the UK and thousands of stores in Italy in partnership with bookstore chain Giunti and the network of Fermopoint and SisalPay stores. The service has also been rolled out to hundreds of Rite Aid stores across the US, a decision that the drugstore retailer might come to regret as Amazon moves further into its category.

Meanwhile, however, the partnership is mutually beneficial. Lord Simon Wolfson, CEO of Next, describes its agreement with Amazon as a way to combine the 'internet's power to offer unprecedented choice with all the convenience of local stores'.[40] Perhaps it's also an indication that he doesn't see Amazon as much of a threat in fashion.

We believe that Amazon will look to strike similar partnerships with other high street retailers around the globe in order to, in Wolfson's words, improve the 'relevance and vibrancy' of bricks and mortar stores. It's all about following the customer – co-opetition will be a key theme for the future.

Notes

1   Thomson, Rebecca (2014) Analysis: Sir Terry Leahy and Nick Robertson on why delivery has become so crucial, *Retail Week*, 6 February. Available from: https://www.retail-week.com/topics/supply-chain/analysis-sir-terry-leahy-and-nick-robertson-on-why-delivery-has-become-so-crucial/5057200.article (archived at https://perma.cc/9Z43-JSCH) [Last accessed 29/6/2018].

2   Keenan, Michael (2021) Global ecommerce explained: Stats and trends to watch in 2021, *Shopify blog*, 13 May. Available from: https://www.shopify.co.uk/enterprise/global-ecommerce-statistics#2 (archived at https://perma.cc/XFG7-7BPA) [Last accessed 20/6/2021].

3   Kumar, Kavita (2018) Amazon's Bezos calls Best Buy turnaround 'remarkable' as unveils new TV partnership, *Star Tribune*, 19 April. Available from: http://www.startribune.com/best-buy-and-amazon-partner-up-in-exclusive-deal-to-sell-new-tvs/480059943/ (archived at https://perma.cc/X6YQ-TUDX) [Last accessed 29/6/2018].

4 McGregor, Kirsty (2015) Pure-play etail will cease to exist by 2020, predicts Planet Retail, *Drapers*, 22 July. Available from: https://www.drapersonline. com/news/pure-play-etail-will-cease-to-exist-by-2020-predicts-planet-retail-/5077310.article (archived at https://perma.cc/BQ7X-KSVJ) [Last accessed 29/6/2018].

5 MDJ2 (2015) Ten things we learned at Retail Week Live 2017. Available from: http://mdj2.co.uk/wp-content/uploads/2016/11/Ten-things-we-learned-at-Retail-Week-Live-2017-1.pdf [Last accessed 29/6/2018].

6 Jiang, Moliang (2017) New retail in China: a growth engine for the retail industry, *China Briefing*, 15 August. Available from: http://www.china-briefing. com/news/2017/08/15/new-retail-in-china-new-growth-engine-for-the-retail-industry.html (archived at https://perma.cc/28TF-XW27) [Last accessed 29/6/2018].

7 Wynne-Jones, Stephen (2017) Shoptalk Europe: an eye-opening journey through the future of retail, *European Supermarket News*, 12 October. Available from: https://www.esmmagazine.com/shoptalk-europe-eye-opening-journey-future-retail/50514 (archived at https://perma.cc/HP9J-N9SM) [Last accessed 29/6/2018].

8 Amazon staff (2020) Fact check: sizing up Amazon, *Amazon's website*, 15 September. Available from: https://www.aboutamazon.com/news/how-amazon-works/fact-check-sizing-up-amazon (archived at https://perma.cc/T523-QTFS) [Last accessed 20/6/2021].

9 Simpson, Jeff, Lokesh Ohri and Kasey M Lobaugh (2016) The new digital divide, *Deloitte*, 12 September. Available from: https://dupress.deloitte.com/ dup-us-en/industry/retail-distribution/digital-divide-changing-consumer-behavior.html [Last accessed 29/6/2018].

10 Del Ray, Jason (2016) 55 percent of online shoppers start their product searches on Amazon, *Recode*, 27 September. Available from: https://www. recode.net/2016/9/27/13078526/amazon-online-shopping-product-search-engine (archived at https://perma.cc/CA9G-QADL) [Last accessed 29/6/2018].

11 Statement by Jeffrey P. Bezos Founder & Chief Executive Officer, Amazon before the U.S. House of Representatives Committee on the Judiciary Subcommittee on Antitrust, Commercial, and Administrative Law (2020). Available from: https://www.congress.gov/116/meeting/house/110883/ witnesses/HHRG-116-JU05-Wstate-BezosJ-20200729.pdf (archived at https:// perma.cc/45Z9-XPSZ) [Last accessed 18/6/2021].

12 Kowitt, Beth (2018) How Amazon is using Whole Foods in a bid for total retail domination, *Fortune*, 21 May. Available from: http://fortune.com/ longform/amazon-groceries-fortune-500/ (archived at https://perma.cc/5MEN-4LPW) [Last accessed 19/6/2018].

13 Reagan, Courtney (2017) Think running retail stores is more expensive than selling online? Think again, *CNBC*, 19 April. Available from: https://www.cnbc.com/2017/04/19/think-running-retail-stores-is-more-expensive-than-selling-online-think-again.html (archived at https://perma.cc/VU55-HQFJ) [Last accessed 29/6/2018].

14 Statement by Jeffrey P. Bezos Founder & Chief Executive Officer, Amazon before the U.S. House of Representatives Committee on the Judiciary Subcommittee on Antitrust, Commercial, and Administrative Law (2020). Available from: https://www.congress.gov/116/meeting/house/110883/witnesses/HHRG-116-JU05-Wstate-BezosJ-20200729.pdf (archived at https://perma.cc/45Z9-XPSZ) [Last accessed 18/6/2021].

15 Meyersohn, Nathaniel (2018) Walmart figured out its Amazon strategy. So why's the stock down 13%? *CNN*, 17 May. Available from: http://money.cnn.com/2018/05/16/news/companies/walmart-stock-jet-amazon-whole-foods/index.html (archived at https://perma.cc/5H4U-2MG7) [Last accessed 29/6/2018].

16 Transcript of Alexandre Bompard's speech (2018) Carrefour, 23 January. Available from: http://www.carrefour.com/sites/default/files/carrefour_2022_-_transcript_of_the_speech_of_alexandre_bompard.pdf [Last accessed 29/6/18].

17 Bohannon, Patrick (2017) Online Returns: A Challenge for Multi-Channel Retailers. Oracle, 27/1. Available from: https://blogs.oracle.com/retail/online-returns:-a-challenge-for-multi-channel-retailers (archived at https://perma.cc/U648-F5U9) [Last accessed 29/6/2018].

18 Wal-Mart Stores Inc. (WMT) Q4 2021 earnings call transcript (2021). Available from: https://www.fool.com/earnings/call-transcripts/2021/02/19/wal-mart-stores-inc-wmt-q4-2020-earnings-call-tran/ (archived at https://perma.cc/Y7RF-SYLA) [Last accessed 20/6/2021].

19 Permission received from Tim Yost.

20 Reagan, Courtney (2017) Think running retail stores is more expensive than selling online? Think again, *CNBC*, 19 April. Available from: https://www.cnbc.com/2017/04/19/think-running-retail-stores-is-more-expensive-than-selling-online-think-again.html (archived at https://perma.cc/VU55-HQFJ) [Last accessed 29/6/2018].

21 Ibid.

22 Pitney Bowes parcel shipping index reports continued growth as global parcel volume exceeds 100 billion for first time ever (2020) *Business Wire*, 20 October. Available from: https://www.businesswire.com/news/home/20201012005150/en/Pitney-Bowes-Parcel-Shipping-Index-Reports-Continued-Growth-as-Global-Parcel-Volume-Exceeds-100-billion-for-First-Time-Ever (archived at https://perma.cc/8Z6S-8JXD) [Last accessed 6/20/21].

23 Droesch, Blake (2021) Amazon dominates US ecommerce, though its market share varies by category, *eMarketer*, 27 April. Available from: https://www.emarketer.com/content/amazon-dominates-us-ecommerce-though-its-market-share-varies-by-category (archived at https://perma.cc/Z37J-8U7V) [Last accessed 6/20/21].

24 Amazon 10-K for the fiscal year ended December 31, 2020. Available from: https://www.sec.gov/ix?doc=/Archives/edgar/data/1018724/0001018724 21000004/amzn-20201231.htm (archived at https://perma.cc/H35D-TDPV) [Last accessed 18/6/2021].

25 McGee, Tom (2017) Shopping for data: the truth behind online costs, *Forbes*, 10 August. Available from: https://www.forbes.com/sites/tommcgee/2017/08/10/shopping-for-data-the-truth-behind-online-costs/#53fdecdfc9d7 (archived at https://perma.cc/8HU7-3CZT) [Last accessed 29/6/2018].

26 Death of Pureplay Retail report (2016) *Gartner L2*, 12 January. Available from: https://www.l2inc.com/research/death-of-pureplay-retail (archived at https://perma.cc/JX8H-HS59) [Last accessed 29/6/2018].

27 Walsh, Mark (2016) The future of e-commerce: bricks and mortar, *Guardian*, 30 January. Available from: https://www.theguardian.com/business/2016/jan/30/future-of-e-commerce-bricks-and-mortar (archived at https://perma.cc/UJE9-MZGN) [Last accessed 29/6/2018].

28 Kim, Tae (2021) Google's ad resurgence makes Alphabet best investment bet among tech giants, Bloomberg, 28 April. Available from: https://www.bloombergquint.com/gadfly/alphabet-s-google-ad-resurgence-is-just-getting-started (archived at https://perma.cc/2CN8-M6NV) [Last accessed 20/6/2021].

29 Southern, Matt (2021) Over 25% of people click the first Google search result, *Search Engine Journal*, 14 July. Available from: https://www.searchenginejournal.com/google-first-page-clicks/374516/#close (archived at https://perma.cc/HZ6T-FFRA) [Last accessed 20/6/2021].

30 Radojev, Hugh (2019) Data: Physical stores 'halo effect' boosts online sales, *Retail Week*, 12 July. Available from: https://www.retail-week.com/data/data-physical-stores-halo-effect-boosts-online-sales/7032402.article?storyCode=7032402&authent=1 (archived at https://perma.cc/F6XA-MMJE) [Last accessed 20/6/2021].

31 Thomas, Lauren (2019) Retail stores get a bad rap, as closures pile up. But here's how stores boost online sales, *CNBC*, 22 July. Available from: https://www.cnbc.com/2019/07/22/icsc-says-theres-a-halo-effect-by-retailers-having-physical-stores.html (archived at https://perma.cc/LW5Z-W9Y3) [Last accessed 20/6/2021].

32   Bhasin, Kim (2012) Bezos: Amazon would love to have physical stores, but only under one condition, *Business Insider*, 27 November. Available from: http://www.businessinsider.com/amazon-jeff-bezos-stores-2012-11?IR=T (archived at https://perma.cc/2UFC-ZAQ6) [Last accessed 29/6/2018].

33   Denham, Jess (2015) Amazon to sell books the old-fashioned way with first physical book shop, *Independent*, 3 November. Available from: https://www.independent.co.uk/arts-entertainment/books/news/amazon-to-sell-books-the-old-fashioned-way-with-first-physical-book-shop-a6719261.html (archived at https://perma.cc/9MVP-3APY) [Last accessed 29/6/2018].

34   Kurtz, Dustin (2015) My 2.5-star trip to Amazon's bizarre new bookstore, *The New Republic*, 4 November. Available from: https://newrepublic.com/article/123352/my-25-star-trip-to-amazons-bizarre-new-bookstore (archived at https://perma.cc/P276-MM3T) [Last accessed 29/6/2018].

35   Del Ray, Jason (2017) One of the most popular mattress makers on Amazon is building an Amazon-powered store, *Recode*, 31 July. Available from: https://www.recode.net/2017/7/31/16069424/tuft-needle-seattle-store-amazon-mattresses-echo-alexa-prime-delivery (archived at https://perma.cc/D88V-PZGC) [Last accessed 29/6/2018]

36   Ibid.

37   Stern, Matthew (2019) How Tuft & Needle found the right balance on Amazon, *RetailWire*, 28 June. Available from: https://www.retailwire.com/discussion/how-tuft-needle-found-the-right-balance-on-amazon/ (archived at https://perma.cc/H4XM-YCYM) [Last accessed: 20/6/2021]

38   Twice staff (2020) 'Amazon Is Working,' Says Kohl's CEO Michelle Gass, Twice, 15 January. Available from: https://www.twice.com/retailing/amazon-is-working-says-kohls-ceo-michelle-gass (archived at https://perma.cc/3FPS-SB2T) [Last accessed: 20/6/021].

39   Wahba, Phil (2021) Kohl's CEO gets small assist in fight with activists, thanks to Amazon partnership, *Fortune*, 3 March. Available from: https://fortune.com/2021/03/03/kohls-ceo-michelle-gass-activist-investors/ (archived at https://perma.cc/V329-PW2P) [Last accessed: 20/6/021].

40   Amazon press release: Amazon Introduces Counter – A New Click & Collect Option At A Store Near You (2019) Available from: https://amazonuk.gcs-web.com/news-releases/news-release-details/amazon-introduces-counter-new-click-collect-option-store-near (archived at https://perma.cc/8ETY-TDZ7) [Last accessed: 20/6/2021].

08

Amazon's grocery ambitions: create a platform to sell you everything else

> 'In order to be a two-hundred-billion-dollar company, we've got to learn how to sell clothes and food.'
> **Jeff Bezos, 2007**[1]

Digital transformation is sweeping across the retail sector, but up until recently three categories – furniture, fashion and food – have been relatively insulated.

These are categories where quality is subjective and cannot always be determined via a screen. These are categories where the desire to see and touch the product traditionally outweighed the convenience of buying online. And therefore, the margin for error in purchasing these categories online was historically higher than when buying commoditized products like books or DVDs, where shoppers knew exactly what they were going to get regardless of where they purchased it.

But that all changed when the pandemic hit. As discussed earlier in the book, the COVID crisis was a boon for online retailers as quarantined consumers turned to the internet in droves. Naturally, the most dramatic shift took place in the one category that everyone needs: food.

Online grocery retail is now at an inflection point. With COVID – not Amazon – as the primary catalyst for change in the grocery sector, retailers were quick to pivot. They commendably adapted to changes in customer demand, increasing online grocery capacity in order to keep the world fed. However, in doing so, they have diverted shoppers to their least profitable channel.

So what does the future hold? Will the customers who perhaps reluctantly turned to online shopping during the pandemic shun their screens as soon as it's safe? Or will newly acquired digital skills outlast the pandemic?

In this chapter, we'll begin to explore Amazon's online grocery strategy in more detail before moving on to its acquisition of Whole Foods Market and broader supermarket ambitions in the next chapter.

US online grocery: a slow burner

The supermarket sector is a notoriously complex, low-margin business with high fixed costs, a fragmented supplier base and product perishability. It only gets more complicated when you add home delivery into the mix. According to Goldman Sachs, it costs supermarkets an astonishing $23 per order to store, pick, pack and deliver groceries, eroding what are already razor-thin margins.[2]

Varying handling and temperature requirements, rejected substitutions and absent customers also add to the complexity. Not even the shopper journey is straightforward – multiple customers may contribute to the basket, adding items right up until the order is picked. Delivering books is a breeze in comparison.

High population density is ideal for any e-commerce operation, but for online grocery it's absolutely essential. You only need to look at the world's most advanced grocery e-commerce markets – South Korea and the UK – for proof. In South Korea, where 83 per cent of the population live in cities, the online grocery penetration stood at an astounding 20 per cent even before the pandemic struck. A large, densely populated and highly connected country is the perfect breeding ground for online grocery, both in terms of driving supply chain efficiencies and consumer adoption (South Korea has the fastest internet in the world).

In countries with large rural populations like the US, such dense coverage becomes harder to achieve. South Korea has 522 people per square kilometre; the US has just 88.[3] In such a vast, sparsely populated country, most American supermarkets have historically found it difficult to achieve the economies of scale required to sustain an online grocery model. This resulted in retailers historically either shunning grocery home delivery altogether or limiting it to cash-rich/time-poor city dwellers.

According to Credit Suisse, there are 13 independent factors that correlate to online grocery adoption and profitability:

- broadband penetration;
- tablet/smartphone penetration;
- online share of retail spend;
- Amazon penetration;
- start-up/independent culture;
- urban driving infrastructure;
- metropolitan areas with >1 million inhabitants (conducive to instore picking model);
- metropolitan areas with >5 million inhabitants (conducive to centralized distribution);
- GDP/capita;
- car ownership;
- prevalence of double-income households;
- density of supermarket space;
- inclement seasonal weather.

In addition to limited access, online grocery adoption in the US had been slow in relation to other markets because of the high fees associated with delivery, which naturally deterred some shoppers from using the service. As recently as 2021, Walmart was still charging a whopping $10 per order.[4] Meanwhile, the typical 'endless aisle' advantage of buying online is less relevant in grocery and many Americans have traditionally been reluctant to let someone else – human or robot – select their produce. The desire to see, touch and even smell fresh food is a key driver to the physical store. Prior to COVID, habits were firmly entrenched and there were barriers aplenty.

Old habits die hard, but they do die. And, as we've all recently learned, if there's one thing that can modify behaviour, it's a pandemic.

Today, 60 per cent of US consumers buy groceries online, compared with 37 per cent in 2019, according to Coresight Research.[5] In 2020, online US grocery sales grew by 54 per cent to $96 billion, giving it a 7.4 per cent share of total US grocery sales. This might not sound terribly impressive, but it's important to bear in mind that as recently as 2018, online grocery share in the US stood at less than 2 per cent.

As discussed early on in the book, the timing of the COVID crisis and subsequent acceleration in the grocery e-commerce sector has been fortuitous for Amazon. In the early stages of the pandemic, orders for groceries from Amazon were as much as 50 times higher than normal levels.[6] If the pandemic had struck just five years earlier, Amazon would have had to just idly watch as Walmart and peers scooped up that trade.

But Amazon's grocery strategy has come a long way in recent years, which meant that when the pandemic hit, it was poised to deliver. As of 2021, Amazon delivered groceries to 5,000 cities and towns across the US (up from 2,000 in 2019). The retailer also launched – and shortly afterwards embarked on a wide-scale rollout of – in-garage grocery delivery during the pandemic, adding another dimension of convenience to the online shopping experience.

So why do we believe that Amazon needs stores to crack grocery? Although grocery e-commerce boomed throughout the pandemic, we should prepare for a deceleration in growth as normal life resumes. By 2023, online grocery sales are expected to make up 11 per cent of total US grocery sales, according to eMarketer.[7] Or, put another way, nearly 90 per cent of US grocery sales will still take place in a bricks and mortar store.

For many shoppers, it's still more convenient – or in some cases enjoyable – to hop into their car and drive to the shop. Don't get us wrong, grocery e-commerce is coming – and it's coming fast – but there will always be a place for the supermarket.

Our view, unsurprisingly, is shared by the country's largest grocery retailer. Walmart CEO Doug McMillon believes that in order to grow a national online grocery business, 'you have to be able to keep perishable products fresh, available and at the right price. To do that, you need a perishable supply chain that supports stores that are near customers'.[8]

In addition to physical stores, McMillon believes that a successful grocery e-commerce business requires 'a lot of general merchandise and apparel to help with the margin mix' as well as 'a lot of scale because volume helps reduce markdowns and throwaways'.[9] Amazon ticks these boxes as well, and is accelerating its incursion into the clothing sector. Remember how earlier we discussed that you cannot look at Amazon's individual categories or business units in isolation and that every service is another spoke on the flywheel? Selling higher-margin clothes, from private label ranges in particular, will help Amazon to offset some of the higher costs of delivering groceries.

Why else does Amazon need grocery stores? Because they'll create a halo effect for the online business through click & collect and same-day delivery, again reinforcing the need for a seamless shopping experience across channels. In many ways, the Whole Foods Market acquisition, in which Amazon picked up 21 million square feet of retail space overnight, was an admission that the grocery category will always require an element of physical retail, albeit one of a more versatile nature.

At the same time, as we've already seen with other sectors, technology will dismantle the barriers traditionally associated with buying food online, automation – from warehouse robotics to driverless delivery trucks – will improve supply chain efficiencies and the rise in third-party delivery services (Instacart, for example) will allow more supermarkets to offer speedy delivery without the hefty investment in infrastructure or systems.

Meanwhile, the customer value proposition for online grocery is exploding; today, consumers benefit from improved mobile phone interfaces, single sign-ons, greater personalization and site navigation, automated lists, recipe inspiration, delivery passes, voice shopping, simplified replenishment, same-day delivery and other alternatives to home delivery such as click & collect, curbside pickup, in-fridge and in-garage delivery, and automated lockers.

Online grocery allows customers to shop on their terms and maximize their time, as technology takes the chore out of shopping for food.

Food: the final frontier and importance of frequency

Food retailing is attractive to Amazon in that it is the biggest non-discretionary sector – and one that is ripe for disruption. As we'll discuss below, it's also vital in that it enables Amazon to finally tap into a high-frequency purchase.

Frequency – a big step closer to retail dominance

It's clear that Amazon can't be the Everything Store without food. Not only is it a major part of the consumer spending bucket, it's also a category that is defined by *frequency* (the average US shopper visits a supermarket 1–2 times per week,[10] according to the FMI) and therefore largely driven by *habit* (85 per cent of the items shoppers put in their carts are the same from week to week).[11] No other sector offers such an incredible customer engagement opportunity.

> '[Grocery is] an everyday way into your life. There's nothing else that happens quite that way.'
> **Walter Robb, former co-CEO of Whole Foods Market**[12]

Data capture aside, there's a very good reason why Amazon limits its wider online grocery offering to Prime members. With grocery, Amazon gets frequency. If consumers are doing their weekly food shop through Amazon, bearing in mind they must first be Prime members, then there's a strong chance Amazon will then become their first port of call for other categories. As the former co-CEO of Whole Foods Market Walter Robb puts it, 'Food is the platform for selling you everything else.'[13]

This is why Amazon's move into grocery should worry all retailers, not just supermarkets. Grocery is the path for Amazon to become its customers' default shopping option. Already, around 15 per cent of US consumers make purchases on Amazon seven times or more a week.[14] If Amazon can crack grocery, it has the potential to further tap into the needs of these superfans (though again not without greater scrutiny from the government).

It's no coincidence that Amazon spent years building out its retail assortment and investing in its Prime offer, adding perk after perk and beefing up the content, before delving into the grocery category. Amazon may be up against some well-established grocery competitors, but the tech giant differentiates in three ways: its ubiquity in the digital space, the effortlessness of buying through its platform and the attractiveness of Prime.

Amazon's food fight: life before Whole Foods Market

The idea of luring shoppers in with food and then tempting them with higher-margin general merchandise is by no means a new strategy. This is the very premise of the hypermarket and superstore model. Walmart began adding food to the mix in the late '80s and in just over a decade became the largest food retailer in the US. Meanwhile, Britain's Tesco started life as a grocer and then in the '60s added general merchandise to its stores, enabling it to eventually become the largest retailer in the UK. 'The principle of what Amazon is doing is almost exactly the same,' says Jack Sinclair, CEO of Sprouts, who previously ran Walmart's US grocery division.[15]

The Whole Foods acquisition was an inflection point for Amazon, but in order to understand the motives for the deal, we must first go back to the beginning.

CASE STUDY

A lesson in the dangers of overexpansion: Webvan and the dot-com bust

One of the most spectacular failures of the dot-com bust was the online grocery service Webvan. The first major online grocery delivery company in the US was co-founded in 1996 by Louis Borders (of the eponymous, now defunct, bookstore chain) and, as with many companies at the time, the mantra was 'Get Big Fast'. In less than three years, the company burned through $800 million in cash, went public, then filed for bankruptcy and closed down its operations.[16] Its meteoric rise and then fall made Webvan the poster child of the dot-com excess bubble.

Some might argue that Webvan was ahead of its time; after all, the snail-like dial-up connections of the late 1990s were hardly conducive to speedy online grocery shopping. Like Amazon, Webvan was placing a big bet on technology's ability to change shopping habits, but its problems ran deeper than that. Its fundamental flaw? Overexpansion without sufficient customer demand.

Webvan shunned the conventional store-based picking model in favour of a centralized approach to online grocery delivery. Not unlike Ocado today, Webvan went on to build state-of-the-art, automated fulfilment centres with the aim of delivering groceries to shoppers within 30-minute time slots. The idea was that its unique technology would drive productivity, enabling Webvan to beat out both online and bricks and mortar rivals.

It wasn't the concept that was bad, it was the execution. Webvan was attempting to simultaneously build a brand and customer base from scratch, while redesigning the very infrastructure of a well-established sector. The capital-intensive plan required Webvan to dish out over $30 million on each large high-tech warehouse, but the lack of customer demand meant that the warehouses weren't running anywhere near full capacity.[17] According to some analysts, Webvan was losing more than $130 per order, when taking into account depreciation, marketing and other overheads.[18]

Richard Tarrant, CEO of MyWebGrocer, said of Webvan in 2013:

> In a low-margin business, where the products can be purchased within three miles by anyone in the United States, they decided to build warehouses and a whole distribution system with delivery trucks, labour, and everything else. But

the 36,000 conveniently located grocery stores on every Main Street in America already had all that.[19]

Under pressure to appease investors, expansion was fast and furious. Covering the launch of Webvan's first mega warehouse in Oakland, California, a 1999 *Wall Street Journal* article stated:

> If it thrives, and even if it doesn't, Mr Borders plans to open another enormous grocery warehouse in Atlanta a few months later. Down the road are plans for at least 20 more such facilities throughout the US in practically every city big enough to support a major-league sports team.[20]

Webvan hadn't worked out the initial kinks with its business model before embarking on an aggressive, and ultimately disastrous, expansion plan. Within 18 months, the online grocer was trading in 10 major metro areas across the US.[21] For comparison, it took Ocado over a decade to open its second fulfilment centre.[22] Webvan 'committed the cardinal sin of retail, which is to expand into a new territory – in our case several territories – before we had demonstrated success in the first market,' said Mike Moritz, a Webvan board member. 'In fact, we were busy demonstrating failure in the Bay Area market while we expanded into other regions.'[23]

In an effort to gain economies of scale, Webvan acquired rival HomeGrocer in 2000. Coincidentally, Amazon owned a 35 per cent stake in HomeGrocer at the time, which provided a first glimpse of Bezos' vision for the grocery category – taking the 'drudgery' out of the experience. In 1999, he commended HomeGrocer for having 'a fanatical eye for the customer experience. Their shoppers pick out better produce than I could for myself... The company really has an unusual attention to detail'.[24]

The HomeGrocer acquisition wasn't enough to save Webvan and within a year it went bankrupt. This had a lasting effect on the US marketplace, souring the appetite for online grocery for years, even decades, to come.

AmazonFresh: rising from Webvan's ashes

Amazon's own online grocery delivery service, AmazonFresh, was born in 2007; though, if you don't live in Seattle, you'd be forgiven for thinking it was a newer concept. Amazon quietly tested the service in its hometown for *five years* before eventually rolling it out to other US cities. If there's one thing Amazon learned from Webvan's crash, it was to nail down its business model before embarking on any kind of expansion.

Leading the AmazonFresh initiative were four former Webvan executives – Doug Herrington, Peter Ham, Mick Mountz and Mark Mastandrea. It's worth highlighting here that Mountz is also the founder of Kiva Systems, the robotics company that Amazon acquired in 2012. Kiva was built on technology originally developed at Webvan and has since become a key part of the AmazonFresh strategy. Interestingly, Webvan was also resurrected in that Amazon purchased the domain – the site was once used to sell Amazon's non-perishable food items, though it's no longer in operation today.

'We had a lot of Webvan DNA in the room and we drew on that experience a lot,' said Tom Furphy, who helped start AmazonFresh with Herrington and Ham before moving on to become a venture capitalist. 'That was a good formula for building the business responsibly.'[25]

But the team had their work cut out for them. As a general merchandise retailer, Amazon's site was – and still is today – designed for targeted search but, of course, shoppers tend to browse grocery categories. And while most online transactions comprise two to four items, the average grocery order is comprised of 50 items.[26] Navigating complexities around supply chain and differences in user experience are key to cracking online grocery.

As Amazon began to make its mark, however slowly, it had two big factors working in its favour – timing and an existing customer base. By the mid-noughties, fast broadband connections and higher smartphone penetration were helping to stimulate demand for online grocery, and, unlike Webvan, Amazon was able to tap into an existing pool of shoppers. However, it's worth pointing out here that Prime was only a couple of years old when AmazonFresh was launched. This was another reason for the tortoise-paced roll-out of online grocery – Prime had to be both mature and compelling enough so that Amazon would be equipped with a loyal, sizeable customer base before it got serious about grocery.

By 2013, AmazonFresh had finally begun to expand operations beyond Seattle and within a few years the service was offered in Chicago, Dallas, Baltimore, Seattle, parts of California (Los Angeles, Riverside, Sacramento, San Diego, San Francisco, San Jose, and Stockton), New York City, northern New Jersey, Philadelphia, Northern Virginia, Connecticut and, outside of the US, London.[27] Today, Amazon delivers groceries to more than 5,000 cities and towns across the US.

Over the years, Amazon experimented with different branding and fee structures in order to make the economics of fresh grocery delivery work. For a while, the service was branded Prime Fresh and offered as part of a bundled Prime membership option for a $299 annual fee – triple the price of a normal Prime membership. This turned out to be too big a pill to swallow for many shoppers who were still getting accustomed to ordering groceries online so, in 2016, the AmazonFresh pricing model was changed – it was still limited to Prime members but as a more palatable $14.99 monthly add-on (as previously mentioned, this has since been incorporated into the broader Prime scheme as a free benefit).

Despite the more favourable market conditions, selling fresh food online was no easy feat, which was why Amazon was simultaneously experimenting with a more familiar category – non-perishables.

Subscribe & Save: a first taste of simplified replenishment

Amazon launched Subscribe & Save in 2007 just several months prior to making its first AmazonFresh deliveries. The subscription programme, which is still running today, allows shoppers to receive automatic delivery of grocery products (from one- to six-month intervals) with discounts of up to 15 per cent. At the time of launch, Amazon's online grocery store, which was separate to the Fresh service, featured over 22,000 non-perishable items from leading brands, including Kellogg's, Seventh Generation and Huggies, as well as a wide selection of natural and organic products.[28]

Subscribe & Save was the first step to locking in grocery shoppers, giving Amazon an incredible amount of insight into their brand preferences and price elasticity – a major criticism of the programme is that, despite the discount, it's still subject to Amazon's dynamic pricing, which can negate the effect of cost savings offered through a subscription.

The launch of Subscribe & Save gave us insight at a very early stage as to how Amazon would disrupt the grocery sector – it would take the chore out of grocery shopping. After all, this is what Bezos had admired in HomeGrocer when it acquired a minority stake years earlier. Subscribe & Save was Amazon's first iteration of a simplified replenishment programme. Amazon would go on to launch a number of entirely new customer touchpoints, physical and digital, that aimed to make the reordering of everyday goods as seamless as possible:

- **Dash Buttons** (now defunct): Wi-Fi-connected one-click reordering buttons placed in shoppers' homes.
- **Dash replenishment service**: device-driven replenishment scheme, ie smart Brita water pitchers that automatically reorder filters or home locks that reorder batteries when running low.

- **Alexa**: AI-powered virtual assistant that allows for voice shopping via Echo.

- **Dash Wand** (now defunct): handheld device that allows for barcode scanning and voice-activated reordering.

- **Dash Virtual Buttons** (now defunct): as the name implies, one-click reordering buttons available on Amazon's app and site.

In the meantime, it's worth calling out here that Walmart filed its own patent to integrate IoT (Internet of Things) into its actual products. Like Amazon's Dash replenishment scheme, this would allow for automatic reordering of items without any input from the customer. The difference, of course, is that Walmart's patent is for product-driven and not device-driven replenishment, which would generate more widespread usage and accelerate the trend.

The automatic replenishment trend will play a significant role in shaping the future of retail. Amazon wants to cut out friction and shorten the path to purchase just as it famously did back in 1999 with its 1-Click purchasing patent. Already today, you can shop without a store or screen. You can ask Alexa to add items to your basket while you're making dinner, and in the future it will become even more seamless as shoppers are able to completely opt out of the purchasing decision. As we go from one-click to no-click, Amazon is best positioned to own the habitual purchase.

As a result, consumers will spend less time buying the essentials in the future, a trend that we will explore in greater detail later in the book, particularly in relation to its impact on the physical space. But for now, it's important to remember that in exchange for the ultra-convenience provided by these technologies, purchases are funnelled directly through to Amazon's retail platform. No other retailer has been so successful at infiltrating the consumer's home.

After several years in operation, Subscribe & Save was bolstered through the 2010 launch of Amazon Mom (now more aptly named Amazon Family) and the acquisition of Quidsi. Amazon Mom allowed customers at a critical life stage to get discounts on nappies if they signed up for regular monthly deliveries; meanwhile, rival Quidsi was the parent company of Diapers.com, Soap.com and BeautyBar.com. While it's not unusual for a retailer to buy one of its rivals, the acquisition of Quidsi was controversial in that many questioned whether Amazon had engaged in predatory pricing. In other words, dropping your prices so you are selling at a loss, forcing competitors to do the same, competitors then go out of business and you can raise your prices again, recouping the previous loss.

According to Congresswoman Mary Gay Scanlon, Amazon was willing to lose $200 million on nappies in just one month.[29]

Despite the acquisition taking place a decade earlier – and Quidsi being shut down by Amazon in 2017 – it remained a focus at the Big Tech antitrust hearing in 2020. Amazon's internal emails, released by Congress, stated that Diapers.com was considered Amazon's '#1 short term competitor' and that Amazon needed 'to match pricing on these guys no matter what the cost'.[30]

The House antitrust report, released in late 2020, concluded: 'In shutting down the company, Amazon eliminated a differentiated online retailer that consumers loved – reducing the number of online options for consumers in the diaper and baby care markets. Further, it eliminated a potential competitor in other verticals such as household goods, toys, and pets.'[31]

Here come the Primes: Pantry and Now

Two more significant launches came in 2014: Prime Pantry, a delivery service focused on household items and non-perishable goods, and Prime Now, one- to two-hour delivery on a variety of grocery and non-food items.

Now it's important to remember that Amazon is constantly experimenting, so it should come as little surprise that both of these offerings have since been integrated into Amazon's wider site and the brands phased out in 2021. In fact, in the first edition of this book, we predicted that Prime Pantry would become obsolete as Amazon eventually consolidated its jumble of grocery services. As for Prime Now, the writing was on the wall when Amazon made same-day grocery delivery a 'free' Prime benefit. With Amazon's delivery times getting faster, it was becoming difficult to differentiate between Amazon's core offering and Prime Now. These initiatives, however, played a vital role in shaping Amazon's current grocery strategy so let's explore how they started out.

Initially catering to the bulky, typically monthly shop, Prime Pantry allowed shoppers to fill a 4-cubic-foot box with up to 45 pounds of non-perishable household goods for a flat $5.99 fee. As shoppers added items to their online shopping basket, they were told what percentage of the box was full. The concept was innovative and relatively low risk – delivering cereal and laundry detergent wasn't foolproof but it was more economically viable than delivering fresh food. It took Amazon half a decade to expand its AmazonFresh grocery service beyond Seattle; Prime Pantry was rolled out across all 48 contiguous states on the first day.

Prime Pantry allowed Amazon to test demand for products that would have been cost-prohibitive to ship for free. The lack of fresh food may not

TABLE 8.1   Amazon's grocery milestones

Year	Amazon's grocery milestones	Category
1999	Acquires 35% stake in HomeGrocer.com	Online grocery
2000	Webvan acquires HomeGrocer	Online grocery
2001	Webvan files for bankruptcy; site folded into Amazon.com	Online grocery
2007	Launches AmazonFresh	Online grocery
2007	Launches Subscribe & Save	Online grocery
2011	Acquires Quidsi	Online grocery
2012	Acquires Kiva Robotics	Online grocery
2013	AmazonFresh expands outside of Seattle	Online grocery
2014	Launches Dash wand	Connected home
2014	Launches Prime Pantry	Online grocery
2014	Launches Prime Now	Online grocery
2015	Launches Dash buttons	Connected home
2015	Launches Dash replenishment service	Connected home
2015	Launches Echo/Alexa for voice shopping	Connected home
2015	Launches Amazon Restaurants	Online grocery
2016	AmazonFresh goes international; inks supply deals with Morrisons and Dia	Online grocery
2016	Launches first private label grocery products	Online grocery
2017	Launches AmazonFresh Pickup	Bricks & mortar
2017	Acquires Whole Foods Market	Bricks & mortar
2017	AmazonFresh is scaled back in select zip codes across nine states	Online grocery
2017	Launches virtual Dash buttons	Online grocery
2017	Launches meal kits	Online grocery
2018	Launches grocery delivery and pickup from Whole Foods Market	Online grocery
2018	Launches Amazon Go	Bricks & mortar
2019	Amazon Fresh expands to more cities with 1- and 2-hr delivery	Online grocery
2019	Grocery delivery from Fresh and Whole Foods Market becomes free with Prime membership	Online grocery
2019	Grocery delivery is available in more than 2,000 cities and towns	Online grocery

(continued)

TABLE 8.1 (Continued)

Year	Amazon's grocery milestones	Category
2020	Launches Amazon Go Grocery	Bricks & mortar
2020	Launches Amazon Dash Cart	Bricks & mortar
2020	Launches Amazon Fresh supermarkets	Bricks & mortar
2020	Expands grocery pickup from Whole Foods Market to all stores nationwide	Online grocery
2020	Amazon launches Key In-Garage Grocery Delivery from Amazon Fresh and Whole Foods Market in select cities	Online grocery
2021	Announces rebranding of Amazon Go Grocery to Amazon Fresh	Bricks & mortar
2021	Grocery delivery is available in more than 5,000 cities and towns	Online grocery
2021	Expands Key In-Garage Grocery Delivery to all cities where delivery from Amazon Fresh and Whole Foods Market is available	Online grocery
2021	Prime Pantry service is discontinued	Online grocery
2021	Prime Now app and website are retired globally, 1- and 2-hr delivery shopping experience moves onto Amazon app and website	Online grocery
2021	Launches Amazon Fresh stores internationally	Bricks & mortar

SOURCE Author research; Amazon

have been a deal-breaker for US customers, but in international markets like the UK, Prime Pantry was less compelling. Consumers expect to do a full grocery shop online, plus the high density of supermarkets and lack of storage space in comparison to US homes means that British shoppers don't 'bulk buy' in the same way as their American counterparts.

But were American Prime members willing to shell out an additional $6 each time a cardboard box of household goods turned up at their doorstep (bearing in mind some of these items were already available through Amazon's main marketplace)? What is more, Prime members had also come to expect two-day shipping but Pantry delivery took up to four business days. Innovative, yes, but it was difficult to see the real value for customers. Amazon went on to tweak the model so that instead of paying per delivery, Prime members were charged $5 per month in addition to their annual Prime membership fee. With Prime Pantry catering to the monthly shop, and

AmazonFresh to the weekly shop, Amazon decided to go after yet another shopping mission – convenience. The introduction of free two-hour delivery with Prime Now (or within the hour for a flat fee of $7.99) exclusive to Prime members changed the game when it came to online shopping; don't forget that same-day delivery was still often a chargeable service ($5.99 for Prime users; $8.99 for others) at the time. Prime Now, originally code-named 'Houdini', was significant in that it enabled Amazon to more effectively target specific shopping occasions – and therefore share of wallet – while completely disrupting the sector in the process.

Despite their best efforts, no Western competitor could offer as vast a range as Prime Now – 20,000 stock keeping units (SKUs) across both grocery and general merchandise categories – delivered in as short a window as one to two hours. They certainly couldn't do it for free.

Tesco came closest with its Tesco Now service, which launched in the UK in 2017 and was quietly discontinued in 2019. Shoppers could have groceries delivered by third-party provider Quiqup within one to two hours, but they could only select 20 items from a range of 1,000 and for a minimum £5.99 fee. Amazon offered 20 times the range at no additional cost to the customer.

Tesco took a second shot at rapid delivery in 2021 with the launch of Whoosh, a one-hour delivery service being trialled in its Wolverhampton Willenhall Express store. Still though, shoppers must pay a fee of £5–7 per order, which may be necessary for the model to be viable but in our view is unlikely to go down well with shoppers who have come to expect convenience without a cost.

Amazon created Prime Now to 'bring a sense of magic to our customers … to give people the time that they need to live their life, rather than go around the town to visit the stores that they need for their grocery shop', explained Mariangela Marseglia, former Amazon Prime director and now heading up the retailer's Italy and Spain operations.

Prime Now went from product idea to launch in less than four months. It started out covering just one zip code in Manhattan because Amazon wanted to perfect the customer experience before rolling it out and Marseglia believed that if Prime Now could work in Manhattan, it would work in any other city. In December 2014, Amazon's first Prime Now order, which was for a video game aptly called Rush, came in at 8:51. By 9:00, the item was picked and packed and by 10:01 it was delivered to the customer.

Christmas Eve is one of Prime Now's most popular days, given Amazon's unique ability to cater to the 'crisis' shopping mission. A customer in Manchester, England placed an order for jewellery, women's perfume and a PlayStation console at 10pm one Christmas Eve and had it delivered by

11pm. Amazon is not only satisfying customers but perhaps saving some marriages in the process!

The two other shopping missions that Amazon learned to better cater for through Prime Now were gifting and top-up grocery, the latter of which is becoming more popular in markets such as the UK. In order to cater to the 'for tonight' shopping mission, Amazon in recent years has pushed its cut-off times to later in the day. In some UK postcodes, shoppers can order as late as 4pm and still have their order arrive that evening.

We'll discuss the mechanics behind Amazon's rapid delivery offerings later in the book, but for now it's important to understand the immediate impact that Prime Now had at Amazon and on the wider market. Within a year of its Manhattan launch, Prime Now was rolled out to over 30 cities – primarily in North America but also London, Milan and Tokyo. By 2016, Prime Now was running in more than 50 cities in nine countries around the globe. It was even used as a vehicle for new market entry; in 2017, Amazon launched in Singapore with Prime Now.

Of all of Amazon's grocery services thus far, Prime Now has hands down been the most disruptive. The price wars have been replaced by the time wars, with many supermarkets around the globe now scrambling to offer not just same-day delivery but increasingly delivery in one hour or less. This has had an impact on even the most advanced online grocery markets like the UK. Despite holding a negligible share of the British grocery sector, Amazon has been a phenomenal catalyst for change when it comes to delivery speed. So how have competitors responded?

- Tesco rolled out same-day delivery nationwide, in addition to its one-hour delivery experiments previously mentioned;
- Sainsburys introduced Chop Chop, a one-hour delivery service, to 50 stores across 20 UK cities;[32]
- Ocado rolled out micro customer fulfilment centres to support the growth of its Zoom one-hour delivery service;
- Waitrose, the Co-op, Aldi, Marks & Spencer and Amazon-owned Whole Foods Market have partnered with food delivery app Deliveroo (in which Amazon has a minority stake);
- Morrisons and Booths have hopped on the Amazon bandwagon;
- We've also seen the emergence of on-demand grocery providers (Weezy, Zapp, Jiffy, Getir, Dija, Fancy, Gorillas) which make even Amazon look like a laggard by delivering groceries in 15 minutes or less.

The UK grocers, we believe, were broadly reluctant to offer same-day delivery prior to Amazon's incursion, as a) shoppers weren't crying out for it and b) it added unnecessary cost and complexity. But Amazon let the genie out of the bottle and now, particularly in the wake of the pandemic, there is no putting it back.

As Amazon so often does, it ignited a new trend in rapid delivery, altering shopping behaviour and expectations to such an extent that some competitors have begun turning to Amazon's very own infrastructure in a bid to stay relevant. It's not just Morrisons and Booths in the UK that sell via Prime Now; Amazon has inked similar supply deals with many national and independent grocers around the world including Dia in Spain and Monoprix in France. Meanwhile, a long-standing supply agreement with US natural food retailer Sprouts was unsurprisingly terminated in 2018 after the Whole Foods acquisition – Sprouts teamed up with Instacart instead.

At the moment, these partnerships are essential for Amazon because, despite their many innovations, Amazon struggles to be perceived as a credible food destination. What good is the infrastructure without a compelling range of stuff? These supply deals, and the Whole Foods acquisition which we'll come on to shortly, give Amazon instant brand recognition and credibility in the competitive grocery category and, crucially, allow Amazon to learn more about how to sell food online.

But this brings up an important point. If Amazon's plan is to differentiate in grocery as it does in non-food – through product choice and convenience – then it needs to take on a host role. It needs to be the gateway to other retailers and brands; it's the marketplace, the infrastructure. In non-food, we're seeing more and more retailers succumb to Amazon's platform because of its undeniable reach. In theory, Amazon could have done the same in grocery – but then it bought Whole Foods Market. At some point, it will need to decide whether it wants to be the supermarket or the marketplace.

Notes

1 Stone, B (2013) *The Everything Store: Jeff Bezos and the age of Amazon*, Bantam Press, London.
2 Kowitt, Beth (2018) How Amazon is using Whole Foods in a bid for total retail domination, *Fortune*, 21 May. Available from: http://fortune.com/longform/amazon-groceries-fortune-500/ (archived at https://perma.cc/BQ8A-L4WS) [Last accessed 19/6/2018].

3 Harris, Briony (2017) Which countries buy the most groceries online? *World Economic Forum*, 6 December. Available from: https://www.weforum.org/agenda/2017/12/south-koreans-buy-the-most-groceries-online-by-far/ (archived at https://perma.cc/ZP7V-UZG3) [Last accessed 19/6/2018].

4 Bowman, Jeremy (2018) Walmart thinks you'll pay $10 for grocery delivery, *The Motley Fool*, 18 March. Available from: https://www.fool.com/investing/2018/03/18/walmart-thinks-youll-pay-10-for-grocery-delivery.aspx (archived at https://perma.cc/JCV7-7RRL) [Last accessed 19/6/2018].

5 Redman, Russell (2021) Online grocery shopping grows amid 'pandemic-induced channel stickiness', *Supermarket News*, 24 May. Available from: https://www.supermarketnews.com/online-retail/online-grocery-shopping-grows-amid-pandemic-induced-channel-stickiness (archived at https://perma.cc/63XP-T77R) [Last accessed 20/6/2021].

6 Weise, Karen and Conger, Kate (2020) Gaps in Amazon's response as virus spreads to more than 50 warehouses, *The New York Times*, 5 April. Available from: https://www.nytimes.com/2020/04/05/technology/coronavirus-amazon-workers.html (archived at https://perma.cc/T45Y-QMCZ) [Last accessed 20/6/2021].

7 eMarketer editors (2021) In 2021, online grocery sales will surpass $100 billion, *eMarketer*, 24 February. Available from: https://www.emarketer.com/content/2021-online-grocery-sales-will-surpass-100-billion (archived at https://perma.cc/YZ9R-E2UL) [Last accessed 20/6/2021].

8 Walmart (2017) Thomson Reuters Streetevents edited transcript WMT – Wal-Mart Stores Inc 2017 Investment Community Meeting, 10 October. Available from: https://cdn.corporate.walmart.com/ea/31/4aa1027b4be6818f1a65ed5c293a/wmt-usq-transcript-2017-10-10.pdf (archived at https://perma.cc/AJ3W-MYZH) [Last accessed 19/6/2018].

9 Walmart (2017) Thomson Reuters Streetevents edited transcript WMT – Wal-Mart Stores Inc 2017 Investment Community Meeting, 10 October. Available from: https://cdn.corporate.walmart.com/ea/31/4aa1027b4be6818f1a65ed5c293a/wmt-usq-transcript-2017-10-10.pdf (archived at https://perma.cc/AJ3W-MYZH) [Last accessed 19/6/2018].

10 Wilkinson, Sue (2017) How my weekly grocery shopping habits relate to U.S. grocery shopper trends, *Food Marketing Institute*, 25 July. Available from: https://www.fmi.org/blog/view/fmi-blog/2017/07/25/how-my-weekly-grocery-shopping-habits-relate-to-u.s.-grocery-shopper-trends (archived at https://perma.cc/EB8S-PKTX) [Last accessed 19/6/2018].

11 Kowitt, Beth (2018) How Amazon is using Whole Foods in a bid for total retail domination, *Fortune*, 21 May. Available from: http://fortune.com/longform/amazon-groceries-fortune-500/ (archived at https://perma.cc/BQ8A-L4WS) [Last accessed 19/6/2018].

12 Ibid.

13 Ibid.

14 Burke, Molly (2021) Addicted to Amazon: Habits of daily Amazon shoppers, Jungle Scout blog, 18 March. Available from: https://www.junglescout.com/blog/addicted-to-amazon/ (archived at https://perma.cc/QZ6P-JREX) [Last accessed 20/6/2021].

15 Kowitt, Beth (2018) How Amazon is using Whole Foods in a bid for total retail domination, *Fortune*, 21 May. Available from: http://fortune.com/longform/amazon-groceries-fortune-500/ (archived at https://perma.cc/BQ8A-L4WS) [Last accessed 19/6/2018].

16 Bensinger, Greg (2015) Rebuilding history's biggest dot-com bust, *Wall Street Journal*, 12 January. Available from: https://www.wsj.com/articles/rebuilding-historys-biggest-dot-come-bust-1421111794 (archived at https://perma.cc/P2BZ-9XM2) [Last accessed 19/6/2018].

17 Anonymous (2001) What Webvan could have learned from Tesco, *Knowledge at Wharton*, 10 October. Available from: http://knowledge.wharton.upenn.edu/article/what-webvan-could-have-learned-from-tesco/ (archived at https://perma.cc/3GYW-6UND) [Last accessed 19/6/2018].

18 Ibid.

19 Bluestein, Adam (2013) Beyond Webvan: MyWebGrocer turns supermarkets virtual, *Bloomberg*, 17 January. Available from: https://www.bloomberg.com/news/articles/2013-01-17/beyond-webvan-mywebgrocer-turns-supermarkets-virtual (archived at https://perma.cc/9VJS-9N6K) [Last accessed 19/6/2018].

20 Anonymous (2001) What Webvan could have learned from Tesco, *Knowledge at Wharton*, 10 October. Available from: http://knowledge.wharton.upenn.edu/article/what-webvan-could-have-learned-from-tesco/ (archived at https://perma.cc/3GYW-6UND) [Last accessed 19/6/2018].

21 Barr, Alistair (2013) From the ashes of Webvan, Amazon builds a grocery business, *Reuters*, 16 June. Available from: https://www.reuters.com/article/amazon-webvan-idUSL2N0EO1FS20130616 (archived at https://perma.cc/7Y9Y-G565) [Last accessed 19/6/2018].

22 Ocado website. Available from: http://www.ocadogroup.com/who-we-are/our-story-so-far.aspx (archived at https://perma.cc/X4AZ-UTEK) [Last accessed 19/6/2018].

23 Barr, Alistair (2013) From the ashes of Webvan, Amazon builds a grocery business, *Reuters*, 16 June. Available from: https://www.reuters.com/article/amazon-webvan-idUSL2N0EO1FS20130616 (archived at https://perma.cc/7Y9Y-G565) [Last accessed 19/6/2018].

24 Amazon press release (1999) Amazon.com announces minority investment in HomeGrocer.com, *Amazon*, 18 May. Available from: http://phx.corporate-ir.net/phoenix.zhtml?c=176060&p=irol-newsArticle&ID=502934 (archived at https://perma.cc/2C9Q-SJZC) [Last accessed 19/6/2018].

25 Barr, Alistair (2013) From the ashes of Webvan, Amazon builds a grocery business, *Reuters*, 16 June. Available from: https://www.reuters.com/article/amazon-webvan-idUSL2N0EO1FS20130616 (archived at https://perma.cc/7Y9Y-G565) [Last accessed 19/6/2018].

26 Kowitt, Beth (2018) How Amazon is using Whole Foods in a bid for total retail domination. *Fortune*, 21/5. Available from: http://fortune.com/longform/amazon-groceries-fortune-500/ (archived at https://perma.cc/BQ8A-L4WS) [Last accessed 19/6/2018].

27 Anonymous (2016) AmazonFresh expands to Chicago, Dallas, *Progressive Grocer*, 26 October. Available from: https://progressivegrocer.com/amazonfresh-expands-chicago-dallas (archived at https://perma.cc/7GMD-E22Z) [Last accessed 29/6/18].

28 Amazon press release (2007) Amazon.com's grocery store launches new Subscribe & Save feature allowing automatic fulfillment of most popular items, *Amazon*, 15 May. Available from: http://phx.corporate-ir.net/phoenix.zhtml?c=176060&p=irol-newsArticle&ID=1000549 (archived at https://perma.cc/PYY3-CTU2) [Last accessed 29/6/18].

29 Nickelsburg, Monica (2020) Documents unearthed by Congress offer new window into Amazon's war against one-time rival, Geekwire, 30 July. Available from: https://www.geekwire.com/2020/hearing-documents-reveal-amazons-aggressive-strategy-beat-diapers-com/ (archived at https://perma.cc/Y4G8-334K) [Last accessed 20/6/2021].

30 Nickelsburg, Monica (2020) Documents unearthed by Congress offer new window into Amazon's war against one-time rival, Geekwire, 30 July. Available from: https://www.geekwire.com/2020/hearing-documents-reveal-amazons-aggressive-strategy-beat-diapers-com/ (archived at https://perma.cc/Y4G8-334K) [Last accessed 20/6/2021].

31 Investigation of competition in digital markets. Majority staff report and recommendations (2020) Subcommittee on Antitrust, Commercial and Administrative Law of the Committee of the Judiciary Available from: https://fm.cnbc.com/applications/cnbc.com/resources/editorial files/2020/10/06/investigation_of_competition_in_digital_markets_majority_ staff_report_and_recommendations.pdf (archived at https://perma.cc/ZS8P-9PRZ) [Last accessed 20/6/2021].

32 Macadam, Dan (2018) Can supermarkets really deliver in a day? BBC, 4 February. Available from: https://www.bbc.co.uk/news/business-42777284 (archived at https://perma.cc/W66U-FNGB) [Last accessed 29/6/18].

09

Supermarkets: a brave new era

'I don't want people goin' away, thinkin' that nothin's gonna change around here. 'Cause things are gonna change. There's just no question about that.'
John Mackey, Whole Foods Market CEO and Co-Founder, 2017[1]

Recognizing that online and offline are no longer mutually exclusive, retailers are now racing to equilibrium. But the big question is, who will get there first? Legacy bricks and mortar chains believe they can successfully crack e-commerce before the online players figure out how to run physical shops. Amazon begs to differ.

The tech giant's $13.4 billion acquisition of Whole Foods Market in 2017 was a pivotal moment for the grocery industry and a sign that after years of dabbling with physical retail, Amazon was ready to commit. Of course, Amazon doesn't just run Whole Foods Market stores these days but it is increasingly building out its own portfolio of supermarkets.

A reflection of the retailer's constant experimentation, it can be difficult to keep up with Amazon's bricks and mortar grocery strategy. Amazon Fresh stores in the US (see Figure 9.1) are different from the Amazon Fresh stores in the UK. And that's not to be confused with Amazonfresh, its online grocery offering. Meanwhile, Amazon Go Grocery has now been rebranded as Amazon Fresh. But we mean the Amazon Fresh in the US, not the UK (that one is more like an Amazon Go).

Amazon has many strengths but branding is not one.

Nonetheless, Amazon is becoming a formidable threat to grocers at home and abroad. In this chapter, we'll explore Amazon's blockbuster acquisition

FIGURE 9.1   The first Amazon Fresh supermarket opened in Los Angeles in 2020

of Whole Foods Market and how Amazon's current bricks and mortar experiments will redefine the supermarket for the 21st-century shopper.

Applying its thirst for invention to the supermarket sector

Based on what we've covered in the book so far, the acquisition of a grocery store operator should come as no great surprise. Just prior to the acquisition announcement, we predicted that, 'without actively acquiring another retailer, [Amazon is] unlikely to have a meaningful impact on the grocery sector for at least another five years'. Weeks later, the Whole Foods deal was announced (see Figure 9.2).

Immediate reaction in the industry was mixed. On the one hand, Amazon's move into the supermarket space would be one of disruption, requiring legacy grocers to significantly up their game and naturally exposing some losers along the way. But on the other hand, the deal was also the utmost validation that bricks and mortar retail has a future. Perhaps even a bright one.

Investors seemed to agree. Following the announcement, Amazon's market cap appreciated by $15.6 billion – about $2 billion more than it paid for the supermarket chain. Amazon essentially picked up Whole Foods for free, while the rest of the supermarket sector lost $37 billion in market value.[2]

FIGURE 9.2 The future of retail is clicks and mortar: the Whole Foods Market acquisition was Amazon's most significant move into physical retailing

Prior to the acquisition, three things were very clear: 1) Amazon's wider appetite for bricks and mortar was growing; 2) without physical stores, Amazon would always be underrepresented in grocery; and 3) Amazon had the potential to revolutionize the customer experience.

At the time, the retailer had been quietly experimenting with two new grocery formats in its Seattle hometown: its checkout-free Amazon Go stores, which we'll come on to shortly, and AmazonFresh Pickup, a service that allows Prime members to drive up to a designated site, untethered to a supermarket, and have their groceries brought out to their cars. On a global scale, AmazonFresh Pickup wasn't exactly revolutionary – French grocers had been operating these 'Drive' concepts for years – but in the US, prior to the pandemic-related explosion of curbside pickup, the idea was still relatively novel. In fact, Walmart was the only retailer actively testing such a service around the same time.

AmazonFresh Pickup was the most logical extension into store-based retailing for Amazon. The retail giant brought its rapid fulfilment capabilities

FIGURE 9.3 Amazon disrupted the convenience store sector with its first checkout-free store, Amazon Go

to bear, putting its own spin on the concept through its established payment process and even using licence plate recognition technology to speed up waiting times. Shoppers can collect their groceries as quickly as 15 minutes after placing an order. Several years after launch, AmazonFresh Pickup is still running today but unlikely to move beyond trial phase in our view. Instead, Amazon will have incorporated the learnings from this concept into its wider bricks and mortar estate. This is particularly important now given that curbside pickup is poised for continued growth in a post-pandemic world.

Although Amazon was always going to have to expand into physical stores, it was never going to slap its logo on a chain of run-of-the-mill supermarkets. The combination of Amazon's customer obsession and thirst for invention meant that the supermarket sector was about to get seriously disrupted. You can always count on Amazon to challenge the status quo and drastically enhance the customer experience, whether that's by delivering groceries to your car or getting rid of queues altogether. But this was just the beginning.

Why Whole Foods Market?

We believe Amazon's end game for grocery is as follows:

1 Democratize online grocery so customers can first and foremost shop on their terms, as they've grown accustomed to doing in general merchandise.

2 Use technology to take the chore out of grocery shopping. Amazon is uniquely positioned to make simplified and automatic-replenishment a reality for functional, routine-driven consumable categories, and will be particularly motivated to develop private label ranges here.

3 The instore experience will use technology to minimize friction during the navigation and payment parts of the shopping journey, while also enabling real-time, hyper-personalized recommendations and rewards. Being a part of the Amazon family takes Whole Foods from 'class dunce' to 'valedictorian', in the words of former Whole Foods' CEO John Mackey.[3]

4 Entire categories will be removed from the physical store, freeing up space for: 1) more emotive categories like fresh and prepared foods; 2) blended experiences – from cookery classes to co-working space; 3) click & collect / return counters; 4) online grocery fulfilment to cater to demand for same-day delivery.

5 Prime, as previously discussed, will underpin Amazon's grocery strategy. After all, the main incentive for Amazon's move into grocery is to reach shoppers weekly, locking them into its wider ecosystem.

With that in mind, particularly the points about freshness and utilizing stores as mini-fulfilment hubs, you can begin to understand why Amazon was attracted to Whole Foods Market. A strong emphasis on perishables, which account for more than two-thirds of the supermarket chain's sales, theatrical merchandising displays and renowned own-label ranges – including within the coveted fresh category – would compensate for Amazon's relative weaknesses. There had previously been rumours of Amazon acquiring a mass retailer like Target or BJ's Wholesale Club. But, in our view, Amazon needed a foodie business, not only to establish credibility in perishables but also because the lack of non-food in Whole Foods stores minimized the potential of range duplication.

Naturally, there was a clear overlap in target customer base, with both retailers having a strong hold among affluent, educated and often time-pressed consumers. In fact, Whole Foods might have done this a little too well – one of Amazon's first moves would be to address its 'Whole Paycheck' reputation by investing in lower prices. This would happen across the board, but with a particular emphasis on sweetening the deal for Prime members, as discussed in Chapter 5.

Whole Foods was also a good fit for Amazon because it had a national presence but it wasn't overstored – Amazon wanted several hundred outlets, not several thousand. This is important, not only because Amazon wants to grow grocery e-commerce sales, thereby lessening the need for physical space, but also because Whole Foods is really a giant test lab for Amazon. It helps to have a more focused, leaner store portfolio as Amazon experiments with pricing, merchandising and layout, iterating on the concept until it finally has a scalable format.

Crucially, Whole Foods is also well represented in urban areas. This means it adds not only a supplemental but a complementary resource to its last-mile infrastructure, providing it with yet another platform from which to deliver groceries within a couple of hours. As we discussed in the last chapter, rapid delivery is one of Amazon's unique competitive advantages in grocery so it's no surprise that it aggressively rolled out this service across Whole Foods stores nationwide. When Amazon bought Whole Foods, it didn't just acquire 460 stores. It acquired 460 mini-warehouses.

But it's worth highlighting here that compared to its global peers, Amazon is behind the curve in this regard. In China, the promise of 30-minute delivery to customers within a three-kilometre radius is a key feature among other online-to-offline grocery concepts such as Alibaba's Hema and JD.com's 7fresh. Unlike Amazon, the Asian giants are moving organically into physical retail, building supermarkets from scratch to suit the modern consumer's needs.

The wake-up call

> 'When Amazon bought Whole Foods, what they did was they sent the signal to the entire grocery/retail landscape that Amazon was coming.'
> **Apoorva Mehta, CEO of Instacart[4]**

Amazon's pace of innovation may be relentless – every week it appears to be disrupting a new sector – but when it comes to implementation, Amazon is notoriously methodical. The entire industry is now watching with bated breath to see if the retail colossus can do one of the most fundamental things in retail – operate stores. Amazon is happy to take its time, quietly experimenting and tinkering with various bricks and mortar concepts as it tackles the steep learning curve that is grocery.

The acquisition meanwhile was a wake-up call for incumbent supermarkets, not only to ramp up their own e-commerce capabilities but also to digitally enhance their store base. To do that, most retailers have had to look externally.

The impetus Ocado was waiting for

Two weeks after the Whole Foods deal, Ocado CEO Tim Steiner was all smiles at the retailer's half-year results meeting in London. One of their biggest threats was also their biggest opportunity. When asked his thoughts on the Whole Foods deal, Steiner noted that it would simply spur on demand for online grocery, which would ultimately help them to grow their business. 'Grocery retailing is changing and we are ideally positioned to enable other retailers to achieve their online aspirations.'[5] Steiner's message echoed that of Instacart CEO Apoorva Mehta who, the same year, called the Amazon-Whole Foods deal a 'blessing in disguise'.[6]

For years, Ocado had been promising investors it would secure an international partner for its grocery delivery technology, Ocado Smart Platform. After missing its first self-imposed deadline of a 2015 announcement, investors began to lose patience as the months and then years rolled on. Perhaps Ocado's ambitions to transition from retailer to global technology provider were inflated?

Ocado finally signed its first long-awaited deal with France's Casino Groupe in 2017 – less than six months after Amazon's Whole Foods acquisition. The agreement enables Casino to have exclusive rights to use Ocado's robotics, online technology and delivery software in France. Since then, Ocado has announced a flurry of deals with global retailers including Sobeys (Canada), ICA (Sweden), Kroger (US), Bon Preu Group (Spain), AEON (Japan) and Coles (Australia). Acquiring Whole Foods cemented Amazon's commitment to the grocery category, acting as an impetus for supermarkets around the world to invest in their own digital offerings.

What is more, Steiner believes that the pandemic has *permanently* accelerated the shift to e-commerce, which could create another opportunity for Ocado – to move away from licensing its tech and perhaps go it alone overseas. 'The next five, 10 years, you may well find that we decide to run a retail business outside the UK,' Steiner said in 2021.[7]

In the meantime, however, Amazon's grocery onslaught has certainly created strange bedfellows. While buying alliances aren't unheard of in Europe, it was shocking to see two of the world's largest food retailers – Tesco and Carrefour – join forces in 2018. The strategic alliance was scrapped in 2021, but some analysts believe that a future merger could still be on the cards.

Tech partnerships are now in vogue, with Google and Microsoft in particular leading the anti-Amazon alliances. Retail acquisitions are also ripe, designed to either keep up with or maintain distance from Amazon. Walmart alone has gobbled up – and spat out – a number of digitally native brands in recent years, from the now defunct marketplace Jet.com to virtual fitting room company Zeekit.

> 'I would agree that for a lot of retailers, whilst they've put up a great fight, ultimately working with the likes of Amazon is probably a good way to tackle the digital space.'
> **Marcus East, former Marks & Spencer executive[8]**

Some are even opting for Team Amazon (see Table 9.1). As we've touched on throughout the book, more retailers are turning to Amazon for their scale and expertise, risking the Trojan Horse element of such partnerships in return for a rapid upscaling of their digital offering. Others, meanwhile, are

TABLE 9.1   Co-opetition examples: how retail brands lean on Amazon

Concept	Retail partners
Marketplace	Under Armour, The Children's Place, Chico's FAS, Adidas, Calvin Klein
Collection lockers	Casino/Monoprix, Rite Aid, 7-Eleven, Stein Mart, Save-A-Lot, Shell, Repsol, Morrisons, Co-op
Rapid delivery (formerly 'Prime Now')	Morrisons, Booths, Dia, Casino/Monoprix, Bio c'Bon
Alexa integration	Ahold Delhaize, Ocado, Morrisons, Dominos, Gousto, JD Sports, AO.com, B&H Photo, Woot
Amazon instore pickup and/ or returns	Kohls, Next, Rite Aid, GNC, Health Mart
Amazon-powered stores	Tuft & Needle, Calvin Klein
Collaboration on exclusive product/service	Best Buy (exclusive line of smart TVs); Tuft & Needle (exclusive mattress)
Amazon Pop Up (formerly 'presented by Amazon')	Featured brands include Mattel, DOVE, Samsung, Hover-1, Nordic Track, Stasher, Seventh Generation, Nature's Way, Burt's Bees, Brita, Green Toys, re-spin by Halle Berry, and more

SOURCE   Author research; Amazon

adamant that teaming up with Amazon is not in their playbook. 'We hate Amazon,' said Tarsem Dhaliwal, MD of UK supermarket chain Iceland, in 2018. 'They'll bully us and do horrible things to us. They'll use us; we don't want anything to do with them.'[9]

Goodbye Whole Foods, hello Amazon Fresh?

It's clear that although Amazon needed to buy its way into the grocery sector, its real passion lies in building an experience from the ground up. An experience that has the potential to revolutionize the way we shop for food by removing friction points and seamlessly merging physical and digital worlds.

It's also clear that despite Amazon's best efforts, Whole Foods Market just doesn't have mainstream appeal. Amazon will have learned a lot from

Whole Foods over the past several years, but if it wants to make serious inroads into the grocery sector, it needs to offer customers more choice in formats. It's a delicate balance that most supermarkets are familiar with – running multiple fascias targeted at different shopping missions without cannibalizing their own sales.

Amazon Go has been its most disruptive format to date, and as of 2021, there were approximately 30 stores in operation (see Figure 9.3). As we've stated previously, we believe there is huge potential for these checkout-less stores, particularly in the travel retail sector, but they do have limitations. The stores are tiny (they average 1,200–2,300 square feet) and are therefore heavily geared towards a top-up/convenience shop.

During the COVID crisis, while most retailers scrambled to keep shelves stocked, Amazon launched new formats – or as a 2021 Bloomberg article succinctly put it: 'Amazon quietly began building a grocery chain during [the] pandemic.'

The Amazon Go Grocery fascia debuted at two stores in early 2020. The larger store was approximately six times the size of the original Amazon Go and with 5,000 SKUs, it offered about five times the range. Shoppers could still 'Just Walk Out', bypassing the checkout altogether.

Later that year, however, came a more significant launch: Amazon Fresh, its first-ever full-sized grocery store. 'Fresh stores are more of an all-in strategy for Amazon. A very strategic, long-term play,' a former Amazon employee told Bloomberg. Ranging in size from 25,000–45,000 square feet, the stores look like a bog-standard American supermarket but with some high-tech features. Most stores do not feature the Just Walk Out technology (difficult to scale although Amazon has now begun to trial this); instead the Fresh stores allow customers to skip the checkout line by using a Dash Cart. Shoppers place their bags directly in the smart cart, sign in using their Fresh QR code in the Amazon app, do their shopping and then exit through the Dash Cart lane to automatically complete their payment.

There are digital price tags as well as Echo Show devices throughout the store so shoppers can ask Alexa, rather than a store associate, which aisle the cereal is in. And naturally, the stores offer same-day delivery and pickup as well as a collection and package-less returns hub for items purchased from Amazon.com. Fresh stores offer competitive prices and more traditional brands like Kellogg's, Kraft and Coca-Cola, in addition to a growing portfolio of Amazon's own brands, as we'll explore in the next chapter.

Let's not forget that Amazon has the power of data to influence decisions, not just online but increasingly in the bricks and mortar world as well. For example, Amazon analyzed the density of Prime members per zip code in order to determine where to locate the first Fresh stores. Several were former Toys R Us locations.

So is this it? Is Amazon's vision of the supermarket of the future coming to fruition? Aside from a few high-tech touches, Amazon Fresh might not seem all that different from a traditional grocery store and perhaps, dare we say, a bit underwhelming to some. But if Amazon is going to scale a grocery format, it has to balance operational efficiencies with customer experience.

Amazon Fresh cuts out the main supermarket friction points – finding and paying for groceries – and the ability to use the store as a fulfilment hub will be hugely relevant to post-pandemic shoppers. The counterargument here is that both of these 'differentiators' are replicable – and legacy grocery stores are catching up quickly.

But Amazon's got one crucial thing up its sleeve: Prime. We've said from day one that Amazon's grocery strategy would be underpinned by Prime. Technology may be imitated, and fulfilment options replicated, but the ability to acquire and retain over 200 million loyal shoppers around the globe is not something that can be easily matched. At least not overnight. Amazon will continue to refine its grocery strategy until it finds the right model for growth – and you can bet that it will be centred around Prime.

Notes

1 McGregor, Jena (2017) Five telling things the Whole Foods CEO said about the Amazon deal in an employee town hall, *Washington Post*, 20 June. Available from: https://www.washingtonpost.com/news/on-leadership/wp/2017/06/20/five-telling-things-the-whole-foods-ceo-said-about-the-amazon-deal-in-an-employee-town-hall/?utm_term=.1e861128178f (archived at https://perma.cc/C5H6-QM2N) [Last accessed 11/7/2018].

2 Meyer, Robinson (2018) How to fight Amazon (before you turn 29), *The Atlantic*, July/August issue. Available from: https://www.theatlantic.com/magazine/archive/2018/07/lina-khan-antitrust/561743/ [Last accessed 11/7/2018].

3 McGregor, Jena (2017) Five telling things the Whole Foods CEO said about the Amazon deal in an employee town hall, *Washington Post*, 20 June. Available from: https://www.washingtonpost.com/news/on-leadership/wp/2017/06/20/ five-telling-things-the-whole-foods-ceo-said-about-the-amazon-deal-in-an-employee-town-hall/?utm_term=.1e861128178f (archived at https://perma.cc/ T2LE-LRJ5) [Last accessed 11/7/2018].

4 Levy, Nat (2017) How Amazon's $13.7B purchase of Whole Foods is a 'blessing in disguise' for Instacart, *Geekwire*, 10 October. Available from: https://www. geekwire.com/2017/amazons-13-7b-purchase-whole-foods-blessing-disguise-instacart/ (archived at https://perma.cc/LDE5-4H3A) [Last accessed 11/7/2018].

5 Rovnick, Naomi (2017) Ocado dismisses fears of increased competition from Amazon, *Financial Times*, 5 July. Available from: https://www.ft.com/content/ f48fecac-6151-11e7-8814-0ac7eb84e5f1 (archived at https://perma.cc/8YNN-ABA6) [Last accessed 9/7/2018].

6 Levy, Nat (2017) How Amazon's $13.7B purchase of Whole Foods is a 'blessing in disguise' for Instacart, *Geekwire*, 10 October. Available from: https://www. geekwire.com/2017/amazons-13-7b-purchase-whole-foods-blessing-disguise-instacart/ (archived at https://perma.cc/PGH2-BUQY) [Last accessed 11/7/2018].

7 Eley, Jonathan and Bradshaw, Tim (2021) Ocado weighs retail opportunities beyond the UK, *Financial Times*, 31 May. Available from: https://www.ft.com/ content/e0e1e9a2-b617-45a6-8dfe-06feeff0b6de [Last accessed 20/6/2021].

8 Dawkins, David (2018) Marks and Spencer told to team up with Amazon to save retailer as stores close, *Express*, 20 June. Available from: https://www. express.co.uk/finance/city/977070/amazon-uk-marks-and-spencer-m-and-s-high-street-online (archived at https://perma.cc/S8GH-TDXN) [Last accessed 11/7/2018].

9 Key, Alys (2018) Iceland Food rules out deal with Amazon as Food Warehouse attracts new customers, City AM, 15 June. Available from: http://www.cityam. com/287618/iceland-sales-heat-up-food-warehouse-attracts-new-customers (archived at https://perma.cc/5YFQ-E5VV) [Last accessed 11/7/2018].

10

A private label juggernaut:
here comes the squeeze

Spotted Zebra. Revly. Stone & Beam. Solimo. Recognize these brands? Probably not.

Amazon has been quietly building up its own portfolio of brands, yet only a handful bear the retailer's name. As of 2020, the retailer offered nearly 23,000 products from over 100 different private brands, more than triple the number of items available in 2018.[1]

> 'Your margin is my opportunity.'
> **Jeff Bezos[2]**

So why the big push into private label? To start, it will help Amazon inch closer to sustained profitability. With its own brands, Amazon can widen margins without raising prices. This is particularly important as Amazon moves deeper into low-margin categories like fresh groceries and other fast-moving consumer goods. Own brands provide shoppers with more choice and greater value – essentially more bang for their buck. These ranges also help to sweeten the deal for Prime members, who benefit from exclusive discounts on and, at times, exclusive access to Amazon's private label ranges.

But perhaps most significantly, own brands give Amazon greater leverage over suppliers. Let's point out here that this is a tried and tested strategy and by no means unique to Amazon, but this is also where things get murky since more than half of Amazon's sales come from third-party products.

With the sheer amount of customer data the tech giant holds, no one is better positioned to understand customer needs and then develop ranges specifically for them.

Amazon's unique dual role as marketplace and retailer has come under increased scrutiny in recent years. Is Amazon playing by its own rules or is it, in fact, just acting like any other retailer? We'll explore this further, but first it's important to understand the context of own label development in the US and why adoption has been slow relative to other markets.

The post-great recession mindset

Americans have historically had a strong affinity for national brands. The country's largest retailer Walmart regularly refers to itself as a House of Brands, and many household products today still go by their brand name – Kleenex, Tupperware, Q-tips, Band-Aids, Saran Wrap, etc.

Yet as far back as half a century ago, retail analysts like Victor Lebow were warning retailers of the dangers of product sameness. In a *Journal of Retailing* essay in 1955, Lebow wrote:

> Quite a few studies have shown that a large proportion of shoppers, when questioned, cannot tell which of several competing variety chain stores, or supermarkets, they have just left. But this sameness of their merchandise, in stores that look like twins, provides the opportunity for different merchandise in stores that look different, individual, with a character of their own.[3]

Lebow was well ahead of his time: it would take over half a century for his advice to take hold. Private label in the US grocery sector has historically been slow to catch on due to a combination of market fragmentation and, up until relatively recently, the lack of grocery discounter presence. You only need to look across the Atlantic to see the opportunity for private label when a market is highly concentrated and swarming with Aldi and Lidl stores; in the UK and Switzerland, for example, own label can account for half of all grocery sales. In the US, however, own label products were traditionally the poor relation to the national brand, often confined to the bottom shelf. Cheap, but not cheerful. As such, growth of own label products was previously limited to periods of economic uncertainty. At the first sign of an upturn, shoppers would quickly abandon private labels and trade back up to national brands.

But something interesting happened at the end of the Great Recession in 2009. This time, many shoppers didn't revert to their old ways; habits seemed to be permanently altered. Frugality went from being shamed to celebrated and the notion of 'smart shopping' took off. So, what was different this time compared with previous recessions? Technology adoption.

This was the beginning of the smartphone era – a technology development that would go on to become all-encompassing and, for many, indispensable. By the end of the Great Recession, consumers had access to information right at their fingertips, creating an unprecedented level of price transparency and therefore empowerment.

Meanwhile, a combination of media fragmentation and supermarket consolidation resulted in a shift in power away from national brands, making it more challenging for them to connect with customers. This was fertile ground for private label development. Many supermarkets saw this as an opportunity to deepen customer relationships by enhancing the quality and messaging behind their own ranges, taking them from generic knock-offs to brands in their own rights. At the same time, the notoriously less brand-loyal Millennials came of age during the Great Recession, creating additional opportunities for retailers to expand into new, higher-margin categories like organics and meal kits.

Amazon's private label ambitions

'Since the first store brands launched in the 19th century, customers have benefited from the value they offer.'
Amazon, 2020[4]

Amazon also recognized this change in behaviour and in 2009 launched its AmazonBasics range. At the time, Amazon had already begun dabbling in private label with a handful of other lines such as Pinzon kitchen gadgets, Strathwood outdoor furniture, Pike Street bath and home products, and Denali tools. But this was the first time Amazon would attach its brand to a product (hardware aside) so it made sense to start out in a low-risk, commoditized category and one that would complement its core product range – electronic accessories.

Priced approximately 30 per cent lower than major brands, the AmazonBasics line was initially limited to accessories like cables, chargers and batteries. But within just a few short years, the brand accounted for nearly one-third of Amazon's battery sales, outselling national brands like Energizer and Duracell.[5] Less than a decade after launch, AmazonBasics had been expanded to dozens of categories – home, furniture, pet supplies, luggage, sports, etc – and today is one of the top-selling brands on Amazon's platform.

This should hardly come as a surprise. Amazon is, as discussed throughout the book, in the enviable position of being the starting point for many product searches. From those searches, and indeed purchases themselves, Amazon can glean an incredible amount of insight into what shoppers want, allowing it to identify and prioritize own label investment in specific categories.

Keith Anderson, SVP of Strategy and Insights at Profitero explains:

> There's a huge difference in the intent signalled in searches on retailer sites versus searches on Google or traditional search engines. What we often find is the context of those searches on a retailer site is much more detailed. It tends to be product benefit or characteristic focused, and Amazon has the potential to analyse what people are searching for and either are finding, or maybe just as importantly, not finding in the selection that's available on the site.[6]

Writing its own rules

So, Amazon already has a head start when it comes to understanding private label requirements. Another massive competitive advantage? Visibility.

In a physical setting, brands buy shelf space to guarantee exposure to the customer. The supermarket then tends to position its own label 'national brand equivalent' alongside the brand leader in a given category. The retailer's goal is to give the best possible placement to its own higher-margin goods for the highest chance of conversion.

The same principle applies to a virtual shelf. For many brands today, there's nothing more important than visibility on the world's most powerful retail platform. The problem is Amazon shoppers don't tend to search by brand; about 70 per cent[7] of all word searches made on the site are for generic items (ie shaving cream rather than Gillette). And for these unbranded or attribute-led searches, Amazon is becoming increasingly comfortable steering shoppers towards its own label items.

Brands can, of course, pay for placement on Amazon – and this is becoming a big business. As we discussed in Chapter 4, as more brands cram onto Amazon's marketplace, the need for visibility becomes greater. And this is where things get muddled – the brands in competition with Amazon's private labels are the same brands paying Amazon to *sell* and, increasingly, *advertise* on its platform. Amazon is the ultimate frenemy.

Advertising may be one of its newer business segments, but Amazon has major clout. And it continues to invest, for example by using deep learning models to show more relevant sponsored products. 'We continue to improve the relevancy of the ads being shown on the product detail pages. And we've seen rapid adoption of the video creative format for sponsored brands, among other things,' said Amazon CFO Brian Olsavsky in 2021.[8]

> 'Customers like our store brands – on average, they have higher customer review ratings, lower return rates, and higher repeat purchase rates than other comparable brands in our store.'
> **Amazon, 2020**[9]

Today, if you search for coffee on Amazon, the first thing you see at the top of the page is a banner ad sponsored by Folgers. But you only need to scroll down slightly to find Amazon's equivalent 'Featured from Our Brands' private label banner as well as other products from its AmazonFresh and Solimo ranges listed on the first page of search results. It's also common for Amazon's private label products to feature a badge denoting that the item is a best-seller, sponsored product or 'Amazon's Choice' (an algorithm-determined recommendation, originally developed for voice shopping via Alexa, based on the item being Prime-eligible, in stock and featuring a review rating of at least 4.0, among other criteria).

Amazon holds all the cards here. While generating revenue from digital advertising, it is simultaneously optimizing the placement of its private label products with the aim of maximizing the conversion of shoppers to its own brands. This is not unlike a brand paying a slotting fee to feature on a supermarket's shelf, only to find the private label equivalent sitting next to it. But here's where Amazon differs – customer reviews. Imagine a grocery shopper at the shelf, trying to decide between a trusted national brand like Heinz or

Coca-Cola and a less well-known own label. The shopper can see there is a cost advantage to buying the own label, but what's the quality like? Will it taste like the national brand? Will the kids turn their noses up at it?

Amazon can help to sway shoppers at this point thanks to its user-generated reviews – online but also increasingly instore through electronic shelf labels (ESL). If that same shopper can see that the own label item generates thousands of 4.5-star reviews, then they're probably going to feel more confident giving it a try. So, to build trust and awareness of its private label items, Amazon has been proactively utilizing its Amazon Vine programme to build up customer reviews of these new items. Under the invite-only scheme, Amazon's most active reviewers post opinions about new and pre-release items in exchange for free products. Although Vine is also open to first- and third-party vendors, Amazon certainly leverages it to nudge customers towards its private brands.

Amazon has to maintain a delicate balance between driving private label sales and giving customers what they want. But for brands and sellers, the gloves are well and truly off. Many have succumbed to selling on Amazon because of its undeniable reach, but as own label becomes a greater focus, so does Amazon's leverage.

And it's only going to get tougher for suppliers as voice shopping takes hold: Alexa produces just two search results. 'When it comes to voice search you go first position or you go home because beyond the first or second place there is no future', says Sebastien Szczepaniak, former Amazon executive who now heads up e-commerce at Nestlé.[10] We'll discuss how Alexa prioritizes search results in the coming chapters, but for now it's important to understand that in instances where the customer's shopping history is unknown, Alexa's recommendation will be an Amazon's Choice product.

There is, however, some good news for brands here. Voice works best when shoppers know exactly what they want, so if that brand loyalty already exists then Alexa will simply shorten the path to purchase and, crucially, remember the customer's preference for the next time.

At times, Amazon has resorted to more aggressive measures to drive private label conversions. For example, the retailer has run advertisements for its own label products on other brands' product detail pages and, in the past, Amazon has disabled the 'hot link' feature (that allows shoppers to quickly view alternatives) on its own brand baby wipes detail page.

Amazon has also used search to steer shoppers towards its own, higher-margin products, an approach that has proved controversial even internally. The retailer reportedly tinkered with its product-search system to give greater visibility to items that are more profitable for the company, which naturally includes its own brands. At one point, Amazon was running own label promotional spots that featured prominently in a user's search results. For example, a search for 'baby food pouches' would bring up a banner of Amazon's own label products under the tab 'Top Rated from Our Brands' at the very top of search results.

'When [proprietary data is] leveraged to promote their private label products, I can see how it would be perceived as unfair and even maybe predatory,' said former Amazon executive Andrea Leigh.[11] Unsurprisingly, this kind of behaviour has not gone unnoticed by lawmakers. For years now, US Senator Elizabeth Warren has been calling to break up big tech companies, claiming that the use of proprietary marketplaces like Amazon's ultimately limits competition.

Antitrust and 'internal competitors'

Surprisingly for Amazon, the retailer continues to pursue an old-school tactic – copycats. Amazon has produced cheaper clone versions of a number of branded items across a diverse range of categories – from bocce balls to pressure cookers and blackout blinds. We've come to expect Amazon to be tough on vendors, but this kind of behaviour doesn't feel like 'starting with the customer and working backwards'. We find it strange that Amazon, a retailer that is typically at the forefront of change and puts the customer at the heart of everything it does, would pursue a copycat strategy that risks devaluing its brand and eroding trust with shoppers. Customers are not exactly crying out for knock-offs. If anything, Amazon's ongoing issues with counterfeits and fake reviews on its site would be enough reason to steer clear of copycat brands.

Imitation is the sincerest form of flattery, at least for those premium and ethical brands that are more insulated from the threat of copycats. After Amazon unveiled a wool sneaker that looked 'strikingly similar' to Allbirds' own wool runner but for about half the price, Allbirds CEO Joey Zwillinger called on Jeff Bezos to 'please steal our approach to sustainability'.[12]

Now it's important that we point out here that Amazon is in many ways just acting like a, well, retailer. In fact, Amazon's chief competitor Walmart had its own Allbirds knockoff sneaker at one point, affectionately dubbed as 'Walbirds' by online reviewers. And Walmart is the goliath here – it generates around $80 billion in own label sales compared with Amazon's $3 billion.[13] In fact, private label products typically account for anywhere from 15 per cent to 90 per cent of a retailer's sales – Walmart falls on the low end of that spectrum (but makes up for it in volume), while an overwhelming majority of goods sold in limited-assortment supermarkets like Aldi and Trader Joe's are own label. Amazon is the outlier – only 1 per cent of all physical product sales come from private label goods.[14]

So what's all the fuss about? Why doesn't Walmart, a company twice the size of Amazon with a considerably larger private label business, get the same amount of negative publicity for its 'Walbirds' or other copycat products?

The difference is that Amazon has access to decades worth of detailed customer data which it can use to its advantage. Amazon can 'see everything about the demographic of the customer that likes [a particular product], which customers have purchased it, how many customers have searched and have not purchased, who clicked on a similar product so that they can serve a product next to it', said Jason Boyce, a former Amazon seller.[15]

According to the European Commission, Amazon knows 'the number of ordered and shipped units of products, the sellers' revenues on the marketplace, the number of visits to sellers' offers, data relating to shipping, to sellers' past performance, and other consumer claims on products, including the activated guarantees'.[16]

We would also highlight that, the 'Walbirds' example aside, when retailers create a product that mimics another brand, it tends to be in generic categories like cereal and laundry detergent. Amazon, however, is producing imitation versions of niche products created by smaller entrepreneurs, many of which rely on Amazon for their livelihood. As of 2020, Amazon had 2.3 million active third-party sellers on its marketplace worldwide and it is estimated that more than one-third of them rely on Amazon as their sole source of income.[17]

'Many big tech companies own a marketplace – where buyers and sellers transact – while also participating on the marketplace. This can create a conflict of interest that undermines competition. Amazon crushes small companies by copying the goods they sell on the Amazon Marketplace and then selling its own branded version.'
US Senator Elizabeth Warren, 2019[18]

When copycatting backfires

San Francisco-based camera and travel manufacturer Peak Design had been selling its 'Everyday Sling' on Amazon for several years when, in late 2020, Amazon unveiled a near-identical version called the 'AmazonBasics Everyday Sling'. In an attempt to raise awareness of Amazon's tactics, the seller released a tongue-in-cheek video titled 'A Tale of Two Slings: Peak Design and Amazon Basics'.

'It looks suspiciously like the Peak Design Everyday Sling but you don't have to pay for all those needless bells and whistles like years of research and development, recycled Bluesign approved materials, a lifetime warranty, fairly paid factory workers and total carbon neutrality. Instead, you just get a bag.'[19]

After the video was posted, Amazon's listing for the private label item was inundated with negative ratings – to the point where reviews had to be temporarily disabled.[20]

This has historically been a thorny issue and highlights the growing scrutiny Amazon will face in being both a seller and the infrastructure. Publicly, Amazon refers to its third-party vendors as 'partners', but behind closed doors they are 'internal competitors'.[21] Amazon has always maintained that company policy prohibits employees from using data on third-party sellers to bolster its own sales; however, in 2020, when Jeff Bezos testified in front of Congress for the first time, he admitted: 'I can't guarantee you that that policy has never been violated.'[22]

The congressional hearing was part of an investigation into whether the once untouchable tech giants are abusing their power and violating antitrust law. Bezos testified alongside the CEOs of other big tech companies – Facebook's Mark Zuckerberg, Google's Sundar Pichai and Twitter's Jack Dorsey. Lawmakers grilled Bezos on Amazon's aggressive competitive practices, homing in on the bombshell report from *The Wall Street Journal* earlier in the year which found that Amazon employees were secretly accessing seller data to discover top-selling products they might want to compete against. 'The executives also developed workarounds to Amazon's internal restrictions to gain access to reports on individual seller data, as part of a practice dubbed "going over the fence",' according to *The Wall Street Journal*.[23]

'You have access to the entirety of sellers' pricing and inventory information, past, present and future, and you dictate the participation of third-party sellers on your platform. So you can set the rules of the game for your competitors but not actually follow those rules yourself. Do you think that's fair to the mom and pop third-party businesses that are trying to sell on your platform?'
Rep. Pramila Jayapal (D-WA) questioning Jeff Bezos before Congress, 2020[24]

The 16-month congressional investigation concluded that Amazon indeed has 'monopoly power over many small- and medium-sized businesses that do not have a viable alternative to Amazon for reaching online consumers' and that it has 'engaged in extensive anticompetitive conduct in its treatment of third-party sellers'.[25] There are now calls for broader reform to antitrust laws, as we'll explore later, which would potentially break up big tech companies like Amazon. At this stage, these are purely recommendations for potential legislation and will not lead to immediate action against Amazon.

> 'We must ensure that dual role platforms with market power, such as Amazon, do not distort competition. Data on the activity of third-party sellers should not be used to the benefit of Amazon when it acts as a competitor to these sellers.'
> **Margrethe Vestager, Executive Vice-President, European Commission[26]**

However, it's clear that certain aspects of antitrust need revamping for the digital era – and this is true outside of the US as well. Amazon has most recently come under fire in Europe: in 2020, the European Commission found that Amazon breached antitrust rules by distorting competition online.[27] The investigation concluded that 'very granular, real-time' data about listings and sales by other merchants were used to influence decisions on new product launches, pricing, how many items to stock and which suppliers to use.[28] Amazon is facing a number of antitrust investigations around the globe, but these are the first formal charges against the retailer – and possibly a sign of more to come.

A fashion powerhouse?

Amazon may not be perceived as the fashionista's go-to shopping destination, but the retailer makes up over one-third of all US apparel purchases made online (and accounts for 11–12 per cent of *all* apparel sold in the country), according to Wells Fargo.

In order to build credibility and offer customers additional choice, Amazon has been quietly building up a portfolio of highly targeted sub-brands – Lark + Ro, Goodthreads, Amazon Essentials, Daily Ritual, to name a few.

As of 2019, private label accounted for 9 per cent of Amazon's first-party sales in the Clothing, Shoes & Accessories category (see Tables 10.1 and 10.2).

TABLE 10.1   Private brand share of total listings

Category	First-Party % of Total Listings	Private Brand % of First-Party	Third-Party % of Total Listings
Consumer Electronics	4%	< 1%	96%
Beauty	4%	< 1%	96%
Home & Kitchen	1%	< 1%	99%
Softlines	8%	< 1%	92%
Books	34%	< 1%	66%
Consumables	3%	< 1%	97%
Toys	9%	< 1%	91%

SOURCE Amazon
NOTES Data based on Amazon's 2019 fiscal year; Softlines includes apparel, footwear and accessories; Consumer Electronics includes smart speakers

TABLE 10.2   Private brand share of total sales

Category	First-Party % of Total Sales	Private Brand % of First-Party	Third-Party % of Total Sales
Consumer Electronics	43%	3%	57%
Beauty	35%	< 1%	65%
Home & Kitchen	33%	4%	67%
Softlines	28%	9%	72%
Books	74%	< 1%	26%
Consumables	41%	2%	59%
Toys	42%	< 1%	58%

SOURCE Amazon
NOTES Data based on Amazon's 2019 fiscal year; Softlines includes apparel, footwear and accessories; Consumer Electronics includes smart speakers

TABLE 10.3 Amazon's grocery and FMCG own label ranges

Year Launched	Brand	Babycare	Food & Beverage	Health, Beauty & Personal Care	Household Supplies	Petcare	Vitamins & Supplements
2009	AmazonBasics				x		
2014	Amazon Elements	x					x
2016	Happy Belly		x				
2016	Mama Bear	x	x				
2016	Presto				x		
2016	Wickedly Prime		x				
2017	AmazonFresh		x				
2017	Whole Foods Market*		x	x	x		x
2017	365 by Whole Foods Market*	x	x	x	x		x
2018	Amazon Basic Care		x	x			
2018	Wag					x	
2018	Solimo		x	x	x	x	x
2018	Mountain Falls**	x		x			
2018	Nature's Wonder**						x
2018	P2N **						x
2018	Cinque Terre**		x				
2018	Kalista **		x				
2018	Le French Pantry **		x				

(continued)

TABLE 10.3 (Continued)

Year Launched	Brand	Babycare	Food & Beverage	Health, Beauty & Personal Care	Household Supplies	Petcare	Vitamins & Supplements
2018	Mix-A-Licious **		x				
2018	Nature's Instincts **						x
2018	Powers & Powers **		x				
2018	Roast Ridge Coffee Roasters **		x				
2018	Simply Sweet **		x				
2018	Zesty Bee **		x				
2018	Super Organics **		x				
2019	Belei			x			
2019	Sugarly Sweet**		x				
2019	Santa Ninfa **		x				
2020	Fresh		x				
2020	Amazon Kitchen		x				
2020	Cursive		x				
2021	Aplenty		x				
2021	By Amazon***		x				

*Acquired Whole Foods Market brands
**Exclusive to Amazon, but not Amazon-owned
***UK-specific

It has the reach, but can Amazon convince shoppers that it's a credible fashion retailer? Does its USP of convenience and choice really lend itself to fashion, a category where it's all about the product? Like grocery, the fashion sector is notoriously fickle. We don't doubt that Amazon can shift a boatload of clothes but selling socks and t-shirts is not the same thing as selling fashion.

> 'The Amazon brand has nothing to do with luxury; the Amazon brand has everything to do with convenience, price, value, speed; it doesn't have any emotional appeal.'
> **José Neves, CEO of Farfetch**[29]

Selling private label clothing helps to improve Amazon's overall margin mix, which will be further pressured as Amazon becomes more grocery focused, while crucially filling merchandise gaps when certain fashion brands are unwilling to sell on Amazon. 'For a long time people thought of Amazon as the place to get toilet paper or cat food', said Elaine Kwon, a former executive at Amazon's fashion business. 'In 2014, many brands were very hesitant to even let it be known publicly that they wanted to work with Amazon.'

But the balance of power is shifting. The pandemic has fast-tracked the shift to buying clothes online, much to the advantage of pure-play fashion retailers like Asos, Zalando and Boohoo. Amazon, meanwhile, is ubiquitous today; it's become a sales channel that can no longer be ignored. But selling through Amazon isn't just about generating greater volumes – it also gives brands greater control of pricing and presentation of their products, since many are already being sold on Amazon via third parties.

> '2020 was a year like no other, but it also confirmed the opportunity lying ahead of us. The pandemic has accelerated change in the fashion industry that has long been in progress.'
> **Zalando shareholder letter, 2021**[30]

Cracking down on such third-party sales was Nike's primary incentive for selling on Amazon – a decision that turned heads when it was announced in 2017. Nike had already been the number one clothing brand on Amazon, according to Morgan Stanley, even though it did not sell directly on the site. As part of the deal, Amazon agreed to monitor its site for counterfeits and no longer allow third-party vendors to sell Nike products.

The collaboration, however, was short-lived as Nike struggled to compete against third-party listings, which would benefit from having more reviews than its own verified listings. Nike cut ties with Amazon after just two years in order to pursue a direct-to-consumer (DTC) model, which has been largely successful for the brand.

The move sparked much debate in the industry – would other brands follow in Nike's footsteps in ditching Amazon? As one of the most valuable brands in the world, Nike might not have needed Amazon – but many others do. Amazon remains the indispensable route to market for most, and Nike's departure demonstrates the delicate balance Amazon must strike in order to attract major brands while simultaneously offering customers breadth of assortment through its marketplace. Make no mistake – Amazon needs established brands in order to grow its fashion business. Private label is important, but it takes a long time to build a brand, and many question whether Amazon's utilitarian image will prevent it from being perceived as a fashion powerhouse. The tech giant must also find its USP in fashion. Near-infinite assortment is powerful, but also overwhelming – a search for a black dress will produce over 40,000 results.

Amazon may not be the go-to destination when browsing for clothes, but it is compensating for its weaknesses through innovations. Again, bearing in mind Amazon is a tech company obsessed with disrupting quo, there are plenty of fashion friction points for Amazon to tackle. We have discussed the launch of Prime Wardrobe, which has removed the barrier of upfront payments and fuelled the 'buy to try' trend. But we expect Amazon to go further in order to improve the experience and, crucially, reduce returns rates. For example, customer education and size recommendation tools can help to instil confidence and Amazon should be encouraged by the fact that customers generally want to get it right the first time.

Amazon's interactive 'View in 360' feature lets shoppers explore styles in 360-degree detail to better visualize fit. It is currently being used in luxury but could be rolled out across the wider apparel category to help make the experience smoother and more engaging. Amazon is very much in experimentation mode here and naturally some things have quietly failed.

For example, its Alexa-powered standalone fashion camera Echo Look was discontinued in 2021. The device would rate a user's outfit and offer fashion advice based on things like past purchases and the weather. That functionality has since been moved to the Amazon shopping app and Alexa-enabled devices.

Amazon has filed a number of fashion-related patents, including a blended reality mirror that lets shoppers try on clothes virtually while being placed in a virtual location, and an on-demand automated clothing factory designed to quickly produce clothing only after an order is placed – a move that would not only propel its own label fashion business but could reinvent the entire supply chain and shake up the whole apparel sector in the process. Amazon also owns Body Labs, which uses artificial intelligence to produce 3D body scans and has developed an AI fashion designer which can make recommendations based on products that appear on Instagram, for example.

'Retail has always been about delivering on and also anticipating customer expectation,' John Boumphrey, Amazon's UK Country Manager who formerly headed up its European fashion business, told the authors. 'What can we do to make sure we're continuing to be relevant? How do we make sure we continue to deliver a great experience for customers?'

If Amazon succeeds in stamping the friction out of fashion, it could revolutionize the way we shop for clothes. We're not writing it off just yet.

The branding conundrum: Amazon's mishmash of grocery brands

In 2014, Amazon launched its first major own label brand for the Fast-Moving Consumer Goods (FMCG) category – Amazon Elements. Many in the FMCG sector feared Amazon's premium range of nappies and wipes was the beginning of its long-awaited own label incursion. But within two months, the nappies were discontinued.

Feedback had been lukewarm, with Amazon citing the need for 'design improvements'. It was a hugely risky category in which to debut its first ever own label FMCG product; quality can be subjective at times but a nappy either works or it doesn't, and brands aren't given many second chances in a category like babycare. Nonetheless, Amazon maintained the Elements brand, using it exclusively for wipes before eventually extending it, somewhat bizarrely, to vitamins and supplements. But remember, Amazon sees failure as an opportunity to iterate and improve, so it wasn't much of a surprise to see own label nappies resurface a few years later – this time under the Mama Bear brand.

The line, which also includes organic baby food, was one of several new FMCG ranges Amazon launched in 2016 prior to the Whole Foods acquisition. Others included: Happy Belly (trail mix, nuts, spices, eggs and coffee); Presto (paper towels, toilet paper, laundry detergent); and Wickedly Prime (gourmet snacks including potato chips, popcorn, soup, tea). Following the Elements fiasco, Amazon trod carefully and steered entirely clear of one big category – perishables.

That changed with the Whole Foods deal, when Amazon inherited its very well-regarded 365 Everyday Value and eponymous line of own label foods. Overnight, Amazon became a credible grocery operator with a compelling range of private label goods. Within four months of the acquisition, 365 took in $10 million in sales, according to Edge by Ascential, making it the second-largest private label available on Amazon.

In addition to all the benefits laid out earlier in the chapter, private label is particularly important for grocers because of the high-frequency/habitual nature of the category. Remember Amazon's goal is to take the chore out of grocery shopping by automating replenishment of everyday goods. That in itself is very powerful, but even more so when it's the retailer's own item that's being replenished.

Since the Whole Foods deal, Amazon has quietly rolled out additional FMCG ranges including Wag, Solimo, Aplenty, 'By Amazon' (UK only), Basic Care and Mountain Falls, among many others (see Table 10.4). Amazon can be excused for being in experimentation mode but at some point it will need to create a more unified and coherent message across its private label portfolio.

This brings up an important point about brand elasticity. Amazon is the king of diversification, but stretching into new sectors and services risks diluting its brand – or even worse, customer backlash. Would shoppers accept Amazon-branded groceries along with their Amazon-branded Echos, Kindles, video and music streaming and, potentially in the future, Amazon-branded pharmacies, hair salons and financial services? In grocery, we believe that Amazon is destined to be a jumble of own brands, but that doesn't make it any less of a threat. Competitors should be prioritizing investment in private label while suppliers ensure they have strategies in place for defending market share. Deeper customer engagement will be essential and, where appropriate, own label production should also be considered.

TABLE 10.4 Amazon's FMCG own label ranges

Year launched	Brand		Category						
		Babycare	Beauty & grooming	Food & beverage	Health & personal care	Household supplies	Petcare	Vitamins & supplements
2014	Amazon Elements	X						X
2016	Happy Belly			X				
2016	Mama Bear	X						
2016	Presto					X		
2016	Wickedly Prime			X				
2017	AmazonFresh			X				
2017	Whole Foods Market*		X	X	X	X		
2017	365*	X	X	X	X	X		X
2017	Engine 2 Plant-Strong*			X				
2018	Basic Care**				X			
2018	Wag						X	
2018	Solimo		X	X	X	X		X
2018	Mountain Falls**		X		X			

*Acquired Whole Foods Market brands
**Exclusive to Amazon, but not Amazon-owned

Notes

1   Kaziukenas, Juozas (2020) 9% of Amazon's sales in clothing are from its private label brands, *Marketplace Pulse*, 17 September. Available from: https://www.marketplacepulse.com/articles/9-of-amazons-sales-in-clothing-are-from-its-private-label-brands [Last accessed 20/6/21].

2   Housel, Morgan (2013) The 20 smartest things Jeff Bezos has ever said, *The Motley Fool*, 9 September. Available from: https://www.fool.com/investing/general/2013/09/09/the-25-smartest-things-jeff-bezos-has-ever-said.aspx (archived at https://perma.cc/8W2G-HEHC) [Last accessed 29/6/2018].

3   Lebow, Victor (1955) Price competition in 1955, *Journal of Retailing*, Spring. Available from: http://www.gcafh.org/edlab/Lebow.pdf (archived at https://perma) [Last accessed 3/9/2018].

4   Amazon staff (2020) Fact check: sizing up Amazon, *Amazon's website*, 15 September. Available from: https://www.aboutamazon.com/news/how-amazon-works/fact-check-sizing-up-amazon [Last accessed 20/6/2021].

5   Creswell, Julie (2018) How Amazon steers shoppers to its own products, *New York Times*, 23 June. Available from: https://mobile.nytimes.com/2018/06/23/business/amazon-the-brand-buster.html (archived at https://perma.cc/GN9X-NFA2) [Last accessed 29/6/2018].

6   Anderson, Keith (2016) Amazon's move into private label consumables, *Profitero* (blog post) 28 July. Available from: https://www.profitero.com/2016/07/amazons-move-into-private-label-consumables/ (archived at https://perma.cc/BSC7-AEKD) [Last accessed 11/9/2018].

7   Ibid.

8   Amazon (AMZN) Q1 2021 earnings call transcript (2021). Available from: https://www.fool.com/earnings/call-transcripts/2021/04/29/amazon-amzn-q1-2021-earnings-call-transcript/ [Last accessed 6/20/2021].

9   Amazon staff (2020) Why customers love store brands like AmazonBasics, 17 June. Available from: https://www.aboutamazon.com/news/how-amazon-works/why-customers-love-store-brands-like-amazonbasics [Last accessed 20/6/2021].

10 Chaudhuri, Saabira and Sharon Terlep (2018) The next big threat to consumer brands (yes, Amazon's behind it), *Wall Street Journal*, 27 February. Available from: https://www.wsj.com/articles/big-consumer-brands-dont-have-an-answer-for-alexa-1519727401 (archived at https://perma.cc/YYQ5-CFJD) [Last accessed 29/6/2018].

11 Kim, Eugene (2019) Amazon quietly removes promotional spots that gave special treatment to its own products as scrutiny of tech giants grows, *CNBC*, 3 April. Available from: https://www.cnbc.com/2019/04/03/amazon-removes-special-promo-spots-for-private-label-products.html [Last accessed 20/6/2021].

12 Salpini, Cara (2019) Allbirds to Amazon: 'Please steal our approach to sustainability', Retail Dive, 27 November. Available from: https://www.retaildive.com/news/allbirds-to-amazon-please-steal-our-approach-to-sustainability/568187/ (archived at https://perma.cc/5BJY-TL22) [Last accessed 20/6/2021].

13 Amazon Staff (2020) Why customers love store brands like AmazonBasics, 17 June. Available from: https://www.aboutamazon.com/news/how-amazon-works/why-customers-love-store-brands-like-amazonbasics (archived at https://perma.cc/FXL7-722X) [Last accessed 20/6/2021].

14 Ibid.

15 Palmer, Annie (2021) Amazon accused of copying camera gear maker's top-selling item, *CNBC*, 4 March. Available from: https://www.cnbc.com/2021/03/04/amazon-accused-of-copying-camera-gearmaker-peak-designs-top-selling-item-.html (archived at https://perma.cc/56TU-8MXG) [Last accessed 20/6/2021].

16 European Commission press release (2020) Antitrust: Commission sends Statement of Objections to Amazon for the use of non public independent seller data and opens second investigation into its e-commerce business practices, 10 November. Available from: https://ec.europa.eu/commission/presscorner/detail/en/ip_20_2077 (archived at https://perma.cc/9RC9-YMEC) [Last accessed 20/6/2021].

17 Investigation of Competition in Digital Markets. Majority Staff Report and Recommendations. Subcommittee on Antitrust, Commercial and Administrative Law of the Committee of the Judiciary (2020). Available from: https://fm.cnbc.com/applications/cnbc.com/resources/editorialfiles/2020/10/06/investigation_of_competition_in_digital_markets_majority_staff_report_and_recommendations.pdf (archived at https://perma.cc/3XEV-J9DM) [Last accessed 20/6/2021].

18 Warren, Elizabeth (2019) Here's how we can break up Big Tech, *Medium*, 8 March. Available from: https://medium.com/@teamwarren/heres-how-we-can-break-up-big-tech-9ad9e0da324c (archived at https://perma.cc/KAQ7-CMKA) [Last accessed 20/6/2021].

19 Peak Design (2021) A tale of two slings: Peak Design and Amazon Basics (online video). Available from: https://www.youtube.com/watch?time_continue=84&v=HbxWGjQ2szQ&feature=emb_logo (archived at https://perma.cc/WD8F-GJG4) [Last accessed 20/6/21].

20 Palmer, Annie (2021) Amazon accused of copying camera gear maker's top-selling item, *CNBC*, 4 March. Available from: https://www.cnbc.com/2021/03/04/amazon-accused-of-copying-camera-gearmaker-peak-designs-top-selling-item-.html (archived at https://perma.cc/U5CX-J7PV) [Last accessed 20/6/2021].

21 Palmer, Annie and Novet, Jordan (2020) Amazon bullies partners and vendors, says antitrust subcommittee, *CNBC*, 6 October. Available from: https://www. cnbc.com/2020/10/06/amazon-bullies-partners-and-vendors-says-antitrust-subcommittee.html (archived at https://perma.cc/YUT5-34L8) [Last accessed 20/6/2021].

22 Buncombe, Andrew (2020) Jeff Bezos says he 'can't guarantee' Amazon has not used third-party data to benefit itself, *The Independent*, 30 July. Available from: https://www.independent.co.uk/life-style/gadgets-and-tech/jeff-bezos-hearing-amazon-net-worth-third-party-data-a9644961.html (archived at https://perma.cc/25Q8-59W8) [Last accessed 20/6/2021].

23 Palmer, Annie (2020) Amazon uses data from third-party sellers to develop its own products, WSJ investigation finds, *CNBC*, 23 April. Available from: https://www.cnbc.com/2020/04/23/wsj-amazon-uses-data-from-third-party-sellers-to-develop-its-own-products.html (archived at https://perma.cc/TYJ8-5VXE) [Last accessed 20/6/2021].

24 Nickelsburg, Monica (2020) What we learned about the antitrust case against Amazon from Jeff Bezos' time in the Congressional hot seat, *Geekwire*, 29 July. Available from: https://www.geekwire.com/2020/heres-jeff-bezos-revealed-antitrust-case-amazon-unwieldy-tech-hearing/ (archived at https://perma.cc/T8V6-52N9) [Last accessed 20/6/21].

25 Investigation of Competition in Digital Markets. Majority Staff Report and Recommendations. Subcommittee on Antitrust, Commercial and Administrative Law of the Committee of the Judiciary (2020). Available from: https://fm.cnbc.com/applications/cnbc.com/resources/editorialfiles/2020/10/06/investigation_of_competition_in_digital_markets_majority_staff_report_and_recommendations.pdf (archived at https://perma.cc/2WNJ-GEUB) [Last accessed 20/6/2021].

26 European Commission press release (2020) Antitrust: Commission sends Statement of Objections to Amazon for the use of non-public independent seller data and opens second investigation into its e-commerce business practices, 10 November. Available from: https://ec.europa.eu/commission/presscorner/detail/en/ip_20_2077 (archived at https://perma.cc/4CUU-5RGA) [Last accessed 20/6/2021].

27 Ibid.

28 Statement by Executive Vice-President Vestager on Statement of Objections to Amazon for the use of non-public independent seller data and second investigation into its e-commerce business practices (2021). Available from: https://ec.europa.eu/commission/presscorner/detail/en/STATEMENT_20_2082 (archived at https://perma.cc/6X3Q-9S5F) [Last accessed 20/6/2021].

29 Shapiro, Eben (2021) Farfetch CEO José Neves on how the pandemic drove fashion sales online, *Time*, 14 February. Available from: https://time.com/5938014/fashion-luxury-farfetch-jose-neves/ [Last accessed 20/6/2021].

30 Zalando Letter to Shareholders (2021). Available from: https://corporate.zalando.com/en/investor-relations/letter-shareholders-0 [Last accessed 20/6/2021].

11

Technology and frictionless retail

> 'We're proud of the differentiation we've built through constant innovation and relentless focus on customer experience.'
> **Jeff Bezos[1]**

In Chapter 6 we began to explore the 'on-my-terms' shopper. We started to discuss the impact of technology on retail and how it is revolutionizing the way we shop – 'on my terms'.

The key to understanding what this really means every day, to the average consumer, starts with understanding how a shopper sets these 'terms' for their shopping journeys. Simply put, rapid technology development has given consumers the tools to shop on their own terms. The digitization of modern life not only underpins our increased appetite for, and ability to seek out, more 'fun' or informed customer experiences over the more functional, weekly grocery type of shop; the so-called 'consumerization' of technology is also fuelling heightened expectations of convenience, immediacy, transparency and relevancy among more and more consumers.

As recent tumultuous global events have shown, people will always need to buy things. So, while any looming retail apocalypse may be overstated, fears for the future of the industry are founded on the fact that many familiar household retail chains have fallen by the wayside. But we contend that, for some their demise was by no means inevitable. That was until COVID hit. They failed to accommodate today's digitally empowered, on-my-terms shopper. This is why any focus on Amazon as a causative agent is unfounded. But, as more retail casualties fail to use technology to digitally transform and differentiate in response to the industry-wide challenge of the on-my-terms shopper, it is worth taking an in-depth look at how Amazon has seemingly been able to stay one step ahead of both the competition and the needs of its customers.

In the next two chapters, we explore how Amazon continues to use technology development in artificial intelligence (AI) and voice as two particularly strong areas of focus in combination with the underlying drivers of change such development responds to, and the next-generation expectations and demand for frictionless retail experiences on the part of today's on-my-terms shopper it helps to meet. Through this exploration, it becomes easy to see how not just Amazon's business, but more so the technology advantage that underpins its execution, will continue to weed out complacent players and push the entire retail industry towards the creation of customer experiences that make shopping instore as effortless as it has become online and turn the functional into something more fun.

Customer obsession

Retailers that do not understand, and adjust their propositions accordingly in response to, the on-my-terms shopper are the very ones whose complacency means they also fail to keep pace with the impact of the technology drivers of change; they fail to recognize how the internet, mobile and subsequent tech-enabled service innovations, such as click & collect or shoppable media, are changing the retail landscape for ever.

Before getting into how the technology itself has developed, let's first examine its overall impact on the wider industry landscape and its role in empowering the on-my-terms shopper. We are about to reach a major tipping point, where over half of the planet has access to the internet via mobile. Widespread adoption of technology as it relates to retail has put the customer firmly in control of the terms of the buying process. This is where it becomes impossible to ignore the spectre of Amazon. We can see how the shifting balance of power from retailers to consumers has not only tracked closely against technology development, but how Amazon has also used this shift to support its growth and evolution. Acknowledging this shift is central to understanding how, just like Amazon, any successful business can use technology to both its own and its customers' advantage. But here, it is also Amazon's desire to 'delight' its customers, as Bezos has put it, that has allowed it to tap its technology advantage. It is also a lesson in putting the needs of the customer at the heart of innovation any business could learn from.

In one of the famous Shareholder Letters, Bezos wrote:

> Look inside a current textbook on software architecture, and you'll find few patterns that we don't apply at Amazon. We use high-performance transactions systems, complex rendering and object caching, workflow and queuing systems, business intelligence and data analytics, machine learning and pattern recognition, neural networks and probabilistic decision making, and a wide variety of other techniques. And while many of our systems are based on the latest in computer science research, this often hasn't been sufficient; our architects and engineers have had to advance research in directions that no academic had yet taken. Many of the problems we face have no textbook solutions, and so we – happily – invent new approaches...

It's hard to believe that was over a decade ago. So, how has Amazon's success tracked so closely against the rise of digital retail in the wake of consumer technology adoption? As we have stated and so strongly suggest, it is because Amazon is a technology company first and a retailer second. But it manages to successfully keep the customer it serves at the heart of the technology innovation it harnesses in support of its business strategy. For example, out of Amazon's 14 Leadership Principles, the first is 'Customer Obsession'. As referenced in Chapter 2, it is this customer-centric ethos that has served it well as consumers have begun to embrace digitally enabled or enhanced technology shopping tools. It cannot be underestimated, however, how much it helps that Amazon's core business is founded on technology innovation. Before looking at this innovation, let's take a step back here, as it wasn't always this way.

Going back to 2002, with necessity truly being the mother of all invention, Amazon Web Services was born of the need for sufficient number-crunching capacity and standardized, automated computing infrastructures on which to run its retail marketplace. Capitalizing on advances in networking, storage, computer power and virtualization, Amazon began reselling its cloud computing capabilities as services in 2006.

However, AWS did not deliver immediate success. During that time shareholders would have been forgiven for wondering if the company would ever make a profit, and its dwindling share price reflected this. In relative terms, it was smaller than Walmart. In the meantime, though, Amazon had quietly been consolidating market share in meeting the fast-growing demand for cloud computing services.

Then, in 2015, in what would be a pivotal year for the company and a decade since going public, it first revealed just how profitable AWS had become, with margins to rival those of Starbucks, and investors saw their Amazon stock start to rise in value. Today, its AWS customers include Netflix (yet another example of a competitor running on Amazon rails),[2] NASA[3] and retailers such as Gilt, Ocado and Under Armour.[4] But even back then, AWS was responsible for two-thirds of Amazon's profits; today, it continues to be Amazon's main profit engine. Don't forget this is why we said Amazon is not your average retailer. It is a technology company first.

The power of obsession

Thinking about the values that have gone on to define Amazon, when it comes to technology innovation, its third Leadership Principle – 'Invent and Simplify' – is the most significant.

Although AWS fulfilled its potential to power Amazon to the behemoth it is today, in the first instance it was not afraid in its quest to invent and simplify its own operations. It then went on to repackage and resell these efforts to businesses and consumers alike. So much so that, a decade after going public its market value had increased more than eightfold to its 2021 market cap, helped in no small part by the world being driven online in 2020. This has also provided its retail business with a massive balance sheet and the vast amounts of computing power required to build out the sophisticated AI-based systems needed to power its extensive, global e-commerce, supply chain and fulfilment operations, as well as the next digital frontiers in retail – automation and voice.

As we discussed in Chapter 2, Amazon itself suggests it can afford to 'be misunderstood for long periods of time'. If the story of how 'AWS came to fruition' isn't clear enough illustration of the fact, then let's take a closer look at Prime Day as another worthy proof point.

Amazon also held its first Prime Day a decade after going public. By then, Prime was already eight years old. While some reports from the inaugural discount day highlighted a lack of blockbuster deals, marketplace management software provider ChannelAdvisor found it boosted Amazon's US sales by 93 per cent and its European sales by 53 per cent. By the second Prime Day, total orders increased 60 per cent year-on-year, striking such a blow for bricks and mortar retail competitors everywhere that even now they struggle to competitively keep up with the annual discount day. By 2020, Prime Day had expanded to 20 countries and had already been offering special incentives to Amazon customers using its Alexa voice assistant for three years. We need to understand how Alexa has come to take such a prominent role and will delve into that later. Here we should pause to recognize that the 2020 Amazon Prime Day generated $3.5 billion. Even so, to put that amount in further perspective, its Chinese competitor Alibaba raked in some $74 billion during its equivalent discount event for the unofficial, annual 11 November Chinese holiday, Singles' Day, in the same year.[5]

Despite its Chinese counterpart making Prime Day look like small change, it does represent a great example of Amazon's phenomenal growth. Putting Amazon's growth into context, it was only in its tenth year that AWS realized profits and it launched Prime Day, but it was also the year that sales exceeded $100 billion for the first time. It was arguably the first year the Amazon flywheel became self-sustaining. Delivering sales growth was the last of Bezos' 'three pillars', where AWS provided for its cost base, while Prime has gone on to power its customer acquisition and retention strategy.

The power of innovation

The first technology trend Amazon has, therefore, taken advantage of is the rapidly growing number of individuals accessing the internet over mobile devices. According to mobile operators, the number of unique mobile subscribers reached 5.8 billion, equivalent to 73 per cent of the world's population, in 2021.[6] Other internet- and mobile-enabled developments that have transformed the way we shop include payment, enabled via online banking and mobile wallets. Debit and credit so-called 'card-not-present' payments and PayPal, which saves time and adds extra security on entering payment information, introduced consumers to online shopping, in the same way as contactless credit and debit cards have paved the way for the rollout of mobile wallet payments instore.

SEAMLESS EXPERIENCES

The common denominator among such innovation is consumer demand for more immersive, portable and personalized experiences. This has led to the objective of eliminating 'friction' in customer experiences, as it relates to the speed, convenience, transparency and relevance throughout the shopping journey. This may be, for example, browsing online, using an app or visiting a store, only to find the item sought is out of stock, or having to join long queues at checkout. Eliminating such friction requires that the retailer enables that customer to perhaps order the desired product online for delivery to home; or, on finding the item, it then facilitates the looking up of reviews or offers to check on the best deal, right through to final, rapid checkout via mobile with express fulfilment. By contrast, anything that introduces unnecessary friction into the customer experience, such as queues, delivery issues or poor sales service, is not compatible with today's on-my-terms shopper. In order to give customers more of what they want, the 'what' of frictionless retail is enabled through the use of digital to improve customer experiences, where the 'how' is provided by technology. This is where Amazon's technology business gives it an unprecedented advantage, and why it is wrong for both traditional and online retailers to compare themselves directly against it.

TECHNOLOGY DRIVERS

Technology is not only transforming the way consumers interact with retailers in this way, it is blurring the physical and digital divide. To understand how Amazon has successfully harnessed its technology advantage to provide a digitally enabled, frictionless shopping experience, it is necessary to first break down the fundamental drivers of technology that underpin the frictionless objectives of the on-my-terms shopper. They are:

1 ubiquitous connectivity;

2 pervasive interfaces; and

3 autonomous computing.

We see the effects of the first of these drivers with the impact of mobile in and out of the home, as well as instore and in other public places. The more that connectivity becomes truly ubiquitous, with the development of fifth-generation (5G) mobile networks, alongside blanket Wi-Fi availability, wireless charging, and whatever device or means that enable us to be always connected and online at faster speeds, the more impatient we become for greater choice, more intuitive search and instantaneous response and fulfilment times.

The context for the second technology driver, towards more 'pervasive interfaces', requires that we go back to the early, pre-internet days of computing, where the idea of a handheld pointing device or 'mouse' was relatively new. For example, in 1984, reporter Gregg Williams wrote of the introduction of the first Macintosh computer that it 'brings us one step closer to the ideal computer as appliance'.

'The Lisa computer was important because it was the first commercial product to use the mouse-window-desktop environment. The Macintosh is equally important because it makes that same very same environment affordable.'
Gregg Williams, 1984[7]

Nearly 40 years later, we're used to using trackpads and balls, pointers, pens and graphics tablets, not to mention other PC peripherals like headphones and microphones, and even smart glasses, watches and other so-called 'wearables'. The common theme linking all of this development has been the search for the means of interfacing with computing devices that is also seamless or frictionless. In this sense, use of the interface becomes so intuitive that it enables the technology itself to essentially 'disappear' into the background, allowing its functionality to come easily to the fore to serve the user's particular needs. Perhaps the most common modern example of a pervasive interface is the touchscreen; so much so that a child born after the launch of Apple's iPhone is more likely to claw at the screen of any computing device they are given to control it, than to look for a button to switch it on.

AUTONOMOUS COMPUTING

Where connectivity and interfaces have, to date, been hardware-based, the third global technology driver is predicated on the development of increasingly 'intelligent' software that can almost think for itself and come up with answers to questions without necessarily being programmed with the necessary information. Instead, autonomous computing systems can cross-reference and correlate disparate data sources, augment their own algorithms, and answer complex 'what if?' sorts of questions. As such, AI, including machine learning, natural language processing (NLP) and deep learning techniques, could not exist without autonomous computing development as the last global technology driver. AI development is, in fact, responsible for many of the functional computing advances of the last 20 years, from search algorithms, spam filters and fraud prevention systems to self-driving vehicles and smart personal assistants.

We can trace the influence of these drivers throughout Amazon's rise to dominance, where it has capitalized on its technology development based on these drivers to bring greater digital capabilities to bear in the quest to provide more frictionless shopping experiences.

The power of foresight

In the case of each technology driver, Amazon's attempts to capitalize on developments outside of its core capabilities (ie cloud computing and retail) have met with varying degrees of success. As discussed earlier in the book, it's important to remember that even Amazon can – and does – get it wrong sometimes. But the bets it places are big enough that when they come off, they are so wildly successful that they more than make up for the failures.

In this context, let's consider the developments by Amazon that have been driven by the quest for ubiquitous connectivity and pervasive interfaces first. There may be some who may remember its ill-fated foray into smartphone manufacturing, a key example we first touched on in Chapter 2. After unveiling the Amazon Fire phone in 2014, the device was met with a swathe of negative reviews that dismissed the device as not only 'forgettable',[8] but also 'mediocre'.[9] In fact, one reporter who declared the device 'forgettable' went on to advise consumers to 'wait for the sequel'.

However, the Fire phone bombed so badly, a sequel was never going to be forthcoming. Just one month after launch and the damaging reviews, Amazon slashed the price of its phone from US $199 (for the 32GB version) to just 99 cents. As if that wasn't admission enough of the device's abject failure, the company also revealed in its tenth anniversary year that it had taken a $170 million loss on its development, manufacture and splashy launch event. Amazon was, perhaps, lucky at the time that the stellar AWS numbers it also revealed that year, which we referenced earlier in this chapter, stole the spotlight.

For a book that aims to deconstruct the secrets of Amazon's success, it is worth taking a moment here to dissect how and why the Fire phone failed; more so because, since then, it has seemingly learned from its mistakes. Taking a consensus view, Amazon's attempts to launch a smartphone at the peak of popularity of Apple's iPhone, where only a handful of Android OS-based devices led by Samsung could compete, were doomed to failure. In a market dominated by two major mobile operating system (OS) players, Amazon needed to clearly differentiate its offering on either price or quality, but it did neither. At the same time, though, we've acknowledged that it quickly recognized this and took ameliorative action.

The Fire phone did, however, reveal Amazon's ambitions to expand its move into PC hardware beyond its first e-reader, the Kindle, which was launched in 2007. As Marcus Wohlsen wrote for *Wired.com* at the time, 'The [Fire phone] project was doomed from the start, because the only one who really needs an Amazon phone is Amazon.'[10] Amazon might have felt it needed the Fire phone to get closer to its customers and add another spoke to its flywheel to lock those customers into its ecosystem. An application called Firefly, which shipped with the Fire phone, was intended to do just that. Firefly was a text, sound and object recognition tool designed to let shoppers identify millions of different products and then buy them online – friction-free, from Amazon, of course. But even after a series of price reductions, the mobile device was subsequently discontinued.

MISTAKES LEARNED

Amazon learned from the failure of the Fire phone, and the misstep certainly did not dampen its ambitions in regard to taking advantage of the rise of technology that could enable more ubiquitous connectivity and pervasive interfaces. After all, it did have the success of its Fire tablet (launched in 2011) to save its hardware development credentials. The tablet, which was already on its fourth generation by the time the Fire phone was launched, built on Amazon's e-book sales and Kindle success and also offers users access to the Amazon e-commerce site directly from its home screen. But it did not enable connectivity beyond the functionality of connecting to the Amazon store, nor did its early versions use the latest touch interface technology, despite the fact that Apple had commoditized the touchscreen with the introduction of the iPhone four years earlier. Latterly, it also acquired tens of millions of Amazon Fire TV users, many of whom access its services using the Amazon Fire TV stick USB device with their internet-connected televisions. Where Amazon has been more successful in applying the first two global technology drivers, though, is in its core retail business, where it historically brought the concepts of ubiquitous connectivity and pervasive interfaces to bear with far more success.

One click to no click

Applying the first two global technology drivers to the Amazon timeline, it is possible to recognize just how important their application has been in facilitating the removal of friction from the online shopping experience it offers. Its '1-click' patent is the preeminent example, even though the patent expired in 2017. Many industry watchers questioned whether its ability to register billing, payment and shipping information details in advance of being able to then add products to a shopping basket and checkout to buy those products with 'one click' should have been granted a patent at all. They argued that it stifled e-commerce competition because it gave Amazon an unfair monopoly, predicated on what amounts to little more than an efficient means of using what quickly became standard e-commerce technology. But, back in 1999, it was perhaps easy to understand how it was then seen as a cutting-edge innovation and a first hint at how Amazon would go on to make shopping friction the enemy while changing the status quo. So, on the patent being granted, Amazon then famously sued the US bookseller Barnes & Noble for having implemented a similar method to the one described in its patent for allowing its customers to make repeat purchases. (The two companies reached an undisclosed settlement in the case in 2002.)

Meanwhile, the patent, and Amazon's rigorous defence of it, afforded the company a significant advantage over its competitors for nearly 20 years, where competitors could either choose to add more clicks to their checkout processes or pay Amazon licensing fees to offer '1-click' checkout. The reason it was such a powerful piece of functionality for Amazon was that the friction it reduced was effective in helping to eliminate shopping cart abandonment.

Just like every e-commerce player in the early days, Amazon could see customers browsing and adding items into their shopping basket. But online retail cart abandonment rates, ie the ratio of the number of abandoned shopping baskets to the number of initiated and/or completed transactions, have always been high. Most recently, analysis of 44 different e-commerce sites in 2020 found the average shopping cart abandonment rate was 69.8 per cent.[11] Unsurprisingly, Amazon doesn't publish its abandonment rates. But merchants selling via Amazon's Marketplace who, understandably, want to remain anonymous have reported that Amazon has managed to consistently maintain lower-than-average rates of abandonment. Another published estimate, which assumed the technology increased Amazon's sales by a relatively modest 5 per cent, put the value of the patent at $2.4 billion annually.[12]

Paying for the privilege

The advantage Amazon gained with its 1-click patent demonstrates just how much a source of friction the checkout process can be in retail, whether online or offline. We only have to think about the times we have been discouraged from completing a purchase in a physical store on seeing a long queue at the checkout – many of us 'just walk out' (we will come to explore the significance of this term later). But here, Amazon has again proved its ability to stay one step ahead of its competition, by not only leveraging its 1-click expertise, but also by developing the functionality required to facilitate payment as well as fulfilment services for the merchants that sell via its marketplace. Past launches, such as 'Pay with Amazon', allow third-party e-commerce sites to give customers the option to check out using the credit card and shipping information they have stored with Amazon (in just the same way as Google or Facebook's single sign-on speeds website registration), shaving the purchase process down to just a few clicks by running on Amazon's e-commerce transactional rails – for a price and the cost of collaborating to compete, of course.[13]

The last, and perhaps the most important, example of how Amazon has defined the development of frictionless shopping and realized its 'Invent and Simplify' Leadership Principle takes us back to its Prime service. We have already examined how much of a barrier to conversion the checkout process can be. But delivery costs are an even greater barrier. Research carried out by the Baymard Institute among US consumers (once those just browsing without any intention to buy were eliminated from the survey pool) found that high extra costs associated with shipping, taxes and fees were the top reason for abandoning a shopping cart.

Amazon has, with its Prime service, solved two key sources of friction in online shopping. By offering a flat monthly or annual fee for expedited shipping, it has eliminated both the hidden cost of shipping before checkout and the perception that shopping online is slower than shopping at retail stores. Add in streaming multimedia on-demand and live events, as discussed earlier in the book, and it is easy to understand why today the scale of Prime membership, at 200 million-plus globally, dwarfs some of the most popular other online subscription services, including Spotify (with 158m premium subscribers) and Apple Music (72m), and has proven such a central, supportive pillar to Amazon's flywheel ecosystem of services.

The transparency of Prime's model and the friction it eliminates are the capabilities that characterize Amazon's most notable innovative digital shopping achievements. Prime also gives Amazon a recurring revenue stream to underpin its competitive offer over the so-called 'last mile' of fulfilment. Taken together with the simplicity and elegance of Amazon's recently expired patent for one-click purchases, these developments could also be said to have laid the groundwork for Amazon's now-defunct Dash Buttons, as well as shopping by voice using its Alexa voice assistant – all of which have been designed to pull the customer further into the Amazon flywheel ecosystem.

EASY AUTO-REPLENISHMENT

As first referenced in Chapter 8, Amazon's Dash Buttons were launched in – yes, you guessed it – 2015. Although now discontinued, they are worthy of note as a major stepping stone in its move from one click to 'no click' online shopping. For the first time, they gave Amazon and its brand partners physical, branded real estate in consumer homes. Launched the day before April Fools, leading some analysts to think it was a prank, some mocked the relatively low-tech idea, which relies on a wireless internet connection to communicate the reorder command, at the press of a button, to the owner's Amazon mobile app. The customer still had to confirm the reorder in-app to avoid any accidental purchases. While Dash buttons, and their 2017 successor the voice enabled, barcode scanning Dash Wand, were discontinued in 2019 and 2020 respectively, the concept built on and augments the subscription success of its Prime fulfilment scheme.

What Amazon learned from the Dash initiative taught it that smart home developments and its Alexa voice assistant and Echo devices have obviated the need for it to offer dedicated auto-replenishment hardware and given it the chance to iterate in adjacent areas. Its 'Subscribe & Save' online feature provides a similar service. Some appliance makers have built the Dash Replenishment Service directly into their products to help consumers quickly reorder associated items. Plus, Amazon recently chose to name its smart grocery store shopping trolley the Dash cart, which we've also examined in relation to its grocery ambitions.

The company has been able to take the learnings about how we shop from its mobile and auto-replenishment device initiatives and bake them into either voice assistant devices or its own mobile app, which is the number one shopping app in many of its markets. Add into this mix the fact that Amazon is now the starting point for over half of US consumers searching for products, and it is easy to see why it has grown to the position of online dominance it commands today. Indeed, among Millennials (many of whom were born after the World Wide Web went live in 1991), Amazon was the number one app they could not live without on their mobile devices.[14] But Amazon has not been content to innovate and develop a business strategy predicated on the ubiquitous connectivity and pervasive interfaces that are revolutionizing the way we live, work and shop, it also has its sights set on making both the physical and digital shopping process even more rapid and intuitive by relying on autonomous computing capabilities.

Notes

1   Amazon Investor Relations (1999) 1998 Letter to Shareholders, 5 March. Available from: http://media.corporate-ir.net/media_files/irol/97/97664/reports/ Shareholderletter98.pdf (archived at https://perma.cc/5FTF-AQKX) [Last accessed 11/6/2021].

2   Amazon Netflix case study (2016) Amazon AWS. Available from: https://aws. amazon.com/solutions/case-studies/netflix/ (archived at https://perma. cc/9MCT-WESP) [Last accessed 16/5/2021].

3   Breeden II, J (2013) The tech behind NASA's Martian chronicles, GCN, 4 January. Available from: https://gcn.com/articles/2013/01/04/tech-behind-nasa-martian-chronicles.aspx (archived at https://perma.cc/E9CX-CDKX) [Last accessed 16/5/2021].

4   Amazon retail case studies (2018) Amazon AWS. Available from: https://aws. amazon.com/retail/case-studies/ (archived at https://perma.cc/DCD7-2YDA) [Last accessed 16/5/2021].

5   Kharpal, Arjun (2020) Alibaba, JD set new records to rack up record $115 billion of sales on Singles Day as regulations loom, CNBC.com, 12 November. Available from: https://www.cnbc.com/2020/11/12/singles-day-2020-alibaba-and-jd-rack-up-record-115-billion-of-sales.html (archived at https://perma.cc/ P9EE-G3A4) [Last accessed 16/4/2021].

6   GSMA Intelligence (2020) The mobile economy 2020, March. Available from: https://www.gsma.com/mobileeconomy/ (archived at https://perma.cc/L3U7-LMPN) [Last accessed 16/5/2021].

7   Dvorak, John (1984) The Mac meets the press, San Francisco Examiner, 2 February, quoted in Owen Linzmayer, Apple Confidential 2.0, p115. Available from: https://books.google.co.uk/books?id=mXnw5tM8QRwC&lpg=PA119& pg=PA119#v=onepage&q&f=false (archived at https://perma.cc/56M5-6CV3) [Last accessed 16/5/2021].

8   Molen, Brad (2014) Amazon Fire phone review: a unique device, but you're better off waiting for the sequel, Endgadget, 22 June. Available from: https:// www.engadget.com/2014/07/22/amazon-fire-phone-review/ (archived at https://perma.cc/8A2F-BQ39) [Last accessed 16/5/2021].

9   Limer, Eric (2014) Amazon Fire Phone review: a shaky first step, Gizmodo, 22 June. Available from: https://gizmodo.com/amazon-fire-phone-review-a-shaky-first-step-1608853105 (archived at https://perma.cc/PS6N-XFZG) [Last accessed 16/5/2021].

10 Wohlsen, Marcus (2015) The Amazon Fire Phone was always going to fail, *Wired*, 1 June. Available from: https://www.wired.com/2015/01/amazon-fire-phone-always-going-fail/ (archived at https://perma.cc/V86J-C3TA) [Last accessed 16/5/2021].

11 Staff researcher (2020) 44 cart abandonment rate statistics, Baymard Institute, 20 December. Available from: https://baymard.com/lists/cart-abandonment-rate (archived at https://perma.cc/8RQF-WMNM) [Last accessed 16/5/2021].

12 Pathak, Shareen (2017) End of an era: Amazon's 1-click buying patent finally expires, *Digiday*, 13 September. Available from: https://digiday.com/marketing/end-era-amazons-one click-buying-patent-finally-expires/ [Last accessed 16/5/202].

13 Brooke, Eliza (2014) Amazon touts reduced shopping cart abandonment with newly expanded 'login and pay' service, *Fashionista*, 16 September. Available from: https://fashionista.com/2014/09/amazon-login-and-pay (archived at https://perma.cc/AA4V-GK3S) [Last accessed 16/5/2021].

14 Lipsman, Andrew (2017) 5 interesting facts About Millennials' mobile app usage from 'The 2017 U.S. Mobile App Report', *comScore*, Insights, 24 August. Available from: https://www.comscore.com/Insights/Blog/5-Interesting-Facts-About-Millennials-Mobile-App-Usage-from-The-2017-US-Mobile-App-Report (archived at https://perma.cc/LW2N-E7GS) [Last accessed 16/5/2021].

12

AI and voice: the new retail frontier

'People are busy taking care of work and family in today's virtual world. They are tired of Zoom and Teams. It's nice to be able to order food and groceries via voice-controlled apps while doing other things, and chat with strangers at any time without having to go on camera.'
Parna Sarkar-Basu, CEO, Brand and Buzz Marketing[1]

To recap what we've explored in regard to the pivotal role technology has had to play in Amazon and the wider retail industry's fortunes so far, we have seen how global technology drivers have helped to facilitate Amazon's growth, and how it would not have been possible for it to take advantage of these drivers were it not, first and foremost, a technology company. It is reliant on the fact the on-my-terms shopper has embraced the internet, touchscreens and mobile apps, among other digital technology innovations. We have also discussed how its technology capabilities then enabled it to apply its significant ability to innovate at the point of divergence in shopping between the functional and fun.

The technology drivers harnessed by Amazon have helped it develop the e-commerce shopping journey and introduce new shopping experiences, including one-hour delivery and automated replenishment. But we have purposefully left the most revolutionary of its innovations for last: that is, voice technology. Having also outlined the impact of the first two global technology drivers (ubiquitous connectivity and pervasive interfaces) on retail as an industry and Amazon's dominance within it, it is here, with voice, that the third driver – autonomous computing – comes into its own.

In order to understand the significance of this third technology driver on Amazon's fortunes, it is important to understand the distinction between technology systems that are programmed to 'automate' and digitize previously manually intensive and error-prone processes, and those technology systems whose programs enable them to solve problems without implicit direction, ie autonomously. These systems are also described as 'machines that learn', spawning the development of interrelated branches of AI, including machine learning, neural networks and NLP.

Autonomous computing development – moving beyond simple automation to eliminating the need for human intervention – would not have been possible without massively networked systems, such as the internet, plus having some network-connected means of accessing the information they store, such as desktop client PCs, as well as smartphones and tablets. The likes of cloud computing, also developed out of the drive towards ubiquitous connectivity and storage access, is also an essential building block of autonomous computing systems. Big Data, generated as the result of increasingly pervasive interfaces that encourage users to digitize more of their lives, from music and messages to memories, feeds these systems with varied and potentially unstructured data needed to derive insight from innumerable 'what if?'-type scenarios.

The most significant manifestation of the drive towards increasingly autonomous computing systems is AI. In turn, AI has made checkout-less stores, chatbots, robotics, driverless cars, drones and voice assistants a reality, and we have only begun to tap its potential. Indeed, the global artificial intelligence in retail market is expected to grow at a compound annual growth rate (CAGR) of 34.4 per cent from 2020 to reach $19.9 billion by 2027.[2] It is no accident, therefore, that AWS, the massive amounts of data Amazon already has on its customers, and its relentless pursuit of simplification in the name of innovation, has supported the company's dominance in the rapidly emerging area of AI and its application through voice systems.

The value of recommendation

Having identified AI as the culmination of the main drivers shaping technology innovation today (stemming from a need for more autonomous computer systems particularly) – and before diving straight into voice technology as its current apotheosis – it is necessary to undertake an examination of how Amazon capitalized on the development of AI systems across its business and not just in its customers' homes, as we have already done with the drivers of ubiquitous connectivity and pervasive interfaces. This adds to our understanding of how it has achieved its aim of removing friction from the average shopping journey and, in so doing, created a virtuous cycle that, in turn, generates even more sales and growth.

In fact, it is AI that underpins the power of its search and recommendation engines. Back in the 1990s, Amazon was one of the first e-commerce players to place heavy emphasis on product recommendations, which also helped it to cross-sell new categories as it moved beyond books. It is a category of technology development that Bezos has described as 'the practical application of machine learning'. Amazon's search and recommendation machine learning capabilities also underpin its sophisticated supply chain proficiency, as well as its most recent voice shopping assistant functionality. In all of these applications, it can use the massive computing power of its AWS division to crunch billions of data points in support of testing a variety of options and outcomes to rapidly work out what will and won't cost-effectively work with customers. Historically, more than a third of Amazon purchases are driven by AI-generated product recommendations.[3] It has also made its AI framework, DSSTNE (pronounced as 'destiny') free, to help expand the ways deep learning can extend beyond speech and language understanding and object recognition to areas such as search and recommendations. The decision to open source DSSTNE also demonstrates how Amazon recognizes the need to collaborate over making gains with the vast potential of AI.

On the Amazon site, these recommendations can be personalized, based on categories and ranges previously searched or browsed, to increase conversion. Equally, Amazon's recommendation engine can display products similar to those searched for or browsed in the hopes of converting customers to rival brands or products. There are also recommendations based on anything 'related to the items you've viewed'. Or they can depend on items that are 'frequently bought together' or by 'customers who bought this item also bought…' with the aim of boosting average order value. In these cases, 'if that, then this' (IFTT) AI-powered decision engines work in the background to match the items in your basket with other complementary products. For example, browsing for a gadget might prompt Amazon to recommend the right-sized cover for it, or a compatible peripheral accessory.

All of this affinity marketing is powered by AI-based machine learning algorithms that can match whoever is using the site dynamically with what they see. This can depend on myriad variables, such as the customer's purchase history and preferences, and what's in stock and what stock needs shifting quickly, in such a way as only AI-based systems are advanced enough to deliver in real time. It is also the foundation of its growing ads-based business.

China's Alibaba Group uses AI-driven product recommendations for shoppers with no previous transaction data. According to Wei Hu, Alibaba Merchant Service Business Unit director of data technology, its engine can consider data points from other browsing and shopping data to match new shoppers with relevant items. Return customers to the Group's Tmall and Taobao platforms are presented with product recommendations based not just on their past transactions, but also on browsing history, product feedback, bookmarks, geographic location and other online activity-related data. During just one of its 'Singles' Day shopping festivals, Alibaba used its AI recommendations engine to generate 6.7 billion personalized Taobao shopping pages based on merchants' target customer data. Alibaba said that this large-scale personalization resulted in a 20 per cent improvement in conversion rate from the 11 November event.[4]

The importance of interaction

One of the last, more mature areas of AI development applied to online customer service specifically are 'chatbots', so called for their use of conversational, AI-based NLP algorithms to manage common issues and questions. Much like the interactive voice recognition (IVR) systems used by businesses to triage customers' calls, Amazon.com customers can chat with the Amazon Assistant online for shopping help. Going one step further, it has tested neural network-based AI systems that can handle common customer service requests automatically and help customer service agents respond to customers more easily.

Most text-based online customer service systems use automated agents to handle simple requests, such as checking the status of an order or initiating a refund. Where these agents are typically governed by rules, if they can't recognize or handle a request, they refer the request onto a human customer service representative.

The neural networks Amazon is using move beyond rules-based autonomous computing, enabling agents to handle a broader range of interactions.

Amazon has said this garners better results and allows its customer service representatives to focus on tasks that depend more on human judgement.

The next stage in the use of chatbots for shopping is also moving beyond answering customer queries into the realms of what's been referred to as 'conversational commerce', where the chat or voice assistant is able to influence a sale. Sephora's virtual artist, an AR-integrated chatbot, offers customers a virtual makeover using selfies. Kik bot, by fashion retailer H&M, is a digital stylist that uses a customer's history to personalize recommendations based on their interests. These bots can also help increase sales by processing payments directly in the chat interface, and are expected to grow in use by 20 per cent year-on-year, according to Deloitte, to more than 10 billion interactions within the next few years.

If retailers and brands have been using chatbots for customer-facing interaction, another, related, space Amazon plays in is the development of bots for business. AWS chatbot AI framework, Amazon Lex, is designed to enable organizations to build bots that increase contact centre productivity, automate simple tasks and drive operational efficiencies. It also powers Amazon Alexa. E-commerce rival Shopify also offers a virtual assistant called Kit that lets you perform tasks like social network ads, sending 'thank you' emails, and creating and promoting discount codes.

Recommendations, personalization and chatbots aside, Amazon's reliance on AI systems to orchestrate its vast business operations as well as its customer-facing ones is diverse. But, as for those that are the most significant in our exploration of best retail practice established by the company, we cannot discuss Amazon and AI without also touching on its supply chain and the introduction of its Just Walk Out checkout-free store technology system.

Supply chain complexity

Again, in order to understand the true significance of Amazon's AI advantage in its supply chain, it is necessary to first grasp what the industry-wide challenges are. Global research carried out by analyst firm IHL Group found that (exacerbated by the disruption of the COVID pandemic), inventory distortion, caused by under- and overstocking in supply chains and stores, amounted to $1.8 trillion in 2020.[5]

When grocery store shelves were left bare by panic buying, and non-essential retailers who were forced to close stores scrambled to make stock available for sale online, even Amazon was not immune to the impact of COVID-19 on supply chains. Early during the outbreak it informed sellers in a number of affected markets that it would no longer accept non-essential products at its warehouses, causing chaos for many.[6] A surge in orders caught it by surprise and it struggled to meet delivery windows, quickly running out of hand sanitizer and paper towels, which meant it had also had to combat widespread price gouging. Like every other operator, it rushed to accommodate necessary operational changes to keep warehouse employees safe without slowing productivity. But that was not before it faced negative press over sacking two employees who spoke publicly about misgivings over the lack of health initiatives for warehouse workers. Even Jeff Bezos was forced to acknowledge the impact of coronavirus on Amazon's supply chain early on. 'The current crisis is demonstrating the adaptability and durability of Amazon's business as never before, but it's also the hardest time we've ever faced', he said.[7]

It is easy, therefore, to see why Amazon has been pushing forward in this space for some time now – right to back when 'predictive analytics' defined the limits of early forays into AI. Its 'anticipatory shipping' patent caused waves for signalling its intent to use AI in order to squeeze even more efficiency out of its supply chain by putting the stock closer to customers before customers even knew they would want to buy it. After all, it arguably has more to lose than its competitors, with its free, two-day Prime delivery promise. The patent enables it to pick, pack and ship the products it expects customers in a specific area will want, before they are ordered – based on previous orders and other factors. The packages wait at shipping hubs or on trucks until an order arrives. Its potential was very quickly apparent to many, including Professor Praveen Kopalle. 'If implemented well, this strategy has the potential to take predictive analytics to the next level, allowing the data-savvy company to greatly expand its base of loyal customers', she said.[8]

Even so, Ralf Herbrich, Amazon's former director of machine learning, remarked that some items are much harder to predict demand for.[9] With clothing, for instance, the company must decide which sizes and colours to stock at which warehouses, depending on nearby buyers' shapes and tastes, as demand can be affected by shifting trends and seasons, as well as exceptional drivers, such as lockdown panic.

The rapid expansion of its Prime commitments has always been a catalyst for Amazon to bring the ubiquitous connectivity of its cloud services to bear on the development of increasingly autonomous, command-and-control operational fulfilment capabilities for many years. In this way, it has also entrusted robots in its warehouses and delivery drones with autonomous functionality to support growth. When Amazon acquired Kiva Systems, the robotics company that had been supplying warehouse robots for Amazon to automate its order fulfilment processes, and which is now the backbone of the company's Robotics division, it clearly signalled its intent to move the dial on its warehouse efficiency. Today, consensus estimates put its total robot fleet at over 200,000. This would mean its robotic fleet constitutes at least 25 per cent of the company's workforce, performing roles with varying degrees of AI-enabled autonomy. Amazon has also tested delivery drones and made its first package delivery using a semi-autonomous drone, with grand aspirations that 'One day, seeing Prime Air vehicles will be as normal as seeing mail trucks on the road.'[10] (We explore the impact of Prime Air in more detail in Chapter 16.)

Just Walk Out

While we also explore the significance of its checkout-free convenience system, 'Just Walk Out', in other chapters, we must include it here as evidence of Amazon's technology-fuelled ambitions not just to embed itself in our homes, on the mobile devices that accompany us everywhere, or through its own supply chain and fulfilment operations. It has now set its sights on conquering the physical retail space. If retailers felt under siege by the inexorable erosion of their store-based market share by e-commerce, then Amazon's checkout-free stores are tantamount to an existential threat to their core bricks and mortar businesses and the people who staff them.

Amazon's Just Walk Out technology system detects which products customers take from or return to the shelves, keeping track of them in a virtual cart so that the customers are automatically charged for the items they leave the store with. Apart from its relevance here to Amazon's use of AI, in combination with computer vision and sensor fusion technologies in pursuit of providing more frictionless retail experiences that can be further monetized through licensing its use to other retailers and in other industrial applications, it is also a great demonstration of how it has used the technology drivers of change to enable this experience, eliminating the function of the checkout process altogether.

Just Walk Out capitalizes on technology drivers of change to serve the on-my-terms shopper:

1   *Ubiquitous connectivity*: view customer activity and attribute spend at every point in their shopping journey – online or offline.

   a) Customers are unable to even enter the store without first registering their personal and payment details with Amazon.

   b) Customers must identify themselves using the Amazon app on their mobile device to gain entry to the store, which also helps to tie their store visit and purchases to their online identity.

2   *Pervasive interfaces*: remove any barriers to shopping, such as technical issues that may arise with scan-as-you-shop, self-service systems that rely on customers to use their own mobile phones or purpose-built handheld devices provided by the retailer, at that retailer's capital expense.

   a) The use of a mobile app is the most friction-free way to ensure a smooth convenience store experience for customers on entry.

   b) The removal of any human interface from the most friction-filled process of any store-based shopping journey, ie checkout, affords the customer unprecedented speed and simplicity.

3   *Autonomous computing*: AI-based computer vision, sensor fusion and deep learning technologies power Just Walk Out technology.

   a) Just Walk Out technology operates without manual intervention, eliminating the need for checkout staff or hardware.

   b) It also eliminates shrinkage as a major source of loss for traditional bricks and mortar retailers. Customers are charged with whatever goods they walk out with, even if they try to hide the fact from the store's extensive computer vision camera tracking systems.

The untapped potential of voice

It's taken a while to get here. But now, within the context of Amazon's track record of capitalizing on technology drivers of change, it is clear to see quite how important a bet it has made on voice – especially when you consider that it is predicted that the number of devices consumers will use to interact with voice assistants will grow 113 per cent from 4.2 billion in 2020 to over

8.4 billion devices by 2024.[11] In fact, David Limp, Amazon Digital Devices SVP, predicted from the outset that 'voice control in the home will be ubiquitous. Kids today will grow up never knowing a day they couldn't talk to their houses'.[12]

Amazon launched its first voice-enabled hardware device, Echo, featuring its AI-powered Alexa voice assistant in – surprise, surprise – 2015. Just as it did with AWS, 1-click, Prime, its mobile app, Pay with Amazon, Dash, drone delivery, robots and Just Walk Out, Amazon has been attempting to define a new mode of pervasive computing interface using sophisticated AI systems that play completely to its strengths, feed its existing ecosystem and embed it further in the everyday functions of the home. Juniper Research predicts voice commerce sales will amount to $164 billion worldwide by 2025, which represents a five-year CAGR of 630 per cent from the $22 billion spent in 2020.[13] The aim of Amazon's Alexa voice assistant is not solely to increase Amazon.com sales per se, but to deepen the reliance on its ecosystem among the on-my-terms shoppers it has so far served so well, and suck them in further. This is why some have said that 'Amazon won by losing the smartphone war'.[14]

The argument follows that, if the Fire phone had been a success at launch, Amazon would have been bogged down in the complexity of updating mobile device hardware and its Fire mobile OS ever since. Perhaps Amazon's management realized it was never going to win the smartphone wars with Apple and Google, whose core businesses are founded on mobile software and hardware development, not retail. Either way, the initial launch of the Echo voice-enabled device, followed by the continually revamped and expanded line of Echo devices it unveils every year, demonstrate a real differentiator for Amazon as well as the culmination of its flywheel strategy, which is based on its three pillars that are, in turn, built on the three global drivers of technology development, and which facilitate more and more frictionless retailing experiences.

First-mover advantage

While the voice assistant device market is still in its relatively early stages of development, Amazon has already consolidated its first-mover advantage, enabling its users to watch shows, sports and movies (with Fire TV), turn on kitchen timers, listen to music, check the weather, even connect the Alexa app on their phone with their car using Echo Auto and, of course, shop on Amazon – all using just their voice and all with the aim of positioning its voice devices as so indispensable that it is able to embed itself ever more firmly into its customers' lives. It's another example of Amazon building out a 'competitive moat' around its customer base and also why antitrust clouds have gathered overhead. It's also worth mentioning here how Black Friday and Prime Day have certainly helped Amazon sell more Echo devices. It uses these artificial promotional events to offer exclusive discounts on orders placed through Alexa in order to get shoppers comfortable with the idea of voice-activated shopping.

Harking back to its Fire phone misstep, Bloomberg's Shira Ovide correctly observed at the time: 'Amazon is building a future untethered from the smartphone, but with all the software intelligence of that gadget and more – with the company at the centre. Amazon can embrace this future because it lost the recent past.'[15] Today, every Alexa-embedded device sale sucks that customer further into Amazon's flywheel ecosystem, as it is very hard not to interact with Amazon when using one, much in the same way as Google and Apple funnel their customers into their respective ecosystems and maximize lock-in by removing friction to ensure the seamless interoperability between their different proprietary products. 'The default option for buying stuff through the Amazon devices is Amazon', Ovide added.

Amazon's ecosystem play lies at the heart of its voice development, and so, perhaps unsurprisingly, it has emerged that shopping is not the main use case for Alexa. The top three shopping-related Alexa commands used by owners related to researching products, adding items to their shopping list and tracking a package.

ACTIVITIES THAT VOICE ASSISTANT OWNERS ALREADY PERFORM VIA VOICE ON A REGULAR BASIS:

51% product research

36% adding items to shopping list

30% package tracking

22% making a purchase

20% providing ratings or reviews

18% contacting support

17% reordering items

Voicebot Smart Speaker Consumer Adoption Report

These findings were supported by research carried out by Strategy Analytics which found smart speaker sales reached 147 million units globally in 2019. Amazon retained the market share crown with 26.2 per cent, down from 33.7 per cent in 2018, followed by Google with 20.3 per cent, which was down from 26 per cent year-on-year. However, it wasn't always this way. Only a few years after Alexa's launch on the Amazon Echo, the top-selling device sold via Amazon during that period to shoppers looking to connect to and control the likes of lighting, security and heating systems in their home via voice was its rival, Google's Nest heating thermostat controller. Amazon subsequently withdrew Nest devices for sale from its site, clearly demonstrating how ruthless it is prepared to be in its attempts to kill the competition.

Voice as the next frontier

The main question on every retailer and brand owner's lips is whether voice will add to or cannibalize sales made in other channels. Unsurprisingly, the rate at which consumers shopped for retail products from home doubled during the height of the COVID-19 pandemic, providing a boost to voice-enabled products and sales. Where 92.4 per cent of consumers watch television, 54.7 per cent own a smart TV, and 17 per cent shop while watching television, nearly a third (32.6 per cent) own a voice assistant and 30 per cent drive a connected car.

To capitalize on increased adoption and headroom for growth, Amazon has been encouraging third parties to build Alexa skills, opening up its Alexa skills store for anyone to create custom Alexa skills. It also introduced the Alexa Knowledge Skills voice app option for developers to integrate product catalogues and build directories and other facts into the voice assistant. User can then simply ask Alexa for information without needing to invoke a specific skill.

With forecasts suggesting that, by 2024, the number of digital voice assistants will outstrip the world population and grow at 4-year CAGR of 19% to 8.4 billion units, Amazon needs to build out its voice ecosystem to maintain market share.[16]

Another question worrying retailers and brands with voice is how it will affect the discoverability of their products when the billions spent on marketing and advertising are not as easily transferable to or discoverable via the voice platform. The fact is that Alexa will only return two results to a search query, as opposed to the pages of results returned when using mobile or desktop Amazon search (along with the ads, recommendations and various other marketing tools that subsume the shopping experience). Based on a consensus of research to date, there are a number of factors that determine which of those two results are returned via voice (Source: One Click Retail):

1 Purchase history – Alexa will offer to reorder the same item if purchased before.

2 If there is no purchase history for Alexa to revert to, it will then offer an 'Amazon Choice' – a dynamic tag assigned to certain items based on a number of factors introduced with the launch of its first Echo device. These include that the product has to be available via Prime, and so will be shipped via its Fulfilment by Amazon service (from Amazon itself or an Amazon seller using FBA); it has to be in stock and replenishable; and it has to have a review rating of 4.0 or higher.

3 In the absence of purchase history or an Amazon Choice, Alexa will return the same top two organic search results that Amazon's search would serve on via mobile or desktop PC.

This means that to win with Alexa for shopping, the good news is that the fundamentals of search – keywords, title and product feature bullets and description – still apply. Put another way, it is the same content and attributes used to describe a product that drives both higher click through, and then sales conversion rates, from both traditional and voice search results that will determine how high up the search ranking that product appears – for now.

Bezos has publicly stated that Amazon designed Alexa with the same principles it used to build its business: by focusing on products that customers are likely to prefer, regardless of whether the products are sold by Amazon or third-party sellers.

He told a US Congressional big tech antitrust hearing: 'There are a variety of ways to shop using Alexa, and Amazon is still in the early stages of learning what is most helpful to customers and designing tools and features that improve their shopping experience. One popular way Alexa helps customers, for example, is by suggesting products that customers frequently purchase based on their past orders, whether those orders are from Amazon or a third-party seller. If a customer has not purchased an item from Amazon's store before, Alexa may highlight a highly-rated, well-priced product. In addition, most Alexa shopping interactions provide product suggestions customers can review later on their phone or computer.'

Bezos also revealed that customers only complete the purchase of a product suggested by Alexa on Alexa a low, single-digit percentage of the time. He said the percentage of third-party sales purchased directly through Alexa more than doubled from launch, accounting for 45 per cent of all sales made through Alexa in 2020. This percentage was lower than overall third-party sales on Amazon (about 58 per cent of physical items) in part, he explained, because customers disproportionately use Alexa to order household consumable items (like paper towels or batteries) for which Amazon's offers are particularly competitive. However, a US antitrust subcommittee report found: 'Voice assistant ecosystems are an emerging market with a high propensity for lock-in and self-preferencing. Amazon has expanded Alexa's ecosystem quickly through acquisitions of complementary and competing technologies, and by selling its Alexa-enabled smart speakers at deep discounts.'[17]

Taking Amazon's growing ads business into consideration, it seems only a matter of time before the company also looks to monetize its reach via voice, despite its repeated intentions for Alexa to remain ad-free. In the meantime, just before stepping down as CEO, Bezos admitted to a US Congressional hearing that 'it wouldn't surprise me if Alexa does promote our own products'.

Nevertheless, voice is a gateway into the Amazon shopping ecosystem that competitors cannot afford to ignore. They have rushed to integrate Alexa skills into their offerings, not unlike the rush to develop mobile apps for Apple and Android app stores in the early days of consumer smartphone adoption. In fact, online grocers like Ocado and Peapod (which was acquired by Ahold Delhaize and integrated into its US Stop & Shop banner) were among the first to integrate Alexa globally. Ocado's Alexa skill lets customers add products to their order, as well as check their order total and ask what produce is in season, for example. When it comes to direct competitors, Google introduced a rival programme called Shopping Actions, which it later renamed to Buy on Google, offering a universal shopping cart for shopping on mobile, PC or via a voice-enabled device. Major retailers, including Walmart, Target, Ulta Beauty, Costco and Home Depot, signed up to the programme to list products across Google Search, in its Google Express shopping service, and in the Google Assistant app for smartphones and on smart speakers like the Google Home.[18]

In spite of competitive challenges, by feeding further into Amazon's flywheel ecosystem, Alexa is just the latest technology-based competitive tool that forces rivals such as Ocado to build on it in order to fulfil the need to remain relevant against a competitor that is helping to drive unprece-dented, technology-fuelled change in the retail space.

'You do not survive in this industry without being a little paranoid and looking over your shoulder,' Carrie Bienkowski, former Peapod chief marketing officer, once commented: 'Ten years ago, just getting your grocer-ies delivered – that was convenient. But one of the things we're really internalizing is the fact that we've got to continue to evolve beyond just the delivery of groceries.'

While the likes of Ocado and Ahold Delhaize could be applauded for embracing 'co-opetition' and developing for Alexa, it is likely that the real winner as a result of their efforts is not the consumer but Amazon. This explains why Amazon has invested to build out its Alexa hardware and software ecosystem beyond just facilitating online shopping, adding calling facilities and a screen (which may seem to run counter to the idea of increas-ingly pervasive computing interfaces that 'disappear' into the background). Its efforts to build out the ecosystem to control more smart devices, from ovens to TVs, have spawned around 100,000 Alexa skills worldwide that can interoperate with a similar number of third-party smart devices.

Spencer Millerberg, founder and former CEO of One Click Retail, there-fore advises that deciding how much investment to put into Alexa voice search is 'all about prioritization. If you're the CEO of a music business, then absolutely, this has got to be one of your first [strategic development] priorities. If you're the CEO of a consumer brand, it's going to end up becoming a little bit less [of a priority], because shopping is not a top Alexa use case; whereas if you're in home automation, maybe it's the middle ground you have to work in. The main thing we have to focus on is the fundamentals.'[19]

Danny Silverman, general manager at Spotlight by Ascential (formerly know as Clavis Insight), adds: 'At the end of the day, [the fundamentals are that] the same things that drive voice search are what drive search on desk-top and mobile. If you have the data and insights to understand what's working or not [as regards search rankings on Amazon.com], and you opti-mize against those for desktop and mobile, you will win with voice at the same time.'

So, while it's hard to chart the evolution of frictionless retail against the drivers in technology development that have enabled it without including Amazon on the map, it is also impossible to envisage its growing influence on the application of AI and voice abating.

Retail technology smarts

But where does this journey of innovation towards truly frictionless retail experiences leave the rest of retail? Indeed, with the retail market reeling from the latest round of profit warnings and administrations in the sector, many retailers will be looking towards digital technology differentiation to ride out challenging times and futureproof their businesses. Uwe Weiss, Blue Yonder chief executive, argued that the 'Amazon Effect' – in the sense of ongoing disruption and evolution of the retail market caused by the consumerization of technology and the on-my-terms shopper – will now increase its influence as retailers fight to retain market share and customer loyalty. When it comes to its impact on brands, for example, the industry is anxiously waiting to see if voice has a tangible impact on brand loyalty and marketing strategies – particularly if voice systems remain ad-free. The need for sophisticated content and attribute-led management to top search rankings could require some drastic reorganization in some companies.[20]

Weiss pointed out that, with Amazon already using AI to deliver personalized shopping recommendations and optimize its supply chains, traditional retailers must be all the more aggressive in their adoption of next-generation technologies if they are to retain market share. 'With the likes of more traditional retailers facing closures, innovation needs to be in the spotlight more than ever,' he said. He highlighted that the field of AI is developing incredibly quickly. Amazon's recommendation system runs on a machine learning-based architecture, so its suggestions on what to buy, watch or read next are 'incredibly smart', and Google's DeepMind division is now giving its AI algorithms an 'imagination' so that it can predict how a certain situation will evolve and make decisions. 'This leads to more conversions and upselling across the business, as well as giving Amazon insight on how to price its products for its customers, and how much stock to hold,' he added.

Rightly so, though Weiss warned against using technology for technology's sake, especially in areas where Amazon's advantage of being a technology company first is insurmountable. While it is clear that the potential of AI to boost levels of productivity, efficiency and personalization in the retail industry is promising, he advised retailers to also be realistic about what they can expect from AI and machine learning. 'AI in retail doesn't predict the future – at least not yet!' he stressed. 'It analyses reams and reams of intricate behavioural and circumstantial data to identify patterns and trends. These trends enable retailers to make informed decisions that result in more accurate stock levels, and pricing that better suits product lifecycles.'

Weiss also pointed out that if traditional retailers, particularly in the grocery sector, are to survive and compete with online giants such as Amazon, they will need to radically adjust their approach to technology and data. 'Retailers need to begin thinking of data as one of their most important assets, and as the key that can enable them to build better relationships with their customers, optimize their supply chain and pricing, and compete against online competitors,' he concluded. For example, research has shown that over half of all Amazon Echoes are located in the kitchen, meaning the opportunity for greater category-specific engagement around recipe preparation and ad hoc basket building for household goods and grocery could initially be higher for operators with relevant businesses and brands. The introduction of a smart camera with the Echo Look, as discussed in Chapter 10, was designed to access the fashion apparel market screen, working in conjunction with an app to offer suggestions on what to wear and share photos and video via social media. But when it was superseded by the Echo Show, which features a screen, it subsequently paved the way for users to make video and voice calls. Also powered by AI and voice, the Style by Alexa Amazon app feature dispenses fashion tips, and any Alexa-enabled device will attempt to help if asked, 'Alexa, what should I wear?' In this way, voice expands on the 'in the moment' shopping trend and may even become the gatekeeper to the shopper, particularly for grocery retailers and FMCG brands from a retail volume point of view. Some have begun integrating voice into their mobile apps, as the latest evolution of the technology's development. The app of US retailer Target lets customers ask about their order status, which is great if you're in the car about to do curbside pickup, for example.

It's perhaps not surprising those grocers that don't want to join Amazon have formed an 'anti-Amazon' alliance with Google over its rival voice assistant, and the internet giant has been more than happy to oblige. Unsurprisingly, Walmart, Tesco and Carrefour were keen to sign up and develop capabilities for their customers to order goods online using Google Assistant via its Google Shopping service. Carrefour, for example, partnered with Google to create an online voice assistant called 'Lea' as part of the French retailer's five-year, $3.5 billion digital transformation plans. 'Lea has been designed to make day-to-day life easier for our customers – they can use it to manage their shopping lists... using just their voice,' the French retail giant stated at the time. It launched a voice-based grocery shopping service using Google Assistant software to connect customers to Carrefour's e-commerce platform in 2020.

Competitive landscape

Google is currently the only viable alternative voice platform to Alexa for shopping. Even though Google trails a distant second to Amazon, the Google Assistant itself can claim far higher penetration levels, and Google has said it is used by over 500 million globally. From January 2018 to September 2020, the number of smart devices supported by Google Assistant rose from around 1,500 to 50,000, from 5,500 manufacturers. These include home appliances from LG, headphones from Bose and a range of speakers from a range of different companies, robot vacuums, smart plugs and, of course, car entertainment systems with Android Auto, as well as all devices running its Android OS. But the supporting Google Express shopping platform is relatively small in scale, scope and fulfilment speed in comparison to Amazon's Marketplace, Fulfilment by Amazon and Prime services.

Other players are also entering the fray. Even Starbucks entered a joint partnership with Shinsegae Group in South Korea to integrate voice recognition ordering with Bixby, Samsung's voice assistant as an extension of Starbucks' mobile order-ahead-and-pay technology. Apple's Home Pod device features its Siri voice assistant. While it offers voice-activated smart home and audio-visual control and device integration, as well as news, weather, calendar and mapping functionality, where you can ask it, 'what's the best vegetarian food nearby?', for example, Apple hasn't yet forged the partnerships or ecosystem required for consumers to do any shopping with it. But the iOS shopping list app Grocery utilizes Siri and is built on top of Apple's Reminders app.

Whether consumers come to trust Alexa and its counterparts to delegate shopping tasks, however, is another matter entirely, given the nature of their operation means some are by design always on and listening, while others require a separate physical interaction with the device before listening for a voice prompt – think Apple and the long home-button press to activate Siri on an iOS device. Instead, a number of reports have suggested that Alexa can mishear words in conversation or even on the TV that it thinks are a cue to leap into action. Such accidental activation has led to reports of Alexa uttering random creepy laughter, or even thinking it had been prompted to record a man and his wife's conversation and then send the recording to one of his employees.[21]

This led to revelations that the AI system powering Alexa needed additional training using human input, where a global team reviews audio clips to help the voice-activated assistant respond to commands.[22] Some have

TABLE 12.1   Amazon technology hardware launches, 2011–2021

Amazon device	Launch date	Price at launch	Functionality
Kindle Fire	November 2011	$199	Tablet computer
Fire TV	April 2014	$70	Smart TV streaming media device
Fire Phone	July 2014	$199	Smartphone (discontinued August 2015)
Dash Button	March 2015	$4.99	One click, auto-replenishment device (discontinued February 2019)
Echo	June 2015	$100	Smart speaker and voice assistant
Echo Dot	March 2016	$50	Mini version of smart speaker and voice assistant
Amazon Tap	June 2016	$80	Smart, battery-powered speaker and voice assistant (discontinued December 2018)
Echo Look	April 2017	$120	Smart speaker, voice assistant and handsfree camera (discontinued July 2020)
Echo Show	June 2017	$230	Smart speaker and screen, voice assistant and videoconferencing system
Dash Wand	June 2017	$20	Battery-powered, voice assistant-enabled grocery scanner (discontinued July 2020)
Cloud Cam	October 2017	$120	Home security camera (discontinued October 2019)
Blink	October 2017	$100	Smart, battery-operated home security camera and door bell
Echo Plus	October 2017	$150	Smart speaker, voice assistant, and connected home device hub (discontinued September 2020)
Echo Spot	December 2017	$130	Smart speaker, voice assistant and digital alarm clock
Echo Connect	December 2017	$35	Telephony connector to Echo devices
Echo Buttons	December 2017	$20	Gaming control extensions to Echo devices
Amazon Fire Cube	June 2018	$119	Voice assistant-enabled 4K TV streaming set-top-box

(continued)

TABLE 12.1 (Continued)

Amazon device	Launch date	Price at launch	Functionality
Ring Alarm	July 2018	$119	Alarm security kit with a keypad, siren and motion sensors
Echo Wall Clock	September 2018	$30	Syncs time to a paired Echo device
Echo Sub	September 2018	$129	Subwoofer that connects to other Echo speakers
Amazon Smart Plug	September 2018	$25	Smart Alexa-controlled plug
Fire TV Recast	November 2018	$280	Digital video recorder with an over-the-air antenna for Fire TV or Echo Show device playback
Echo Link	December 2018	$199	Smart, mains-powered voice assistant speaker with output ports and volume control
Echo Link Amp	May 2019	$299	Smart, mains-powered voice assistant speaker and amplifier
Echo Auto	September 2019	$25	Smart, Bluetooth-enabled Alexa in-car mobile app connector
Echo Loop	September 2019	$179.99	Wearable smart ring for Alexa activation
Echo Flex	November 2019	$25	Smart, mains-powered Alexa speaker
Echo Buds	October 2019	$130	Wireless earbuds with Alexa integration
Echo Input	December 2019	$100	Smart, mains-powered voice assistant input device with no on-board speakers
Echo Studio	December 2019	$199.99	Smart Alexa speaker with 360-degree and Dolby sound
Luna Game Controller	September 2020	$49.99	Amazon Luna gaming platform cloud-connected controller
Always Home Cam	September 2020	$250	Aerial indoor security camera
Amazon eero 6	September 2020	$129	App-controlled wireless mesh router
Echo Frames	December 2020	$249.99	Wearable Alexa-enabled smart glasses with mobile device
Ring Car Alarm, Cam & Connect	December 2020	$59.99 to $199.99	Smart in-car security system

SOURCE Author research

questioned whether this adds weight to the case that, apart from the obvious privacy concerns, Amazon has an unfair advantage by potentially having access to customer recordings.

Similar concerns were raised when Amazon bought internet router provider Eero, which had become known for its focus on privacy. But to the retail tech giant, getting into the consumer Wi-Fi business is just another step in its development of a smart home ecosystem of devices that further embeds itself into our lives. But this attitude has also stoked voice-related antitrust concerns. For example, Patrick Spence, Sonos CEO, accused Amazon, alongside Google, in congressional testimony of using their respective search and e-commerce to subsidize the smart speaker market and, potentially, unfairly dominate the market for other smart home and voice-activated devices.

The other unknown is how the use of voice may play out in the store, which we explore in greater depth in the next chapter. Meanwhile, Amazon was the first to strike a landmark deals with Toyota and BMW to integrate Alexa into cars. Even satellite navigation manufacturers have got in on the act, like Garmin, which offers cameras that also come with Alexa integration. This enables the use of voice commands to get directions, play music, make phone calls, control smart devices in a connected car, and place orders for products and services, like takeaway delivery or collection. But here, Amazon is having to compete with car manufacturers' own voice prompt systems, as well as the significant traction that Apple has gained with its CarPlay system to connect Apple's iOS devices to a car for navigation, music and voice prompt-based integration – not to mention the prospect of Apple launching its very own car.[23]

If we have learned anything from our study of Amazon's pivotal role in the development of AI and its use in voice applications in the pursuit of a more frictionless retail experience, it is that AI holds the ability to improve return on investment both instore and online, by simplifying shopping journeys, improving inventory accuracy and optimizing the supply chain in order to support growth. It is the culmination of development of the technology drivers of change with the use of data generated by the digital shopping tools that technology innovation and development has enabled. The reason AI has become so important in this way is because the likes of Amazon are using it to provide greater convenience, immediacy, transparency and relevancy for today's on-my-terms shopper, who is seeking to make the functional expedient and bring the fun parts of shopping to the fore. It is clear that retailers should see technology, specifically AI and digital tools and data, as critical in helping them keep pace with online disruptors in the race to adapt to today's digitally enabled consumer expectations. In the meantime, it should now be easy to understand why Amazon has, so far, shown them the way.

Notes

1   Council Member Expert Panel (2021) 15 B2B technology marketing trends to watch in 2021, Forbes Communication Council, Forbes.com, 5 May. Available from: https://www.forbes.com/sites/forbescommunicationscoun cil/2021/05/05/15-b2b-technology-marketing-trends-to-watch-in-2021/ (archived at https://perma.cc/DJ75-6UJL) [Last accessed 31/5/2021].

2   Staff researchers (2020) AI in retail – global market analysis (2020–2027), ResearchAndMarkets.com, 29 July. Available from: https://www.businesswire.com/news/home/20200729005453/en/AI-in-Retail---Global-Market-Analysis-2020-2027-by-Product-Application-Technology-Deployment-and-Region---ResearchAndMarkets.com (archived at https://perma.cc/3668-CRZB) [Last accessed 16/5/2021].

3   Mackenzie, Ian, Meyer, Chris and Noble, Steve (2013) How retailers can keep up with consumers, *McKinsey & Company*, October. Available from: https://www.mckinsey.com/industries/retail/our-insights/how-retailers-can-keep-up-with-consumers (archived at https://perma.cc/5UNY-YGM2) [Last accessed 16/5/2021].

4   Erickson, Jim and Wang, Susan (2017) At Alibaba, artificial intelligence is changing how people shop online, *Alizila*, 5 June. Available from: https://www.alizila.com/at-alibaba-artificial-intelligence-is-changing-how-people-shop-online/ (archived at https://perma.cc/C5Q9-9BAU) [Last accessed 16/5/2021].

5   Staff researchers (2020) Anyone see Canada? Retail's $1.8t inventory distortion issue, IHL Group, 6 August. Available from: https://www.ihlservices.com/product/inventorydistortion/. (archived at https://perma.cc/3WBN-MUY7) [Last accessed 16/5/2021].

6   Amazon.com seller FBA shipping update (2020) Temporarily prioritizing products coming into our fulfillment centers, Amazon Seller Central, 17 March. Available from: https://web.archive.org/web/20200326061039/https://sellercentral.amazon.com/gp/help/external/help.html?itemID=GF37V7QBB8W SVF43&tag=bisafetynet2-20& (archived at https://perma.cc/3KDB-AF8D) [Last accessed 12/6/2021].

7   Amazon press release (2020) Amazon.com announces first quarter results, Amazon Investor Relations, 31 March. Available from: https://s2.q4cdn.com/299287126/files/doc_financials/2020/Q1/AMZN-Q1-2020-Earnings-

Release.pdf (archived at https://perma.cc/YR4H-D8VF) [Last accessed 12/6/2021].

8 Kopalle, Praveen Prof (2014) Why Amazon's anticipatory shipping is pure genius, *Forbes*, 28 January. Available from: https://www.forbes.com/sites/onmarketing/2014/01/28/why-amazons-anticipatory-shipping-is-pure-genius/ (archived at https://perma.cc/6DF9-D7Q5) [Last accessed 16/5/2021].

9 Staff writer (2018) In algorithms we trust: how AI is spreading throughout the supply chain, Economist Special Report, 31 March. Available from: https://www.economist.com/news/special-report/21739428-ai-making-companies-swifter-cleverer-and-leaner-how-ai-spreading-throughout (archived at https://perma.cc/4BFX-ME9U) [Last accessed 16/5/2021].

10 Amazon (2018) Amazon Prime Air, *Amazon.com*, Available from: https://www.amazon.com/Amazon-Prime-Air/b?ie=UTF8&node=8037720011 (archived at https://perma.cc/VHB7-BC2S) [Last accessed 31/5/21].

11 Staff researcher (2020) Number of voice assistant devices in use to overtake world population by 2024, Juniper Research, 28 April. Available from: https://www.juniperresearch.com/press/number-of-voice-assistant-devices-in-use (archived at https://perma.cc/U9SK-5KKX) [Last accessed 31/5/21].

12 Harris, Mark (2017) Amazon's latest Alexa devices ready to extend company's reach into your home, *Guardian*, 27 September. Available from: https://www.theguardian.com/technology/2017/sep/27/amazon-alexa-echo-plus-launch (archived at https://perma.cc/5CEA-MH3T) [Last accessed 31/5/2021].

13 Maynard, Nick and Sadler, Alexandria (2020) Smart home payments: Segment analysis, use cases & market forecasts 2020–2025, 9 November. Available from: https://www.juniperresearch.com/researchstore/fintech-payments/smart-home-payments-market-research (archived at https://perma.cc/AU8H-LPSY) [Last accessed 12/6/2021].

14 Ovide, Shira (2018) Amazon won by losing the smartphone war, *Bloomberg*, 28 September. Available from: https://www.bloomberg.com/gadfly/articles/2017-09-28/amazon-leaped-ahead-on-gadgets-by-losing-the-smartphone-war (archived at https://perma.cc/P6ET-T2B3) [Last accessed 31/5/2021].

15 Ibid.

16 Report (2021) How we will pay 2020, PYMNTS.com and Visa, 18 January. Available from: https://www.pymnts.com/study/visa-how-we-will-pay-2020-home-as-consumers-commerce-command-center (archived at https://perma.cc/W8QT-MBEZ) [Last accessed 12/6/2021].

17 Bond, Slade (2020) Investigation of competition in digital markets, US Congressional Subcommittee on Antitrust, Commerical and Administrative Law of the Committee of The Judiciary, 10 June 2020. Available from: https://fm.cnbc.com/applications/cnbc.com/resources/editorialfiles/2020/10/06/

investigation_of_competition_in_digital_markets_majority_staff_report_and_
recommendations.pdf (archived at https://perma.cc/FGQ9-G5F9) [Last
accessed 12/6/2021].

18 Blog (2018) Help shoppers take action, wherever and however they choose to
shop, *Google Inside Adwords*, 19 March. Available from: https://adwords.
googleblog.com/2018/03/shopping-actions.html (archived at https://perma.
cc/3GW5-KVYZ) [Last accessed 31/5/2021].

19 Clavis Insight (2018) One Click Retail: the double click episode (video
podcast), 15 March. Available from: https://www.youtube.com/
watch?v=218LelVkGDQ&t=11s (archived at https://perma.cc/8RNP-HVN2)
[Last accessed 31/5/2021].

20 Weiss, Uwe (2018) 'Amazon effect' will grow as retail challenges increase, says
Blue Yonder, RetailTechnologyReview.com, 23 April. Available from: https://
www.retailtechnologyreview.com/articles/2018/04/23/amazon-effect-will-grow-
as-retail-challenges-increase,-says-blue-yonder/ (archived at https://perma.
cc/4ZW9-CR6R) [Last accessed 31/5/2021].

21 Chokshi, Niraj (2018) Is Alexa listening? Amazon Echo sent out recording of
couple's conversation, *New York Times*, 25 May. Available from: https://www.
nytimes.com/2018/05/25/business/amazon-alexa-conversation-shared-echo.
html (archived at https://perma.cc/9J2K-NQJY) [Last accessed 31/5/2021].

22 Day, Matt, Turner, Giles and Drozdiak, Natalia (2019) Amazon workers are
listening to what you tell Alexa, Bloomberg, 10 April. Available from: https://
www.bloomberg.com/news/articles/2019-04-10/is-anyone-listening-to-you-on-
alexa-a-global-team-reviews-audio (archived at https://perma.cc/MP3Q-SYF3)
[Last accessed 12/6/2021].

23 Staff (2021) Apple Car, MacRumours, 8 June. Available from: https://www.
macrumors.com/roundup/apple-car/ (archived at https://perma.cc/RAB8-
UYGK) [Last accessed 12/6/2021].

13

Store of the future: how digital automation will enrich the customer experience

'Essentially, you sign in to your Amazon app, you shop and you walk out.'
Jeff Helbling, vice president of Amazon Fresh Stores[1]

We've seen how Amazon's technology innovation and first-mover advantage have given it the edge online with the development of its e-commerce services and functionality, as well as in the home, through its various hardware devices and Alexa voice assistant. Here, Amazon has used digital shopping tools applied with AI-based capabilities to remove the friction from online shopping and personalize the experience with tailored recommendations. So much so, that the ease with which Amazon can enable shopping online and delivery right to you for free within 48 hours has fuelled constant debate over its role in the impending death of the physical retail store. We've already declared our view that physical retail is far from in terminal decline, and the majority of sales are still being completed in stores.

We would, however, contend that over a quarter century on from Amazon's Day 1, chain retailers have as much to learn from the way Amazon is bringing its digital automation and innovation skills to bear to bricks and mortar retailing as Amazon has to gain by mastering the physical sales territory that traditional chain retail has dominated for over 40 years. We will argue that the lessons Amazon still has to learn about retail are based on the very advantages of the physical store it has tried to overcome online: the ability to touch, feel and try; the instant gratification of being able to walk out with purchases immediately; the chance of human interaction delivered by competent customer service specialists and knowledge experts. These physical advantages are precisely why so many sales are still fulfilled instore, even if ordered online. It is also the major reason why Amazon has had to make the inevitable move offline with its Amazon 4-Star, Books and pop-up stores, alongside its various convenience and grocery store banners and formats, including Whole Foods, Amazon Go and Amazon Fresh if it is to sustain anything near its current levels of growth into the future. The impact of blended online-to-offline services also features heavily in our examination of Amazon's fulfilment strategy in Chapter 15. But for the purposes of our look at how the store of the future may develop, its operators could – and arguably post-pandemic must – certainly learn a thing or two from Amazon and its e-commerce counterparts about making the physical shopping experience a more attractive one that is not fraught with crowds, queues or empty shelves.

Ironically, Amazon's move into bricks and mortar also reveals the skills it so desperately needs that are prized by physical retailers: marketing and merchandising a brand or multiple brands within a finite space and the merchant art of curation through seasonal and sale events, as opposed to the 'endless aisle' search results associated with the Amazon.com shopping experience; the buying, planning and forecasting required to maximize product and staff availability while minimizing inventory exposure and customer throughput time; and the ability to surprise and delight through the overall experience instore. It is these inherent physical store advantages, applied with skill, that retailers need to channel and develop to compete with Amazon, and which can all be blended, enhanced or augmented by bringing the three technology drivers of change – ubiquitous connectivity, pervasive interfaces and autonomous computing – to bear through digital automation.

As we shift our focus into the store, we see both how Amazon is taking a lead in bringing digital automation and innovation to bear on common tangible retail friction points, such as product selection and checkout, and how its competitors are exploiting their bricks and mortar presence through technology deployments that can also enrich the customer experience to overcome the Amazon effect. In this context, we will look at how Amazon has influenced the search, browse and discovery stages of the typical shopping journey and, in this way, where other retailers can use similar blended digital tools in their stores to learn from and capitalize on both Amazon's e-commerce and growing physical retail impact.

Research online, buy offline

We need to take a step back to understand why the traditional store, with its purely transactional focus, is under threat. Many consumers in the first wave of e-commerce development discovered the internet and online shopping via PCs and laptops with the effect that e-commerce sales have grown and eaten into traditional store sales and footfall. Despite the accelerated shift to digital caused by lockdowns across the world because of the pandemic during 2020 (as a great test of consumer attitudes towards physical stores), motivations behind purchase channel selection remained broadly the same during the first half of that year compared with previous years. Convenience was still the number one factor across most retail categories and home delivery and availability were also key. Some 86 per cent of consumers said the convenience of online was key to their choice to shop online (up 3 per cent from 2019), while 69 per cent said the same for stores, which was down only 8 per cent year on year.[2]

All over the world, the current and next waves of consumers are now discovering e-commerce via mobile first, where there are no physical boundaries to where you can shop online. When you add social media, mobile payments, voice and apps into the equation, retailers have had to develop – some say transform – their digital presence in order to compete. They have certainly been sure to capitalize online by launching their own e-commerce channels. Some have even begun to join these up with online-to-offline services, such as click & collect. But this is why mobile apps and other mobile-enabled areas of digital automation also have a central role to play in the store of the future, for their ability to bring the speed, convenience, transparency and relevance associated with the online shopping journey in customers' hands directly into the store.

Yet again, though, when it comes to mobile, Amazon has a head start; nearly half of all Millennials have their Amazon app accessible on their home screen, according to a survey conducted by a US media analytics company.[3]

Amazon's online dominance in the markets where it operates will continue to exert heavy influence on the online research phase of any shopping journey, regardless of where the shopper's search takes place, as well as potentially stealing that sale from a physical rival. However, thinking about the two-thirds of shoppers who like to shop exclusively instore or in combination with online, the popularity of ROBO – research online, buy offline – or 'webrooming' as it is also known, favours the physical retailer. Nearly half

(45 per cent) of consumers buying a product instore pre-pandemic said they had first researched it online. By 2020, 75 per cent of people using digital channels for the first time indicated they would continue to use them when things returned to 'normal', according to a McKinsey survey.[4] So, it could be said that a retailer may lose as many sales online to Amazon in the search phase as it may win instore via the ROBO trend.

'webrooming'

noun, informal

Definition: When shoppers research items online so they can check out and compare lots of options, but then head to a physical store to complete their purchase, leading it to also become known through the practice of researching online to buy offline (ROBO). Often, consumers will use this method when they want to see exactly what the product looks like in real life before they make the final purchase.

With ROBO, the retailer must win during the search phase of the shopping trip, by beating Amazon on either price, product range and information or location – the first of which we already know, given the online giant's dominance, is far easier said than done. Playing to the ROBO trend, Amazon established an early advantage when it came to price with the introduction of its Price Checker barcode scanning app. It even offered a one-off 5 per cent discount (up to $5) on each of three items for a total of $15 off purchases for one day at the end of 2011 to encourage shoppers to use the app. It also asks customers to report advertised instore price and location information back to Amazon to ensure it is offering the most competitive deals. It has even launched an Amazon Shopper Panel, rewarding customers who send in their receipts for any purchases made at non-Amazon retailers.

Amazon's early-mover advantage in recognizing the power of customer ratings and reviews to enhance available product information has also informed the company's move offline. A survey by Podium suggests 82 per cent of consumers read reviews before making the buying decision, while 93 per cent of consumers say online reviews impact their buying decision. Being a forerunner in its pre-eminent use of customer product and marketplace seller reviews as a determining factor in how high a product appears in its search rankings, Amazon has an obvious advantage over retailers with less well-developed equivalent e-commerce features. But a retailer can still exploit online reviews to its own advantage. One e-commerce systems provider has suggested that 50 or more reviews per product can generate a 4.6 per cent increase in online conversion rates, while a customer is 58 per cent more likely to convert after interacting with a review.[5]

It's easy to see why, given its pioneering role in persuading consumers to buy products online before trying them, Amazon put its customers' ratings and reviews front and centre of its first foray into physical retail with its Amazon Books stores. It also equipped store staff with handheld mobile devices to offer customer service. In Chapter 7 we touched on the way its format sacrificed range for aesthetics and upended booksellers' traditional approach to merchandising, favouring mobile-enabled digital service to access more information and choice.

But it's worth calling out here that having been accused of killing off the traditional bookstore, some in the industry were quick to point out that Amazon's move into their territory betrayed a lack of experience of retailing in physical spaces. In comparison, say, to Apple's expansive and glass-lined 'Town Square' stores, commentators also highlighted Amazon Books stores' relatively utilitarian look and feel.

Amazon's bookstore may have been a soulless loss leader. But in the wider context of the store of the future, it is easy to see how its objective was not necessarily to make money but to test how it could transfer the best of its online experience offline and start building out physical spokes on its flywheel. Here we see how crucial a role mobile has to play. The point here is that this instore, mobile-enabled view of the customer, which we will come to understand as a major enabler of Amazon's customer-centric proposition, has become Amazon's physical differentiator. Just as it allows Amazon to match a customer identified instore by their purchase history and preferences to the offers and recommendations it gives them online, so it can accurately measure attribution, across both online and the store, and refine its physical offer according to how customers actually shop the store, as well as what it can offer each individual store customer in terms of pricing, product information and promotions.

Amazon's aim, from the outset, has been to create a physical retail environment where customers readily identify themselves, so it can iteratively use the data they then share to personalize their experience and tailor it, so it complements whatever stage they're at during their shopping journey. By pushing pricing and other such information to an app that lives on a customer's personal device, Amazon can potentially personalize every offer, recommendation and price to each customer in real time, whether they are in an Amazon or a rival store, to optimize acquisition, conversion and retention.

Location as a proxy for relevance

Even though ratings and reviews had been the preserve of the e-commerce pureplay to inform the research phase of the shopping trip, we can see how Amazon has transposed them via mobile into its Amazon Books store environment to personalize and so enhance the customer experience. But it has also used the data its customers generate from their shopping activities online to inform every aspect of these stores – from ranging and merchandising, to pricing and promotions – so it can then tie the offline results back to its online execution and vice versa in what should become a virtuous loop of constant refinement and improvement.

Bear in mind that under the influence of digital, marketers now view the research phase of the shopping journey as a 'zero moment of truth' (or ZMOT, a term coined by Google in 2011).[6] By virtue of the fact that shoppers can look for products anonymously online, just as they can do instore, it should come as no surprise to see Amazon exporting such features, which can positively influence this ZMOT by promoting conversion, offline. When it comes to exploiting the store's physical advantage at the ZMOT – to potentially aid a ROBO sale for example – location-based or 'near me' search is a powerful tool at the bricks and mortar retailer's disposal that capitalizes on the store's physical advantage of being able to provide instant gratification (if the sought-after product is in stock). This is because, in the days before Amazon even existed, location has always been a powerful proxy for relevance and why, therefore, the world's largest retailers have such extensive and, in some cases, densely located store networks.

As Google itself has suggested, 'near me' search is no longer just about location; it is about connecting people to things in a timely manner as much as it is about finding a place in and of itself. The search giant has called out the fact that 'near me' searches containing variants of 'can I buy?' or 'to buy' terms grew 150 per cent prior to the pandemic.[7] This is because shoppers will often use searches to find answers to an immediate need, where Google has also said nearly a third of all mobile searches are related to location. So, when it comes to immediacy, the store will trump online nearly every time – especially if the retailer also offers the opportunity to 'save the sale' on out of stocks by making online inventory available to order instore. This is another reason why customers expect to see the same range and have an equivalent experience instore as is on offer online – the digital experience enables it, so why doesn't the retailer's store?

However, location, as we saw during the pandemic, cemented the role of store as a fulfilment hub. Some 80 per cent of all online orders were fulfilled at the kerbside, confirming the importance of having and leveraging physical infrastructure in digital era. It's also given rise to the 15-minute delivery and one-hour click & collect services referenced earlier in the book, adding further weight to the evolving role of stores as an essential component of e-commerce fulfillment.

This is also why the digital presence of a physical store must not neglect basic search engine optimization (SEO) requirements to ensure it and its inventory can be found. Other Google features, such as its patented Knowledge Panel feature that appears to the right of its search results, are designed to help discover brands or locate businesses; and, like Amazon, its paid search and Shopping Express platform can make a bricks and/or clicks business discoverable in the moment, where Amazon's rapid delivery range does not yet stretch. We explore how Google is further capitalizing on its 'What Amazon Can't Do' (WACD) advantages through fulfilment in Chapter 15.

Ramping up this pressure on Amazon and other retailers whose businesses are online first or online only, Google introduced shoppers to the power of local store inventory search with a tool called See What's In Store (SWIS). Shoppers can search for a specific product and discover which local stores have that item in stock, or search a single store's entire available inventory when using Google's main search bar or Google Maps. Selecting the closest store location will generate a second search bar in the Google Knowledge Panel where shoppers can search that store's inventory, available as a feature that Google currently offers for free. Shoppers can also type the name of a specific product into the Google Shopping search bar, and the results will show which local stores have that item in stock. However, stores must pay to show up in these Local Inventory Ads results. Although the advertising costs may be prohibitive to smaller, local businesses and the capability hasn't taken off among consumers, a number of technology products have been developed to help retailers associate store inventory with a Google Business listing.

'E-commerce wins a lot because people don't know where to find stuff. That's a major disadvantage local stores have to Amazon. If you knew something was available one block away, or that you could pick it up in a local store without having to wait for shipping, you might not choose to order it online.'

Mark Cummins, CEO of Pointy, a Dublin-based tech firm acquired by Google to power SWIS[8]

Amazon may not yet have an extensive store network to match the physical networks of its global grocery and general merchandise rivals, but no matter how hard Google tries to level the playing field with features like Local Inventory Ads and SWIS, Amazon is still dominant when it comes to product search. When asked why, though, price was not the stand-out reason (Figure 13.1), suggesting again that there are more ways to compete with Amazon in the ROBO wars.[9]

When it comes to winning the ZMOT, we cannot think about the research phase of the journey without considering the advent of visual search. Technology provider Slyce delivers visual search engine image recognition for numerous retailers including Home Depot, Urban Outfitters and Tommy Hilfiger in the US and UK, for example. The company says the quality of its image recognition is superior to the likes of Amazon and Google as it builds

FIGURE 13.1   The top reasons why US consumers begin their product searches on Amazon[10]

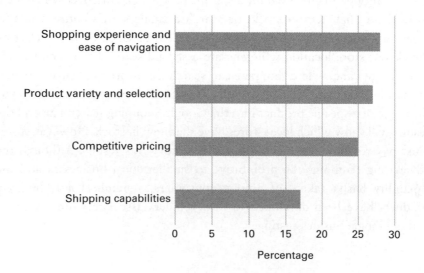

classifiers and detectors, which are the initial level of recognition. Machine learning is employed to train the software to recognize user-generated photographs of variable quality. It claims retailers see average order values increase by 20 per cent and conversion rates are 60 per cent higher when integrating the technology with their own e-commerce website or mobile app searches.

Here, Amazon had a head start back when it first used its image recognition and machine learning AI capabilities to launch a visual search solution in its app, Amazon Remembers, aimed at scanning the barcodes of books, debuting it in-app as an additional camera search feature called Flow. It then integrated it as an app called Firefly with its ill-fated Fire phone, before also introducing it to its Kindle Fire HD device, and expanding the visual capabilities of the Amazon app to recognize almost any item a few years ago.[11] This visual search app functionality has continued to grow thanks to a partnership with Samsung to embed the functionality into one of the handset maker's flagship Galaxy S smartphone range. Using the Galaxy S camera with the Samsung assistant Bixby, shoppers can snap a photo of an item or barcode to reveal relevant results from Amazon's catalogue of products. It has also partnered with Snapchat to let users take a photo of an object to buy it on Amazon.com, capitalizing on the social commerce trend we first highlighted in Chapter 3.

Another visual search tool, reverse image search, can arguably aid online shopping activities as much as it could be used to steal a store sale. The ability to search inventory that closely resembles an item in a picture uploaded by a shopper is a capability Amazon has seized on, enabling third parties to write dedicated apps for its tablet devices, and there are quite a few Google browser extensions to enable customers to use Google image search to find items on Amazon.com when using Chrome. Its significance could be brought to bear in combination with live on-shelf inventory visibility to drive customers to store. But only retailers that are both online and on the High Street can compete using this tool if their customer, inventory and order views are constantly in sync. So, features like visual search can help bridge the offline-to-online gap both remotely and instore to enhance the customer experience, introducing the opportunity to browse a selection of similar products according to their visual attributes. It's no surprise then that Microsoft's Bing search engine has its own Visual Search capability and even Pinterest got in on the act with its launch of Lens. The point here is that the store retailer must now consider how to use such digital tools to make them discoverable in the online world, where their location, range and availability, in combination with price, may be enough to steal a potential Amazon sale. If it is not, then they must also now be able to compete online too.

The store as a showroom

All of the developments we have so far explored can take place anywhere outside, as well as inside a store. The significance of mainstream mobile adoption means that search can take place anywhere, but it also has a significant influence on the shopper's purchasing decision while they are inside a store. Whereas ROBO refers to the search and purchase phases of a shopping journey, where browsing is a purely virtual experience, the idea behind the concept of 'showrooming' places the browsing phase squarely inside the store. Unlike ROBO, though, it is the store that loses out on the sale.

'showrooming'

noun, informal

Definition: When customers visit a shop to check out a product, but then actually complete the purchase online, sometimes at a lower price. Essentially, the store acts as a product showroom for online shoppers.

It should come as no surprise, then, due in part to its prevailing online dominance, that Amazon has been used twice as much as Google for showrooming.[12] Targeting Prime users particularly, Amazon uses its data and AI smarts to work around exclusive merchandise SKUs and serve up comparable, competitive items, powered by its recommendations engine. This works better for functional items, in books or grocery household categories for example, which can easily be matched by brand or description, compared with sectors such as fashion or electronics, where the look and feel of the item are more important.

Amazon also recognized this limitation with its anti-showrooming patent.[13] Having exploited the trend to its own ends, the patent is designed to prevent customers from showrooming in its own stores. It describes a mechanism to identify what content a shopper is accessing via a browser connected to its store Wi-Fi network. If the content is deemed as product or pricing information from a competitor's website, Amazon can take any number of actions, from comparing the product searched for to what's available instore and then sending price comparison information or a coupon to your browser, to suggesting a complementary item or even blocking content outright. Of course, it also means Amazon stands to benefit from any future attempts by technology providers or retailers to develop similar systems, serving as a reminder of the extent of its competitiveness.

The same visual search capabilities of mobile apps and devices that contain image recognition functionality and features can be used to win the sale at that 'zero moment' (ZMOT) in both 'research online, buy offline' (ROBO) shopping journeys, as well as in response to showrooming inside the store. Augmented reality (AR) relies on similar image recognition and machine learning AI capabilities that shoppers use for image searches in combination with additional computer vision and geolocation mobile developments. It is so-called because, in comparison to the complete immersiveness of virtual reality (VR) headsets and controllers, AR overlays images, text, video, graphics and other media onto the view that a smartphone camera sees of the real world. AR is an area where retailers and brands have only begun to exploit its true potential, but in the store of the future, it has the potential to really enhance marketing and merchandising during the browsing phase of the shopping journey both inside and outside the store.

IKEA, for example, was one of the first to use AR in the home sector with its AR feature for visualizing 3D models of its furniture in customer homes. The furniture firm has also been one of the most extensive retail users of Apple's AR software development kit (SDK) for its iOS mobile operating system (OS) with the IKEA Place app, which enables 3D renderings that can be viewed from different angles. Most recently it launched a feature to help people design entire rooms using the LiDAR sensors built into Apple's iPhone. Wayfair and Home Depot have rolled out similar features to help users design and decorate their home. But not to be outdone, Amazon's similar View in Your Room feature available in its app offers AR views of products in its Amazon Home department.

JD.com's Yihaodian, China's largest online grocery store, has experimented with the idea of AR convenience stores, allowing customers to use its mobile app to shop virtually at the designated locations. Lego installed AR kiosks in its stores to allow customers to see how a finished model would look superimposed on its box when held up to the kiosk screen, and launched a Lego X app for enthusiasts to build 3D brick models on their phone. Japanese apparel retailer Uniqlo worked with AR specialist Holition to introduce a 'Magic Mirror' to some of its stores to let customers see how they would look wearing an item they have tried on but in different colours. Meanwhile, cosmetics brand Max Factor worked with Blippar, an AR web browser, to make all of its products interactive and enable shoppers to reveal multimedia content tailored to each product using the Blippar app.

The application of AR to maximizing conversion on purchases as subjective as home decor, fashion and makeup is obvious. But most recently, Nike became one of the biggest footwear retailers to introduce an AR-powered feature to its Nike Fit app that can use computer vision, data science, and AI-based machine learning and recommendation algorithms to measure the full shape of your feet. Another shoe retailer, UK-based Hotter, is doing something similar. Both companies report the AR feature enables customers to buy online with confidence, and also reduces returns.

The digital customer experience

Even if they're not showrooming using the Amazon app, or 'blipping' products at the shelf edge to access AR content, consumers are developing ever more sophisticated expectations around the level of digital interaction or self-service available when instore, set by their shopping experiences online. Here, Wi-Fi is the prerequisite enabler for meeting these expectations. Yes, admittedly, it facilitates showrooming, but so does the shopper's own mobile data plan if coverage is available in the store. The difference is that Wi-Fi is also the essential connectivity required by retail store owners looking to maximize returns on investment from any customer-facing digital touchpoints instore. Recalling the reasons why retailers have adopted Wi-Fi in their stores, one once (anonymously) commented that the inability of mobile data signals to penetrate the depths of their wireless network-unfriendly store sites meant that, if they didn't offer Wi-Fi, they'd lose the sale to Amazon anyway because a showrooming customer would leave the store to get a mobile data signal, perform their price check and then never come back.

Also, although mobile data coverage and speeds will continue to increase as new networking protocols and spectrum for bandwidth develop, a key driver for instore Wi-Fi adoption has been to facilitate even more digital touchpoints that can enhance the physical shopping journey and dissuade the shopper from completing their purchase elsewhere. At least with Wi-Fi, the retailer can ensure ZMOT can be anywhere in the store, including the shelf edge, where the retailer or brand can exert the most influence. We've already talked about how the in-built camera functionality of a mobile device can help shoppers find similar products they are looking for in the offline world online. But the geolocation features in these mobile devices mean mapping functionality has come a long way too.

Accurate real-time, location-based and mobile-optimized information about the store and its offer can persuade consumers to pay a visit but, once inside, retailer mobile-optimized websites and apps that include 'wayfinding' can help them quickly navigate their way to the right shelf edge and find the products they are looking for more quickly. French grocer Carrefour has trialled an in-app service that allows shoppers to receive directions, via their mobiles, to promotions in a store – often linked to individual preferences. It has used 600 Bluetooth Low Energy (BLE) beacons in its 28 Romanian hypermarkets to connect to an app on shopper smartphones or retailer-supplied shopping carts equipped with Samsung tablets. Carrefour's Euralille hypermarket in Lille, France also installed 800 programmable Philips LEDs as part of a major refit not only to save energy but to also use Philips visual light communication (VLC), which encodes light waves with data about products and promotions and transmits the information straight to the camera on a shopper's smartphone. An app then displays the directional information, which helps to guide the consumer to a product location.

Intelligent space

The benefit of owning the network connectivity instore is the intelligence it can provide from the data it generates. For example, retailers have traditionally relied on people counting systems that tracked footfall based on infrared camera imagery or the numbers of shoppers entering or leaving the store as they cross its threshold. The store of the future will use data garnered from Wi-Fi and mapping systems alongside other footfall-monitoring technologies to improve store design and layout in line with how their customers shop, particularly in stores with regularly updated assortments and ranges.

In 2017 Apple introduced an AR software development kit (SDK) for its mobile OS – ARKit for iOS – to add immersive virtual and 3D features to its mapping functionality and make up ground on rival Google Maps. Taken with developments like VLC and visual search, AR mapping can also be used to gamify shopping instore. Shopkick was an early pioneer in this regard, working with US retailers Best Buy, JCPenney, Target and Macy's to make location-based rewards and offers available to shoppers for checking in at participating stores and scanning barcodes of specific items. Starbucks and telco retailer Sprint collaborated with Nintendo to add Pokémon Go AR 'lures', called PokéStops, and drive footfall by enticing players into their stores. Other retailers have experimented with the gamification of AR-based marketing initiatives with scavenger hunts, for example.

When it comes to digitizing every instore experience, electronic shelf labels (ESLs) are not new technology. But they do typify the reason Wi-Fi should be basic hygiene in a store of the future that employs technology to build digital touchpoints into the customer experience at the ultimate ZMOT in the discovery phase of the shopping journey. Apart from the fact that a major ESL study found that for 80 per cent of consumers, price has the greatest influence on buying decisions at the shelf edge, for 67 per cent of retailers the cost of manually managing labelling or signage changes related to pricing and promotions instore amounts to a staggering 1–4.99 per cent of average monthly store turnover.[14]

Coupled with the costly inefficiencies of swapping out paper shelf-edge price labels, which include a band of store associates armed with the pre-printed labels or belt-worn label printers, the inaccuracies that are more liable to occur with old-fashioned pricing methods may also lead to breaches of regulations around the accuracy of pricing[15] and product information[16] if the store is located in the European Union, for instance. But the time it takes to manually change prices also means the traditional store's ability to react quickly to competitor discounts is severely limited, putting it at a disadvantage to the might of Amazon's AI-driven dynamic pricing algorithms that mean it can change prices on millions of items a day. This is compared with the mere tens of thousands of total price changes made by the likes of Best Buy and Walmart in an entire month.[17]

Given that the ESL study also found accurate pricing is the main type of information shoppers wish to see displayed (82 per cent), with only 43 per cent always trusting that the prices on display will be the same paid at the till, ESLs can enhance the customer experience by also increasing shoppers' confidence in the accuracy of shelf-edge pricing. Coupled with the improved capabilities of AI computer vision software, facial recognition at the shelf can even help to personalize the experience. Intel showcased its RealSense technology for ESLs, supporting AMW Smart Shelf and Automated Inventory Intelligence software being trialled by The Hershey Company and Pepsi in a number of Walmart stores. The software enables digital shelf labelling to recognize when people are passing by the shelves and to display pricing. When nobody is close by they show promotional imagery instead. Kroger also has its own smart shelf solution, which it said allows it to seamlessly change prices and offer a personalized experience to shoppers.

The bi-directional, wireless communication capacity required to update ESLs can also be turned towards the customer to connect with their mobile devices via Wi-Fi, Bluetooth beacons or the same near-field communications (NFC) technology used by mobile wallets and contactless credit and debit cards. In future, harnessing this connection at the shelf edge to deliver complementary product recommendations, reviews and offers to inform the customer experience will become more important. An ESL can drive further positive engagement by offering more detailed pricing, origin and allergy information, etc than is possible to display on a traditional shelf-edge label. Some retailers have already deployed large-sized ESLs for their capacity to present more information, accompanied with QR codes that direct customers to more information online. European home improvement retailer Leroy-Merlin deployed ESLs to solve the accuracy, productivity and pricing velocity challenges already associated with paper-based labels. But it also used its ESLs to offer customers automatic and real-time geolocation of products inside the store. Amazon has been using ESLs in some of its stores for some time now. But it introduced them to its latest convenience and grocery formats only recently.

Digital points of purchase

Wi-Fi, beacons, VLC, ESLs and AR can all turn various elements of the store into digital points of purchase. Ted Baker in the UK tested mannequins fitted with beacons that can send out promotions, for example. Bidoo uses them to make digital billboards change to display the face of a shopper as they pass alongside offers tailored to their preferences. Its micro-location app allows shoppers to accept and then redeem offers at nearby outlets. Meanwhile beacons have also been used in the drive-through space. Diners can use voice control technology in their car to place a Pizza Hut order, and the restaurant receives an alert of their impending arrival using beacons. Payment is completed via Visa, whose system is integrated into the car dashboard.

Another key area is interactive digital signage. Samsung offers its Nexshop cloud-based digital store software platform with real-time behavioural sensing using IP and mobile devices, as used by business-to-consumer facing brands as diverse as audio manufacturer HARMAN, carmaker BMW and hairdressing chain TONI&GUY. In addition to analysis capabilities, it allows stores to interact with customers using cloud-based content via tablets or interactive displays for a more engaging customer experience. A number of luxury brands, including L'Oréal, Luxottica and LVMH, use

MemoMi smart mirror technology from Finish Line and Elo, which allows customers to take a photo of themselves wearing new clothing items and superimpose the image on a variety of backgrounds. The screen can text the image to the customer, allowing for easy social sharing of the image.

US-based 1-800-Flowers has gone one step further by adding conversational commerce powered by AI to its instore innovation, telephone ordering, e-commerce, and mobile and social media. It was the first retailer to launch a Facebook Messenger purchasing bot, has an AI-powered concierge named GWYN ('Gifts When You Need'), and has partnered with Amazon and Google to allow customers to make purchases with just their voice.

But use of voice in the store of the future has started to emerge, where Amazon and its Alexa voice platform are leading the way. For example, SmartAisle, a voice-powered instore shopping assistant developed by The Mars Agency, was recently trialled in the US by BevMo! liquor stores. The standalone system, consists of an Amazon Echo smart speaker, navigational LED lights and custom-made POS built into a merchandise display. Once directed with the command 'Alexa open SmartAisle', the customer is guided through a series of simple questions about their preferences (for whisky in the trial), such as type and taste, before Alexa suggests a shortlist of three products, highlighted by shelf lights.

It is, however, in its own physical stores that Amazon is leading by example and extending points of interaction and purchase beyond its JWO checkout-free technology. It introduced the Amazon Dash Cart with its larger-format Amazon Fresh grocery stores, enabling customers to skip the checkout line by applying the same JWO capabilities to anything placed in the cart, as well as new Alexa features to help customers manage their shopping lists and better navigate its aisles. Customers can use Alexa and Alexa shopping lists to find items in the store. On arrival they can access their Alexa shopping list through the Amazon app or on the Amazon Dash Cart's in-built screen, enabling them to quickly navigate aisles and check off items as they shop. There are even Amazon Echo Show devices available throughout the store for customers to ask Alexa for help. Amazon suggests they simply say, 'Alexa, where can I find the hot sauce?'

The store of the future will certainly offer digitally empowered assistance. But with an emphasis on self-service, where does this leave most retailers' frontline staff? One retail IT director, who shall (for obvious reasons) remain unnamed, was at a corporate event a few years ago lamenting that 'the customers were coming into the store armed with more information on their mobile than our store associates'. Here, the digital version of a 'Black Book' system used in luxury retail to serve high-value customers, called 'clienteling', can empower store staff with digital devices to assist in high-value, high-touch, consultative sales in sectors including health and beauty, consumer electronics, automotive and luxury. Health and beauty retailer, Boots introduced its MyBeauty app to help associates show product information, ratings and reviews, look up inventory online and make personalized customer recommendations based on online analytics. Another beauty retailer, Sephora, worked with ModiFace to develop its Virtual Artist technology, available in its app as well as in select stores. While customers reportedly visit the app several times per month to check everything from content to personalized messaging, they can also engage in a more digitally augmented consultation in person with an associate instore.

The importance of the human touch

The role of staff in the store of the future will therefore be to facilitate more digitally enabled consultative than transactional services. They must become true brand ambassadors. Like clienteling, staff can also be deployed with queue-busting capabilities, using integrated handheld product barcode scanners, card payment and PIN entry machines particularly for cashless sales. But practical consideration must be paid to the bagging and security de-tagging process. More widely used in grocery particularly are self-scan and checkout systems. While they increase customer speed and throughput at checkout, they also shift the entire burden of the shopping journey onto the customer, compounding the fact by asking customers to scan loyalty cards as part of the payment process, just before they leave the store! Indeed, the refrain, 'unexpected item in bagging area', has spawned many an internet meme, betraying a strong dislike among consumers for the systems, while retailers have had to accept the increased risk of theft their use carries with them. Walmart dumped its 'Scan & Go' mobile app in 2018 due to low take-up, while rumours had it that it was also subject to high levels of theft. However, Sam's Club and Costco offer similar instore scan and payment apps, and Starbucks enables payment using the stored value card functionality of its app, customers can also order ahead for quicker pickups. It is also worth noting that Walmart was arguably forced to re-introduce scan & go functionality via its Walmart+ app during the pandemic in September 2020 due to sheer demand for safer, low-touch, self-service store environments.

So, the final phase of the shopping journey focuses on checkout and payment, where the next stage of development is from unmanned checkout to unmanned stores, and 'checkout-less' or 'checkout-free' shopping. Here, China leads the way. F5 Future Stores runs 24-hour unmanned convenience stores in China's Guangdong province that are entirely managed by robotic arms. A typical store is made up of three vending machines and an automatic cleaning machine. The first vending machine sells FMCG products, such as canned drinks, and it takes 7 seconds to complete the order on average; the second sells fresh food, such as noodles and minced fish balls, taking about 50 seconds to serve the dish; and the third machine sells beverages such as hot coffee on the spot, which it can complete in 20 seconds. Other unmanned store examples include Auchan China's Minute and BingoBox stores and the self-driving Wheelys MobyMart, which rely on the customer using an app to access the store and pay for goods by scanning QR codes, or computer vision that debits the customer's account on exit. There's also the 7-Eleven Signature concept in South Korea and even a huge Tmall car vending machine that looks more like a building from Alibaba in Guangzhou.

These rivals to Amazon have been setting the standard, but it is unlikely we will see future store formats dominated by unmanned, robot-run boxes. The high cost of the technology involved limits them to small-footprint, convenience formats, and the human touch will always be most prized in sectors that require more consultative sales. But Walmart and Portugal's Sonae have also both tested autonomous shopping carts for shoppers with limited mobility.

When it comes to the role of robots in the store, examples such as Simbe's Tally, tested by Target, may take over the repetitive and laborious task of shelf auditing to identify out-of-stock, low-stock and misplaced items, and pricing errors. Others, like the LoweBot, used by US home improvement retailer Lowe's, are capable of limited customer interaction. LoweBot can understand multiple languages and uses a 3D scanner to detect people in the stores. Shoppers can seek the robot's help to search for any product, either by talking to it or by typing items onto a touchscreen on its chest. The robot then guides them to the products using smart laser sensors. Woolworths in Australia is using a hazard-detecting robot called Millie. But unlike a similar robot, called Marty, which is being used in Giant and Stop & Shop stores in the US, instead of merely alerting employees to the spills, Millie can also clean them up. Softbank's Pepper robot has been deployed in multiple customer-facing situations, including taking Pizza Hut orders in Asia, and electronics retailer MediaMarktSaturn has deployed a robot called Paul to greet and guide customers. The German retailer is also among many retailers around the world testing autonomous robotic delivery vehicles developed by Starship. Even so, robots won't be replacing humans altogether inside or to and from stores anytime soon.

Micro-fulfilment is another area of robotics development inside the store that is not designed to be seen by shoppers. Walmart, for example, relies on robotics systems supplied by Alphabot to speed up the fulfilment of customers' online orders, retrieving products by rolling along rails surrounding storage bins containing food and climbing up the three-storey storage structures. Its smart store concept, called the Intelligent Retail Lab, has a suite of ceiling-mounted cameras to monitor inventory levels for out-of-stocks and shelf dates. In this way, retailers are applying technology drivers to not only enhance the customer experience in-store but also improve store and staff productivity.

From self-checkout to no checkout

So, we come to Amazon's checkout-free store concept, which first opened its doors in Seattle in 2018. The computer vision-equipped, sensor fusion, AI-powered store uses Amazon's patented 'Just Walk Out' technology to enable customers to literally walk out with their goods without having to go through any checkout process at all. Customers have to scan their Amazon app to gain entry and register a form of payment that is charged when they leave according to what the computer vision and sensor fusion systems detect they have taken from the shelves. Its beauty is Amazon knows precisely who is in its store and what they do at every move, while the technology eliminates shrink. The success of the checkout-free model, particularly in attracting repeat customers,[18] means more stores have been rolled out across the US and in London. But the store is hardly unmanned, as staff are on hand to restock shelves and prepare fresh items, grant verified access to age-restricted goods, such as alcohol, and man the click & collect desk for online orders; and it relies heavily on densely populated, high-traffic locations to make its higher-margin convenience format offset the high-tech costs.

The cost equation has also come into greater focus with the introduction of the Amazon Dash cart to its larger format Amazon Fresh grocery store, designed for small to mid-sized trips. Unlocked via a Prime app QR code, the cart uses a combination of computer vision algorithms and sensor fusion to identify items put in the cart. When the customer exits through the store's Amazon Dash Cart lane, sensors automatically identify the cart and payment is processed using the credit card on their Amazon account. It also includes a screen at the top to access an Alexa Shopping List, check items off, view the cart's subtotal and with a coupon scanner.

Another related initiative, the Amazon One scanner, enables customers to pay by scanning the palm of their hand. As it was trialled at two of Amazon's Seattle stores, Amazon also said it was in discussions with other companies to resell the system. Amazon said it could become an alternate payment or loyalty card option, or even be for access control to enter a location such as an office or stadium.

In spite of cost being a barrier to adoption, Just Walk Out, the Dash cart and Amazon One have raised the game for rival retailers, particularly when the post-pandemic consumer has become accustomed to mobile-enabled self-service and low-touch shopping environments, where the investment had previously been measured against productivity gains, such as checkout throughput. Ahold Delhaize also trialled a checkout-less concept, where purchase is made by tapping a contactless card against ESLs to verify transactions. Meanwhile, Sainsbury's briefly tested the ability for customers to bypass the till and pay for goods using their mobile phone. UK rival Tesco experimented with 'scan and go' technology to enable customers to pay for groceries via the retailer's Scan Pay Go smartphone app in its Express convenience store at its own Welwyn Garden City HQ, and tech giant Microsoft worked on a checkout-less store concept that works by attaching cameras to shopping carts in order to track purchases as customers walk the aisles. JD.com actually beat its US rival to open the already-referenced BingoBox in 2017 as the first automated, unmanned store in partnership with Auchan (although remote customer service is available, and the store is manually restocked daily). The first unmanned and checkout-less D-Mart c-store opened at JD's company headquarters in the same year. This so-called Smart Store is equipped with an Intel-based responsive technology suite that includes smart shelves, intelligent cameras, gateways and sensors, smart counters for checkout-free shopping and smart digital signage. The JD solution offers low-cost wholesale or incremental customization flexibility to allow traditional retail store owners to upgrade their operations in a 'low touch' and cost-effective way. It also supports JD.com founder and chief executive Richard Liu's ambitions to open a modern convenience store in every village in China within the next few years.[19] Albertsons and Sam's Club in the US are also trialling checkout-free technology across multiple stores.

But both JD.com and Alibaba's offline moves arguably deserve more credit than that afforded Amazon's Just Walk Out system for the fact that they offer more accessible digitally enabled experiences to new as well as existing customers. With a focus also on fresh, convenience and food service, JD.com's 7fresh concept and Alibaba's Freshippo Supermarkets also blend the best of the physical with QR codes, app-based digital touchpoints including ESLs, and payment. Again, mobile payment is playing a key role in enabling the store of the future where – if retailers are serious about automating this final, most friction-filled part of the shopping journey – they also get to tie the customer's identity back to the final transaction and basket. Increasingly, identity verification is moved beyond personal identification numbers (PIN) and even facial recognition scanning, to use more sophisticated biometric systems, undaunted by related security and privacy concerns. Both Visa and MasterCard showcased biometric payments to enable customers to bypass queues at the checkout. KFC in China, in cooperation with Alibaba-owned Ant Financial Services, introduced the first 'smile-to-pay' payment system in China. Alipay customers can authenticate their payments through a combination of facial scanning and inputting their mobile phone numbers, which means they need not reach for their wallets – or even smartphones – anymore. 7-Eleven's Signature store in Seoul uses 'HandPay', a biometric verification system that scans palm vein patterns.

While many established store-based retailers are facing the reality of slowing sales and being overspaced, other digital-first players have recognized the critical importance of gaining a physical presence. Stores help support the omnichannel proposition by providing extra flexibility in terms of order collection, returns, service and a physical environment to showcase the brand. So, retailers should bring pervasive tech interfaces, ubiquitous connectivity, and autonomous computing of digital and mobile to bear so the store can support every stage of the shopping journey, off- and online, from search and browse through to discovery and payment phases in ways that match the speed, accessibility and availability of online.

Stores for digital players play a different role from the primary role of the traditional store simply selling products. We believe that these players, with their strong skills and capabilities in technology, are the ones that will really push forward the vision of the digitally enabled and automated store of the future to enhance its role as a powerful, tangible engagement point within their wider customer ecosystems.

Notes

1 Redman, Russell (2020) Amazon unveils first Amazon Fresh grocery store in Woodland Hills, *Supermarket News*, 27 August. Available from: https://www.supermarketnews.com/retail-financial/amazon-unveils-first-amazon-fresh-grocery-store-woodland-hills (archived at https://perma.cc/X4V6-46RD) [Last accessed 13/6/2021].

2 Allen, Emily and Smidt, Frank (2020) 8 ways consumers in the U.K. adapted their shopping behaviour this year, *Think with Google*, August. Available from: https://www.thinkwithgoogle.com/intl/en-gb/consumer-insights/consumer-trends/consumers-adapted-shopping-behaviour-covid/ (archived at https://perma.cc/Q9VP-KMSP) [Last accessed 1/6/2021].

3 Lipsman, Andrew (2017) 5 interesting Millennials' mobile app usage from the '2017 mobile app usage report', *comScore*, August 24. Available from: facts about https://www.comscore.com/Insights/Blog/5-Interesting-Facts-About-Millennials-Mobile-App-Usage-from-The-2017-US-Mobile-App-Report. (archived at https://perma.cc/D7Z7-MKLD) [Last accessed 6/9/2018].

4 Staff researchers (2021) McKinsey COVID-19 US Digital Sentiment Survey April 2020, 13 May. Available from: https://www.mckinsey.com/business-functions/marketing-and-sales/our-insights/survey-us-consumer-sentiment-during-the-coronavirus-crisis (archived at https://perma.cc/6PDK-TNUK) [Last accessed 4/6/21].

5 Cullinan, Emily (2017) How to use customer testimonials to generate 62% more revenue from every customer, every visit, *Big Commerce*, 2 April. Available from: https://www.bigcommerce.com/blog/customer-testimonials/ (archived at https://perma.cc/L64H-2RCB) [Last accessed 4/6/2021].

6 Lecinski, Jim (2011) Winning the zero moment of truth ebook, *Google*, June. Available from: https://www.thinkwithgoogle.com/marketing-strategies/micro-moments/zero-moment-truth/ (archived at https://perma.cc/28GT-XMWC) [Last accessed 4/6/2021].

7 Agarwal, Shirish (2019) How to leverage the rise of "near me" searches, HubSpot, 24 May. Available from: https://blog.hubspot.com/marketing/how-to-leverage-near-me-searches (archived at https://perma.cc/74TX-A3KF) [Last accessed 13/6/2021].

8 Peterson, Haylet (2018) Google now lets you see what's on shelves at stores near you, and it's a powerful new weapon against Amazon, *Business Insider UK*, 12 June. Available from: https://markets.businessinsider.com/news/stocks/google-see-whats-in-store-vs-amazon-2018-6-1026877001 (archived at https://perma.cc/699M-938W) [Last accessed 4/6/2021].

9 Murga, Guillermo (2017) Amazon takes 49 percent of consumers' first product search, but search engines rebound, *Survata*, 20 December. Available from: https://www.upwave.com/amazon-takes-49-percent-of-consumers-first-product-search-but-search-engines-rebound/ (archived at https://perma.cc/M6BK-QWMZ) [Last accessed 4/6/2021].

10 Ibid.

11 Press release (2016) Three, Two, One...Holiday! Amazon.com launches Black Friday deals store and curated holiday gift guides, *Amazon*, 1 November. Available from: https://press.aboutamazon.com/news-releases/news-release-details/three-two-oneholiday-amazoncom-launches-black-friday-deals-store (archived at https://perma.cc/G4GT-EPFQ) [Last accessed 4/6/2021].

12 Mason, Rodney (2014) Dynamic pricing in a smartphone world: A shopper showrooming study, *Parago*, 4 January. Available from: https://www.slideshare.net/Parago/dynamic-pricing-30010764 (archived at https://perma.cc/6WWJ-PTRB) [Last accessed 4/6/2021].

13 Amazon Technologies, Inc. (2017) Physical store online shopping control, US Patent No. 9665881, 30 May. Available from: http://patft.uspto.gov/netacgi/nph-Parser?Sect2=PTO1&Sect2=HITOFF&p=1&u=/netahtml/PTO/search-bool.html&r=1&f=G&l=50&d=PALL&RefSrch=yes&Query=PN/9665881 (archived at https://perma.cc/AF8X-6DJW) [Last accessed 4/6/2021].

14 Displaydata press release (2018) Analogue to automated: retail in the connected age, *PlanetRetail RNG*, May. Available from: https://www.businesswire.com/news/home/20180522005419/en/New-Research-from-Displaydata-and-Planet-Retail-RNG-Estimates-That-Global-Retailers-Spent-104-Billion-on-Manually-Changing-Price-Labels-in-2017 (archived at https://perma.cc/U23Z-SJP2) [Last accessed 4/6/2021].

15 Official Journal of the European Communities (1998) Directive 98/6/EC of the European Parliament and of the Council on consumer protection in the indication of the prices of products offered to consumers, *EUR-Lex*, 16 February. Available from: https://eur-lex.europa.eu/legal-content/EN/TXT/?uri=celex%3A31998L0006 (archived at https://perma.cc/6VEE-4FSP) [Last accessed 4/6/2021].

16 Official Journal of the European Communities (2011) Regulation (EU) No 1169/2011 of the European Parliament and of the Council of 25 October 2011 on the provision of food information to consumers, *EUR-Lex*, 25 October. Available from: https://eur-lex.europa.eu/eli/reg/2011/1169/oj (archived at https://perma.cc/53A2-RM3K) [Last accessed 4/6/2021].

17 Profitero (2013) Profitero Price Intelligence: Amazon makes more than 2.5 million daily price changes, *Profitero*, 10 December. Available from: https://www.profitero.com/blog/2013/12/profitero-reveals-that-amazon-com-makes-more-than-2-5-million-price-changes-every-day (archived at https://perma.cc/R44Y-JZLM) [Last accessed 4/6/2021].

18 Dastin, Jeffrey (2018) Amazon tracks repeat shoppers for line-free Seattle store – and there are many, *Reuters*, 19 March. Available from: https://ca.reuters.com/article/technologyNews/idCAKBN1GV0DK-OCATC (archived at https://perma.cc/AK7F-FFM6) [Last accessed 4/6/2021].

19 Liu, Richard (2018) Interview conducted by broadcaster and Plenary session moderator of World Retail Congress, Munchetty, N, Madrid, 17 April.

14

Redefining the store: shifting from transactional to experiential

> 'Physical spaces need to provide a value that you can't get from your couch.'
> **Rachel Shechtman, Founder of Story**[1]

What is the role of a store? Previous chapters have aimed to illustrate how the instore experience will become more frictionless and hyper-personalized through technology. Addressing customer bugbears like product navigation and waiting in line at the checkout will allow retailers to finally take the physical store into the 21st century, achieving a level of convenience and ease that was traditionally only associated with online shopping.

The urgency for retailers to reinvent the physical space will be reinforced as more categories move online. Shoppers can buy literally anything online today and, thanks to Prime, usually have it delivered the same or next day. Amazon has taken every effort out of shopping. In the future, this will go one step further as rapid delivery providers make one-hour delivery or less the norm in cities and, longer term, certain household products move towards simplified and auto-replenishment. As our homes get smarter, shoppers' lives will get easier. The average adult currently makes a whopping 35,000 decisions every day,[2] but in the future our connected homes will do all the low-level, mundane reordering of household products, freeing up time to focus on more enjoyable tasks. Shoppers will no longer have to traipse down supermarket aisles when they run out of bleach or toilet paper. They will spend less of their valuable time buying the essentials and we believe the impact on the physical store will be immense; retailers today should be rethinking store layout, trip drivers and the broader purpose of the store.

In the future, we will see a greater divergence between functional and fun shopping. No one does functional like Amazon, so competitors must focus on the fun element. Winning in retail today means excelling where Amazon cannot, and therefore focusing less on product and more on experience, services and expertise.

WACD – What Amazon Can't Do – has become a recognized acronym in the retail industry as competitors desperately seek ways to survive in the age of Amazon. Even the very terminology – words like 'retailer', 'store' and 'sales associate' – must be reconsidered: these days, Apple refers to its outlets as 'town squares' and cycling chain Rapha, 'clubhouses'. In a similar vein, many shopping malls are actually ditching the m-word in favour of phrases like 'village', 'town centre' and 'shoppes'.[3] Others have taken the notion of experiential retail to the extreme – UK department store retailer John Lewis lets shoppers stay overnight in an instore apartment – and even has plans to become a residential landlord – while US home furnishings retailer West Elm has branched out into running hotels.

Not all retailers will have the means or incentive to go to such extremes, but one thing is clear – stores must be repositioned as genuine destinations. It can no longer be just about product; instead, retailers must tap into purpose and community, providing an experience that is compelling enough to ditch our screens for. Even before COVID struck, Angela Ahrendts, former SVP of Retail, observed that 'while people are more digitally connected than ever, many feel more isolated and alone.' The physical store is well-positioned to cater to a growing consumer desire for social connectedness in today's post-pandemic digital age.

Let's not discount the importance of disconnectivity in this digital era. Over the next decade, expect more retailers to invest in experiences that enable customers suffering from screen fatigue to unplug from their devices, to slow down and enjoy the moment. This is one of the reasons behind the recent resurgence of physical bookstores, a format that at one time was thought to be on the path to extinction. As terms like 'forest bathing' enter the mainstream, how might this translate in a retail setting? Just as we have quiet coaches on trains, could we see digital detox zones instore in the future? Mindfulness classes? More green spaces?

We are entering an era of participation. There's an untapped opportunity for retailers to build a sense of belonging among shoppers in a way that instore yoga classes and potato peeling workshops (yes, that is a real thing) never could. But in order to find their tribe, retailers need to be bold about who they are and what they stand for. The days of being everything to everyone are over.

We've already talked extensively of the trend towards a more blended retail experience as online and offline continue to merge. But bricks and mortar retailing will also become more blended in the sense that retail space won't just be about retail. The future, particularly for malls and larger formats like department stores, is mixed-use development, which will open doors for collaboration with all kinds of unconventional partners. These aren't entirely new concepts: retailtainment (or retail theatre) and positioning retail as a leisure activity have featured in retailers' playbooks for the past century. Mr Harry Gordon Selfridge himself once said that 'a store should be a social centre, not merely a place for shopping'.[4]

This is sound advice for retailers today. For all its perks, shopping on Amazon is still a very utilitarian experience. In fact, transacting is perhaps a more accurate depiction of the Amazon experience. And although this is entirely deliberate on Amazon's part, it also presents an opportunity for competitors to distance themselves by injecting some personality and soul into their stores, further blurring the lines between retail, hospitality and lifestyle.

The store of the future won't just be a place to buy, collect and return stuff but also a place to transcend the transaction. It will be a place to eat, play, discover, even work. It will be a place to rent products, learn new skills and connect with others. It will be immersive, memorable and, in the words of John Denver, it'll fill up your senses. In an increasingly digital world, the role of the physical shop will have no choice but to move from transactional to experiential.

Prior to the pandemic, 'experiential retail' had been positioned as the catch-all solution to the physical store's problems. We believe it will come back with a vengeance, although retailers must take less of a scattergun approach. Now before we make our case for it, let's debunk a few myths because, let's face it, 'experience' can be a fluffy word.

First, as we said right at the beginning of this book, experiential retail is not about throwing some gyms and brow bars into your stores and carrying on as usual. It requires a titanic cultural shift, where sales associates are equipped with new skills and are incentivized to provide outstanding service.

Second, experiential retail must go beyond the flagship store. While there is arguably a greater need for experiential retail in cities, this is about enhancing the customer experience across the entire estate. Don't underestimate the importance of consistency here.

Critics will argue that not every retailer needs to create an all-singing, all-dancing version of their stores if they can genuinely offer the best value for money or the most convenient experience. There is some truth to this – we don't believe Aldi or Lidl, for example, will look very different by 2030. However, even retailers like Primark are recognizing the need to incorporate experiences into some of their stores – from hair salons to Disney-themed cafés – in a bid to stand out from their online rivals.

From shop to lifestyle centre: ensuring brand values align

Adding a social dimension to the brand can help retailers to stand out from both on- and offline competition but it's vital that such diversification is aligned with the retailer's own brand. It might sound obvious, but you only need to cast your mind back to a decade ago when Tesco began filling its stores with artisan cafés, restaurants, upmarket bakeries, yoga studios and even gyms. By 2016, it had sold off all the companies it had begun investing in just a few years earlier: Harris + Hoole, Giraffe and Euphorium.

There were various reasons for the 180 in strategy: new leadership; the need to rationalize non-core assets in order to turn around the core grocery business; plus these concessions were largely loss-making. We would argue that the strategy was fundamentally flawed in that the partner brands' aspirational stance was misaligned with Tesco's own positioning as a low-priced, mass-appeal grocer. After buying a freshly ground piccolo macchiato, shoppers would turn to face a swathe of red and yellow signs shouting about 3-for-2 deals.

Tesco might have failed to reinvent the superstore concept at the time, but it certainly learned a great deal through the experimentation. Today, it has successfully filled excess space by partnering with other retailers which have included Holland & Barrett, Arcadia Group (before its brands were sold to ASOS and Boohoo), Currys (formerly known as Currys PC World), AO.com and Next. Sure, there is some overlap in product categories but the concessions create a point of differentiation for Tesco while the brands benefit from the supermarket's regular footfall.

A decade ago, Tesco wouldn't have dreamed of teaming up with competitors but today they have a shared enemy in Amazon. Co-opetition allows them to better serve the customer and jointly fend off the Seattle behemoth.

Despite the previous branding misalignment, Tesco's intentions to turn its stores into an under-one-roof shopping, leisure and foodservice destination were not far off the mark. It was perhaps just a few years too early with such a radical reinvention plan.

A place to eat

Food: fashionable footfall driver

> 'Whilst a screen will deliver products, ultimately people will still want to try things on, feel the fabric and experience a service which is unique to the shop, and there is no better way to bring people into shop than food.'
> **Richard Collasse, president of Chanel Japan[5]**

Today, retailers are fighting for their survival and scrambling to redefine the retail space. A tried-and-tested method of driving footfall and increasing dwell time is through the addition of cafés and restaurants. From McDonald's in Walmart stores to the glitzy KaDeWe food halls of Berlin, foodservice has always been a natural extension of retail. This is particularly true for department stores and other big-box concepts such as IKEA, for example, whose Swedish cuisine has become as famous as its Billy bookcase.

'We've always called the meatballs "the best sofa-seller",' says Gerd Diewald, head of IKEA's US food operations, 'because it's hard to do business with hungry customers. When you feed them, they stay longer, they can talk about their [potential] purchases, and they make a decision without leaving the store.'[6]

So what's new? The roster of retailers is growing and so is the breadth of their offering.

Earlier in the book, we discussed how fashion retailers have been hit particularly badly by the pandemic; plus, they're under constant pressure from more nimble online fashion chains. ASOS alone adds 5,000 new products each week. What high street retailer can compete with that?

It's no surprise then that many fashion chains are now turning to food and drink experiences as a way to differentiate from their online rivals and entice shoppers through the doors. Millennial favourite Urban Outfitters pioneered this trend back in 2015 when it acquired the Philadelphia-based Vetri Family group of restaurants. The unprecedented move raised eyebrows at the time but since the deal, more and more clothing retailers around the globe have added dining options to their stores. Uniqlo shoppers in Manhattan and Chicago can grab a Starbucks coffee instore. In the UK, Next has added Italian restaurants to some stores. Meanwhile, even fast fashion chains are jumping on the bandwagon – H&M's Flax & Kale à Porter restaurant in Barcelona features a variety of organic and vegetarian food.

> 'Until they invent actual replicators like on Star Trek, e-commerce is not a threat to the restaurant business.'
> **Jeff Benjamin, co-founder of Vetri Family (restaurant chain sold to Urban Outfitters)[7]**

Department stores are also upping their game in this area. Saks Fifth Avenue launched a version of French eatery and celebrity magnet L'Avenue in its renovated flagship store, while competitor Neiman Marcus offers a vegan café run by celebrity chef Matthew Kenney. 'In the past, the restaurants were developed to keep customers in the store longer and spend more', said Marc Metrick, president of Saks Fifth Avenue. 'Now restaurants are a way to attract people into store.'[8]

Food: beyond fashion

Looking beyond fashion now, incorporating food and drink experiences has also been a powerful tool (and logical extension) for supermarkets. Grocery retailers around the world should be taking inspiration from the likes of Eataly and Whole Foods Market, flexing their fresh credentials with food emporiums, cookery classes and grow-your-own initiatives. In China, online giants are redefining the physical supermarket for today's modern shopper with tech-infused stores that place a strong emphasis on freshness and experience. For example, Alibaba's Freshippo chain allows customers to select their own live seafood and have it prepared by instore chefs, while instore dining accounts for around half of rival JD.com's 7Fresh supermarket's sales.[9]

During the pandemic, coffee shops were forced to pivot due to a slump in demand at its city-centre and travel retail locations (we touched on Pret's move to sell on Amazon's marketplace earlier). But what about physical shops? Despite the risk of devaluing their brands, both Pret and high-end Italian café chain Carluccio's decided to follow the footfall – partner with the supermarkets. Shoppers can now find Pret concessions in Tesco stores and Carluccio's cafés and deli counters in Sainsbury's. In fact, in Sainsbury's Selly Oak superstore, in 2021 the retailer launched the 'Restaurant Hub', a multi-brand offer featuring a whole host of grab-and-go and delivery options, with Caffè Carluccio's, GBK, Slim Chickens, Harry Ramsden's and Ed's Easy Diner. Meanwhile, in Italy, Co-op's 'store of the future' features a restaurant that cooks only with their own-label products, reinforcing both quality and provenance. More upmarket supermarkets like Waitrose and Publix have long capitalized on their higher-end positioning and reputation for instore experience with cookery classes. Meanwhile, Germany-based Metro became the first retailer in Europe to implement instore farming and Whole Foods Market has experimented with rooftop greenhouses.

The Markt Halle concept from Real, also owned by Metro, is a fantastic example of how large hypermarkets and superstores can distance them-selves from both their online and discounter rivals through a greater focus on fresh foods and hospitality. The aim of the store is to convey the atmos-phere of a traditional market hall and as such, the food/non-food split has gone from 60/40 per cent to 70/30 per cent. An internal dining area and winter garden can host nearly 200 people and customers can enjoy seasonal food that is freshly prepared in front of them. Some foods like pasta are made instore and shoppers can also take part in culinary-related activities like sushi workshops. USB-enabled device-charging points are also offered, encouraging shoppers to spend more time instore, whether that's socializing, shopping or even working.

A place to work

Retail isn't the only sector being redefined by technology. Although at the time of writing there is much uncertainty about the future of the office, it's safe to assume that there will be no return to the old normal. The pandemic has for ever changed the world of work, disrupting embedded routines and accelerating the shift towards a more hybrid, flexible workplace.

Pre-COVID, the traditional 9–5 office-based routine was already being tested as increased connectivity enabled employees to start working in a more flexible way. Today, nearly half of jobs in the US can be done remotely, but in 2010, according to the U.S. Census Bureau, a mere 7 per cent of workers worked largely out of their homes, and roughly 10 per cent worked from home one day a week.[10]

The pandemic has solidified the transition to flexible working. The 'work near home' concept will become even more relevant in the future as companies shift towards a hybrid office model. According to real estate experts JLL, 30 per cent of all office space is expected to be consumed flexibly by 2030.[11]

> 'I think flexible working will be more apparent than it's ever been.'
> **Pano Christou, CEO, Pret A Manger**[12]

The rise in remote working, co-working spaces, hot-desking and third spaces is transforming consumers' lives – and creating opportunities for retailers in the process. As with the Real example, major European food retailers have been becoming more hospitable in a bid to increase dwell time, offering free Wi-Fi and device-charging points while enhancing their foodservice options. Carrefour Urban Life, a concept that debuted in Milan in 2017, marked the European retailing giant's move into co-working. Carrefour describes the store, which also features a meeting room and lounge bar serving more than 200 Italian and international beers, as an innovative solution for busy city dwellers 'who seek more than ever to combine pleasure, work and socialization'.[13]

In the future, we believe hybrid store concepts will become a common sight in urban areas around the globe, although we must acknowledge the pandemic-induced exodus of city dwellers, made possible in part by new remote working opportunities. A 2020 survey from the World Economic Forum revealed that nearly half of all US adults would prefer to live in a small town or rural area.[14] Most urban cities in the US are now shrinking, with The Bay Area, New York, Los Angeles and Chicago among the biggest losers.[15]

That said, cities remain home to most of the world population today. Rapid urbanization in developing countries like China and India, for example, shows no signs of deceleration. In Africa, less than 20 per cent of people lived in cities in 1950;[16] by 2020, that number had more than doubled to 43 per cent. The UN expects 60 per cent of the world's population to live in urban areas by 2030.[17]

Meanwhile, we believe the 15-minute city concept, where most essentials (work, retail, leisure) are within a 15-minute walk or cycle from your home, will gain momentum as cities around the world re-engineer themselves for post-pandemic life. Paris has championed this concept, which is based on four principles: proximity, diversity, density and ubiquity. Paris is tackling the climate emergency head-on by taking drastic measures to reduce car use and enable safer, greener, more active travel, and in doing so, the French capital is being transformed into a collection of neighbourhoods. Hyper-localism is here to stay.

'We need to reinvent the idea of urban proximity,' says Carlos Moreno, the Sorbonne professor who developed the 15-minute city concept. 'We know it is better for people to work near to where they live, and if they can go shopping nearby and have the leisure and services they need around them too, it allows them to have a more tranquil existence.'[18]

Collaboration with shared office providers will help give malls and department stores, in particular, a much-needed new lease of life. As discussed earlier in the book, the biggest challenge for these retail channels today is making use of surplus space as spending shifts online. In London, John Lewis is looking to convert 45 per cent of its flagship Oxford Street store into office space, while Westfield plans to convert two-thirds of a former House of Fraser department store into co-working space.

In 2020, WeWork opened its largest building in Canada – in a Hudson's Bay department store. 'We will drive those millennials through our entrances and create excitement and interest around our locations,' said Richard Baker, executive chairman of Hudson's Bay. 'We've been focused on rein-venting the old, tired stores we bought, and one of the ways to do that is to bring new uses into the stores.'

Not only does converting dead retail space into offices provide an alter-native source of income, it drives traffic, increases dwell time and, as is the case with other services like click & collect, there is a very good chance of additional spend once people are instore. Plus, shared office space is a natu-ral extension of services found in most malls and department stores – cafés and free Wi-Fi.

A place to play

Co-working spaces may help department stores to stay relevant, but they are just one small cog in a very big wheel. Perhaps inspired by experiential marketing strategies of fitness brands like Sweaty Betty, department stores have turned to instore fitness, with mixed success, as a way to put the leisure back into shopping. Although much innovation in this space has naturally been put on hold due to the pandemic, we believe there is an opportunity to pick this up again as part of a broader push into health and wellness.

In recent years, we've witnessed Saks offering a fitness centre with salt rooms and a vegan nail salon; Debenhams, while still trading, experimenting with instore gyms with specialist Sweat!; and Selfridges launching boxing gyms, skate bowls and even cinemas in its stores. With demand for home fitness skyrocketing during the pandemic, John Lewis partnered with Peloton for instore concessions, while Nordstrom joined forces with Tonal, allowing shoppers to see a demo of the gym or try a workout firsthand.

Meanwhile, London's Oxford Street is undergoing radical change. We've already seen now defunct department stores (BHS sites, for example) reincarnated as fitness centres, bowling alleys, crazy golf centres and cinemas. In the future, around one quarter of the ground floors in the area will change to include more gaming lounges, galleries and athletic-focused products.[19]

The world's biggest high street will also become greener and more people-friendly with the creation of two pedestrianised piazzas. At the same time, neighbouring Regent Street, home to more than 75 international flagship stores, has widened pavements, added new seating areas and benches, implemented cycle lanes, planted 60 semi-mature trees and constructed over 300 planters. This is how you do high streets in a post-pandemic digital era.

If Elon Musk has his way, his Tesla supercharger stations across the US will feature upmarket convenience stores alongside climbing walls, outdoor cinemas and 1950s-style drive-in restaurants with waiting staff on roller skates – giving customers something to do during the 30 minutes it takes to recharge their vehicles.[20] It's not quite colonizing Mars, but it's certainly blurring the lines between retail and entertainment.

We believe more brands will make the leap from selling a product to selling a lifestyle – and this has implications for both the physical and the digital space. Lululemon's $500 million mid-pandemic acquisition of at-home fitness company Mirror is a great example of a retailer that is transcending the transaction by tapping into something that shoppers can't put a price on: community. Similarly, DTC brand Eve Sleep doesn't describe itself as a mattress retailer but as a 'sleep wellness brand'. Imagine how different the bricks and mortar space would look if more stores adopted this mentality.

Shopping malls meanwhile are looking to rather unconventional ways to fill space such as hotels, entertainment (from laser tag to full-scale concert arenas) and kid-oriented experiences like KidZania or the Crayola Experience. Some are even positioning themselves as resort-style destinations where shoppers can spend a day out with their family. Rushden Lakes, for example, is the UK's first shopping centre combined with a nature reserve. The Northamptonshire centre features a first-of-its-kind lakeside setting where shoppers can go canoeing or explore the adjacent nature trails by foot or bike in addition to playing golf, trampolining and indoor climbing. 'We genuinely believe we are redefining the UK retail landscape – where else can you come to shop by canoe?' said Paul Rich, centre manager of Rushden Lakes.

It's also worth looking to Miami, which is set to become home to America's largest shopping mall. Spanning 6 million square feet, the 'American Dream' complex is expected to open in 2025 and will feature a water park with a giant indoor pool, ice climbing wall, artificial ski slope, 'submarine' rides, 2,000 hotel rooms and up to 1,200 stores.

Meanwhile, in Houston, we've seen a struggling Bed, Bath & Beyond store converted into an interactive art museum, while in Las Vegas an 'experience mall' called AREA15 opened in 2020. The 126,000-square-foot hybrid retail-entertainment complex has been described as a '21st-century immersive bazaar' and features attractions like escape rooms and virtual reality, a bamboo-filled sanctuary, festivals, themed events and live events (everything from concerts to Ted talks). Post-pandemic escapism at its finest.

Catering to pint-sized customers

No one is better positioned to embrace the fun factor than high street toy retailers. The problem is these are few and far between these days. Over the past decade, we've seen the famous FAO Schwarz store close on 5th Avenue, in addition to the demise of entire chains like KB Toys and, more recently, Toys R Us and baby goods and toy retailer Mothercare.[21]

It would be easy to just blame e-commerce for the toy specialists' problems, but let's not forget that supermarkets and big-box retailers have been chipping away at the specialists' business for decades. The internet, of course, lends itself to toy retailing, and during the pandemic it was one of the only ways to buy toys. Lego, for example, saw site visits to LEGO.com double in 2020. Toys are a commodity category where, like books and DVDs, shoppers generally know what they're getting without having to see the product in person. A Hatchimal is a Hatchimal regardless of where you buy it. What is more, the use of augmented reality is helping to instil even greater confidence in online shoppers – for example, the Argos app allows shoppers to see full-scale versions of select Lego toys before buying them. It's no surprise then that the toy category has one of the highest online penetration rates – and is poised for continued post-pandemic digital growth.

When you factor in the growing trend towards same-day delivery, bricks and mortar retailers lose their one remaining USP – immediacy. In toy retailing today, you need to be cheap, convenient or fun. Online and mass retailers may deliver on the first two, but there is still very much a place for specialists to inject some fun into the offering.

This was where Toys R Us went wrong. In the fast-moving sector, it fell behind in delivering on each of these areas, leaving it stuck in a retail no man's land. As a specialist, the Toys R Us experience had high potential to be a magical one with instore events, dedicated play areas and product demonstrations. The reality was a soulless shed with very little innovation or technology to draw shoppers in. Private equity ownership was a big factor here – saddled with debt, it was simply unable to adapt to a changing retail environment. It's also worth mentioning, as this is a book on Amazon after all, that another pitfall of Toys R Us was outsourcing its e-commerce business to Amazon in the early days, giving one of its biggest competitors an incredible insight into its customers' toy buying habits. Co-opetition isn't always good for business.

We believe there is an opportunity to put the joy and magic back into toy stores – or any type of retail geared towards children and families. This seems like common sense retailing. Why doesn't Tesco offer mum and baby classes in its large superstores? Why didn't Mothercare offer soft play for toddlers? Why didn't Toys R Us roll out play zones to let kids interact with the toys their parents were going to buy? In fairness, they did begin testing this in 2015 but sadly it was too little, too late.

In the US, Disney is redesigning its stores to make shoppers feel like they're on vacation – daily parades at Disneyland in California and Walt Disney World in Florida are being streamed live to cinema-sized screens instore. During the parades, customers can sit on mats and purchase cotton candy and light-up Mickey Mouse ears, as if they were in the theme park themselves.

When it comes to retail theatre, Lego steals the show with instore experiences that are consistently entertaining and engaging. Product is intentionally placed at eye level and within reach of its target consumer, and Lego famously lets both pint-sized and grown-up customers build instore, offering imaginative and creative spaces that cannot be replicated in a digital setting. And it's working. Lego continued to open hundreds of stores during the pandemic.

'People are looking for unique and memorable physical brand experiences, so we will continue to invest to expand our global retail footprint, as well as elevate our instore shopping experiences.'
Niels Christiansen, Lego CEO[22]

In 2021, Hasbro took over the former Paperchase flagship on London's Tottenham Court Road to launch Monopoly Lifesized, an immersive experience played on a giant Monopoly board. Meanwhile, British toy retailers such as The Entertainer regularly hold events where children can meet famous characters like Poppy and Branch from Trolls, while Smyths offers Magformers demonstrations and Barbie dress-up days, and Hamleys runs a mini theme park in its Moscow store.

CASE STUDY
Westfield's Destination 2028

The shopping centres of the future will be 'hyper-connected micro cities' driven by social interaction and community, according to Westfield.

The leading shopping centre laid out its vision for the future of retail with a concept called Destination 2028. Although this was created prior to the pandemic, we believe that COVID has only accelerated the need for a more digitally enabled, experience-led shopping centre. AI-infused walkways and hanging sensory gardens feature in an environment designed to cater to the growing importance consumers will place on experience, leisure, wellness and community. New technologies, from AI to drones, will blend seamlessly with back-to-basic concepts such as 'classroom retail'. The makers and process behind any product will take centre stage – from craftspeople creating a masterpiece in front of a live crowd to resident artists painting in the live gallery. New stage areas will host a series of showpiece interactive activities and events.

Technology will enable the shopping centre of the future to become more frictionless and personalized. Dubbed 'extra-perience' by Westfield, eye scanners will bring up information on entry about a visitor's previous purchases and recommend personalized fast lanes around the shopping centre. Magic mirrors and smart changing rooms will allow shoppers to see a virtual reflection of themselves wearing new garments while other innovations, like smart toilets that can detect hydration levels and nutritional needs, will enhance the overall experience.

Wellness is a key theme of Destination 2028. A 'betterment zone' allows customers to reflect in a mindfulness workshop, while reading rooms will be available for shoppers to unwind and tranquil green space will be featured both indoors and outside. The addition of allotments and farms gives shoppers the opportunity to select their own produce for their meal, while a network of waterways will not only offer an alternative route around the shopping centre but also access to watersports – one of the many leisure activities available.

Westfield's 'Destination 2028' concept also highlights the rise of the sharing economy, with 'rental retail' expected to become the norm for post-millennials seeking to rent everything from clothes to exercise gear. Pop-ups, temporary retail, and co-working spaces are also likely to emerge in the future of retail, according to Westfield.

A place to discover, a place to learn

Bricks and mortar retailers, therefore, must not overlook the importance of discovery as they aim to differentiate from online rivals. Although e-commerce has not traditionally posed a threat to discovery-led retailers, social media channels – Instagram in particular – are becoming more commerce-minded, potentially encroaching on the physical store's last remaining USPs. The good news for bricks and mortar retailers is that the pandemic has largely put 'browsing' on hold and we believe there is much pent-up demand for shoppers to come back to stores to 'have a mooch', get inspired and, crucially, take a break from their screens. Therefore, the need to surprise and delight shoppers instore has never been greater, whether through conventional methods like a Costco-style treasure hunt or more high-tech measures such as augmented and virtual reality.

Discount supermarkets like Aldi and Lidl do a fantastic job injecting excitement into what is otherwise a very functional shopping experience. The thrill of the middle aisle, where the shoppers find a rotating assortment of non-food goods, is a traffic driver in its own right. Going in for milk and walking out with an ice cream maker and set of *Harry Potter* DVDs is just something you can't get online.

Like the budget supermarkets, TJX (through its TJ Maxx/TK Maxx, Marshalls, HomeGoods and HomeSense stores) keeps the instore experience interesting by constantly refreshing its ranges – stores receive new shipments several times a week. And during the pandemic, it was a haven for shoppers looking to escape their homes for a bit. 'Customers tell us that part of the reason they shop with us is for some stress relief, particularly during these times, and some "me time", which we expect to continue into the future,' said Ernie Herrman, CEO of TJX, in 2021.[23]

One brand that has ditched traditional retail norms and embraced the art of discovery is New York City-based Story, which describes itself as 'the store that has the point of view of a magazine, changes like a gallery, and sells things like a store'. As its name implies, the focus is on stories – not products. Every six to eight weeks, the 2,000-square-foot store gets a make-over with a new design, curated range and fresh marketing messages. 'If time is the ultimate luxury and people want a higher return on investment of their time, you need to give them a reason to be in a physical space', said Story Founder Rachel Shechtman.[24]

It's worth calling out here that the Story brand was acquired by Macy's in 2018 in an attempt to stay relevant to younger shoppers and differentiate from its peers. It didn't appear to work. Story concept shops were rolled out across 30-plus Macy's stores, but a large number were shut in 2020, coinciding with the launch of another new format, Market by Macy's. At 20,000 square feet, the stores are about one-tenth the size of a regular Macy's store. The concept is Macy's ticket out of the main mall. Instead they will open in neighbourhood shopping centres and strip malls and, as such, look to tap into discovery, community and convenience. The stores feature event spaces that can accommodate a range of 'community-driven programming, from cooking tutorials and book signings to crafting and fitness classes'. Whether that is enough to save a struggling department store remains to be seen, but you can't fault Macy's for experimentation.

Personal shopping and merchandise-free stores

An increasingly popular way to tap into the art of discovery is through personal stylists. Once reserved for elite shoppers, personal shopping has become democratized both on- and offline. The rise of online styling services like Stitch Fix and Trunk Club have led major retailers like Amazon and ASOS to create their own versions of 'trying before you buy'. Amazon and ASOS' iterations currently lack the personal styling element – they are argu-ably more about instilling confidence in buying clothes online – but this would be a logical future move for both retailers.

Instore, everyone from H&M to Agent Provocateur now offers personal styling; however, some retailers have gone to the extreme of getting rid of products altogether in order to focus on the experience and customer service.

Men's fashion brand Bonobos, previously a pure-play online retailer and now owned by Walmart, wanted to allow its online shoppers to try before they came up with the concept of 'guideshops'. Here's how it works: shoppers come in for a personalized visit where they are fitted and provided with individual measurements. They can try anything on instore – Bonobos keeps all sizes, colours, fits and fabrics in stock at all times (only one of each item variation) – but they can't walk out with any merchandise. Shoppers can either pay for clothes instore and have them shipped, or order online when they get home.

Department store retailer Nordstrom, meanwhile, continues to roll out what it refers to as its Nordstrom Local 'service hubs', another example of retailers shying away from the word 'store'. At just 3,000 square feet, the stores do not carry their own inventory, though you can get items from nearby full-line stores within hours. What the Nordstrom Local stores lack in merchandise, they certainly make up for in amenities – personal styling consultations, clothing alterations, manicures and a bar serving beer, wine and pressed juice. The stores also serve as a convenient hub for online collection and returns, putting Nordstrom in an enviable position for future e-commerce growth. During the pandemic, online sales jumped from one-third to about half of the retailer's total sales, and the retailer expects this to be a permanent shift.[25]

The no-inventory model sounds wacky, but there is certainly some merit to it. Without massive piles of stock, these showrooms can trade from a significantly smaller footprint – which means a significantly lower rent bill. And without any shelves to restock, employees can devote more attention to the customer with the ultimate aim of driving sales and decreasing the likelihood of returns. The customer meanwhile gets the perfect fit and doesn't have to worry about carrying clothes home. 'Nordstrom Local customers who engage with our services at a Local including curbside pick-up, returns, alterations and styling spend more than two-and-a-half times compared to other customers,' said Ken Worzel, the company's Chief Operating Officer.[26]

Education, guidance and inspiration

When we think of retailers as educators, Apple workshops immediately spring to mind. Apple was doing experiential retail well before it went mainstream; however, even they are upping their game in this area. Remember the town square concept? Apple's blueprint for the future of retail places an even greater emphasis on experience and Apple stores now offer coding lessons to kids and host additional educational workshops and events, such as sessions for photography, music, gaming and app development.

John Lewis meanwhile runs 'discovery rooms' where shoppers can learn new skills or get advice on a variety of topics – how to choose the right camera, how to light a room, improve their garden or how to get a perfect night's sleep. In select stores shoppers can have one-to-one or group style consultations, receive beauty and makeup advice and also indulge in after-noon tea.

Ethical beauty retailer Lush, meanwhile, creates a completely sensory experience through its use of smell and colour, while the lack of packaging allows shoppers to engage directly with the products. Demonstrations are a core feature of the instore experience as staff are encouraged to show how products work (and justify the $14 price tag that comes with a bottle of shampoo).

Beyond the famous bath bomb demos, Lush employees are trained to recognize and respond to individual customer behaviours, allowing them to deliver a superior, tailored customer experience. For example, if a customer seems inquisitive, staff will spend the time getting to know their needs, explaining the product origins and demonstrating how they work; however, staff are also expected to identify and efficiently serve those who want to get in and out quickly. It might sound straightforward, but the ability to distin-guish between two very different customer types in a discovery-led setting is vital.

Known for going the extra mile, Lush employees are also empowered to make their own decisions to better connect with the customer, whether that's giving away a free sample or changing the merchandising mix to reflect the weather (ie putting out more colourful, cheery products on a rainy day). The result is a more meaningful, more memorable experience – and certainly one that goes beyond the transaction.

A place to rent

Last but not least, we believe that, as we inch closer to 'peak stuff', the store of the future will be a place to borrow. The sharing economy has already disrupted transportation and tourism but has yet to make its mark on the retail sector – shops naturally want to sell, rather than lend, to their customers. Well, the times are a-changing.

We are entering an age where access will trump ownership. This is due to the combination of a growing population, unprecedented connectivity and shifts in consumer values and priorities. We are no longer defined by our material possessions; instead we're opting to spend less on stuff and more on experiences. This is particularly pertinent among Millennials and, increasingly, Gen Z shoppers who are forgoing ownership of homes, cars, bicycles, music, books, DVDs, clothes, furniture and even pets. The World Economic Forum predicts that by 2030 products will become services and the notion of shopping will become a 'distant memory'.[27]

'We have an ownership society now, but we're moving toward an access society, where you're not defined by the things you own but by the experiences you have.'
Airbnb co-founder and CEO Brian Chesky[28]

The category most familiar with rental retail is fashion. Luxury retailers have spearheaded the trend, with pioneer Rent the Runway describing itself as the world's largest dry cleaner. In 2020, UK department store retailer Selfridges moved into this space, partnering with wardrobe sharing platform Hurr for its first ever luxury rental collection allowing customers to 'access high fashion at fast fashion prices'. Shoppers can now rent items for up to 20 days across both Selfridges' physical and online stores.

Rental retail, however, is no longer limited to luxury. Clothing rental subscriptions have become more mainstream in recent years, particularly in the US where a whole host of mass-appeal brands – American Eagle, Ann Taylor, Banana Republic, Express, Urban Outfitters – has dabbled in this space. The stigma attached to renting, or buying secondhand, is disappearing due to both financial and environmental concerns, particularly among younger generations. Meanwhile, the benefit to retailers is clear: a recurring revenue stream, increased loyalty, and it may even help to stamp out one the industry's newer problem – 'wardrobing' (the ugly, unintended consequence of free delivery and returns).

'Our goal is to slow down fast fashion and remove the need to buy wear-it-once items.'
Victoria Prew, CEO of Hurr[29]

From renting clothes to renting couches? IKEA now offers a furniture rental scheme in over 30 markets around the globe. This might sound like a radical departure for the flatpack king, but let's not forget that IKEA was one of the first retailers to address the rather thorny topic of 'peak stuff', a difficult acknowledgement for any business that is designed to sell. The retailer has since set the ambitious goal of using only renewable and recycled materials in its products by 2030. In some markets, IKEA already buys back used furniture so the rental scheme was a natural extension.

And it's not alone. In the US, West Elm has partnered with Rent the Runway for a similar furniture rental scheme, while start-ups like Feather and Fernish bring brands like Crate & Barrel to Generation Rent. In Japan, shoppers can rent Muji furniture for just $7 (800 yen) a month. Meanwhile, British shoppers can rent desks, chairs, dining tables and sofas for up to a year through John Lewis, thanks to a partnership with the world's largest product rental marketplace Fat Llama. 'Attitudes towards renting items and the sharing economy have dramatically shifted in recent years, and we know that renting, reselling items and recycling them is a growing priority for our customers,' said Johnathan Marsh, Director of Home at John Lewis.[30]

Outside of fashion, electricals retailer Dixons Currys has talked of a membership scheme where shoppers would pay for access to durable goods like a washing machine, for example, including installation and repairs – but without actually owning it.

In the future, it will be essential to create deeper relationships with customers as the focus shifts from product to service. This explains why a retailer like IKEA acquired TaskRabbit in 2018. The online marketplace connects 60,000 freelance 'taskers' with consumers looking to hire someone to do chores such as furniture assembly. Today you can buy a Stuva wardrobe without the anxiety of putting it together.

We believe there's an opportunity for hypermarkets and superstores, as a large store format with regular footfall, to consider library-style concessions where shoppers could borrow select items. This would be well suited to products that are expensive to buy outright, infrequently used and/or difficult to store – for example, sewing machines, tents, drills.

In southeast London, the Library of Things is a 'borrowing space' social enterprise that stocks everything from kitchenware to wetsuits. It's free to join and members can borrow up to five items each week, most of which can be rented for less than £4.[31] An instore 'library of things' could be part of the solution for those retailers who are struggling to fill dead space. Not only would it drive traffic to stores, but more importantly it would allow retailers to tap into the local community and develop a much deeper bond with customers.

In summary

Today, retail really is everywhere – in stores, our phones, our homes, in objects, even in media.

Online retailers like Amazon may have given shoppers unrivalled accessibility and near-instant gratification but, in doing so, they've taken the touch and feel out of shopping. Bricks and mortar retail must evolve to serve a purpose beyond just shifting product. Stores need to become special and fulfilling again. They need to tell a story, and to appease a growing desire for human connection in an increasingly digital world. Stores need to be focused on the community and provide a sensory experience that cannot be replicated online. The aim should be to make the physical space so compelling that shoppers might even be willing to pay an admission fee, as they do when going to an amusement park or the theatre.

Retailers must continue to break down silos, abandon old schools of thought and reinvent the measures of store success. We started off this chapter pondering the role of the store in today's digital era. Well, if the role of the store is no longer purely about selling, why are we still measuring things like sales densities and like-for-like sales growth?

Retailers, perhaps falsely, take comfort in the fact that this data is tangible. It's easy to understand. And it's how it's always been done. But as we all know now, 'business as usual' is possibly the most dangerous phrase a retailer could utter in today's rapidly changing world. We need a new set of metrics that are reflective of 21st-century shopping.

So, if the role of the store is, in part, to offer an experience that shoppers can't get online, then we should be measuring dwell time (its 'discoverability' factor), staff satisfaction and the number of meaningful, and ideally tech-enabled, engagements with customers. We should also be measuring how the store stacks up in its role as a hub for fulfilment. While the current

KPIs inherently measure the physical store *against* e-commerce, retailers must change gears to measure the success of the physical store *alongside* e-commerce. We need to start measuring KPIs such as digital purchase intent, percentage of online orders fulfilled by the store, the role of bricks and mortar in relation to returns (footfall, incremental spend) as well as the ability to utilize the store for rapid delivery.

Now, let's move on to explore the store as fulfilment hub in more detail.

Notes

1   Parisi, Danny (2021) After Story closures, Macy's tackles new experiential retail concept, *Glossy*, 20 February. Available from: https://www.glossy.co/fashion/inside-macys-plans-for-its-market-by-macys-concept-stores/ (archived at https://perma.cc/C8D8-BLXA) [Last accessed 20/6/2021].
2   Microsoft Office 365 (2017) Introducing Microsoft To-Do, now in Preview (online video). Available from: https://www.youtube.com/watch?v=6k3_T84z5Ds (archived at https://perma.cc/DC53-JLE4) [Last accessed 1/7/2018].
3   Thomas, Lauren (2017) Malls ditch the 'M word' as they spend big bucks on renovations, *CNBC*, 24 October. Available from: https://www.cnbc.com/2017/10/24/malls-ditch-the-m-word-as-they-spend-big-bucks-on-renovations.html (archived at https://perma.cc/YN77-MLUX) [Last accessed 29/3/2018].
4   Selfridges (nd) Selfridges loves: the secrets behind our house. Available from: http://www.selfridges.com/US/en/features/articles/selfridges-loves/selfridges-lovesourhousesecrets (archived at https://perma.cc/VT8Y-XF4L) [Last accessed 6/9/2018].
5   Abrams, Melanie (2017) Come for the shopping, stay for the food, *New York Times*, 26 October. Available from: https://www.nytimes.com/2017/10/26/travel/shopping-in-store-restaurants.html (archived at https://perma.cc/N4R5-8BEQ) [Last accessed 30/6/2018].
6   Ringen, Jonathan (2017) IKEA's big bet on meatballs, *Fast Company*. Available from: https://www.fastcompany.com/40400784/Ikeas-big-bet-on-meatballs (archived at https://perma.cc/CVP7-E5VU). [Last accessed 12/9/2018].
7   Henninger, Danya (2015) Vetri to sell restaurants to Urban Outfitters, *Philly*, 16 November. Available from: http://www.philly.com/philly/food/Vetri_to_sell_restaurants_to_Urban_Outfitters.html (archived at https://perma.cc/A3B6-DAJW) [Last accessed 30/6/2018].

8   Abrams, Melanie (2017) Come for the shopping, stay for the food, *New York Times*, 26 October. Available from: https://www.nytimes.com/2017/10/26/travel/shopping-in-store-restaurants.html (archived at https://perma.cc/N4R5-8BEQ) [Last accessed 30/6/2018].

9   Ryan, John (2018) In pictures: how China's ecommerce giants Alibaba and JD.com have reinvented stores, *Retail Week*, 5 June. Available from: https://www.retail-week.com/stores/in-pictures-chinas-alibaba-and-jdcom-reinvent-stores/7029203.article?authent=1 (archived at https://perma.cc/PYM4-X7KL) [Last accessed 30/6/2018].

10 Florida, Richard (2020) The forces that will reshape American cities, Bloomberg, 2 July. Available from: https://www.bloomberg.com/news/features/2020-07-02/how-coronavirus-will-reshape-u-s-cities (archived at https://perma.cc/F6KX-6NRH) [Last accessed 20/6/2021].

11 Tron, Jesse (2020) Post-COVID environment will drive demand for flexible office space, JLL press release, 14 July. Available from: https://www.us.jll.com/en/newsroom/post-covid-environment-will-drive-demand-for-flexible-office-space (archived at https://perma.cc/UQD5-TPCZ) [Last accessed 20/6/2021].

12 Anonymous (2020) Coronavirus: Pret boss says demand in city centres may never recover, *Sky News*, 4 September. Available from: https://news.sky.com/story/pm-mass-infrastructure-projects-crucial-for-uk-as-construction-begins-on-hs2-12063373 (archived at https://perma.cc/N7QW-VKVY) [Last accessed 20/6/2021].

13 Translated from French.

14 Roper, William (2021) COVID-19 is pushing Americans out of cities and into the country, *World Economic Forum*, 19 January. Available from: https://www.weforum.org/agenda/2021/01/rural-life-cities-countryside-covid-coronavirus-united-states-us-usa-america/ (archived at https://perma.cc/VQ6Y-3X3Q) [Last accessed 20/6/2021].

15 Kolko, Jed (2021) The most urban counties in the U.S. are shrinking, *The New York Times*, 4 May. Available from: https://www.nytimes.com/2021/05/04/upshot/census-new-results-county.html (archived at https://perma.cc/U6HT-KZBR) [Last accessed 20/6/2021].

16 Buchholz, Katharina (2020) How has the world's urban population changed from 1950 to today?, *World Economic Forum*, 4 November. Available from: https://www.weforum.org/agenda/2020/11/global-continent-urban-population-urbanisation-percent/ (archived at https://perma.cc/Z8E2-QJRN) [Last accessed 20/6/2021].

17 United Nations Department of Economic and Social Affairs No. 2020/2 (2020) Policies on spatial distribution and urbanization have broad impacts on sustainable development. Available from: https://www.un.org/development/desa/pd/sites/www.un.org.development.desa.pd/files/undes_pd_2020_popfacts_urbanization_policies.pdf (archived at https://perma.cc/962G-FWEH) [Last accessed 20/6/2021].

18 Willsher, Kim (2020) Paris mayor unveils '15-minute city' plan in re-election campaign, *The Guardian*, 7 February. Available from: https://www.theguardian.com/world/2020/feb/07/paris-mayor-unveils-15-minute-city-plan-in-re-election-campaign (archived at https://perma.cc/54YA-4QVJ) [Last accessed 20/6/2021].

19 Amaro, Silvia (2021) London's iconic Oxford Street is rethinking retail as it deals with Covid-fueled closures, *CNBC*, 9 February. Available from https://www.cnbc.com/2021/02/09/londons-iconic-oxford-street-is-rethinking-retail.html (archived at https://perma.cc/MH69-CZ4E) [Last accessed 21/6/2021].

20 Taylor, Kate (2018) Tesla may have just picked a spot for Elon Musk's dream 'roller skates & rock restaurant' – here's everything we know about the old-school drive in, *Business Insider*, 13 March. Available from: http://uk.businessinsider.com/elon-musk-tesla-restaurant-los-angeles-2018-3 (archived at https://perma.cc/T94S-SMDE) [Last accessed 1/7/2018].

21 Anonymous (2018) Mothercare confirms 50 store closures, *BBC*, 17 May. Available from: http://www.bbc.co.uk/news/business-44148937 (archived at https://perma.cc/T8KN-EVG5) [Last accessed 1/7/2018].

22 Lego 2020 annual results (2021) The LEGO Group delivers strong growth in 2020, 10 March. Available from: https://www.lego.com/en-us/aboutus/news/2021/march/2020-annual-results/ (archived at https://perma.cc/9H3L-QD5A) [Last accessed 20/6/2021].

23 The TJX Companies' (TJX) CEO Ernie Herrman on Q4 2021 results – earnings call transcript (2021) Available from: https://seekingalpha.com/article/4408679-tjx-companies-tjx-ceo-ernie-herrman-on-q4-2021-results-earnings-call-transcript (archived at https://perma.cc/2GCE-N4Z9) [Last accessed 20/6/2021].

24 Hoand, Limei (2016) 7 Lessons for retail in the age of e-commerce, *Business of Fashion*, 13 September. Available from: https://www.businessoffashion.com/articles/intelligence/concept-store-story-rachel-shechtman-seven-retail-lessons (archived at https://perma.cc/U82K-JAGA) [Last accessed 1/7/2018].

25 Wahba, Phil (2021) How Nordstrom's strategy is changing now that 50% of its sales come online, *Fortune*, 4 February. Available from: https://fortune.com/2021/02/04/nordstrom-sales-online-strategy-retail/ (archived at https://perma.cc/REC6-YSGY) [Last accessed 20/6/2021].

26 Nordstrom press release (2020) Nordstrom expands convenience for Los Angeles customers with two new Nordstrom Local service hubs, 27 October. Available from: https://press.nordstrom.com/news-releases/news-release-details/nordstrom-expands-convenience-los-angeles-customers-two-new (archived at https://perma.cc/7Z8Q-JKYM) [Last accessed 20/6/2021].

27 Parker, Ceri (2016) 8 predictions for the world in 2030, *World Economic Forum*, 12 November. Available from: https://www.weforum.org/agenda/2016/11/8-predictions-for-the-world-in-2030/ (archived at https://perma.cc/5KXX-98WS) [Last accessed 1/7/2018].

28 Taylor, Colleen (2011) Airbnb CEO: The future is about access, not ownership, *Gigaom*, 10 November. Available from: https://gigaom.com/2011/11/10/airbnb-roadmap-2011/ (archived at https://perma.cc/AYN9-ZTUC) [Last accessed 12/9/2018].

29 Nazir, Sahar (2020) Clothing rental services - a viable option for UK consumers?, *Retail Gazette*, 3 September. Available from: https://www.retailgazette.co.uk/blog/2020/09/clothing-rental-services-fashion-waste-consumers-recycling-uk-retail/ (archived at https://perma.cc/89A6-V89Z) [Last accessed 20/6/2021].

30 John Lewis press release (2020) John Lewis partners with Fat Llama to test furniture rental service, 17 August. Available from: https://www.johnlewispartnership.co.uk/media/press/y2020/jl-partners-with-fat-llama.html (archived at https://perma.cc/6Y99-3LMF) [Last accessed 20/6/2021].

31 Balch, Oliver (2016) Is the Library of Things an answer to our peak stuff problem? *Guardian*, 23 August. Available from: https://www.theguardian.com/sustainable-business/2016/aug/23/library-of-things-peak-stuff-sharing-economy-consumerism-uber (archived at https://perma.cc/TXQ7-LMUM) [Last accessed 1/7/2018].

15

Retail fulfilment: winning the customer over the final mile

'You do not want to give Amazon a seven-year head start.'
Warren Buffett, US business magnate[1]

In Chapters 13 and 14, we saw how the store of the future will have to evolve to simultaneously increase automation to reduce friction and become more experiential. The influence of digital on the shopping journey has also increasingly seen the role of the store develop as an online fulfilment hub. Before e-commerce, the major supply chain logistics a retailer had to worry about were getting products from suppliers to the distribution and fulfilment centres, and then into their stores.

The promise to deliver

In the early e-commerce days, retail executives recalled exasperated calls from store managers demanding to know if online returns they had to accept instore would 'come off their targets'. It was then that established bricks and mortar retailers making their first forays online began to realize the true impact of e-commerce on their stores. They recognized that they could turn the fact that they had not foreseen online returns impacting their bricks and clicks presence into an advantage over the likes of then-pure play Amazon by managing both the fulfilment process and the returns instore. They were happy to embrace this new store role if it meant shoppers eliminating the delivery costs when they came in to pick up their orders, which the retailers themselves would otherwise incur, particularly when they had to reschedule missed deliveries. This is a particular challenge for e-commerce operators when you consider return rates can be as high as 40 per cent in sectors such as fashion, and one study found that 1 per cent or more of all revenue can be lost due to delivery fraud alone.[2] Little did they know how popular these so-called 'click & collect' services, or buy online pick up instore (BOPIS), would become.

Although we discussed click & collect earlier in relation to COVID-19's impact on shopping trends, it is necessary to understand how this fufilment service was able to come to the rescue of so many store-based retailers at the height of global lockdowns.

Many European countries were first to see the widespread adoption of click & collect. This is due to a number of factors: prohibitively high e commerce delivery charges; the geographic density of its populations, where they were never far from a retail chain's store; high internet broadband penetration and mobile access; and consumers' relatively mature acceptance of alternatives to cash payment, with card-not-present and cash-on-delivery transactions facilitating the remote shopping model of e-commerce in the first place. The click & collect operations of French grocers and other retailers give 80 per cent of the population access within 10 minutes to some thousands of pickup points. Known as 'click and drive' or 'curbside pickup', the fulfilment method already accounted for 50 per cent of supermarket chain E. Leclerc's total sales in the run up to the pandemic.[3] UK consumers are also enthusiastic click & collectors; the number of UK stores offering click & collect grew by 32 per cent year-on-year in response to 2020's lockdowns, while 41 per cent of consumers intend to increase their use of click & collect in future.[4]

In the US, click & collect 'Drive Up', curbside pickup has also grown in popularity. But Walmart's kiosk concept that we referenced earlier in the book helps the retail giant balance the higher fulfilment costs of its e-commerce growth with the ability to incentivize store visits and drive potential additional footfall. Some estimates also put the proportion of 2020's pandemic-induced increase in online sales fulfilled at the curb as high as 80 per cent, proving that collection services may have saved bricks and mortar retailers at the height of global lockdowns.[5]

As we touched on earlier in the book, before it could even think about acquiring a physical grocery chain, Amazon made its first foray into click &

collect via lockers. The first Amazon Lockers appeared in Amazon's home town of Seattle, as well as New York and London, in 2011. Customers can choose any locker location for their delivery and receive a unique pickup code via email or text message to retrieve their orders, which they enter on the touchscreen of their assigned locker to open its door. Amazon has scaled its locker service by partnering with retail property owners to place the lockers in shopping malls, and in the stores of retailers such as 7-Eleven and Spar, as well as Co-op and Morrisons in the UK. Amazon Lockers can also be found in Canada, France, Germany and Italy, while the company is not opposed to using less traditional locker locations, including public libraries[6] and urban apartment complexes and even the Coachella music festival, offering festival goers a convenient way of sourcing a last-minute phone charger or sunscreen, with its locker-based Amazon Hub service.[7] As of 2021, Amazon Lockers were located in more than 900 cities and towns across the US alone.

Remote pickup convenience

The beauty of lockers is that they eliminate specific last-mile fulfilment issues, such as theft, missed deliveries and the need for redelivery, as well as the associated additional costs. Customers can also return unwanted goods using the system. But not every third-party Amazon seller can make use of the locker option if the item or the carrier they use relies on a system that requires a signature to confirm receipt of delivery (although Amazon Hub delivery lockers accept parcels from all carriers). There is also the fact that Amazon Lockers are also unsuitable for perishable goods. With a larger online grocery market, Europe has led in the development of temperature-controlled click & collect lockers. Here, emmasbox is worthy of note. The Munich, Germany-based start-up supplies its refrigerated pickup stations for online food order fulfilment to the country's public transport authority, Deutsche Bahn, as well as other transit locations, such as Munich Airport and grocery retailers Edeka and Migros. French retailer Auchan introduced 250 temperature-controlled click & collect lockers for groceries in the Saint-Etienne area a few years ago, shortly after discounter Lidl began installing pickup points for online grocery orders in Belgium. Other models, such as DHL/Deutsche Post's Packstation in Germany, La Poste's Cityssimo in France and ByBox in the UK, are based on the provision of full-blown pickup locations in or near transport hubs or other high-traffic footfall urban areas, rivalling the role of the traditional post office or FedEx and

UPS retail outlets. Up until 2021 Amazon UK customers could also pick up their parcels from Doddle's 400-plus locations, for example. In the US, Lowes Foods is working with retail automation company Bell and Howell to provide temperature-controlled lockers at office buildings to bring grocery deliveries to customers' workplace. But, as discussed previously, it's not just about lockers these days. We've seen click & collect lockers spring up in diverse settings and partnerships between Amazon with the likes of Next in the UK and Kohl's in the US.

When it comes to performance targets, many retailers now measure the impact of e-commerce by factoring the order location into store-based or regional sales. This is why industry consensus still credits around 80 per cent of global retail sales as being 'completed' in a store. A customer may order and pay for a product online, but then choose to collect it from a local store or third-party location at a time that's more convenient for them, while also often allowing them to forgo the premium of a delivery charge. When it comes to delivery charges, Amazon was one of the first to use free delivery as a lure for more customers in 2002. It introduced its Super Saver shipping offer, lowering the threshold from $100 to $25. Outside of its Prime membership scheme, Amazon today offers free shipping on orders of $25 or more of eligible merchandise.

So, the retail industry has had to become increasingly obsessed over the 'last mile' since internet access became ubiquitous and interfaces pervasive, and as demand for near-instant fulfilment has soared. Traditionally a term used by telecommunications network providers to refer to the infrastructure that physically reaches the end-user's premises, the 'last mile' has been adopted by retail to refer to the last stage in the product or service fulfilment process. Replenishment to store, home delivery, or a hybrid of the two: fulfil-to-store for click & collect, or lockers on third-party premises, for example (see Figure 15.1).

FIGURE 15.1   New fulfilment options driving heightened complexity in retail supply chains

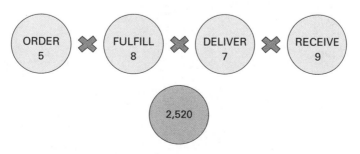

FIGURE 15.2 The growing complexity of fulfilling e-commerce customer orders

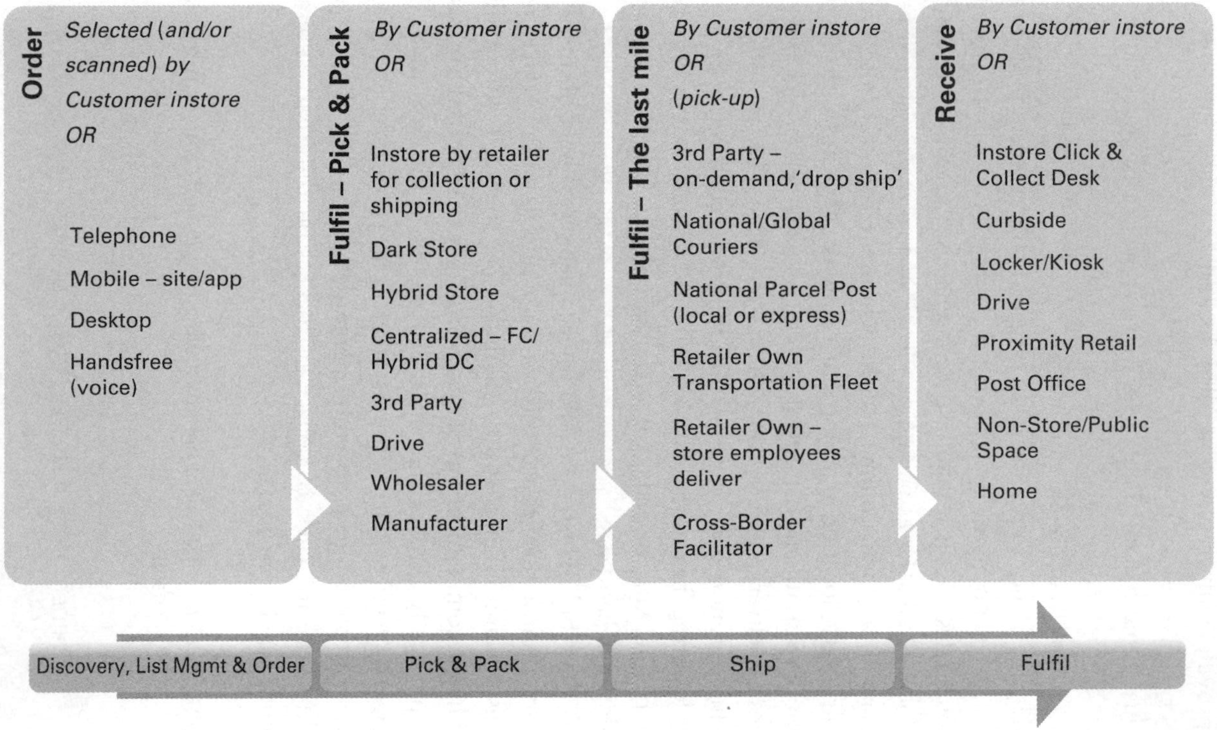

Order

Selected (and/or scanned) by Customer instore

OR

Telephone

Mobile – site/app

Desktop

Handsfree (voice)

Fulfil – Pick & Pack

By Customer instore

OR

Instore by retailer for collection or shipping

Dark Store

Hybrid Store

Centralized – FC/ Hybrid DC

3rd Party

Drive

Wholesaler

Manufacturer

Fulfil – The last mile

By Customer instore

OR

(pick-up)

3rd Party – on-demand, 'drop ship'

National/Global Couriers

National Parcel Post (local or express)

Retailer Own Transportation Fleet

Retailer Own – store employees deliver

Cross-Border Facilitator

Receive

By Customer instore

OR

Instore Click & Collect Desk

Curbside

Locker/Kiosk

Drive

Proximity Retail

Post Office

Non-Store/Public Space

Home

Discovery, List Mgmt & Order | Pick & Pack | Ship | Fulfil

This is when you consider the proliferation of options the consumer now has, alongside the traditional shopping trip, where the customer picks, packs and receives their own goods in a store. Supply chain capabilities have had to rapidly evolve beyond traditional hub-and-spoke, distribution and fulfilment centres to store networks to enable shoppers to access products however, wherever and whenever they want them. The 'terms', as we have referred to them in this book, of the 'on-my-terms' shopper are dictated by the order (Figure 15.2).

With the consumer in control, the variations of the traditional supply chain are multiplying rapidly. These variations are driving heightened complexity in retail and manufacturing supply chains. But historically the supply chain has been considered a cost centre for many organizations. Even those retailers deemed 'essential' during the height of COVID-19 lockdowns, who benefited from unprecedented online sales growth, saw margins eroded by increased last mile-costs and supply chain delays. So, when considering the Amazon effect, now more than ever, supply chain models – which dictate where an order will be picked, packed and fulfilled over the last mile, in support of new paths to purchase – will be one of the most critical growth enablers for both retailer and manufacturer organizations. This is because Amazon has already been winning over the last mile for some time now.

Developing the last mile

Winning the last mile increasingly dictates who wins the overall race to reach the consumer – success means also beating the competition on frequency, as well as relevancy, and, ultimately, loyalty. Amazon's fulfilment infrastructure is its competitive engine, in service of the speed and convenience that powers its flywheel. Without it, its two biggest supply chain-based growth generators – Prime and Fulfilment by Amazon (FBA) – could not be successful. In winning the last mile, Amazon is well known for wanting rapid delivery to be the norm, where its customer proposition also makes it just as easy to order whatever you want. In that, it is a genuine disruptor.

Take, for example, YouTuber Rob Bliss, who decided to use his Amazon Prime subscription to deliver goods to the homeless community around New York City. He asked each person what they needed and ordered them. Donations included socks, shoes, sleeping bags, long johns, and other hygienic items. Within hours, the items were delivered, while his videos and idea went viral.[8]

In Chapter 8 we saw how much of its last-mile strategy has also been built on the foundations Amazon is using to gain ground in the grocery market. But it's worth restating how its massive AWS computing capability powers the complex algorithms that orchestrate its massive logistics capability and manage the complexity of getting an order processed, picked, shipped and packed to a street corner in downtown Manhattan within a matter of minutes. The AWS pillar underpins Amazon's delivery mechanisms in the most literal sense.

If you look at the final part of the online shopping process in isolation, it starts from the time that the customer decides to buy an item and place an order. This is whether they are using their own device to place the order and complete the purchase or one belonging to the retailer instore, including checkouts with e-commerce integration, kiosks, or other 'endless aisle' applications. Here, we've already seen how Amazon has enticed Prime members into its book and 4-Star stores with preferential pricing. It also highlights the ease of using their existing online accounts to speed payment, just as it set the standard for 1-click purchasing, which simplifies the most laborious parts of the online checkout process – filling in delivery and payment information. As we also acknowledged earlier, Amazon directly influenced the widespread adoption of this feature with its 1-click patent, while its simplified voice assisted auto-replenishment services, as well as embedding Alexa in its technology hardware range, can all perform the search, browse and discovery stages of the online shopping process hands free, right through to the order and putting items in the customer's basket for checkout. Amazon has even enabled Alexa users to pay to refuel their vehicles with their voice.

When it comes to checkout, Amazon has also built a major play. Amazon Payments, the online payments gateway gives Amazon.com customers the option to pay with their Amazon accounts on external merchant websites. Just like its rivals Google Checkout and PayPal, Amazon Payments effectively enables customers to use one account from a trusted provider for all their online payments, while merchants are charged a percentage of the transaction and a transaction fee. One of the reasons third-party merchants like Amazon Pay is that its customers never leave the merchant's website during the checkout process and can pay using any method supported by Amazon. It is also device agnostic and merchants receive a customer's name and verified email at check-in. It has also built API integrations to some of the e-commerce platforms that are popular with mid-sized merchants, such as BigCommerce, Magento and Shopify, as well as payment service provider

FIS (through its acquisition of Worldpay), so their users can activate a free plug-in to add the Amazon Payment option to their checkouts.

In the race for the online payments space, however, Amazon Payments cannot claim market dominance, although its client base makes it a major player. It can access 300 million-plus active customer accounts, while payments gateway rival PayPal has around 400 million. Meanwhile, the competition from social media is mounting. Facebook has over 1.88 billion daily active users and, although its payments processing revenue is a tiny proportion of its earnings in comparison to its advertising revenues, it earned $1.8 billion in payments and other fees in 2020 from sources including in Facebook Payments and Marketplace.[9] But you need not necessarily register payment details in order to use the social network, unlike some of the others. Despite this, while most of the others – with the exception of PayPal – have larger user bases, Amazon is the only retailer with this extended capability (though Apple has retail stores to sell its own consumer electronics products and services, and also offers Apple Pay). The only real online rival in both size, scale and sector in this regard is Alibaba subsidiary AliPay, which had a whopping 1.3 billion annual active users as of 2020, processing $17 trillion worth of transactions in mainland China during that year.

Checkout to go

The main reason for considering purchase as part of the fulfilment process and its influence over the last mile is to put Amazon's Just Walk Out checkout-free system into proper context here. Completely eliminating the need for checkout and payment points the way towards store of the future concepts that are more focused on fulfilment. The previous two chapters focused on how retailers can look to reduce friction at every stage of the shopping journey – from search and browsing to discovery. But, in terms of those processes that may discourage conversion instore, checkout and payment loom front and centre; retailers should take a tip from Amazon and see stores as a way of letting customers get hold of the products they want with as little effort and inconvenience as possible.

UK grocer Waitrose has trialled a cashless store in its 'little Waitrose' format, while Walmart and Kroger certainly heeded the Amazon Go threat in the US, with both developing checkout-less shopping services but with differing fortunes. Walmart initially tested a 'Scan & Go' mobile app that allowed customers to scan the barcodes of selected products and then check them out without having to complete an additional stop at a checkout – although those customers did have a dedicated Express lane to exit the store with their purchases, for security purposes. Then, just before Amazon revealed its Just Walk Out store technology to the world, Walmart expanded its app after successfully implementing a similar service at its wholesale chain, Sam's Club. But, just as suddenly as it made its announcement, six months later it said it was abandoning the rollout due to low uptake. Some in the industry said customers found it difficult to manage their device, the product they were scanning, and their basket, trolley or shopping bag; that theft was also an issue. Walmart continued to offer its Scan & Go service using proprietary handheld scanning guns, with lower risk of them running out of battery life, and dedicated trolley holders until, as previously referenced, reintroducing the app during the pandemic. Kroger rolled out a similar mobile app and handheld scanner-based service it calls 'Scan, Bag, Go'. In fact, where Sainsbury's in the UK saw more than half of all store sales go through its SmartShop app during the middle of the pandemic, many retailers have accelerated their scan & go mobile app rollouts. It's also worth noting that Waitrose was first to roll out proprietary handheld scanning guns … two decades ago!

Amazon's checkout and payment strategy also ensures it has a role to play in the ordering and payment processes of other retailers as it continues to revolutionize this part of the shopping journey from a physical perspective too. Although it does not include these services in its third-party Marketplace financials, let's not forget this part of the flywheel in our consideration of Amazon's role in the order, pay and fulfilment process, where Amazon provides the entire e-commerce front-end, online shopping service for third-party merchants.

Where every part of the Amazon infrastructure, offering and ecosystem reinforces its core aim, to sell 'more stuff', its last-mile proposition very much reinforces the core values of its offer: choice, convenience and speed. The multi-track Amazon last mile extends from auto-replenishment to Prime and its free, unlimited two-day delivery offer, or same day depending on the delivery location.

It's worth considering how well Amazon fares in using the mechanics of subscription to drive increased sales among members too. Certainly, led by Amazon's example with Prime, subscription services have been growing in popularity for a while. Apart from being a proxy for a loyalty scheme with the added benefit of recurring revenue, convenience (42 per cent) tops consumers' list of benefits for subscribing to a product or service instead of owning it, followed by cost savings (35 per cent) and variety (35 per cent). Over two-thirds (78 per cent) of consumers have subscription services and 75 per cent believe that in the future, people will subscribe to more services and own less physical 'stuff'. But consumers want to pay for what they use. Nearly three-quarters (72 per cent) would prefer the ability to pay for what they use rather than just a flat fee.[10]

Recurring revenues

Melanie Darvall, director of marketing and communications at UK postal delivery company Whistl, commented that the key to launching a successful subscription service is finding the right balance to make the offering beneficial for both parties – the retailer and consumer. 'Ensuring the quality of product or value of discount is high enough to make your customer base loyal and consider spending money outside of what is essentially a monthly "taster" service can certainly be a challenge, but once you've cracked that side of things, you'll reap the rewards and hopefully retain a happy customer base', she commented.[11] To Darvall's point, a notable Amazon advertising campaign used the slogan 'Amazon Prime Delivers More', in reference to the free video and music streaming Prime members have access to, alongside free delivery, among its many other benefits. Now Amazon's growing Prime subscriber base is driving its fulfilment capacity demands.

So, in the rest of this and the next chapter, we'll look at how it is building out its last-mile fulfilment logistics proposition, including current and future innovation through Prime lockers and ultra-rapid delivery by drone, as well as FBA, but also how its supply chain strategy is evolving to encompass added online-to-offline capabilities in a growing array of other sectors, including fashion and, of course, grocery too.

Building out the last mile

Amazon was actually a relative latecomer to the rapid delivery space. At launch, industry watchers questioned whether Amazon could afford to dump money into a war over the last mile with the rash of on-demand start-ups springing up to challenge traditional retail fulfilment models in response to consumers' insatiable appetite for instant gratification. The rise of 15-minute delivery rivals noted in earlier chapters has only served to further raise the stakes when it comes to winning with customers over the last mile.

Others suggested it had no choice but to go head-to-head with the Postmates, Uber Eats, Instacarts and Deliveroos of this world, where these competitors own no products and fulfil customer orders on behalf of their retailer clients who are also playing catch-up to Amazon on same-day.

But competitors were quick to respond. eBay, for example, enables sellers to make Express delivery options available when listing products, perhaps targeting third-party sellers who feel cut out of Amazon's own Prime delivery promise, which prioritizes listings of those using its FBA services, as well as its own private label products, as already discussed.

Amazon has also seen its rapid Prime promise to deliver face more competition from one-hour and 10- to 15-minute carriers, as we examined earlier and on which the jury is still out as regards profitability. London-based Dija, for example, uses its own fleet of directly-employed riders on electric bikes and offers three months' worth of free deliveries if its misses its 10-minute delivery window. Drawing comparisons with the likes of the gig economy's Instacart, Deliveroo and Uber Eats, Chad West, Dija's director of brand marketing, says its success is all down to a hyper-local, data-driven model and that the company buys its groceries wholesale to sell retail. 'We're not just going to a supermarket and filling a basket,' he said.[12]

Competitive context

Google, in comparison with eBay, was quicker to launch a same-day and overnight delivery service from local and national US retailers with its Express service. Delivery is carried out via branded vehicles and third-party courier firms and customers must have a Google Play account. Although the retailers can add delivery surcharges, it has seen gradual expansion, in part because its voice assistant integration offers retailers a capable alternative to Amazon's Alexa, signing deals with Walmart, Costco, Target and Carrefour (as referenced in Chapter 11). It has also doubled down on its competitive position to Amazon by partnering with Shopify to give the e-commerce platform's more than 1.7 million merchants the ability to reach consumers through Google Search and its other services, which could include Google Express.

Given rivals Google and eBay's apparent lack of speed to market or ability to rapidly scale their rapid fulfilment efforts, it's easy to understand the space that third-party rapid delivery firms have filled in helping retailers win customers over the last mile. It's the most expensive stage of getting online orders to their buyers.[13] In 2014 the free shipping (and rapid Prime delivery) that Amazon uses to delight its customers and best the competition cost more than $4.2 billion or nearly 5 per cent of net sales. By 2020, this cost amounted to $61 billion, which was also up 61 per cent on the previous year. Stephenie Landry, Amazon grocery vice president, addressed questions about the cost of meeting its rapid delivery promise.[14] 'Ultra-fast shopping is an expensive proposition', she admitted. 'It isn't easy to do but the only way to learn about it is to be in the game.' But, in the true spirit of living the Amazon Leadership Principles, Landry added, 'As leader of this business, I don't spend much of my time thinking about delivery costs; I really think about customer love – how do I make a customer love this product? I would take a cost problem over a customer love problem any day.'[15]

Food takeaway expansion

In addition to consolidating the wider benefits of Prime within Amazon's ecosystem – feeding the flywheel – Amazon has also played in the food delivery space with its Restaurants service. But in the spirit of its test-and-learn ethos, it was discontinued after it likely realized it was too late to the party to use its tech smarts to provide significant differentiation. Its one-hour delivery used a business model comparable to those of Just Eat, Delivery Hero, foodpanda, foodora and a whole host of other restaurant food delivery intermediaries. Interestingly, arguably the king of fast-food giants, McDonald's, has been operating its McDelivery service in 25 countries; it launched in the US in 1993, predating the rapid food delivery gold rush. The latest McDelivery development, however, shows just how disruptive third-party delivery intermediaries have become, rolling out in the UK via Just Eat and Uber Eats.

Deliveroo is worth a mention here, not only for the fact it shares similarities in its rapid restaurant food delivery model with the Just Eats of this world but that it has taken on some of the food production as well. Deliveroo has gone on to launch its pop-up Editions 'dark' kitchens. The so-called 'RooBox' takeaway-only kitchens prepare branded food from the likes of Thai chain Busaba Eathai, US-style MEATLiquor diners and Franco Manca pizza parlours, from locations such as industrial estates and disused car parks, to reduce the set-up costs in comparison with a full-service restaurant. Despite this, in an ironic turn of fortunes, it was Amazon that bailed out the failing company in the middle of the pandemic by increasing its investment stake in the company after the deal was approved by the UK's Competition Commission, which gives Amazon unfettered access to its IP and data.

Also, like Deliveroo, Instacart has been learning from the clients it serves in very similar ways to how Amazon likes to own retail's rails. Brittain Ladd, industry consultant and former Amazon executive, wrote:

> Instacart is given complete and unfettered access to every detail and costs of the retailers who signed them. Instacart has been actively increasing the amount of capital they raise so that they can become a grocery retailer, wholesaler, and manufacturer of private label products. The grocery retailers who viewed Instacart as being their saviour taught Instacart their business, including their strengths and weaknesses. As Instacart expands their business model, they'll be able to use their knowledge of their grocery customers to their advantage.[16]

Driving last-mile demand

So, we can see how the expansion of rapid fulfilment services responds to growing sector opportunities, as well as rapidly evolving consumer demand driven, in part, in reaction to disruptive global events. The likes of Amazon Prime and Fresh may have the company's scale behind them to add significant momentum to its flywheel, but they must also compete against increasingly diverse rivals.

One area where Amazon has sought to stay ahead of the competition when it comes to the differentiation of Prime is, of course, the actual online shopping experience. A good example of this is its in-app order tracking capability, which gives customers a real-time map of their delivery's journey, as well as how many other stops or deliveries your courier will make before theirs. The system is only compatible with parcels fulfilled by its own logistics network and not those handled by the US Postal Service, UPS or FedEx. We'll come on to Amazon's often fraught relations with its third-party logistics partners in the next chapter, which examines the last mile infrastructure responsible for orchestrating the delivery of all of those smiling boxes behind the scenes. Many other retailers and carriers have gone on to develop similar features to maintain their promise to deliver while attempting to safeguard margins. But Amazon is still reaping the rewards from its early and pioneering role in winning customers over the last mile.

Notes

1 Video (2017) 'You do not want to give Jeff Bezos a seven-year head start,' *Warren Buffet archives*, 8 May. Available from: https://buffett.cnbc.com/video/2017/05/08/buffett-you-do-not-want-to-give-jeff-bezos-a-seven-year-head-start.html (archived at https://perma.cc/U73F-8R4X) [Last accessed 5/6/2021].

2 Lexis Nexis (2014) Annual Report: True cost of fraud study: post-recession revenue growth hampered by fraud as all merchants face higher costs, *LexisNexis*, August. Available from: https://www.lexisnexis.com/risk/downloads/assets/true-cost-fraud-2014.pdf (archived at https://perma.cc/3QRQ-JVRP) [Last accessed 5/6/2021].

3 eMarketer Editors (2019) For consumers in France, click-and-collect is an option … but not the only one, eMarketer Insider Intelligence, 15 July. Available from: https://www.emarketer.com/content/for-consumers-in-france-click-and-collect-is-an-option-but-not-the-only-one (archived at https://perma.cc/A4MN-8WHJ) [Last accessed 13/6/2021].

4 O'Carroll, Derek (2020) Five hidden trends that will shape UK e commerce in 2021, Retail Technology Innovation Hub, 2 December. Available from: https://retailtechinnovationhub.com/home/2020/12/2/five-hidden-trends-that-will-shape-uk-e-commerce-in-2021 (archived at https://perma.cc/AYF6-D9X9) [Last accessed 13/6/2021].

5 Kodali, Sucharita (2021) Alt-Control-Delete: The reboot of retail, Manhattan Associates Momentum Connect event, 26 May [Virtual presentation].

6 Gov.uk (2016) Case study: Amazon lockers in libraries, *Gov.uk*, 5 January. Available from: https://www.gov.uk/government/case-studies/amazon-lockers-in-libraries (archived at https://perma.cc/W8EK-RM5L) [Last accessed 5/6/2021].

7 Schlosser, Kurt (2017) Amazon's new 'Hub' delivery locker system is already a hit in San Francisco apartment building, *GeekWire*, 25 August. Available from: https://www.geekwire.com/2017/amazons-new-hub-delivery-locker-system-already-hit-san-francisco-apartment-building/ (archived at https://perma.cc/4Q5Q-KZEU) [Last accessed 5/6/2021].

8 Lang, Cady (2017) How you can use Amazon Prime to help people in need this holiday season, *Time*, 12 December. Available from: http://time.com/5061792/amazon-prime-charity/ (archived at https://perma.cc/UA9L-LRWU) [Last accessed 5/6/2021].

9 Tankovska, H. (2021) Facebook: annual revenue 2009–2020, by segment, *Statista*, 5 February Available from: https://www.statista.com/statistics/267031/facebooks-annual-revenue-by-segment/ (archived at https://perma.cc/LRP3-26LD) [Last accessed 7/4/2021].

10 Press release (2021) Subscription business revenue grows 437% over nearly a decade as consumer buying preferences shift from ownership to usership, Zuora, 3 March. Available from: https://www.businesswire.com/news/home/20210303005291/en/Subscription-Business-Revenue-Grows-437-Over-Nearly-a-Decade-as-Consumer-Buying-Preferences-Shift-from-Ownership-to-Usership (archived at https://perma.cc/VAV9-FW37) [Last accessed 13/6/2021].

11 Morrell, Liz (2018) British consumers spending more than £2 billion a year on delivery subscriptions, *edelivery*, 14 May. Available from: https://edelivery.net/2018/05/british-consumers-spending-2-billion-year-delivery-subscriptions/ (archived at https://perma.cc/R282-6F8B) [Last accessed 5/6/2021].

12 Plummer, Robert (2021) Shopping in 10 minutes: The new supermarket battleground, *BBC News*, 23 April. Available from: https://www.bbc.co.uk/news/business-56720044 (archived at https://perma.cc/9PK8-7B78) [Last accessed: 14/6/2021].

13 Wienbren, Emma (2017) Two-hour deliveries will be normal, says Amazon Prime Now VP, *The Grocer*, 20 March. Available from: https://www.thegrocer.co.uk/channels/online/two-hour-deliveries-will-be-normal-says-amazon-prime-now-vp/550248.article?rtnurl (archived at https://perma.cc/PHM2-3DS9) [Last accessed 5/6/2021].

14 Galloway, Scott (2015) The future of retail looks Like Macy's, not Amazon, *LinkedIn*, 1 May. Available from: https://www.linkedin.com/pulse/future-retail-looks-like-macys-amazon-scott-galloway/ (archived at https://perma.cc/5MR4-EW4L) [Last accessed 5/6/2021].

15 Bernal, Natasha (2021) Amazon took a chunk of Deliveroo. Then things got interesting, *Wired.com*, 11 February. Available from: https://www.wired.co.uk/article/deliveroo-pandemic-amazon (archived at https://perma.cc/Q5K7-59WD) [Last accessed: 14/6/2021].

16 Ladd, Brittain (2018) The Trojan Horse: Instacart's covert operation against grocery retailers, *LinkedIn*, 18 March. Available from: https://www.forbes.com/sites/brittainladd/2018/07/01/__trashed-2/?sh=47018188e4d1 (archived at https://perma.cc/L3GL-MGUZ) [Last accessed 5/6/2021].

16

The last-mile infrastructure

'Amazon makes money differently from a conventional publisher. It is an infrastructure player.'
Nick Harkaway, novelist[1]

Having seen how Prime expands Amazon's reach across categories and acts as a conduit for the introduction of new services to strengthen its flywheel effect and fuel its relentless growth, it is important to think about how the cost of satisfying such impatient and varied demand impacts Amazon's broader fulfilment logistics strategy. Over the years, Amazon's logistics have had to keep pace with and support its growth. Here, we'll look at the strategy and scale being relentlessly pursued to serve its business. When it started to target rapid delivery in urban centres, for example, its executives said delivery workers would walk, take public transportation, bike or drive deliveries to customers – the inference being that they'd do whatever it takes to meet Amazon's Prime promise to deliver.

As an example of how Amazon's innovation extends into its supply chain and logistics operations, Amazon's Prime fulfilment centre (FC) locations are miniature 'Hubs', rather than full-blown Amazon FCs. They are smaller: for example, the Prime Now Kenosha, Milwaukee hub covers 25,000 square feet, which is equivalent to around twice the size of an average urban grocery store. Compare this in size to its mega 1 million-square-foot FC in Dunfermline, Scotland or the 1.27 million-square-foot FC in Phoenix, Arizona, which is large enough to fit 28 football pitches. In the absence of a substantial physical store network in a given location, these FC hubs shorten the last-mile fulfilment costs in densely populated urban areas, where transit times can be severely impacted by traffic. More importantly, they also serve as Amazon's next-best means of competing with the instant gratification of a local retail store visit, with the advantage of your purchases being brought to you. When Amazon phased out its Prime Now one- or two-hour delivery and absorbed it into Prime, the move enabled the company to focus on its main strategic goal of being able to reach 90 per cent of shoppers with same-day or next-day delivery. It's easy to see why when you compare this to the fact that the average distance of a US consumer to a Walmart, as Amazon's biggest competitor, is 6.7 miles.[2]

Prime 'pickers' – so-called in the logistics industry because they pick and pack orders – use mobile handheld barcode-reading devices to locate items. Space is saved by using a 'random stow' system, instead of designated stock areas that more automated warehouse management systems require. While this can lead to some incongruous items being stored alongside each other, where items are put on the aisles of shelving is left down to the pickers to maximize use of space. An Amazon spokesperson reported that random stow enhances picking accuracy; it might be easier to make a mistake if many different versions of the same item were stored in the same location.

Prime FCs also feature easily accessible 'high-velocity pallets' for frequently ordered items, such as toilet paper and bananas, and walk-in refrigerator and freezer units for chilled and frozen goods that might also be ordered through Amazon Fresh household and grocery services. After picking, orders are prepared for dispatch via what Amazon calls its 'SLAM' line, which is an acronym for 'scan, label, apply, manifest'. Orders are then fulfilled using a number of delivery methods as referenced above.

Last-mile labour

From the perspective of last-mile labour costs, servicing Prime requires a different approach from the rest of Amazon's fulfilment infrastructure in its intensive use of pickers, as well as its random stow system. This makes it more reliant on more human labour than in its larger FCs, where its Kiva warehouse robotic sortation systems take on more of the traditional sortation tasks. Its use of express courier services to deliver Prime orders is also another extra labour-intensive expense Amazon must absorb for the price of having the fastest and most extensive last mile. This is why it also introduced Amazon Flex, a platform for independent contractors to provide rapid delivery. The platform capitalizes on the expanding gig economy popularized by Uber and other express delivery rivals to first meet demand. In the same way as Uber matches drivers with what it calls 'riders' and Instacart matches customers with 'shoppers', the Amazon Flex Android-based app directs 'Flexers' to delivery locations within a radius local to them.

Flex is interesting for two main reasons: the first is that its entry into the 'gig economy' by employing independent contractors over its last mile hasn't exactly proved the most customer-centric solution to last-mile express delivery Amazon might have hoped for. True, it gives Amazon end-to-end control, where it can share its last-mile visibility with customers through its delivery tracking app feature. But the fact that Flexers use their own vehicles and initially wore nothing that identified them as working for Amazon, led to an initial backlash by worried neighbourhood watch activists, who were 'creeped out' by these strangers coming to their door.[3] Like Uber, Amazon has also had to defend contractor lawsuits brought by ex-Flexers, who argued that they took home less than minimum wage after costs associated with running their own vehicles. Some plaintiffs who were sub-contracted by Amazon.com via Amazon Logistics and local courier firms, claimed Amazon should pay them as full-time employees because they worked out of its warehouses and were highly supervised by Amazon, who also provided their customer service training.[4]

Perhaps staff working for its Whole Foods subsidiary could carry out deliveries after work to lessen the litigious risk from gig economy-based models, just like Walmart has trialled? In yet another attempt to cut e-commerce fulfilment costs, Walmart can exploit not only its extensive store estate to promote click & collect, but also began looking to its large store staff base to carry out home deliveries. The retailer was offering to pay staff extra to use an app that could direct them to deliver up to 10 customer orders per commute. 'It just makes sense', said Marc Lore in a blog post when he was Walmart US e-commerce president and CEO. 'We already have trucks moving orders from fulfilment centres to stores for pickup. Those same trucks could be used to bring ship-to-home orders to a store close to their final destination, where a participating employee can sign up to deliver them to the customer's house.'[5]

Third-party carrier custom

The second reason for singling out Flex is that Amazon's gig-based initiative reveals a fulfilment logistics strategy that seeks to redouble its efforts to lessen its reliance on the US Postal Service, FedEx, UPS and other third-party parcel delivery services. Bear in mind that multiple different partners currently ship billions of Amazon parcels a year. Cost management is an obvious priority, where Amazon can realize efficiencies by gaining end-to-end visibility over its entire supply chain. Entrusting the last mile to third parties cedes control over the most visible customer-facing part of that chain and is at odds with its customer-driven ethos. But this has also fuelled anti-trust criticisms of the company's dominance that have grown louder as Amazon has grown bigger in its home market, particularly in relation to its threat to the federal government's loss-making US Postal Service (USPS).

By the height of global lockdowns in July 2020, Amazon had increased the volume of packages it delivered itself to 67 per cent, or 415 million packages, compared with 54 per cent a year before. This proportion is set to rise yet further, to 85 per cent by the end of 2022, according to consulting firm MWPVL International. To achieve this swift scaling, the consultancy also tracked a 71 per cent surge in the number of Amazon's US delivery stations to over 275. While its hundreds of vast suburban FCs still make up the largest chunk of its domestic physical footprint, the opening of these smaller facilities has made Amazon the fourth largest parcel carrier in the US. As we discovered earlier in the book, Amazon's net sales increased nearly 40 per cent on the year before, leading the company to invest roughly $44 billion in capital expenditures. At the time, Brian Olsavsky, Amazon's chief financial officer, told investors that its fulfilment centre footprint also grew by 50 per cent year-on-year. 'In a [fulfilment centre] world, it's hard to turn that capacity on quickly, so it generally means you may have to overbuild to protect the customer experience,' he said. As part of its efforts to launch its own delivery network, we'll also examine its growing fleets of airplanes, delivery drones and vans later in the chapter.

For now, it should be said that volume growth for every carrier was also much higher during the pandemic for reasons we've already broken down at length; and it could be argued that USPS's particular woes are down to reasons that have less to do with Amazon and more to do with the fact that it charges below market rate for package delivery, where Amazon undoubt-edly has the scale to negotiate the best possible price. But its falling revenues are actually attributable to the slowdown in direct mail demand rather than package deliveries.[6] Amazon has in the past also had spats with FedEx and UPS over how much business it puts through their USPS rival. But they have, in turn, also been critical of the amount of fixed costs they are required by law to cover with revenue from their competitive parcel business – FedEx and UPS argue that at least 5.5 per cent is not enough when its competitive business now accounts for well over a third of their total revenues, up from 11 per cent from nearly 15 years go.

Other competitive logistics challenges of note have come from direct retail rivals, Walmart and Target. There have been reports that Walmart told a number of its contracted carriers that it may choose not to do business with them if they were also doing business with Amazon,[7] such is the demand for third-party fulfilment capacity driven by US e-commerce sales growth. Walmart took a similar stance with those suppliers using AWS. Target's acquisition of grocery marketplace and same-day delivery platform Shipt was seen as a direct challenge to Amazon's ability to fulfil same-day deliveries, while also giving the retail chain a greater capability to overcome inventory challenges associated with click & collect. In a company blog about its purchase, John Mulligan, Target's chief operating officer, cited the acquisition as part of a series of measures aimed at 'making shopping at Target easier, more reliable and more convenient' for its customers, which included expanding ship-from-store capabilities to more than 1,400 stores nationwide, launching its next-day delivery and curbside collection services, and acquiring last-mile transportation technology company Grand Junction.[8] Target's declared aim was to bring same-day delivery to about half of its stores. By 2021 it had reached 600.

> 'I have 1,800 mini warehouses across the country. 460 feature backrooms converted into online order fulfilment centres. Employees who are cross-trained to work the sales floor and the backrooms pick online orders from stores' shelves or inventory and pack them at the store. UPS picks up the orders and delivers them to hub-and-spoke distribution centres.'
> **Brian Cornell, Target Chairman and CEO[9]**

We've seen how Prime helps power Amazon's flywheel, and how new additions such as Amazon Fresh and Wardrobe add scale and breadth to the wider Amazon ecosystem. But we've also begun to explore how these additions have also put increased pressure on its supply chain and fulfilment logistics. All of this expansion must be fed by its ever-growing distribution and fulfilment network.

Amazon laid the foundations for Prime with a traditional FC and logistics network model, using third-party carriers, as already discussed. But it has continued to innovate, using its substantial AWS computing power to boost the ability to orchestrate its huge logistics network so it can yield greater levels of automation, efficiency and productivity. It started its business with two FCs in Seattle and Delaware and over the next two and a half decades has been growing this estate to nearly 200 FCs worldwide, covering more than 150 million square feet and more than 230 points of presence, serving 245 countries and territories around the globe.

Growing physical infrastructure

Looking at its data centre estate, this vast computing resource is rarely discussed as it is the Amazon business, developer toolset and internet traffic running on top that people care about. With some of the world's biggest media and social networks, streaming services, publishers and retailers all running on the AWS cloud, it's very difficult to estimate how much of the world's internet traffic flows across it. Recent estimates put the proportion at around half. Amazon is also particularly tight-lipped about its AWS data centre infrastructure, never offering tours of any of its facilities. Its website only displays rough approximations of the locations of their data centres, divided into 'regions', each region containing at minimum two 'availability zones' which are home to a handful of data centres. It locates these data centres as near as possible to internet exchange points, which transfer content traffic, and builds its own accompanying electric substations, each of which can generate as much as 100 megawatts or more – enough to power tens of thousands of the densest servers per site, or millions globally. Having set up its first AWS data centre in northern Virginia, US in 2006, as the centre of this infrastructure, by 2020 it had 81 availability zones across the world. It operates much of this estate through a subsidiary company, Vadata Inc.

Data as the oil

The fact that Amazon runs not only its own businesses on its AWS cloud infrastructure but those of so many others has added to antitrust calls for the company to potentially be broken up into its constituent parts. For AWS, it is a market leader with a dominant position. Where the top ten providers account for 80 per cent of the worldwide cloud services market, the share held by AWS amounts to nearly a third, according to Synergy Research Group. Microsoft Azure has about 20 per cent, followed by Google Cloud with 9 per cent and Alibaba Cloud with 6 per cent. Apart from its market share, some have questioned (in the same way we looked at its private label and advertising ambitions) whether having potential access to the world's data creates an inevitable conflict of interest between safeguarding client security and privacy and the potential use of its access to the world's data to unfairly (and potentially unlawfully) advantage its own interests.

When it comes to piping data around the world, it's also worth calling out the growing environmental impact of its meeting of our growing appetite for internet-enabled access to goods and services and how this is likely to affect the data smarts that drive Amazon's vast logistics network too. Take the two new data centres Amazon is building in Ireland, for instance. (We'll take a closer look at this market in relation to Amazon's logistics a bit later in this chapter.) But for the purposes of looking at AWS growth, Amazon's two Drogheda data centres would require a combined 96 MW when operational. To put that into context, planning documents revealed Amazon had committed to offtake power from three renewable wind farm projects in Cork, Donegal and Galway, which could add 229 MW of energy to the Irish grid each year, or the equivalent needed to power 185,000 homes. In addition to access to large amounts of renewable energy, Ireland is ideally located as a transatlantic connection point for communications and data transmission.

Nevertheless, when Amazon revealed its impact on the environment, it was emitting 44.4 million metric tons of carbon dioxide equivalents into the atmosphere – roughly equivalent to the annual emissions of Norway. It has also made a series of commitments that add up to an overall net zero carbon target of 2040 – 10 years before the 2050 net zero target needed to meet the requirements of the Paris Agreement. Amazon does not break out the carbon footprint of its parcel deliveries, but it is rolling out 100,000 electric delivery vehicles to its fleet that it says will save 4 million tons of carbon annually by 2030.[10]

The rise of Amazon Logistics

In much the same way as it has built its AWS services by rapidly scaling its global data centre infrastructure, Amazon has used similar blitz tactics to build out and support its physical last-mile fulfilment network through its

Amazon Logistics operations. Since starting with just those two original FCs, it has been ramping up its supply chain and logistics footprint aggressively since the launch of Prime, and now some 80 per cent of its total global real estate is dedicated to data centres and warehouse facilities. Indeed, some of its North American FC roll-out strategy can be tracked against those states that offer the most tax-friendly breaks for retail sales.

But, as each state started to implement tax fairness policies, Amazon had already moved its focus to serving more urban areas to minimize transportation costs over its last mile and nurture its ever-growing Prime ambitions. Marc Wulfraat, President and Founder of supply chain, logistics, and distribution consulting firm MWPVL International Inc., commented in an email to the authors, 'If you sort the US metro population in descending sequence, you can see that Amazon clearly started to build out FCs close to major metro markets.' It operates a variety of different types of fulfilment and distribution centres, including those that handle small sortable, large sortable, large non-sortable, speciality apparel, footwear and small parts, and return items, as well as its third-party logistics outsourced facilities. It also has a network of ambient and cold-storage grocery DCs to serve its Amazon Fresh operations.[11]

Amazon's leasing patterns have also emphasized last-mile warehouses driving proximity to the consumer in the latest phase of its warehouse network expansion. Amazon now splits its logistics warehouse investment between six types of facility:

- Non-sortable FC: a large warehouse (typically 600,000 to 1 million square feet) that receives large or bulky items, such as garden and outdoor equipment and furniture, and employs around 1,000 full-time associates.

- Sortable FC: at around 800,000 square feet in size, these FCs manage most other customer orders, such as books, toys and housewares, employing around 1,500 full-time associates, some of whom work alongside its fleet of Kiva mobile fulfilment robots that operate in a caged area, shuttling totes of smaller goods to pickers ranged around the cage's edge for maximum efficiency.

- Sortation Centres (SCs): these centres pre-sort packages for carriers, as well as Sunday deliveries. (The SCs are usually adjacent to and/or connected via conveyor belt to an FC.) These facilities sort packages by final destination and consolidate them onto trucks for handoff to the carrier responsible for final delivery. From there, the carrier performs last-mile delivery to the customer. Sortation centres also ship packages to

Amazon's extensive Delivery Station Network, which represents the final node in the Amazon distribution network. Sortation centres can handle packages for a regional area on behalf of one or more FCs.

- Receive Centres: at about 600,000 square feet in size, these centres support customer fulfilment by taking in large orders of the types of inventory that Amazon expects to quickly sell and allocating it to FCs within the network. These facilities are often located near major ports to manage international goods and minimize inbound ground transportation expense from the port to the facility.

- Speciality: Amazon's fulfillment network is also supported by additional types of buildings that handle specific categories of items or are pressed into service at peak times of the year such as the holiday season.

- Delivery stations: sometimes an FC is close enough to a metro area to support Prime deliveries. In other regions, Amazon opens a specific Prime Hub. The Hubs complement an additional subset of metro Delivery Station facilities to service a Delivery Station Network. These smaller, 100-square-foot locations are for the sorting and dispatching of orders prepared for last-mile delivery to customers via local courier firms and Amazon Flex couriers.

Experts recognize these buildings are key enablers to moving away from its reliance on third-party carriers, so packages can be delivered by strategic partners, local couriers and, ultimately, itself. If you're thinking that Amazon could spin out its logistics prowess into another business beyond serving other marketplace sellers and consumers, you're not alone. This is something we'll examine more closely now, and which we can't do without understanding Amazon's insatiable real estate appetite.

Real estate demand

The rise of e-commerce, bolstered by Amazon's inexorable expansion in the US and Europe in particular (as well as Asia and the Indian subcontinent), has been heating up the industrial real estate market. One report listed fulfilment centres and warehouses as the top two sectors with investment potential, where their average size has increased from 24 to 34 feet in height to cater for e-commerce fulfilment.

As warehouse roofs have grown taller, so Amazon has also embraced multi-storey warehouse structures that large delivery trucks can access by ramps, and which are commonplace in Europe and Asia. This is testament to unprecedented cost and competitive pressures to reduce delivery times in congested cities. Home Depot is investing in a similar facility in the US, while Target, for example, is relying on a dense urban network of stores to act as distribution hubs.

Amazon has also been on a shopping spree, buying and converting disused shopping malls across the US to turn them into distribution centres. Over a three-year period to 2019, Amazon turned some 25 shopping malls into DCs, according to an analysis by Coresight Research. Then rumours spread it was in talks with the biggest mall owner in the country, Simon Property Group, to turn bankrupt JCPenney and Sears department stores into FCs. Retail Darwinism at it finest. As we touched on in the previous chapter, the trend towards repurposing some or all of the existing store footprints is not new. Target and Walmart have also turned some space in their own stores into mini FCs.

Pandemic aside, Amazon also has to contend with trade disruption in its third biggest market outside of its own and Germany – thanks to Brexit. When the UK officially exited the European Union at the end of January 2021, just like every other business Amazon had to reorganize its UK distribution and fulfilment capabilities to avoid extra shipping charges and logistics delays for goods it moves across the Irish Sea.

For example, Irish orders had typically been fulfilled in the UK. But the year before Brexit, Amazon opened a 70,000-square-foot delivery warehouse for Prime orders at Rathcoole in County Antrim, Northern Ireland, to act as an intermediary, where a local delivery partner could pick up orders arriving from the UK. Then it emerged that data centres would be far from the only sheds in Ireland that Amazon owns, as it was in the process of securing a 650,000-square-foot warehouse in west Dublin in order to establish its first FC in the market and the biggest in the country – giving Irish sellers direct access to its local marketplace and logistics for the first time. But it may also be that Amazon's Brexit response will characteristically seize the opportunity it affords it to expand in Ireland than allow itself to be derailed by political intra-continental squabbles in one of its largest markets. Further reports at the time of writing could also see it open its first DC near to Shannon Airport in the west of Ireland.

Amazon has said its warehouses can ship millions of items a day during busy times and that a typical Amazon delivery requires just one minute of human labour.[12] That said, Amazon has also come under fire for working conditions in its warehouses such as onerous screening and tracking procedures, long hours and distances travelled per shift with highly regulated bathroom and work breaks, and relatively low levels of remuneration. So much so that it has faced (and will continue to face) increasing employers' rights challenges and union-led threats over pay and working conditions, with pressure from strikes in Germany from as early as 2013. It faces increasing pressure from unions over workers' rights in the US, despite its reputation for stifling any attempts by them to organize challenges to its pay and conditions. Amazon has been quick to point out to the authors how its expansion has provided flexible work options available to even the likes of engineers and small company directors laid off during the pandemic particularly.

Nevertheless, we've already referenced the negative publicity it received about warehouse workers' safety during this period in relation to supply chain complexity in Chapter 10. Here, in relation to real estate, workers' conditions also affected its French operations. Amazon was forced to closed all six of its French warehouses in April 2020 after a French court issued a ruling that threatened to fine the company €1 million per item for shipping anything other than medical supplies, hygiene products and food. The court ruling came after a complaint from French unions representing Amazon's warehouse workers, who argued that conditions were overcrowded and that it wasn't doing enough to protect them from the coronavirus. After citing the complexity of operations and the risks of attempting to only ship products that met the court ruling, its warehouses only reopened gradually a month later with extra social distancing and safety measures in place. Interestingly, when the authors toured another of its warehouses, it was keen to show its social distancing innovation, which used computer vision systems linked to proximity sensors that overlaid two-metre-wide circles onto anyone entering the facility displayed onto a video screen of the footfall, with an alarm to alert individuals when they got too close together.

'The factory [or warehouse] of the future will have only two employees: a man and a dog. The man will be there to feed the dog. The dog will be there to keep the man from touching the equipment.'
Warren Bennis[13]

Let's not also forget, as referenced in our exploration of automation development, Amazon bought Kiva Systems, the company that manufactures its robots. As referenced in Chapter 12, current estimates suggest they now make up one-quarter of the Amazon workforce and also reduce warehouse operating costs by 20 per cent. As also referenced earlier, robots are responsible for moving proprietary shelving 'pods' along a predefined grid to workstations where Amazon picking staff pick, pack and prepare the items for shipment, loading them onto a network of conveyor belts that can handle some 400-odd orders per second. Its warehouse management software also matches the right sized box with each order and handles the application of shipping labels.

The parts of the process managed by the Amazon Robotics system are claimed to be five to six times more productive than manual picking and eliminate the need for human-scale aisles, taking up half as much space as a traditional, non-automated warehouse. Their flexibility also means they can be used to constantly reconfigure the warehouse space based on sales data, so high-velocity items can be retrieved more quickly. The robots, however, can only handle relatively small items that fit in the pods they transport, in comparison to traditional retail and wholesale warehouses which rely on carrying and stacking most of the inventory on pallets with fork-lift trucks. For larger items, large robotic arms known as 'robo-stows' (manufactured by Thiele Technologies) handle these, moving and packing boxes at Amazon's larger FCs. Another warehouse technology feature is the vision system that can unload and receipt an entire trailer of stock in as little as 30 minutes, while the company has also created a team to guide its use of driverless-vehicle technology, for the deployment of self-driving forklifts, trucks and other such vehicles that can build on its existing automation efforts.

With such a huge supply chain and fulfilment logistics network, and a constant drive to improve performance and cut delivery cost and time, it was perhaps inevitable that Amazon would also enter the transportation market. Indeed, transportation and logistics could be the next billion-dollar opportunity for e-commerce companies, according to industry research.[14] The global shipping market, including ocean, air, and truck freight, is a multi-trillion-dollar industry. With so much at stake, legacy shipping companies, which have been able to capitalize on the boom in parcel delivery as e-commerce spending has risen, are under increasing pressure from Amazon and the likes of Alibaba, JD.com and Walmart. Amazon and its rivals have to date focused on building out last-mile logistics fulfilment capabilities but are increasingly going after the middle and first mile of the fulfilment supply chain.

Amazon has been offering outsourced consolidation for international sellers for years, leveraging bulk discounts for cheaper US import rates. Then it emerged that it had been negotiating to lease 20 Boeing 767 jets for its own air-delivery service, had registered to provide ocean freight services in China, and had purchased thousands of truck trailers to ship merchandise between distribution facilities.[15] Amazon China then registered to provide ocean freight services, essentially pushing Chinese sellers to use its services for shipping to Amazon US customers and giving it control over the significant trading routes between China and the US. Amazon Maritime, Inc. holds a US Federal Maritime Commission operating licence, as a non-vessel-owning common carrier (NVOCC).

Amazon as a carrier

When Amazon received options to purchase up to 19.9 per cent of Air Transport International's stock and began scheduled operations with 20 Boeing 767 aircraft, a year later, it unveiled its first branded cargo plane and announced that Amazon Air would make Cincinnati/Northern Kentucky International Airport its principal hub. It also received tax breaks to the tune of $40 million for the construction of a 920-acre facility with a 3-million-square-foot sorting facility and parking space for over 100 cargo aircraft at an estimated total cost of $1.5 billion. According to plans filed for an onsite sorting facility, 440 acres was scheduled for completion in 2020, while the remaining 479 acres will be developed by 2025–2027 during a second phase, by which time it is planned to handle freight from 100 aircraft based at the hub and operate over 200 flights daily. This move also complements the set of cargo-handling facilities built out at smaller airports to enable connectivity between its Air Sortation Centre in Hebron, Kentucky and major cities with FCs. MWPVL International Inc. refers to these as 'air sortation hubs'. They are positioned close to airport runways for the purpose of handling and receiving freight packages being shipped to the Hebron Air Hub. Most recently, it paid $131 million to increase its stake in Air Transport Services Group Inc.

In addition to its disruptive moves with same-day and one-hour delivery, managing its own fleet of couriers, trucks, cargo ships and planes, and reducing its reliance on third-party providers, Amazon has also introduced its own app for truck drivers, designed to make it easier to pick up and drop off packages at Amazon warehouses.[16] Giving Amazon direct access to millions of truck drivers across the country, it is also thought to be working on a similar app that would match truck drivers with cargo. Another, slightly more leftfield innovation is the patent Amazon holds for delivery trucks equipped with 3D printers that would enable it to manufacture products on the way to the customer destination.[17] A further patent it filed covered the eventuality of cutting the manufacturer out of the equation altogether by taking custom orders for 3D-printed items to get them made and have them delivered to or collected by the customer.[18]

Fulfilment by Amazon

If Amazon really is looking to cut the middleman out of the fulfilment process and take end-to-end control of its supply chain, it is impossible to view any moves to expand its global logistics footprint as anything other than an extension of its 'Fulfilment by Amazon' service, which stores, picks, packs and ships products and handles returns sold by third-party merchants on the Amazon.com marketplace, and also includes Amazon Pay. Sellers can, of course, opt to use Fulfilment By Merchant (FBM) where they are in control of the entire handling and shipping process. Instead of paying a service fee and shipping inventory to Amazon to handle, the seller uses their own resources to sends the items directly to the buyer. But FBA is sold as the best way to optimize the end customer's buying experience, but it can also serve to meet their strict shipping and delivery timelines, and consideration for listing among Prime-eligible products. FBA is available in the US, Canada, the UK, Germany, France, Italy, Japan, China and India.

Boosted in part by ever-increasing speed and scale that Amazon has dedicated to its last mile with Prime, the number of merchants actively selling via the Marketplace and using FBA now accounts for two-thirds, although it does not disclose the revenue it generates from its Fulfilment by Amazon service. Meanwhile, the number of items Amazon sold on behalf of third-party sellers doubled during the same period. From a B2B perspective, we should also consider the impact of Amazon Business (formerly known as AmazonSupply). This competitive marketplace for B2B products on Amazon.com serves procurement business needs across a variety of product categories, such as laptops, computers, printers, office supplies, office furniture, hand tools, power tools, safety equipment, office kitchen essentials and cleaning supplies. RBC Capital Markets managing director Mark Mahaney estimated Amazon Business would surpass $52 billion in gross sales by

2023.[19] From this perspective, given the sheer volume of products handled by both FBA and Amazon Business and, taken with its most recent moves into air cargo, ground transportation and ocean freight, Amazon is already a major global logistics player.

Even here, though, Amazon has experimented with services to make products available for rapid delivery directly from merchants to avoid overwhelming its own warehouses with additional inventory. The service, called Stellar Flex at launch, was tested in India and on the US West coast and was designed to take Amazon's logistical reach beyond its FCs to those of its merchants. The latest iteration, FBA Onsite, gives Amazon greater flexibility and control over the last mile, while saving money through volume discounts and avoiding FC congestion. This comes after some industry insiders hinted a few years ago that Amazon was a victim of its own and FBA's success by sometimes throttling order throughput due to capacity issues. At the same time, some estimates have suggested the cost savings of having sellers hold merchandise in their own facilities is as high as 70 per cent. So, extending FBA into sellers' facilities is another way of adding both capacity and scale to its growing logistics demands.

As referenced throughout, Amazon has experimented to optimize the costly returns process. The relevance here of Amazon's willingness to partner with Kohl's to accept Amazon returns from customers is that it points to its insatiable fulfilment need to extend its customer-facing physical points of presence in the absence of a significant store estate. The retailer's store staff pack and ship eligible items back to an Amazon fulfilment centre for free.[20] Kohl's Chairman, President and CEO Kevin Mansell, commented a few months into the partnership: 'One thing is for sure: the experience is amazing, and people are using the service. If the customer responds, they think it's a great experience, they use the service, but very importantly, it drives incremental traffic, then we're going to look to expand it.'[21] It should also be noted here that it has a similar partnership for collections with Next in the UK and operates Amazon Hub, a worldwide network of pickup locations that enables businesses with a physical location to offer secure package pickup and returns. Amazon's own recent store launches also feature Counter pickup and return services.

Race for the last mile

By comparison, Walmart's expanding transportation and logistics operations are driven largely by cost savings, required to balance the rising cost of fulfilling its e-commerce business with its vast, global store network. The grocer started leasing shipping containers to transport manufactured goods from China and is making greater use of lockers and instore pickup options mentioned earlier to cut down on delivery costs. In 2017, Cristy Brooks, Walmart Senior Central Operations Director, outlined how the company is also tackling on-shelf availability in its larger stores. Out-of-stocks have been an issue the retailer has been urgently addressing in recent years. Its so-called Top Stock system stores inventory on the top shelves of the sales floor. This, Walmart claims, enables it to maintain 'fuller shelves while keeping a better in-the-moment read on inventory'. Benefits include a reduction in Walmart's use of rented temporary inventory trailers and the freeing up of back-room space, which has allowed the retailer to also integrate services like online grocery pickup, according to Brooks. This free space is also being used to provide staff training. Brooks cites its Morrisville, NC store as reducing its back-room inventory by 75 per cent in two months after implementing Top Stock and using the new space to open an associate training academy.[22] It also stole a march on Amazon and its Kohl's returns programme by updating its own online returns process in its stores via an update to the Walmart app. The update meant some of its items for sale online, such as health and beauty products, were available for instant refunds without the need to visit a store.[23]

Amazon already offers instant refunds on some first-party and third-party purchases, and items below a certain value do not need to be physically returned. But Walmart has sought to keep pace in the fulfilment stakes with this returns initiative, which builds on its online grocery pickup, pickup towers, and free two-day shipping services – the latter of which it notably stresses is available without a membership fee outside of Walmart+.

Alibaba also leases containers on ships, similar to Amazon's ocean freight initiative. This means that Alibaba Logistics can now facilitate first-mile shipping for third-party merchants on its marketplace. It is worth comparing the Alibaba logistics model with Amazon's. Alibaba's joint launch of the China Smart Logistic Network, also known as Cainiao, with eight other financial services and logistics companies predates Prime. Today, the $10 billion logistics affiliate subsidiary network is made up of 3,000 logistics partners and 3 million couriers, including the top 15 delivery firms inside China and 100 international operators. The Chinese giant is investing $15 billion in its global logistical capabilities in coming years. It is building this capability using drones and robotics technology to deliver anywhere in China within 24 hours and anywhere in the world within 72 hours.

Considering Cainiao fulfils 100 million orders a day, the sheer dominance of Alibaba in its home market means it can wield significant power over the region's logistics network. Much like Amazon, it bases this power on technology investments that provide the supply chain visibility and data integration required to efficiently orchestrate fulfilment processes across this network. Despite the US, as the world's largest consumer economy, providing a base to its global operations, Amazon's market share is a fraction of the already mature US e-commerce market. By comparison, Alibaba's market share in China is over 50 per cent, where traditional trade still accounts for over 40 per cent of the world's second-largest and most rapidly growing consumer economy.

Alibaba rival JD.com has also been busy building out its own logistics network. Following a model similar to that used by Amazon, it has created a network of fulfilment centres and over 1,000 warehouses across China, including the world's first fully automated example in Shanghai, and thousands of local delivery and pickup locations. JD.com has a number of international fulfilment outposts around the world, including Hong Kong, Los Angeles and New York. Most notably for JD.com, its Europe–China freight train is able to carry goods that it can market to its domestic customers as soon as they are logged and on board. The first China Railway Express train, which travels 10,000 kilometres from Hamburg, Germany to Xi'an, the capital of central China's Shaanxi province, where JD operates one of its most important distribution hubs for cross-border imports, took 35 fewer days than ocean freight alternatives at a cost 80 per cent cheaper than air transport.

Liu Han, General Manager of International Supply chain at JD Logistics, said in a statement at the time, 'Through our use of a train from Germany to China fully dedicated to carrying goods destined for JD.com, we are dramatically reducing the time to market for European retailers and suppliers and providing our consumers with even more product choices at cheaper prices. With demand for imported European products soaring on JD, we expect to launch a regular service.'

Whole Foods and the future

Having examined the effect of rapid delivery and its impact on fulfilment demand and capacities on different continents, we come to the final major area of Amazon's fulfilment strategy, which takes us back to where we started this chapter – where Amazon did not have a significant physical retail presence of its own outside of its bookstore network, and so could not offer extensive, end-to-end online-to-offline services from order to delivery, such as click & collect, like its US rivals Walmart and Target or others across Europe and Asia. That was until it began to build out its physical retail footprint by acquiring Whole Foods Market and, by extension, not just its 450+ stores but also Whole Foods' retail grocery distribution network that serves them.

> 'When you think about [stores] doubling as warehouses, they're already profitable, they're already there, product is getting to them in full truckload quantities. It's the most efficient way to get product forward deployed.'
> **Mark Lore, former Walmart US e-commerce division CEO[24]**

As discussed in Chapter 9, the acquisition of Whole Foods' distribution network, which is largely focused on perishables merchandise for its retail stores in each major market region served, will support the fulfilment of more third-party and own-label ranges while its store network gives it direct exposure to more urban retail locations. Some reports, however, highlighted how existing customers were unhappy that some stores' parking had been allocated to Prime delivery vehicles and that workers picking orders on the shop floor were competing for products and space with customers.

Given the relatively muted online-to-offline success it has enjoyed with this acquisition, plus the last-mile distribution and fulfilment advantages that came with it, speculation that it may be on the lookout for a similar acquisition in Europe that would provide it with another 1,300 stores 'doubling as warehouses', remains just that – rumours. In the meantime, it has partnered with a number of European retailers, including Casino banner Monoprix in France, Morrisons, Booths and Celesio pharmacies in the UK, Dia in Spain, and the Rossmann drugstore chain in Germany.

Having mentioned dark kitchens in the last chapter, in relation to winning hospitality customers over the last mile, it's necessary to also examine growing interest in the role of dark stores.

While not a new concept (Tesco in the UK was first to deploy one over a decade ago), Amazon opened its first dark store in New York in the middle of the pandemic to squeeze more margin out of its online grocery fulfilment. Dark stores enable retailers to get products closer to customers for delivery and, often featuring automated micro-fulfilment centre (MFC) systems, can also address labour challenges, competition for warehouse space and existing instore fulfilment challenges.

The beauty of MFC systems developed by the likes of Fabric, Dematic and Alert Innovation is that they can be installed in space carved out of an existing store, as well as in dark stores, giving bricks and mortar retailers, including Walmart and its Alphabot picking system referenced earlier, a potential advantage here. For context, grocery stores can typically fulfil only about 100 orders per day. Fabric claims its MFC robotics can increase that capacity by 5–10 times in a space that can be as small as 10,000 square feet.

Interestingly here, UK online grocer Ocado has 'done an Amazon' and is now reselling its Ocado Smart Platform (OSP) to other retailers. Kroger in the US, Sobey's in Canada and Group Casino in France are building much larger-scale MFC versions that use similar autonomous picking systems. The OSP's high-speed bots pick products for customers' orders from atop a 3D grid of crates packed with items. Claiming 99 per cent picking efficiency, Ocado's 'USP' is that its cost to serve is significantly cheaper than that of traditional bricks and clicks retailers' methods.

But with its current supply chain and store network strategy, moves to grow an ever greater supply of goods through it that includes fashion and grocery, and the means to drive demand with auto-replenishment and Alexa, what's next for Amazon fulfilment? One thing is for sure, it is likely to continue innovating in order to keep breaking records over the last mile, shrinking delivery windows and continuing to delight customers by living up to its promise to deliver.

Remote innovation

We haven't mentioned them yet but, having now explored Amazon's last-mile ambitions, we can now think about other interesting areas of development around not just fulfilment but also instant gratification outside of the traditional store format. The Amazon Treasure Truck gives Amazon app users access to daily discounts and exclusive products by registering to be notified when it is nearby. Another express fulfilment initiative, Amazon Fresh Pickup, can also now be understood in its full context. The initiative raises the stakes even higher by making available items ready for delivery to your car within 15 minutes of placing an order. Again, customers must be Prime members who can refresh their app near an Amazon Instant Pickup location to see available items.

Chinese logistics firm Cainiao's new Xiao G delivery cart goes one step further than bringing your orders to your car. The 3 foot by 5 foot automated smart vehicle negotiates traffic using 360-degree sensors to bring them to your door. Picking up packages from Cainiao's depot in Hangzhou and touring a nearby neighborhood, customers meet the driverless cart at their nearest delivery point and type in a reference number to gain access to the vehicle's lockers and retrieve their orders.

Amazon has also introduced in-home and in-car deliveries with Amazon Key. It gives Prime members in eligible urban areas the option to have Amazon Flex contractors drop deliveries off in their homes using a one-time entry code. At launch, customers were required to have specific manufacturers' smart locks and a capable version of Amazon's security cameras. To confirm delivery and protect against potential claims of fraud, the camera records as the courier uses the entry code to gain entry and until they exit, sending an image of the activity to the customer's smartphone. The Amazon Key app also enables remote door locking and unlocking, as well as for its users to issue virtual keys. But when Amazon ramped up its commitment in this and the wider Connected Home space with the acquisition of smart camera and doorbell manufacturer, Ring, for $1 billion, the investment is accelerating efforts to increase the reach of its in-home delivery initiative, in a bid to one day perhaps consign missed deliveries to the history books and link the camera and audio equipment in Ring's doorbells to its proliferating Alexa voice-enabled Connected Home ecosystem.

Amazon Key In-Car allows owners of compatible vehicles to get packages delivered in their vehicle's trunk, as long as they are in the same areas served by Amazon Key's in-home delivery. Customers must park their cars in a publicly accessible area but they require no additional hardware. Like the in-home delivery, customers are given a four-hour delivery window.[25] It remains to be seen whether either in-home or in-car delivery proves popular enough to overcome any privacy and security concerns. But, as an extension of the locker concept and its last-mile advantages, Amazon has been developing the requisite technology for several years and can exploit a first-mover advantage. Future developments could see it capitalize on alliances it may forge to embed its Alexa voice assistant into car operating systems.

The final frontier, as far as Amazon's journey to fulfil orders ever faster is concerned, is drone technology. Jeff Bezos revealed plans to commercialize drone delivery some years ago now. A mere three years from announcing its plans, Amazon revealed that Prime Air had completed its first fully autonomous drone delivery. Flying from a Prime Air fulfilment centre in the Cambridge area with no pilot, it took 13 minutes from click to delivery.[26] Eligible items must be less than five pounds in weight, small enough to fit into the drone's cargo box and be delivered to within 10 miles of a participating FC. In addition to the Cambridge centre in the UK, the company has development centres in the US, Austria, France and Israel. The plans reveal the scale of Amazon's fulfilment ambitions, but are still only a concept, as it only recently gained approval from the Federal Aviation Administration (FAA) to conduct unmanned delivery of goods with its fleet of Prime Air drones. But it's actually the third company, behind Google parent's Alphabet-owned Wing and UPS, to receive the requisite certification.

In the meantime, Alibaba's own food delivery app Ele.me recently started using drones for food deliveries in China, while JD.com is well on its way to exploiting the vast continent's geographical scale to ramp up its use of drones too. JD had announced it was planning to build 150 airports for unmanned aerial deliveries, representing a significant strategic commitment to the technology. To date, it claims the world's first Delivery Drone Scheduling Centre in Suqian and a 300-kilometre radius low-altitude general aviation logistics network in Shaanxi. Its drones can currently carry up to 50 kilograms, although it is said to be working on drones that can carry 500kg. However, the investment will only support its limited application in the remote, mountainous Sichuan Province where long-range, radio-controlled communications are most effective. Battery life has also improved enough now for drones to fly almost continuously. But, practically speaking, the most advanced drones designed for commercial use today can fly for, on average, up to about 100 minutes with a flight range of some 35km. Even with such limitations, it is easy to see why JD.com is forging ahead with drone delivery, given its aim for this fulfilment method is to help cut freight costs by 70 per cent.

It's worth considering that while not necessarily fully relevant when it comes to the last mile, all of these e-commerce giants – Amazon, Alibaba's Cainiao and JD – have also been forging ahead in the area of self-driving trucks to squeeze more efficiency from distribution logistics operations. Even USPS is getting in on the act with trials using a truck modification system designed by TuSimple.

Whoever wins the race to mass autonomous vehicle deployment, one thing's for certain – it won't be the last innovation in the race to own the cheapest and fastest last mile.

Notes

1 Harkaway, Nick (2012) Amazon aren't destroying publishing, they're reshaping it, *Guardian*, 26 April. Available from: https://www.theguardian.com/books/2012/apr/26/amazon-publishing-destroying (archived at https://perma.cc/K4BV-KB7F) [Last accessed 14/6/2021].

2 Holmes, Thomas J (2005) The diffusion of Wal-Mart and economies of density, *Semantic Scholar*, November. Available from: https://pdfs.semanticscholar.org/947c/d95a37c55eefb84ccab56896b4037f5c2acd.pdf (archived at https://perma.cc/K5YQ-Y8A2) [Last accessed 14/6/2021].

3 Consumerist (2016) Amazon Flex Drivers are kind of freaking customers out, *ConsumerReports*, 7 October. Available from: https://www.consumerreports.org/consumerist/amazon-flex-drivers-are-kind-of-freaking-customers-out/ (archived at https://perma.cc/L6FY-QF4U) [Last accessed 14/6/2021].

4 Bhattacharya, Ananya (2015) Amazon sued by delivery drivers, *CNN Tech*, 29 October. Available from: http://money.cnn.com/2015/10/29/technology/amazon-sued-prime-now-delivery-drivers/ (archived at https://perma.cc/C5L4-A3DX) [Last accessed 14/6/2021].

5 Lore, Marc (2017) Serving customers in new ways: Walmart begins testing associate delivery, *Walmart Today* (Blog), 1 June. Available from: https://blog.walmart.com/innovation/20170601/serving-customers-in-new-ways-walmart-begins-testing-associate-delivery (archived at https://perma.cc/9BCZ-C7L5) [Last accessed 14/6/2021].

6 US Postal Accountability and Enhancement Act 2006.

7 Jaillet, James (2017) Walmart pressures its carriers against doing business with Amazon, *ccjdigital*, 17 July. Available from: https://www.ccjdigital.com/wal-mart-pressures-its-carriers-against-doing-business-with-amazon/ (archived at https://perma.cc/VX3S-PV99) [Last accessed 14/6/2021].

8 Target (2017) Here's how acquiring Shipt will bring same-day delivery to about half of Target stores in early 2018, a bullseye view (Blog), 13 December. Available from: https://corporate.target.com/article/2017/12/target-acquires-shipt (archived at https://perma.cc/SJN7-HVWB) [Last accessed 14/6/2021].

9 Waldron, J (2016) Bullseye! The Power of Target's Fulfilment Strategy, *eTail*, 20 June. Available from: https://etaileast.wbresearch.com/bullseye-the-power-of-targets-fulfillment-strategy (archived at https://perma.cc/YX7F-GZGH) [Last accessed 14/6/2021].

10 Reynolds, Matt (2020) Jeff Bezos wants to fix climate change. He can start with Amazon, *Wired.com*, 18 February. Available from: https://www.wired.co.uk/article/jeff-bezos-climate-change-amazon (archived at https://perma.cc/48P5-UX5Q) [Last accessed: 14/6/2021].

11 Wulfraat, Marc (2018) Amazon Global Fulfilment Centre Network, *MWPVL International Inc.*, June. Available from: http://www.mwpvl.com/html/amazon_com.html (archived at https://perma.cc/G6VX-T9VH) [Last accessed 14/6/2021].

12 Sisson, Patrick (2017) 9 facts about Amazon's unprecedented warehouse empire, *Curbed*, 21 November. Available from: https://www.curbed. com/2017/11/21/16686150/amazons-warehouse-fulfillment-black-friday (archived at https://perma.cc/AFT9-YXHK) [Last accessed 14/6/2021].

13 Wikiquote (nd) Warren Bennis. Available from: https://en.wikiquote.org/wiki/ Warren_Bennis (archived at https://perma.cc/G625-X8CD) [Last accessed 14/6/2021].

14 Smith, Cooper (2016) The Future of Shipping Report: Why big ecommerce companies are going after the legacy shipping industry, *Morgan Stanley*, June. Available from: https://www.businessinsider.com/shipping-could-be-the-next-billion-dollar-opportunity-for-e-commerce-retailers-2016-6?r=US&IR=T (archived at https://perma.cc/6ZKN-QQHM) [Last accessed 14/6/2021].

15 Greene, Jay and Gates, Dominic (2015) Amazon in talks to lease Boeing jets to launch its own air-cargo business, *Seattle Times*, 17 December. Available from: https://www.scattletimes.com/business/amazon/amazon-in-talks-to-lease-20-jets-to-launch-air-cargo-business/ (archived at https://perma.cc/N3HG-KHQ3) [Last accessed 14/6/2021].

16 Kim, Eugene (2017) Amazon quietly launched an app called Relay to go after truck drivers, *CNBC*, 16 November. Available from: https://www.cnbc. com/2017/11/16/amazon-quietly-launched-an-app-called-relay-to-go-after-truck-drivers.html (archived at https://perma.cc/PNN8-VJGG) [Last accessed 14/6/2021].

17 Amazon Technologies, Inc. US Patent Application (2013) Providing services related to item delivery via 3D manufacturing on demand, US Patent & Trademark Office, 8 November. Available from: https://bit.ly/1aQfBvU (archived at https://perma.cc/65AN-FS32) [Last accessed 14/6/2021].

18 Brohan, Mark (2020) Amazon Business succeeds by dominating B2B logistics, DigitalCommerce360.com, 29 September. Available from: https://www. digitalcommerce360.com/2020/09/29/amazon-business-succeeds-by-dominating-b2b-logistics/ (archived at https://perma.cc/J9ZZ-JHNE) [Last accessed: 14/6/2012]

19 Amazon Technologies, Inc. US Patent Application (2018) Vendor interface for item delivery via 3D manufacturing on demand, US Patent & Trademark Office, 2 January. Available from: http://pdfpiw.uspto.gov/.piw?Docid=09858604 (archived at https://perma.cc/QNB3-X2YA) [Last accessed 14/6/2021].

20 Amazon has also rolled the same service out at Whole Foods to Amazon.com customers since its acquisition.

21 Gurdus, Elizabeth (2018) Kohl's CEO says 'big idea' behind Amazon partnership is driving traffic, *CNBC.com*, 27 March. Available from: https:// www.cnbc.com/2018/03/27/kohls-ceo-big-idea-behind-amazon-partnership-is-driving-traffic.html (archived at https://perma.cc/Y2JV-LSG9) [Last accessed 14/6/2021].

22 Brooks, Cristy (2017) Why smarter inventory means better customer service, *Walmart Today*, 16 August. Available from: https://blog.walmart.com/ business/20170816/why-smarter-inventory-means-better-customer-service (archived at https://perma.cc/6LF2-XFHM) [Last accessed 20/6/2018].

23 Walmart (2017) Walmart reinvents the returns process (blog post), *Walmart*, 9 October. Available from: https://news.walmart.com/2017/10/09/walmart-reinvents-the-returns-process (archived at https://perma.cc/97PH-NDZ4) [Last accessed 14/6/2021].

24 Nusca, Andrew (2017) 5 moves Walmart is making to compete with Amazon and Target, *Fortune*, 27 September. Available from: http://fortune.com/2017/ 09/27/5-moves-walmart-is-making-to-compete-with-amazon-and-target/ (archived at https://perma.cc/44XR-5RVH) [Last accessed 14/6/2021].

25 Amazon (2018) Press release: Buckle up, Prime members: Amazon launches in-car delivery, *Amazon*, 24 April. Available from: https://www.businesswire. com/news/home/20180424005509/en/Buckle-Up-Prime-Members-Amazon-Launches-In-Car-Delivery (archived at https://perma.cc/D5VN-AHAC) [Last accessed 14/6/2021].

26 Amazon (2016) First Prime Air delivery (video). Available from: https://www. amazon.com/Amazon-Prime-Air/b?ie=UTF8&node=8037720011 (archived at https://perma.cc/Q6KJ-AFMA) [Last accessed 14/6/2021].

Conclusion: peak Amazon?

'We must make our choice. We may have democracy, or we may have wealth concentrated in the hands of a few, but we cannot have both.'
Supreme Court Justice Louis Brandeis, 1916–1939

Amazon's relentless dissatisfaction with the status quo has been the key to its success. It has capitalized on the advent of pervasive tech interfaces, ubiquitous connectivity and autonomous computing embraced by the on-my-terms shopper to become one of the most dominant retail forces the world has ever seen.

But it couldn't have achieved this without its 'Always Day One' mentality. Obsessing over and anticipating customer needs, acceptance of failure, embracing the future, innovating at scale – these are all valuable lessons for the wider industry as it reconfigures for the digital era.

Throughout this book we have explored how the pandemic-fuelled shift towards a more digital world has bolstered every aspect of Amazon's business model, allowing it to tighten its grip on consumers. But Amazon's astronomical growth, at a time when many retailers were muddling through, hasn't gone unnoticed in Washington. 'As we continue to shift our work, commerce, and communications online, these firms stand to become even more interwoven into the fabric of our economy and our lives,' states the House Antitrust Report on Big Tech.[1]

Amazon will continue to benefit from post-pandemic tailwinds, as high-margin revenue streams such as cloud computing and advertising allow the tech giant to continue investing in its core retail offering. This is a pivotal moment for the tech giant as it enters a new phase of profitability.

But just how long will this phase last? The net is closing in on Big Tech, and even Bezos himself recognizes that it's only normal that a sprawling empire like his attracts greater regulatory attention. 'I believe Amazon should be scrutinized. We should scrutinize all large institutions, whether they're companies, government agencies, or non-profits,' Bezos stated before

Congress in 2020. 'Our responsibility is to make sure we pass such scrutiny with flying colours.'[2]

Amazon had historically evaded such attention from lawmakers because antitrust law 'assesses competition largely with an eye to the short-term interests of consumers, not producers or the health of the market as a whole,' according to Lina Khan, chair of the Federal Trade Commission and author of the highly influential paper 'Amazon's Antitrust Paradox' published in *The Yale Law Journal*.[3] Instead, antitrust doctrine views low consumer prices to be evidence of sound competition.

With Amazon, it's difficult to demonstrate any harm done to consumers in the form of higher prices or lower quality. Ripping shoppers off is hardly conducive to Amazon's mission to become Earth's most customer-centric company. Such a strategy wouldn't have supported its growth to become worth nearly five times more than Walmart,[4] the world's largest retailer in revenue terms and Amazon's biggest bricks and mortar counterpart. 'It is as if Bezos charted the company's growth by first drawing a map of antitrust laws, and then devising routes to smoothly bypass them. With its missionary zeal for consumers, Amazon has marched toward monopoly by singing the tune of contemporary antitrust', said Khan.

Amazon's dominance has come at a cost – one that most normal retailers could not bear – and now there are growing calls for existing legislation to be rewritten for the digital age. The House antitrust report on Big Tech concluded that despite delivering clear benefits to society, companies like Amazon 'engage in a form of their own private quasi regulation that is unaccountable to anyone but themselves'. The report found that Amazon:

- has monopoly power over many small and medium-sized businesses that do not have a viable alternative to Amazon;
- achieved its current dominant position in part by acquiring its competitors and those operating in adjacent markets in a bid to 'shore up its competitive moats';
- engaged in 'extensive anticompetitive conduct' in its treatment of third-party sellers;
- through early leadership in the voice assistant market, has collected highly sensitive consumer data which it can use to promote its other businesses;

- through AWS, provides critical infrastructure for many of its competitors, which creates the potential for a conflict of interest.[5]

> To put it simply, companies that once were scrappy, underdog startups that challenged the status quo have become the kinds of monopolies we last saw in the era of oil barons and railroad tycoons.'
> **House Antitrust Report on Big Tech**

The playing field has been tilted since day one, from the moment that Bezos convinced his early investors that a growth-over-profits strategy would yield results in the long run. Amazon is a gatekeeper; it has always played by its own set of rules. The result today? It is uncatchable.

Its competitive advantage only deepens as Amazon relentlessly diversifies into new services and upends entire sectors. This is, after all, the whole premise of Amazon's flywheel. But how much is too much? Not just for politicians and regulators but for also consumers. No other retailer has so successfully embedded itself into the consumer's life and physical home. Amazon has become ubiquitous. Through its ecosystem, Amazon is an indispensable resource, a way of life for many shoppers – but as Amazon moves into new consumer-facing sectors like grocery, pharmacy and fashion, its brand elasticity is being tested. Consumers will sacrifice many things for convenience (price and privacy, for example), but we believe that sentiment would quickly change if Amazon became too powerful, too pervasive. Are we perhaps nearing peak Amazon?

At the same time, Amazon's platform has become a dominant e-commerce enabler. Amazon is the world's largest product search engine. Its algorithms promote its own products. Its various devices seamlessly funnel purchases through to its platform. Amazon has access to data unlike any other retailer in the world. For decades, it wasn't subject to the same tax laws as its bricks and mortar counterparts. Its retail business is subsidized by higher-margin segments like AWS, Marketplace and advertising. You don't need to be an antitrust guru to recognize that Amazon has reaped the rewards of an uneven playing field. In our view, Amazon is rapidly moving towards becoming a utility for commerce.

So, will it be regulated? Could Amazon be broken up? Could it be forced to spin off its AWS division to appease both regulators and competing retailers (a growing number of which refuse to dance with the devil)? The Congressional report on Big Tech recommends creating laws to restore competition in the digital economy – essentially breaking up Big Tech companies and making it harder for them to pursue acquisitions – as well as strengthening antitrust laws and their enforcement. But at the time of writing in mid-2021, these recommendations were just that. There will be no immediate action against Amazon, and there may never be. Investors certainly aren't spooked by the prospect of changes to antitrust regulation.

Writing in *The Atlantic*, Stacy Mitchell, co-director of the Institute for Local Self-Reliance, makes the point that while there has not been so detailed an investigation of monopoly power in the lifetimes of most Americans, we can look to history for guidance on what might happen next.

'In 1938, for example, Congress set up a commission to examine concentration across multiple industries. Its findings led the federal government to file a major antitrust case, change the patent laws, and, in 1950, pass sweeping legislation to restrict mergers,' Mitchell wrote.[6] Change may be coming, but the reining in of Big Tech is not going to happen overnight.

In the meantime, Amazon faces a second existential threat – going from disruptor to disrupted. For a company whose success is predicated on *how* it sells, rather than *what* it sells, it's essential Amazon continues to move the dial in terms of the customer experience. Fortunately for Amazon, this is in its DNA. But as the retail industry becomes more tech-centric, Amazon's proposition becomes less unique. Shopify is 'arming the rebels' against Amazon. Retailers are finally leveraging their stores as fulfilment hubs. The 15-minute supermarkets are giving Amazon a taste of its own medicine. Instagram is bridging discovery and community with the effortlessness of online shopping. It's important to remember that Amazon generates transactional, not emotional, loyalty with its shoppers, which may ultimately be its downfall.

Bezos himself has admitted that, one day, Amazon will fail. 'If you look at large companies, their lifespans tend to be 30-plus years, not a hundred-plus years,' he said.[7]

But Amazon isn't going anywhere just yet. Amazon is and will always be a technology company first, retailer second. Understanding where it applies its technology expertise to remove friction from the most functional shopping experiences can help rivals keep pace. We believe retailers can co-exist with Amazon if they stick to these five basic principles:

1 Curate: don't try to out-Amazon Amazon.

2 Differentiate: go (way) beyond selling.

3 Innovate: think of your stores as assets and not liabilities.

4 Don't go it alone.

5 Move quickly.

This is not to say that there won't be some short-term pain along the way. We must brace ourselves for further rounds of store closures, bankruptcies, redundancies and consolidation as the sector reconfigures for the post-pandemic digital age. Time is of the essence – there will be no second chances for retailers that fail to adapt, as the climate is simply too unforgiving. Ultimately, the retailers that survive digital transformation will be those that follow the customer, ensuring they remain relevant in the age of Amazon.

Notes

1 Investigation of competition in digital markets. Majority staff report and recommendations. Subcommittee on Antitrust, Commercial and Administrative Law of the Committee of the Judiciary (2020). Available from: https://fm.cnbc. com/applications/cnbc.com/resources/editorialfiles/2020/10/06/investigation_of_ competition_in_digital_markets_majority_staff_report_and_recommendations. pdf [Last accessed 20/6/2021].

2 Statement by Jeffrey P. Bezos Founder & Chief Executive Officer, Amazon before the U.S. House of Representatives Committee on the Judiciary Subcommittee on Antitrust, Commercial, and Administrative Law (2020). Available from: https://www.congress.gov/116/meeting/house/110883/witnesses/ HHRG-116-JU05-Wstate-BezosJ-20200729.pdf (archived at https://perma.cc/ J4TZ-G9TP) [Last accessed 18/6/2021].

3 Khan, Lina (2017) Amazon's antitrust paradox, *Yale Law Journal*, 3 January. Available from: http://digitalcommons.law.yale.edu/cgi/viewcontent. cgi?article=5785&context=ylj (archived at https://perma.cc/T2NP-XL7K) [Last accessed 7/7/2018].

4 Author research based on June 2021 market cap of $386bn vs 1.76T

5 Investigation of competition in digital markets. Majority staff report and recommendations. Subcommittee on Antitrust, Commercial and Administrative

Law of the Committee of the Judiciary (2020). Available from: https://fm.cnbc.com/applications/cnbc.com/resources/editorialfiles/2020/10/06/investigation_of_competition_in_digital_markets_majority_staff_report_and_recommendations.pdf (archived at https://perma.cc/K5AA-VH3C) [Last accessed 20/6/2021].

6   Mitchell, Stacy (2020) Amazon Is a Private Government. Congress Needs to Step Up, *The Atlantic*, 10 August. Available from: https://www.theatlantic.com/ideas/archive/2020/08/americans-can-barely-imagine-congress-works/615091/) [Last accessed 21/6/2021].

7   Kim, Eugene (2010) Jeff Bezos to employees: 'One day, Amazon will fail' but our job is to delay it as long as possible, *CNBC*, 15 November. Available from: https://www.cnbc.com/2018/11/15/bezos-tells-employees-one-day-amazon-will-fail-and-to-stay-hungry.html (https://perma.cc/K5AA-VH3C) [Last accessed 21/6/2021].

INDEX

1-click shopping 23, 85, 115, 131, 132, 184–87, 266
3D printing 288
4-Star stores 75, 89, 113, 214, 266
15-minute city concept 46, 244

advertising 56–57, 158, 200, 219, 301
agility 11, 35, 36, 41, 85, 102
Alexa
   'Amazon's Choice' 158, 159
   introduction 198
   pandemic effects 57, 58
   powered by Lex AI framework 194
   rivals/competitors 202, 205–06
   role in Amazon ecosystem 198
   in stores 151, 228
   third party integration 150, 200, 202–03
   see also Echo devices
Alibaba 54, 78, 97, 105, 147, 180, 193, 233, 242, 267, 281, 290–91, 295
'Always Day One' philosophy 11, 299
AmazonBasics range 156–57, 162
Amazon Books stores 74, 75, 111, 112, 114, 217, 218
Amazon Business, B2B selling 288–89
Amazon ecosystem, role of voice technology 198, 199, 202
'Amazon Effect' 5, 76, 86, 204, 265
Amazon Fire see Fire phone; Fire tablet; Fire TV
Amazon Flex, independent delivery contractors 276–77
AmazonFresh online 129–31, 133, 134, 136
AmazonFresh Pickup 112, 144–45, 293
Amazon Fresh stores 55, 113, 135, 142, 143, 151–52, 228, 231
Amazon Go stores 142, 144, 145, 151
Amazon Hub services (The Hub) 104, 112, 262, 289
   see also lockers
Amazon Key 294
Amazon Lex 194
Amazon mobile app
   in Amazon stores 113, 151, 197, 213, 215, 224, 228, 231
   Amazon Wallet 14
   Dash Buttons 132, 187

fashion advice 169, 205
image recognition 221
Luxury Stores 54
order tracking 272
price checking barcode scanner 216, 217–18
QR code scanning to shop 115, 151
reach in UK 84
View in Your Room AR 223
Amazon One scanner 59, 232
Amazon Payments 266–67
'Amazon's Choice' products 158, 159, 201
Amazon Web Services (AWS) 22–23
   AI applications 192, 194
   antitrust issues 280 81, 301
   importance to Amazon 20, 21, 78, 178, 180
   logistics role 266, 280
   pandemic effects 60
   physical infrastructure 280
   powering Just Walk Out technology 60
   profitability 23, 60, 178–79
   worldwide importance 280–81
anticipatory shipping 195
anti-showrooming strategies 99, 222–23, 224
antitrust issues 132–33, 160–63, 201–02, 209, 280–81, 299–302
apparel
   selling clothes versus fashion 167
   see also fashion retail; Nike
Apple
   Apple Music subscribers 186
   Apple Pay 84, 267
   AR software development kit 223, 225
   car applications 209
   ecosystem 199
   education 252–53
   Home Pod and Siri voice assistant 206
   iPhone 182, 183, 184, 209, 223
   'town square' stores 217, 237, 252, 267
artificial intelligence (AI) 182, 190–98, 226
   autonomous computing 182, 191
   body scans and fashion designer 169
   chatbots 193–94
   conversational commerce 228
   dynamic pricing algorithms 226

artificial intelligence (AI) (*continued*)
  image recognition 221, 223
  importance in frictionless retail
      experience 209–10
  Just Walk Out stores 196–97
  personalized shopping assistant 26
  potential in retail 204, 209
  prerequisite structures 191
  search and recommendation
      functions 192–93, 204, 222
  supply chain and fulfilment system 179,
      194–96
  voice system applications 191, 197–98
  see also Alexa
augmented reality (AR)
  Apple software development kit 223, 225
  bricks and mortar retail 223–24
  fashion retail 102, 194, 223
  hair and beauty 111, 113, 115, 194
  online shoe purchasing 224
  pandemic effects 42
  potential in physical retail 223
  shopper confidence 246
automated checkout technology *see*
      checkout-free shopping; Just Walk
      Out technology
automation
  autonomous computing distinction 191
  online customer services 193–94
  vehicles 294, 295
autonomous computing 181, 182, 188,
      190–91, 197, 233
  see also artificial intelligence; Just
      Walk Out
autonomous physical devices 196, 230–31,
      293, 294–95
auto-replenishment of goods 25, 105,
      131–32, 134, 146, 170, 187, 207
AWS *see* Amazon Web Services

B2B selling, Amazon Business 288–89
banking services 77–78
beauty retail 35, 54, 115, 229, 252
Bezos, Jeff 2, 9–10, 15
blended retail experience 102–06, 146,
      214, 238
Bluetooth beacons 225, 227
BORIS (Buy Online Return In Store) 104
borrowing and rental 252–55
Boumphrey, John 10, 52, 56, 83, 115, 169
branding 130–31, 142–44, 169–71
brand loyalty 155–56, 159, 204
brands
  elasticity 170

fashion 163–64, 167–69
grocery 169–71
private labels 154–75
promoting own brands over third-
      party 157–63
shifting view of national brands 156
Brexit 284
bricks and mortar retail 25–26
  4-Star stores 75, 89, 113, 214, 266
  advantages 106
  Amazon's transition 3, 54–55, 96–121
  apocalypse 1, 82, 86, 87, 91, 176
  automation in stores 213–35
  bookstore resurgence 237
  checkout 101
  convergence with online 98–106
  customer expectations 85
  customer experience 41–43, 224–33
  differentiated ideas 111
  digital technologies 100–102, 227–29
  effect of e-commerce fulfilment and
      returns 260–61
  evolution of Amazon's presence 112–13
  fulfilment role 292
  future role of staff 229
  global importance 96
  importance to e-commerce 39–41
  intelligent space 225–26
  less demand 86
  location 218–19
  navigation/finding products 101, 225, 228
  online shopping effects 213
  oversupply of retail space 82, 83,
      87–88, 233
  post pandemic effects 34, 38
  Prime applicability 74–76
  redefining the store 236–59
  relevance 87–91
  research online buy offline 215–17,
      218, 223
  stores closing 82–83
  stores as showrooms 222–24
  use of mobile devices 99–102
  workspace 243
  see also Amazon Books; Amazon Fresh
      stores; Amazon Go; department
      stores; grocery retail; shopping malls;
      superstores
Buy Online Pick Up Instore (BOPIS) 261
  see also click & collect
Buy Online Return In Store (BORIS) 104

Carrefour 35, 40, 88, 103, 149, 205, 225,
      243, 270

cars
    in-car deliveries 69, 70, 294
    voice control technology 198, 206, 208,
        209, 227, 294
cash shopping 77
category killers 86
chatbots 193–94
checkout
    digital points of purchase 227–29
    online 184–85, 266–67
    physical stores 185–86
    reducing friction 101, 184–85
checkout-free shopping 230, 231–33
    pandemic effects 38–39, 55, 59–60
    pioneer stores 38, 267–68
    see also Amazon Go; Dash Cart; Just
        Walk Out technology
children
    Alexa Reading Sidekick 57
    experiential retail 245–46, 246–48
cities, trends in size and function 46, 243–44
click & collect 24, 39–41, 103, 126,
    261–63, 289, 292
click & collect 'Drive Up'/click and
    drive 261
    see also AmazonFresh Pickup; curbside
        pickup
clienteling 42, 229
collaboration
    Amazon with other companies 104, 106,
        115–17, 289
    collection and returns 104, 116
    gamification of physical spaces 225
    use of retail spaces 238, 244
competition see anti-trust issues
connectivity, see also ubiquitous connectivity
consumption/consumerism 43–45
contactless payments 39, 101, 227, 232
conversational commerce 194
co-opetition
    joining with Amazon 27, 116, 117, 150,
        203, 247
    retailers teaming up with competitors
        against Amazon's threat 239
copycats, clone versions of branded
    products 160–62
core principles 8–18
coronavirus see COVID-19 pandemic
cost of borrowing money 17
Costco 2, 6, 66, 202, 229, 249, 270
counterfeits 54, 160, 168
COVID-19 pandemic 33–49
    Amazon's response 50–64
    Amazon's success 50–57, 299

change in online fashion buying 167
click & collect helped store-based
    retailers 261
flexible working effect 242–43
long-term effects on retail 33–34, 39–46
online grocery effects 122–23, 124, 125
shift to digital world 1, 3, 34
short-term effects on retail 33, 35–39
supply chain challenges 194–95
voice-enabled product boost 200
warehouses staff safety 195, 285
curbside pickup 39–40, 103, 144–45, 205,
    219, 261–62
customer acquisition costs 110
customer benefits from changing retail
    market 24
customer-centric ethos 9–10, 15, 177–78
customer data 18, 57, 58, 73, 116, 152, 155,
    161, 192, 193, 205, 217–18, 300
customer ratings see product reviews and
    customer ratings
customer relationships with employees 42
customer services, automated
    systems 193–94

dark kitchens 271
dark stores 43, 292–93
Dash cart 113, 135, 151, 187, 228, 231–32
Dash initiative (buttons/wand/replenishment
    service) 57, 131, 132, 134, 186,
    187, 207
data access
    third-party seller activity 160, 161,
        162–63
    see also customer data
deep learning techniques 158, 182, 192, 197
Delhaize, Ahold 150, 202, 203, 232
Deliveroo 137, 270, 271
delivery
    costs 70, 276–77
    Flexers 276–77
    in-home/in-garage and in-car
        deliveries 69, 70, 294
    issues in grocery retail 123, 133, 135–36
    paying store staff to do deliveries 277
    restaurant food 271–72
    semi-autonomous/autonomous
        vehicles 196, 231, 294–95
    third-party carriers 277–80
delivery speed
    grocery retail 43, 136–37, 147
    rapid delivery 2, 18, 26, 42–43, 65
    ultra fast 43, 89, 137, 219, 269–70
demand prediction 195

department stores 34, 87–88, 89–91, 110, 116, 237, 238, 240, 241, 244–45, 250, 251, 253, 284
digital customer experience in stores 224–33
digital detox in stores 237
digital displays in stores 102
digital (mobile) wallets 14, 72, 84
digital points of purchase 227–29
digital signage in stores 227
dot-com bust 16, 128–29
'Drive' concept
    in France 40, 144
    see also curbside pickup
driverless vehicles 294
drivers of technology 181–82, 190, 214, 233
drive-through 40, 111, 227
drones 196, 290, 294–95
DSSTNE artificial intelligence framework 192

early days of company 14–16
eBay 270
Echo devices 198–200
    Echo Auto 198, 208
    Echo Look/Echo Show 169, 205, 207
    introduction 134, 198, 207–08
    in kitchens 205
    pandemic effects 58
    selling promotions 17–18, 199
    in stores 151, 228
    success due to failure of Fire phone 198, 199
    see also Alexa
Eero 57, 209
electronic shelf labels (ESLs) 102, 159, 226–27, 232, 233
employees
    customer relationships 42
    future role of sales associates 229
    paying store staff to do deliveries 277
    Prime pickers 276
    sales associates needing new skills 238
    warehouses staff working conditions 195, 285
    workforce growth 1–2
entertainment
    Prime Video 51–52, 67–69
    in stores 238, 245–46, 247–48
environmental issues 44–45, 281
ESLs see electronic shelf labels
Europe
    15-minute city 46
    Amazon partnerships 292
    Amazon's tax structure 19

Brexit 284
buying alliances 149
click & collect 261, 262
competition concerns 161, 163
retailers redefining stores 243
tax issues 18–21
trade links with China 291
see also Carrefour
experiential retail 42, 236–59
    children 245, 246–48
    discovery and learning 249–52
    fitness and lifestyle 245–46
    foodservice 240–42
    guidance and inspiration 251–52
    nature 245–46
    personal styling 250–51
    Westfield's Destination 2028 248–49

failures
    demise of status-quo retail 35–36, 86, 176, 247
    dot-com bust 16, 128–29
    mistakes made by Amazon 14, 168–69, 183–84
fashion retail
    Amazon 76, 163–64, 167–69
    augmented reality 102, 223
    department stores 91
    different to selling socks and t-shirts 167
    environmental issues 44, 253–54
    foodservice 241
    guideshops 251
    magic (smart) mirrors 228
    offering food and drink 241
    private label versus brands 167, 168
    rental 253
    technology 102, 168, 205–06
    see also Next
Fast-Moving Consumer Goods (FMCG) 165–66, 169–71, 205, 230
FBA see Fulfilment by Amazon
FBM see Fulfilment By Merchant
FCs see fulfilment centres
FedEx 277, 278–79
Fire phone 14, 183–84, 198, 199, 207, 221
Fire tablet (Kindle Fire) 184, 207, 221
Fire TV 52, 115, 184, 198, 207, 208
first-mover advantage 24, 51, 198–99, 204, 231, 294
fitness centres in stores 239, 245
Flex/Flexers, independent delivery contractors 276–77
flywheel effect 5, 7–8, 15, 21, 23, 56, 67–68, 78, 125, 186–87, 198, 265, 275, 279

food, *see also* grocery; takeaway
foodservice, food and drink experiences in
    stores 240–42
footfall, counting and increasing 225
frictionless shopping, convergence of online
    and offline 39, 41, 98–106, 126, 150
frugality 10, 156
fulfilment 260–74
    flexibility 289
    online/offline convergence 103–04
    physical infrastructure 281–83
    see also click & collect; curbside pickup;
        delivery; 'The last mile'; lockers
Fulfilment by Amazon (FBA) 22, 201,
    288–89
Fulfilment By Merchant (FBM) 288, 289
fulfilment centres (FCs) 275–76, 278, 280,
    282–86
    see also micro-fulfilment centre systems
fulfilment hubs 39–41, 146, 147, 152
functional shopping
    fun shopping divergence 25, 237
    technology streamlining 146, 176–236
fun shopping 25, 237, 245–49
furniture retail 157, 223, 254

gig economy 270, 271, 276–77
global operations 53–54, 66–67, 68–69
global shipping 286–87
Google
    as competitor to Amazon 270
    ecosystem 199
    finding products and businesses 219–20
    rapid delivery service 270
    universal shopping cart across
        platforms 202
Google Assistant 202, 205–06
Google Nest 200
grocery retail 26
    Amazon influence on market 3, 26,
        148–49
    Amazon's aims 146
    Amazon's own stores 55, 150–52
    branding/own labels 165–66, 169–71
    challenges with online 123–24
    COVID-19 pandemic effects 122–23,
        124, 125
    delivery issues 123, 133, 135–36
    delivery speed 43, 136–37, 147
    early attempts 129, 131, 134, 144–45
    fee structures online 130–31, 133,
        135–36
    food plus general merchandise 125, 127
    foodservice 242

foodservice in stores 242
    need for stores 125, 126
    online 54–56, 122–41
    own brands 155–56
    physical stores 55
    shopping habits 71–72, 89, 126
    supermarkets 142–53
    third party selling online 138
    Webvan 128–30, 134
    see also Amazon Fresh; Amazon Go;
        Whole Foods Market
growth prioritized over profit 12, 13, 14–15
guideshops 251

hair salons 115
healthcare 8, 43, 54
home automation 198, 200, 203,
    206, 209
    see also Internet of Things; smart home
        ecosystem of devices; voice assistants
home design and decor, augmented
    reality 223
hypermarkets 88, 127, 225, 242, 254
    see also superstores

Iceland (grocery chain) 35, 150
identity verification 59, 232, 233
IKEA 42, 44, 223, 240, 254
image recognition 220–21, 223
industrial real estate 283–84
in-home/in-garage and in-car deliveries 69,
    70, 294
Instacart 126, 138, 148, 270, 272, 277
intelligent space in stores 225–26
internal competitors *see* third-party sellers
Internet of Things (IoT) 105, 132
invention, passion 8–10, 23, 143, 145–46,
    179
inventory systems 102, 107, 290
IoT *see* Internet of Things

JD.com 147, 223, 232–33, 242, 291, 295
Just Walk Out (JWO) technology 39,
    59–60, 113, 151, 196–97,
    231–33, 267
    see also checkout-free shopping

Kindle e-readers 17, 24
Kindle Fire devices 184, 207, 221
Kiva Systems, robotics 130, 134, 196, 276,
    282, 286
knockoffs, clone versions of branded
    products 160–62
Kohl's 112, 116–17, 289

'the last mile' 263–798
  Amazon development 265–67
  infrastructure 275–98
  options and complexity 263–65
  problems and costs 256, 262, 270–71, 276–77
  store purchases and checkout 267–69
  ultra rapid delivery 43, 89, 137, 219, 269–70
  see also click & collect; lockers
leadership principles 10–11
leisure activities in stores 245
library of things concept 255
lifestyle centres, redefining the store 239–40, 245–46
Local Inventory Ads, Google 219, 220
localism 45
locating products offline 219, 220
lockers 24, 104, 111, 112, 150, 262–64, 290, 294
long-term orientation 2, 9, 12, 14–17, 23
loss leaders 17–18, 217
lower-income shoppers 77
low profit margins 14, 17
loyalty 2, 8, 155–56, 159, 204, 302
loyalty cards and schemes 14, 22, 26, 44, 71–72, 73, 75, 101
  see also Prime
luxury sector 54, 167, 168, 227–28, 229, 253

machine learning 182, 191, 192–93, 195, 204, 221, 223, 224
Macy's 40, 88, 103, 105, 250
magic (smart) mirrors 102, 228, 248
malls see shopping malls
market capitalization of US companies 6
Marketplace 21–22
  see also third-party sellers
measuring success 8, 15, 41, 255–56, 263
merchandise-free stores 251
micro-fulfilment centre (MFC) systems 231, 292–93
mistakes, Amazon's failures 14, 168–69, 183–84
mobile devices
  Apple iPhone 182, 183, 184, 209, 223
  augmented reality 223
  checkout-free stores 197
  data signals in stores 99
  Fire phone 14, 183–84, 198, 199, 207, 221
  importance in shopping 84, 85, 99–102, 156, 177

  increasing connectivity 84, 85, 130, 177, 180
  online shopping apps 215
  payment methods 39, 72, 84, 180
  personalized price offers 217–18
  range of devices 84–85
  visual search technology 220–21

national brands, US affinity 155
natural language processing (NLP) 182, 191, 193
navigation, finding products in store 101, 225, 228
Netflix 2, 6, 68, 179
neural networks 191, 193–94
Next 41, 104, 117, 241, 289
Nike 2, 6, 42, 168, 224
NLP see natural language processing
no-inventory models 251

O2O see online to offline
Ocado 129, 137, 148–49, 202–03, 293
offices, in underused retail space 36, 244
omnichannel retail 97–99
one click shopping 23, 85, 115, 131, 132, 184–87, 266
online to offline (O2O) 96–121, 147, 214, 215, 233, 292
'on my terms' shoppers 83–85, 176–77, 181, 197, 265, 299
order tracking 199, 272, 277
out-of-stock issues 98, 100, 180, 219, 230, 231, 290
overspaced, bricks and mortar retail 87–88, 233
own brands see private labels
ownership, changing to access 252–53

pandemic see COVID-19 pandemic
patents
  1-click shopping 85, 132, 184–85, 186, 266
  3D printing solutions 288
  anticipatory shipping 195
  anti-showrooming technology 222–23
  fashion-related technology 169
  Google Knowledge Panel 219
  Just Walk Out technology 231
  Walmart Internet of Things integration 132
Pay with Amazon 186, 198
payment methods 77, 84, 180, 186, 194, 229–30, 266–67
PayPal 84, 266, 267

Peak Design 162
'peak stuff' 252, 254
perishable goods
    delivery costs 70
    supply chain 125
    temperature-controlled click & collect
        lockers 262–63
    Whole Foods acquisition 146–47, 170,
        292
personalization of shopping experience 101,
    193
personal styling (and personal shopping) 42,
    250–51
pervasive interfaces 181–82, 183, 184,
    188–89, 191, 197, 233
physical infrastructure
    Amazon Web Services 280
    fulfilment network 281–83
    see also bricks and mortar retail
'pickers', locating items to pack 276
predictions 25–27, 76
predictive analytics 193
price checking, online/offline 216
Prime 65–81
    advantages to customers 186
    competition 74
    exclusive products 70
    fees 65–66, 70, 73, 77, 78
    flywheel effect 67, 68, 78, 186, 279
    fulfilment centres 275–76
    grocery shopping 127, 130–31, 133,
        135–38, 146
    importance and scope 22
    as a loyalty programme 71–72
    number of members 2
    origins 65
    pandemic effects 51–53
    physical stores 74–76
    profitability 17
    speed of development 14
Prime Air 196, 294–95
Prime Day 71, 179–80, 199
Prime Now 14, 133, 136–38
Prime Pantry 133, 135–36
Prime Video 51–52, 67–69
Prime Wardrobe 69, 76, 168, 279
private labels 154–75
product availability 40–41, 102
product reviews and customer ratings 159,
    217, 218
product search, see also research...
product search results, Alexa 200–201
profit margins, online versus in-store
    purchases 107

profits
    Amazon Web Services 23, 60, 178–79
    building growth first 12, 13, 14–15
pure-play e-commerce, no longer viable 25,
    96–97

QR codes in stores 39, 115, 227, 230, 233

random stow system, Prime fulfilment
    centres 276
recessions 155–56
relevance, importance 1, 3, 87–91, 303
rent not buy 252–55
researching products
    online 215–18, 223
    visual search technology 220–21
    voice assistants/Alexa 199
research online buy offline (ROBO) 215–17,
    218, 223
research phase of shopping, zero moment of
    truth 218, 220, 223, 224, 226
restaurant food delivery 271–72
retail apocalypse 1, 82, 86, 87, 91, 176
retail Darwinism 1, 35–36, 87, 284
retailtainment (retail theatre) 238
retail trends, pandemic effects 34, 35
retail versus services 27
returns
    collaboration 104, 116
    increasing rate 103–04
    partnerships 289
    problems and costs 109–10
    to stores 99, 103, 104, 260
reverse image searching 221
reviews see product reviews and customer
    ratings
robotics
    fulfillment roles 196, 231, 276, 282, 286,
        292–93
    Kiva Systems 130, 134, 196, 276, 282,
        286
    in stores 230–31

Sainsbury's 137, 232, 242, 268
sales versus profits 12
scanning, see also barcodes; QR codes
scanning palm of hand, identity
    verification 59, 232, 233
scanning shopping (barcodes/scan & go/self-
    checkout), in stores 30, 74, 101, 197,
    216, 221, 225, 229, 232, 267–68
seamless (frictionless) shopping, convergence
    of online and offline 39, 41, 98–106,
    126, 150

search engine optimization (SEO) 219
search and recommendation functions,
    artificial intelligence 192–93,
    200–201
See What's In Store (SWIS), Google's
    inventory search tool 219, 220
SEO *see* search engine optimization
shareholder letters and message 9, 15–16,
    167, 178
sharing economy 252–55
shipping costs 78, 107–08
shopping malls 36, 87, 108, 111, 113, 237,
    244, 245–46
'showrooming' 99, 222–23, 224
Siri voice assistant, Apple 206
smart homes
    Amazon's innovations 57
    door locking/unlocking 294
    ecosystem of devices 209
    Internet of Things 105, 132
smart mirror technology (magic
    mirrors) 102, 228, 248
smartphones *see* mobile devices
smart speakers
    discount selling 199, 202, 209
    Google 202
    number of devices 197–98, 200
    see also Echo devices
software architecture 178
sortation, human versus robotic 276
speed of purchases 5
Steiner, Tim 148, 149
stores *see* bricks and mortar retail
Subscribe & Save 131–33, 187
subscription services 268–69
    rental retail 253
    streaming services 186
    see also Prime
supermarkets
    Amazon redefining 3, 142–53
    see also grocery retail
superstores 87–89, 127, 225, 239, 242, 254
supply chains
    artificial intelligence 193–96
    challenges 194–95
    grocery retail 125, 126, 130
    increasing complexity 263–65
    logistics 260–74
    making to order 169
    production to order 169
sustainable moats round companies 17
SWIS *see* See What's In Store

takeaway food services 242, 271–72
Target 2, 6, 40, 91, 103, 147, 202, 205, 225,
    230, 270, 279, 284
tax issues 3, 18–21, 282, 287, 301
technology
    Amazon's effect on retail market 204–05
    checkout-free stores 196–97
    drivers 181–82, 190, 214, 233
    frictionless retail 176–89
    hardware launches 207–08
    roots of Amazon 2, 8, 23–24, 27,
        178–79
    voice applications 190–212
temperature-controlled click & collect
    lockers 262, 263
Tesco 54, 88, 96, 127, 136, 137, 149, 205,
    232, 239–40, 242, 292
third-party carriers/delivery services 126,
    270, 271, 272, 277–80
third party licencing, Just Walk Out
    technology 59–60
third-party sellers
    Amazon accessing data 155, 160, 161,
        162–63
    Amazon's relationship 154–55, 160–62
    branded fashion products 167–68
    customer payments 186, 266, 268
    Fulfilment by Amazon 22, 201, 288–89
    Fulfilment By Merchant 288, 289
    Marketplace 21–22, 27
    product suggestions from Alexa 201–02
    revenue stream 8, 22
    sales tax 19
threats to Amazon 301–02
three pillars of Amazon business
    (Marketplace/Prime/AWS) 21–23
tiered pricing, Prime versus non-customers in
    stores 75
toy stores 246–48
try-before-you-buy services 76, 117, 251
    see also Prime Wardrobe
Tuft & Needle 115–16
Twitch 52, 69

ubiquitous connectivity 36, 84, 181, 183,
    184, 187–88, 190, 191, 192, 195–96,
    197, 233
UPS 277, 278–79
urban landscape changes 46, 244
US Postal Service (USPS) 277, 278
USP (unique selling proposition) of
    Amazon 5

videoconferencing 57, 58
video streaming, Prime Video 51–52,
    67–69
Vine programme, reviews 159
virtual assistants 194
    see also chatbots; voice assistants
virtual reality (VR) 102, 105, 223, 249
    see also augmented reality
visibility of brands 157–58
visual light communication (VLC) 225, 227
visual search technology, product
        research 220–21
VLC *see* visual light communication
voice-activated devices 200, 209
    in stores 228
    see also echo; smart speakers
voice assistants 197–206
    controlling homes 198, 200, 206, 209
    effects on retail industry 204–05
    number of devices 197–98, 200
    outside the home 209
    see also Alexa
VR *see* virtual reality

WACD *see* What Amazon Can't Do
Walmart
    comparison to Amazon 1–2

deliveries 277, 279
    moving inventory to shelf-tops 290
    own labels and copycats 161
    transportation and logistics 289–90
wardrobing (buy/wear/return) 76, 253
warehouses
    industrial real estate 283–84
    robotics 196, 276, 282, 286
    staff working conditions 195, 285
webrooming 215, 216
Webvan 128–30, 134
weekly shop, death of 71–72, 89
Weiss, Uwe 204–05
Westfield's Destination 2028 248–49
What Amazon Can't Do (WACD) 1, 25,
    219, 237–39
Whole Foods Market 54, 75, 112, 126–27,
    134–35, 138, 142–46, 150–51, 165,
    242, 292
Wi-Fi in stores 99, 224, 225–26
working, remote working and co-working in
    retail spaces 243–44
'working backwards' from benefit to
    customer 11

zero moment of truth (ZMOT) 218, 220,
    223, 224, 226